Praise for

WHEELING
THROUGH
TORONTO

"Koehl's *Wheeling through Toronto* presents a lively account of the rise, fall, and rebirth of cycling in Toronto between 1896 and the present. People moving from home to work and, outside working hours, to play created a tense contest among automobile owners, transit users, and cyclists – which motorists appeared to be winning. But the recent rediscovery of cycling in the face of a growing environmental catastrophe opens a new chapter in Toronto's transportation history."

Glen Norcliffe, Professor Emeritus of Geography and Senior Scholar, York University

"In *Wheeling through Toronto*, Albert Koehl shows us three things. First, the bicycle has long been an important part of the city's transportation and social history. Second, bicycles are a big part of the present day largely because of decades' worth of cycling advocacy and activism. Third, bicycles must and will be a critical part of Toronto's sustainable, efficient, and fun mobile future."

Shawn Micallef, author of *Stroll: Psychogeographic Walking Tours of Toronto* and co-founder of *Spacing*

"Albert Koehl's book is an important synthesis of Toronto's cycling history. It allows riders like me to understand fully the riding landscape that I travel through every day. Frustratingly, some of the same old anti-cycling practices and rhetoric keep returning to public discourse. But ultimately, Koehl's work shows how the bike and the city are continuing to grow together."

Matthew Pioro, editor, *Canadian Cycling Magazine*

WHEELING THROUGH TORONTO

A History of the Bicycle and Its Riders

ALBERT KOEHL

ÆVO UTP

Aevo UTP
An imprint of University of Toronto Press
Toronto Buffalo London
utorontopress.com

© Albert Koehl 2024

Library and Archives Canada Cataloguing in Publication

Title: Wheeling through Toronto : a history of the bicycle
and its riders / Albert Koehl.
Names: Koehl, Albert, author.
Description: Includes bibliographical references and index.
Identifiers: Canadiana (print) 20240292928 | Canadiana (ebook) 20240292995 |
ISBN 9781487549572 (cloth) | ISBN 9781487549602 (PDF) |
ISBN 9781487549589 (EPUB)
Subjects: LCSH: Cycling – Ontario – Toronto – History.
Classification: LCC HE5739.C3 K64 2024 | DDC 388.3/47209713541 – dc23

ISBN 978-1-4875-4957-2 (cloth)   ISBN 978-1-4875-4958-9 (EPUB)
ISBN 978-1-4875-4960-2 (PDF)

Printed in Canada

Cover design: Val Cooke
Cover images: (*front*) Paul Martchenko/Shutterstock.com, anatskwong
/iStockphoto.com; (*back*) leonardo255/iStockphoto.com

We wish to acknowledge the land on which the University of Toronto Press operates. This land is the traditional territory of the Wendat, the Anishnaabeg, the Haudenosaunee, the Métis, and the Mississaugas of the Credit First Nation.

University of Toronto Press acknowledges the financial support of the Government of Canada, the Canada Council for the Arts, and the Ontario Arts Council, an agency of the Government of Ontario, for its publishing activities.

Canada Council
for the Arts

Conseil des Arts
du Canada

ONTARIO ARTS COUNCIL
CONSEIL DES ARTS DE L'ONTARIO

an Ontario government agency
un organisme du gouvernement de l'Ontario

Funded by the
Government
of Canada

Financé par le
gouvernement
du Canada

Canadä

MIX
Paper | Supporting
responsible forestry
FSC
www.fsc.org
FSC® C016245

*To Emily
and to Eduard*

Contents

Preface

The bicycle continues to provoke curiously powerful emotions. What is it about this simple machine that it should be so loved by some yet despised by others, often including the very civic leaders entrusted with ensuring the safety of its riders? *Wheeling through Toronto* offers a 130-year ride from the Bicycle Craze in the 1890s to the pandemic of the 2020s to help answer this and other timely questions.

Today's bicycle looks and functions very much as it did in the 1890s, even when it has been modified for electric assist or converted to cargo functions, sometimes with more than two wheels. During its history in Toronto, the bicycle's place on the roads and in public esteem has fluctuated wildly: flaunted as fashionable, disparaged and derided (more so for its rider), rescued from looming obscurity, or promoted as a way to respond to the challenges of the day, most recently the climate crisis and the COVID-19 pandemic. The bicycle reminds us that our transportation system wasn't shaped by a simple, dispassionate assessment of choices between available technologies but by public perceptions of the user (influenced by marketers), corporate interests, and government priorities.

Since the 1920s, the cyclist has competed, usually without success, with the motorist for attention and space. It is no surprise that in the telling of history, the bicycle often goes unnoticed, even when it is directly in the frame. During many recent decades, cyclists were largely distinguished by their lower-economic status and younger age, providing a cue for politicians to ignore their safety on the roads. How much easier it would have been to write this book if only the poor drove cars and the rich rode bicycles.

Instead of an austere chronology, this book highlights eras of the bicycle, with the spotlight directly on utilitarian cycling – to go to work, to school, to shop, and to visit – except when cycling for sport or leisure is important to the context of the story.

In 1896 (chapter 1), the Bicycle Craze was at its peak in Toronto – the cyclist now seated comfortably on the so-called safety instead of the precarious height of the high-wheel (also known as the "penny-farthing" or "ordinary"). Although cycling for sport and leisure among the upper classes had initiated the craze, it was being transformed by the growing popularity of the bicycle for everyday use. The utilitarian cyclist benefited from the political influence wielded by the established bicycle clubs in the city, many of them members of the powerful Canadian Wheelmen's Association. The bicycle's prospects depended on better roads, which were slowly improving, although many cycling advocates, impatient for action, called for dedicated bicycle strips and paths.

By 1910 (chapter 2), the bicycle as fashion had passed. For the upper classes, the bicycle had become "too popular to be popular." The bicycle's fall from fashion in 1899 was dramatic, but its survival nonetheless assured, though with less fanfare (and lower prices), by its utility for everyday travel and commercial use. The average resident, accustomed to walking, had many options to get around and beyond the city, including electric streetcars and radials, the railways (that offered suburban stops), and bicycles. The motorcar had made an appearance, but its own prospects were poor, given the public hostility that it and its typically well-heeled driver provoked.

By 1929 (chapter 3), cyclists had returned to the front pages of newspapers ... as victims of road tragedies. Motorcars dominated city streets, even while serving only a minority of Toronto residents. In fact, when "the wheel" was mentioned in the late 1920s, it was no longer in reference to the bicycle; "Killer at the Wheel" meant the motorist. Public outrage at road casualties, the "slaughter of innocents," failed to slow the motor juggernaut. Amidst, and despite, the carnage, many people were convinced by slick advertising that motorcar ownership elevated their status, while implicitly lowering – since prestige and status are relative terms – the place of other road users, notably the person on a bicycle. City Hall and Queen's Park reordered their priorities, and spending, to satisfy the motor lobby's demand for more, better, and wider roads, an appetite that has yet to be sated.

In 1953 (chapter 4), when the provincial government created the Regional Municipality of Metropolitan Toronto as a federation of the City of Toronto with its fast-growing suburban neighbours, a key goal was to facilitate the building of motorways. In Metro Chair Fred Gardiner the motor lobby found its champion, a man who would let nothing stand in the way of the motorist – neither cost nor sidewalk, neither hill nor river valley. The mania for road building and widening that followed didn't include the cyclist, even as an afterthought. The bicycle, a reliable friend during the Second World War, had been quickly abandoned, even if not by a core population of children, young adults, including messengers, and other adults who might be dismissed as too poor, eccentric, or odd. Most people were willing to accept death – at least of other road users – as the cost of modern transportation.

The bicycle revival (chapter 5) dating from the early 1970s brought adults back to cycling, not for recreation and sport but for travel to everyday destinations, including work. The sporty ten-speed bicycle allowed riders to be "cool" and to distinguish themselves from previous generations of cyclists. There were other reasons to believe that a new transportation model, without toxic air, disfigured cities, or a high casualty toll, was possible. The province's cancellation of the southward extension of the Spadina Expressway in 1971 was a defeat for the car juggernaut on a North American scale, opening the way to rethink the place of neglected travel modes, including the bicycle. But the absence of safe places to ride quickly became apparent, and the car's extravagant need for public space ensured that motorists, and their political champions, were rarely in a mood to share.

By 2019 (chapter 6), the need for a new way to get people from A to B in the city was abundantly clear, although the inertia of a system based on and dominated by cars – and served by entrenched "traffic" experts in government bureaucracies – prevented change from happening at a pace that matched the urgency of problems, including the frightening fact of climate change. The traffic jam continued to be a scream for attention, far louder than what community groups could achieve in their calls for cycling, walking, and transit infrastructure and improvements. The slow pace of action belied the fact that in Toronto in 2019, which since amalgamation in 1998 included the old city and its former Metro suburbs, more people were using car-free alternatives, which rivalled, then edged past, driving as the dominant mode. Indeed, the growing population density, and a city of almost three million people, was making it increasingly difficult to rationalize the spectacular amount of space devoted to cars, with parking space alone often exceeding the living space of the average city resident.

During the global pandemic, old ways of sharing public space in Toronto came up against the social distancing imperative of the COVID-19 virus, forcing a re-evaluation of the privileged place of the motorist. Some road space was quickly, and with little opposition, repurposed for people on bikes and on foot, providing a glimpse of what the city might look like if the convenience of motorists was no longer among leading City Hall preoccupations.

Today, crossing over the monstrous width of Highway 401 and living amidst the masses of cars and trucks that dump millions of tonnes of greenhouse gases into our atmosphere each year, an obvious question presents itself: "How did we get here?" It is a question that current problems force us to try to answer, quickly. When we understand how we got here, finding a way out becomes easier. That is the story of this book, taking the reader on a bicycle ride into the past in order to understand the present, and to chart a path forward where the bicycle and the rider are neither loved nor hated, but simply respected and appreciated as a key element of our transportation system – and part of the answer to the climate crisis.

Enjoy the ride.

Albert Koehl, January 15, 2024

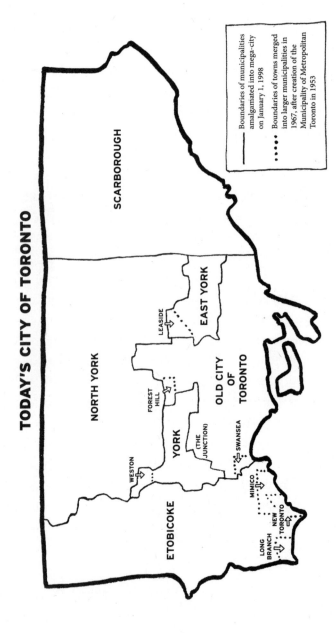

TODAY'S CITY OF TORONTO

SCARBOROUGH

NORTH YORK

ETOBICOKE

YORK

WESTON

FOREST HILL

(THE JUNCTION)

SWANSEA

MIMICO

NEW TORONTO

LONG BRANCH

EAST YORK

LEASIDE

OLD CITY OF TORONTO

Boundaries of municipalities amalgamated into mega-city on January 1, 1998

Boundaries of towns merged into larger municipalities in 1967, after creation of the Municipality of Metropolitan Toronto in 1953

Image 1: Map of today's City of Toronto, which – since amalgamation in January 1998 – encompasses all the municipalities, including the (old) City of Toronto, of the former "Metro," formally the Regional Municipality of Metropolitan Toronto. From its inception in 1954 until amalgamation, Metro Council, with representatives from each municipality, had authority over cross-boundary issues such as arterial roads and expressways. (Artist: Maggie Prince)

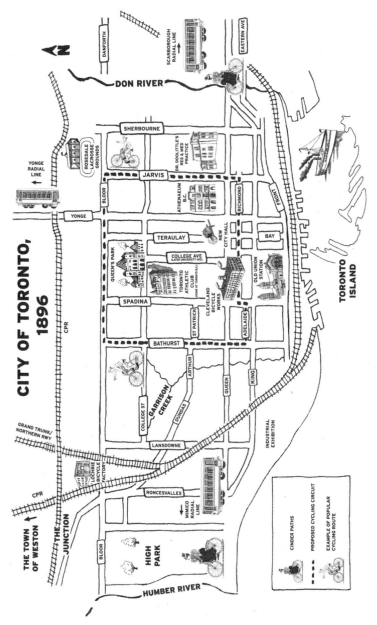

Image 2: Map sketch of Toronto in 1896, highlighting important cycling reference points, including the proposed city cycling circuit and some of the cinder paths beyond the city. (Artist: Maggie Prince)

Timeline of the Bicycle in Toronto

Laufmaschine ("running machine") invented by ——————— **1817** ——
German Baron Karl von Drais for utilitarian purposes,
then converted to leisure use as the so-called dandy horse
or hobby horse. (No record of its use in Toronto, then
known as Town of York.)

High-wheel (a.k.a. penny-farthing or ——————— **1878** ——
ordinary) arrives in Toronto. It is used
mainly for racing and touring by daring,
affluent, young men. Some men (and women)
ride elaborate, but expensive, tricycles, including
chain-driven versions.

Canada Cycle & Motor Company (CCM)
combines five biggest bicycle-makers in
Toronto area; operations soon consolidated
in The Junction, before later moving to ——————— **1899** ——
Town of Weston.

Bicycles remain common for
everyday travel, far outnumbering
the city's motorcars. Motorists are ——————————— **1910** ——
generally detested.

City Hall introduces the bicycle licence,
anticipating substantial revenues
from an estimated 30,000 bicycles.
Bicycle messengers remain common.
The rise of cars since 1916 has made
roads more dangerous. ——————— **1929** ——

Image 3: An illustrated timeline for the bicycle in Toronto, pre–Second World
War and post–Second World War. (Artist: Maggie Prince)

1869 — A new version of the baron's invention has a pedal crank on the front wheel – a vehicle later remembered as the "boneshaker." The first true "bicycle" is greeted with euphoria in the city, at least on indoor rinks, but not on sidewalks.

Toronto Bicycle Club (TBC) formed. In 1882 TBC is a founding member of Canadian Wheelmen's Association (CWA) (a sporting organization that still exists today as Canadian Cycling Association).

1881 —

1896 — Bicycle Craze in full swing after the "safety," featuring equally sized wheels and chain drive, is improved with pneumatic tires, and adapted for women with dropped centre bar. Bicycles, electric streetcars and "radials," steam trains, and ships offer abundant local and regional travel options.

1914–1918 — Canadian Corps Cyclist Battalion serves in WWI. Recruits train along Humber River.

1944 — Police estimate 50,000 bikes on city streets every day, including cyclists from surrounding communities. In 1942 alone, over 40,000 bike licences are issued by the city.

Rise to popularity among children of high-rise bikes, including CCM's popular Mustang with banana seat and monkey handlebars. ——————— **1960s**

Toronto's first bike lane installed on Poplar ——————— **1979**
Plains Road, four years after City Cycling Committee is created. But vehicular cycling approach, which rejects bike lanes, begins to dominate. Ontario's Sam the Safety Duck tells children to "drive" your bike.

Advocacy for Respect for Cyclists (ARC) calls for a coroner's review of cycling deaths. In 1998, coroner recommends network of bike lanes. ——————— **1996**

Bike Plan is adoped by newly amalgamated city, setting out total of 500 km of bike lanes within ten years. Bike Plan has little ———— **2001**
funding or support (outside downtown). "Bike Lanes on Bloor" becomes a rallying cry for grassroots activists. Annual Bells on Bloor parades beginning in 2007 become city's largest-ever advocacy rides.

Toronto Cyclists Union (now Cycle Toronto) formed — first ——————— **2008**
membership-based cycling advocacy group in city since the Toronto Cyclists' Association in 1890s.

1953 — Regional Municipality of Metro Toronto is formed as a federation of City of Toronto and its neighbours (Scarborough, East York, North York, York, and Etobicoke) to address cross-boundary issues, including transportation.

1971 — "Bicycle Revival" is part of growing environmental consciousness and concern about smog. The sporty ten-speed fuels the revival. Extension of Spadina Expressway is cancelled by Queen's Park. Metro Council in 1974 adopts plan to move cyclists from arterials to off-road trails.

1991 — City of Toronto begins planning, then building, bike lanes on secondary roads under its jurisdiction.

1998 — Amalgamation of Toronto with former parts of Metro into the new mega-city of Toronto, bringing together car-dependent suburbs with more densely populated areas where travel on foot, bike, and transit remains strong.

Global pandemic reaches Toronto. Community push for reallocation of public space leads to 30 km of new bike lanes by year's end, a record accomplishment for City Hall. During pandemic, food delivery by bike soars, while electric bikes proliferate.

2020 —

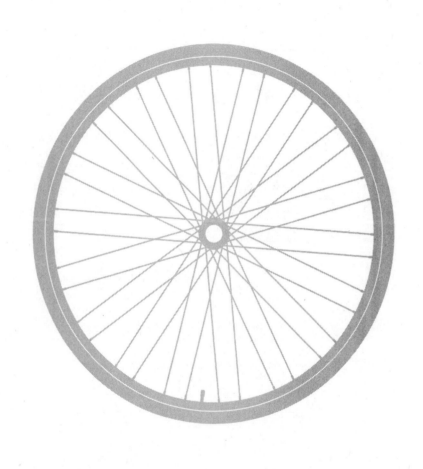

1896

The Bicycle Craze

August 13, 1896 – A good year for wheelmen

It's been a busy year for Dr. Perry Doolittle, Toronto's "pooh-bah and prime mover in everything of a cycling nature." The doctor has helped lead the fight against a municipal bicycle licence, overseen the posting of sign boards to guide city cyclists heading into the countryside, and rallied cycling groups in the call for better roads. Dr. Doolittle also wants to make sure that Mayor Robert Fleming's recent promise of improved cycling conditions in the city is transformed from words to action.

Last year, Dr. Doolittle's renown among cyclists helped him win the coveted presidency of the Canadian Wheelmen's Association (CWA). When his term ended at this year's annual meeting in April, he stood before 500 delegates, some arriving by rail from as far away as Vancouver, at the elegant Toronto Athletic Club on College Street. The Globe devoted three full pages to the "great gathering," describing it as "the most momentous in the annals of the association." The Evening Star listed doctors, lawyers, politicians, "silver-tongued orators, and oily-tongued speakers" among attendees. The Telegram, Mail & Empire, Toronto News, *and the* World, *as well as some US papers, all gave accounts of the meeting.*

After the CWA annual meeting, thirty-five-year-old Dr. Doolittle quickly took up the top post of the Toronto Cyclists' Association, a group that includes the influential Toronto Bicycle Club. In the fight for Sunday streetcar service, the Toronto Cyclists' Association has been courted for its support, although many cyclists are just as happy to have the devil strip (the generally smooth space between the tracks) to themselves on the Sabbath.

The doctor's credentials among wheelmen even makes him a valuable promoter for commercial products. "GENTLEMEN – As an old bicycle racing man, I can heartily endorse the chewing of Tutti-Frutti Gum in long hard races, as it very much diminishes the dryness and thirst which are so distressing at such times."

Riding a bicycle certainly doesn't require chewing gum, or an interest in racing – in fact there is growing agreement that the bicycle has "passed the period in which it was considered only for speeding or amusement." The standard use of pneumatic tires has further smoothed the transition to popular everyday use, including among women. The doctor has marvelled at the transformation brought about by the arrival of the safety, its chain-drive obviating the need for the giant front wheel of the high-wheel – an "out-of-date aristocratic mount," as the doctor now describes it. "To have foretold ten years ago that the bicycle to-day … would be the carriage of the patrician and the peasant; and would fluctuate the stock markets of railway systems and transport companies, would have placed one in the position of a dreamer." If there is today an upper limit to the bicycle's popularity in Toronto, or in the Dominion, it isn't yet in view.

In fact, in two days, the bicycle will take Dr. Doolittle across the Atlantic, at least as a business venture. Today, the doctor will travel by horse-drawn carriage (his bicycle would do just as well if he didn't have luggage) from his elegant east-end home on Sherbourne Street to Union Station. Once in Montreal he will board the S.S. Mongolian steamship bound for England. If all goes well, he'll be in London in eight days, secure investors for his coaster brake innovation, and return home in time to spend Christmas with his wife and two young children.

THE "SAFETY" (BICYCLE) … IN NUMBERS

"[E]verybody's talking about cycling," wrote *Saturday Night* publisher Edmund Sheppard in the spring of 1896. The *Globe* added that "although the snows of winter are with us still yet already we are talking bicycle, thinking bicycle and dreaming bicycle." Sheppard proposed, at least mischievously, a vocabulary for cycling discourse. "Refer to this means of locomotion always as cycling. Never call it bicycling, nor tricycling, nor wheeling, nor rubbering, nor biking, nor gittin' there. All these expressions suggest vulgarity, or, what is worse, a lack of blasé-ness."

The count of bicycles conducted by the *Mail & Empire* in the commercial district on a weekday in October 1895, between 9 a.m. and 6:30 p.m., confirmed Dr. Doolittle's view that cycling was transitioning from amusement to everyday transportation. Newspaper staff, stationed at a window overlooking the street, counted each cyclist riding east or west along King Street, between Bay and Yonge Streets. The highest bicycle traffic was recorded at the end of the workday with 395 cyclists in the thirty-minute interval after 6 p.m. Over 3,500 cyclists were counted during the

Image 4: Yonge Street, looking north from Queen Street, c. 1895. A large, vertical BICYCLE sign (right, foreground) advertises one of many such retailers in the area. There are at least six cyclists in the photo, as well as a horse-drawn wagon at the curb on the left. Most people go about on foot, although electric streetcars, dating from 1892 in the city, are common. An 1896 bike count on nearby King Street recorded over 3,500 cyclists in under ten hours. (Courtesy Musée McCord Stewart, MP-0000.25.179)

nine-and-a-half-hour period (a figure that would put King Street among the busiest cycling routes in the city even today). "There can be no doubt," observed the reporter, "that the bicycling furore has struck Toronto with considerable vehemence."

The excitement for bicycles somewhat depended on one's perspective. One citizen on foot, who twice had to abort attempts to cross the intersection at King and Yonge Streets because of heavy bicycle traffic, complained: "This is too much of a good thing ... this city's getting overrun with these darned wheels." A passing cyclist countered that he "would not be without a wheel for any money. You're independent, and see the time it saves." He counselled City Hall to improve side streets as an alternative to the busy King and Yonge intersection for cyclists – and warned aldermen to "look out for themselves if they're going to try to put us down."

As tensions between cyclists and pedestrians grew, the *Daily Star* playfully, perhaps unhelpfully, suggested that it was pedestrians that should be regulated, using a fictional crash between a visiting farmer on foot and a cyclist as its premise. "See, here, young man," complained the farmer, "I've been dodgin' trolleys all day and I'm not goin' to submit to being run down by one of you." The cyclist replied: "Why, sir, there's 5,000 of us in Toronto. You ought to be glad the whole lot weren't on top of you at once." The *Daily Star* continued the jest, proposing a pedestrian code of conduct, including an obligation to sound a bell or horn upon noticing a cyclist. Taxes were also to be imposed on pedestrians, turning on its head calls to tax cyclists.

Cycling to work had become so popular that bicycle rooms, sometimes with over 200 parking spots, were created, or planned, at a number of office buildings and institutions, including the then

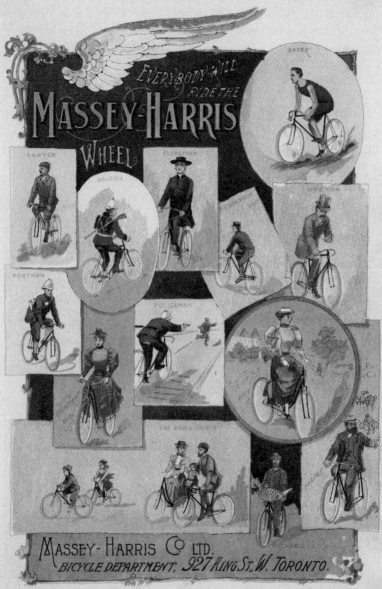

Union Station (just west of its current location), the music conservatory, and at Confederation Life on Richmond Street where Mayor Fleming had his business office. The plans for Toronto's new City Hall (completed in 1899) included two bicycle rooms. The Board of Trade, to dissuade employees and tenants from parking in the building's corridors, was planning to add a room for 100 bicycles. At the twelve-storey Temple Building, the city's tallest skyscraper at its completion in 1896, cyclists could park their vehicles and, for a small fee, have them repaired and cleaned.

In 1895, an estimated 18,000 bicycles were sold in Toronto – an impressive number for a city that counted 196,000 people. Some buyers were repeat customers replacing old bicycles to keep up with year-over-year changes. The city's 1896 directory listed eighty bicycle shops, but other enterprises such as drug and hardware stores also sold bicycles to take advantage of the growing demand.

By 1896 prices for bicycles had begun to fall. The Griffiths Cycle Corporation on Yonge Street was selling bikes for $65 (and $35 by 1898), while the T. Eaton Co. advertised women's bikes for $70, and other bikes for $49. The Toronto Bicycle Exchange on Adelaide Street, touting their "business wheel," offered new bicycles for sale, or for exchange with an older model. Second-hand bicycles

(Opposite) **Image 5:** "Everybody Will Ride the Massey-Harris Wheel." This bicycle catalogue cover, c. 1897, suggests the potential market for bicycles, namely, almost everyone. The illustration lists a lawyer, soldier, clergyman, messenger boy, racer, doctor, postman, country girl, policeman, city girl, children, family of three, mechanic, and farmer. Massey-Harris started making bicycles in Toronto in 1895 to respond to the surging demand. (City of Toronto Archives, Series 2508, File 9, Item 11)

were a more economic option, as were creative options between parties such as an exchange of goods and services, including guitar lessons, for a bicycle.

A reporter's account of a Massey Hall concert to finance bicycle paths suggested that the composition of the audience demonstrated that "the love of cycling has permeated all classes of the community, from the rulers of the financial world down to the individual who holds the rein over a dust-stained coal cart during the day, and drives the dust off of his lungs in the evening by taking a spin in the country." But although bicycle prices were falling, even to almost half of the $100 that had been standard earlier in the decade, bicycles remained out of reach for many people, no matter that retailer John Griffiths Cycle Corporation touted bicycles as "no longer a luxury, but almost a necessity." While professionals, businesspeople, and others of at least middle-class means could afford bicycles, it wasn't likely that sales clerks, telegraph and telephone operators, or domestic, hotel, and restaurant staff could afford one. This did not stop one retailer on Yonge Street from advertising men's and lady's bikes for $85 and $90, respectively, under the title "Even the Poor May Ride."

The factory worker, who might take home $400 in a year, could perhaps rent a bicycle for a few hours – but not on Sundays, the worker's day off, when shops were closed – for the novel experience. Ellsworth and Musson offered 125 bicycles for rent. At many livery stables in the city, the demand for bicycles outstripped that for horses. "The sign 'Bicycles to rent' can be seen adorning nearly every other store window," claimed one newspaper report.

The demand by residents for bicycle riding academies and schools confirmed the keen interest. When the Remington Cycle School opened in February 1896, nearly 1,000 people dropped in "to inspect the school, its spacious well-lighted riding-hall, and its perfect appointments." Most large retailers and bicycle-makers actually provided riding schools above their showrooms. After its Yonge Street retail shop proved too small, H.A. Lozier & Company, maker of Cleveland bicycles at its factory in the Town of West Toronto Junction (which became part of the City of Toronto in 1909, and is today known as The Junction), rented the Granite Club Rink on Church Street to offer cycling lessons. An innovative device, an extra set of wheels to be attached to either side of the rear axle for balance, offered stability to novice riders without the helping hand of a paid instructor.

Young clergymen considered the bicycle "an indispensable part of their equipment," more so for visits beyond the city. "By means of the noiseless steed, which has no need for a digestive apparatus, the preacher can fulfil his country appointments and visit his sick parishioners." Some church leaders, however, fretted, amidst falling attendance at Protestant churches, that parishioners were being lured from the church pew to the bicycle seat. *Saturday Night*'s Sheppard suggested that the church had failed to recognize the cycling trend, but to tackle the issue now would create a "storm of indignation ... more apt to ruin the church than to tie up the wheel." Sheppard said the church would do better to treat the bicycle as a useful conveyance for the faithful, perhaps even providing a bicycle shed for storage, especially given that streetcars were banned on Sundays until a May 1897 municipal plebiscite.

Toronto police also welcomed bicycles to carry out their duties, inaugurating a fleet of five imported Tangent bicycles in 1894, adding ten more in 1896, some to be used by its detectives. Chief Constable Grasett praised the brand in Tangent ads, claiming they had

Image 6: Bicycle Storage Room at the Toronto Lithographing Company in 1898. With many people cycling to work in the city, bicycle storage rooms became important facilities at workplaces, as well as other institutions. (City of Toronto Archives, Fonds 1137, Item 0007)

"required no repairs, though the state of the roads has been such as to impose a more severe test upon them." Bicycles also didn't need to be stabled or fed, offering savings relative to horses.

CYCLING IN THE CITY

The War on Dogs, and the Devil's Temptation

The city had a long-standing battle with its stray dogs, punctuated by declarations of war on an otherwise loved creature. One solution, police poisoning of strays, hadn't sat well with the public, and stricter enforcement of the dog licensing by-law was generally the preferred, albeit marginally effective, option. A passing cyclist presented dogs with an appealing opportunity for a pursuit, but the days when packs of dogs freely roamed the streets was over. In 1894, a City Hall committee renewed the "War on Dogs" with measures that allowed for the seizure of dogs running at large – an initiative undoubtedly appreciated by cyclists.

The poor quality of roads remained the greatest challenge for cyclists. The relatively smooth, narrow swath of the road between opposing streetcar tracks, known as the "devil strip," offered a strong temptation for cyclists, but with an obvious risk when streetcars approached from opposite directions. Toronto's streetcar system, or more precisely, the devil strips along the routes, provided an unofficial cycling network. Cyclists had an obvious interest in seeing the devil strips well maintained, and in the city's engineer, Edward Keating, they found a supporter. He believed that paving the devil strip with brick should be the norm.

By 1894, the horse-drawn cars of the city's streetcar system had all been replaced by electric cars, part of a streetcar network that had grown to 80 miles (129 kilometres). The longest continuous route on the "cars" (the term for streetcars until appropriated for motorcars) was from Victoria Park in the east to Toronto Junction. Cyclists had good reason to cheer the arrival of the electric cars, which eliminated horse droppings, or "road apples," although the greater speed of electric cars gave cyclists good reason for caution.

Cyclists using the devil strip also had to keep an eye out for other cyclists. The custom was that eastbound and southbound cyclists had the right-of-way. (The province codified this rule in 1897, albeit only for Toronto.) *Saturday Night* offered its own sardonic advice for crashes between cyclists: "an effort should be

made to ride over the prostrate enemy as gracefully as possible."
Cycling at night along streetcar routes likewise required a rider's
full attention, even if those streets benefited from lighting, whether
powered by gas or, increasingly, by electricity.

Bicycle outings by couples (sometimes on a tandem) had
become both fashionable and a pleasant way to enjoy the cooler
evening air, especially if the daytime temperature hit 91 degrees
Fahrenheit (33 degrees Celsius), as it did on July 2, 1896. Lawyer
Thomas Rowan's Methodist religion and family background placed
him squarely within Toronto's establishment but not beyond the
danger of its streetcars. He had suffered a broken leg in a crash
with a streetcar in 1893. On this July evening, around 10:30 p.m.,
his small cycling party, including his wife, Gertrude, were heading
back to their elegant home on Bloor Street. On reaching the intersection of Harbord Street and Spadina Avenue, they looked north
and south for the single, bright light or "bull's eye" of an approaching car to ensure a safe route.

Once on Spadina, Rowan cycled within the north-bound
tracks, his wife within the opposite tracks, and their companion
in the devil strip. As they cycled north, a car travelling at 16 mph
(26 km/h) – despite the regular and established rate of not more
than 8 mph (12 km/h) – rounded the bend behind them at Knox
College Crescent, closing quickly. The couple's companion managed
to abandon the tracks in time, while Mrs. Rowan could only watch
in horror as the car dragged her husband under its fender for almost
200 feet (60 metres). The webbed cow-catcher on the front of the
car, originally designed to knock aside wayward cows, was of little
benefit to Rowan who was rushed to a nearby physician's home.

Rowan recovered from his injuries and filed a lawsuit against
the Toronto Railway Company (TRC) for the negligence of its

motorman. The case was heard in early 1897, and ultimately decided by the Supreme Court of Canada. Rowan got $1,500 in damages from the TRC in a decision in which the judges emphasized the cyclist's right to ride within the space of the tracks.

"Muddy York" No More, but Not Quite Buffalo

When the City of Toronto, which succeeded the Town of York, was incorporated in 1834, it counted less than 9,300 inhabitants. Since then the city had slowly, but not completely, moved beyond the insult "Muddy York," especially when spring rains turned some roads, especially those that were little more than compacted dirt paths, into muddy ones, and then, once they dried, into a great source of dust. The sprinkling of water along streetcar tracks and on roads helped to suppress dust, but created slippery pavement for cyclists. There were geologic reasons for the mud, given the city's location on the bed of ancient Lake Iroquois, its clay and sand foundation offering good conditions for mud. The steep slope of the lake's shoreline exhausted cyclists heading to new parts of the city beyond Bloor, which in the mid-1880s still formed most of Toronto's northern boundary. Other contributions to the roadway muck were of more recent vintage, including sewage run-off from some homes, droppings from animals on their way to slaughterhouses, and spillover from carts carrying refuse, including offal from the city's many butcher shops.

Cyclists could skirt holes in the road (the word "pothole" came later), animal waste, or other obstacles, but avoiding the dust and odour was more difficult. The quality of roads was an obvious constraint on the future prospects of the bicycle. By 1896, when the safety's popularity was soaring, only half of the city's 260 miles

(418 kilometres) of roads were paved – with cedar blocks, asphalt, macadam, or brick.

Toronto residents often looked with envy at the wealthy City of Buffalo, which by 1894 boasted over 100 miles (160 kilometres) of asphalted roads, compared to less than 14 miles (22 kilometres) in Toronto. Fortunately for cyclists, who appreciated how smoothly their pneumatic tires rolled over asphalt, City Engineer Edward Keating and most city newspapers favoured asphalt. In "Toronto the Good" – a term used mockingly, proudly, or somewhere in between – asphalt fit nicely with ideas of hygiene, aesthetics, and propriety.

Tree-lined Jarvis Street, the city's first asphalted road in 1888, ranked among the best cycling streets, better still after regular street cleaning began. On a single evening in April 1896, Alderman James B. Boustead claimed to have observed from his verandah 200 children, many with chaperones, riding down Jarvis. Boustead had good reason to notice cyclists: he had been a founder of the Toronto Bicycle Club in 1881 and the CWA in 1882. For his part, Dr. Doolittle considered St. George Street as a rival to Jarvis for the title "select swell street of the city."

Macadam also had its admirers, among them the province's official instructor for road building, A.W. Campbell. He considered it the best surface for cycling, listing among its qualities that it wasn't slippery when wet. University Avenue, Bloor between Yonge and Avenue Road, as well as routes in High Park, all had macadam surfaces.

The choice of road surface was an intensely political question in Toronto, while expertise in paving was rudimentary and the quality of paving materials varied. When cedar blocks (cut to uniform lengths and stood side by side on a solid foundation), which were once considered *de rigueur* in Toronto, became wet, they were slippery and hazardous for cyclists – and when gouged by wagon wheels, they were susceptible to water absorption and rot. Asphalt wasn't yet of a quality that, despite its high cost, made it generally water-resistant. Infiltration of water led to deterioration. (It would take until the 1920s for high-quality asphalt to be developed.)

Sidewalks made of plank boards, and newer ones of concrete, were a tempting refuge for cyclists, although discouraged by a $1 fine and the wrath of pedestrians. For the genteel members of the older bicycle clubs, sidewalk-riding could sully one's reputation. In May 1895, the press reported that R.A. Robertson, a former chair of the CWA Racing Board and "the idol of the cyclists in Hamilton, has fallen from grace" for riding on a sidewalk. In downtown Toronto, cycling on sidewalks was a poor option given the crowds of pedestrians, vendors selling produce, craftsmen, and children at play, including ones who didn't go to school. A motion by city council to allow sidewalk riding during early morning hours, sometimes rationalized as benefiting doctors making house calls, failed.

Cyclists had an obvious interest in good roads not only in the city but for their excursions into the countryside – and therefore good reason to support Ontario's Good Roads Association, created in 1894 with strong support from farmers. Cyclists nonetheless had to be motivated to take the matter of country roads seriously, perhaps because, unlike farmers on their way from farm to market, they could pick and choose their routes. In 1895, Andrew Patullo, who concurrently chaired the CWA's roads committee and the Good Roads Association, rebuked CWA members for their lack of enthusiasm for the cause. (A few years later another commentator complained about the poor state of the roads leading out of

Toronto and the failure of cyclists to exert their influence, lamenting an "all prevailing desire on the part of wheelmen apparently to leave these matters to anybody and of course that means nobody.") In its defence, the CWA had cautioned that it might do more harm than good as leader of the good roads movement because rural audiences would treat their role as "an agitation to help out a lot of dude wheelmen." The CWA did, however, devote substantial energy to the posting of sign boards, albeit with no protection from "anyone with an axe," along roads leading out of the city, offering information about distances, directions, and steep hills. "Good roads, abundantly sign boarded," was a favourite slogan of Dr. Doolittle.

No Regulations, Please – We're Cyclists

The proliferation of bicycles soon led to public demands for regulation. As early as April 1890, Toronto Alderman John Swait called for a bill "to regulate the running of bicycles on the public streets and avenues." At the time, City Hall didn't have the requisite authority, which wasn't granted by the province until 1895. In the meantime, a judicial interpretation of Ontario's *Municipal Act* to include bicycles in the definition of "vehicle" gave municipalities at least some authority to pass cycling by-laws.

Organized cycling groups, including the CWA, the Toronto Cyclists' Association (TCA) – which replaced the Inter-Club Association in May 1896 – and the more established bicycle clubs, were always quick to rally against any regulation, often labelling such restrictions as a nuisance – a point of view shared by many city councillors. In March 1896, a Board of Works subcommittee that had been established by council to meet with cycling groups was quick to provide the assurance, as reported in the *Globe*, that nothing was further from the minds of civic leaders than the "licensing, tagging, belling, braking, or of doing anything obnoxious to the wheelmen." On this occasion, although this was not always the case, a bicycle tax was opposed even if it was dedicated to the building of cinder paths for cyclists. The groups were more receptive to proposed regulation of "reckless" cycling, which they considered as applying to other cyclists, not their own members.

The danger posed by cyclists was increased by the fact that brakes had been slow to catch up with other advances of the bicycle. On the high-wheel, brakes had usually been limited to plunger or spoon-like devices, controlled from a lever on the handlebars to push down on the front wheel, albeit with unwanted wear on the tire. Braking was more often limited to the rider resisting the forward rotation of the pedal crank (like today's brakeless fixed-gear bikes), an exercise with marginal success on downhills. The development of the freewheel on the chain-driven safety created new braking possibilities, including the coaster or hub brake, which allowed the rider to stop the bicycle by pushing back against the pedals, engaging a device in the rear hub. The "Doolittle Brake," for which the doctor was seeking investors overseas, was an adaptation of existing brakes on the market in 1896.

In early 1894, both the Executive Committee and the Board of Works of city council proposed that bicycles be equipped with lamps and bells, the latter "to give warning to all persons in danger of being run down." Cycling groups opposed the initiative. "I think a note of warning should be sounded, but I would not call it a bell," argued Dr. Doolittle, adding, "I also do not think a light necessary. It would look like a glow-worm in our electric-light streets." Advocates often hinted that regulation could undermine the growing bicycle industry and its contribution to the local economy, and on this occasion, noted the imminent start of large-scale bicycle manufacturing in the city. The generally upper-class status of cycling advocates ensured a sympathetic hearing at City Hall, both because many politicians were themselves wheelmen or they travelled in the same social circles. Indeed, an invitation for a politician to speak at a gathering of cyclists was usually accepted with gratitude.

The proposals for lamps and bells failed, although Chief Constable Grasett, in his annual report for 1894, reiterated the call, as well as action to address reckless cycling. (The Board of Works again proposed bells and lamps in April 1897, forcing cycling groups to repeat their "usual performance" at council and suggesting that aldermen would do better to devote their energies to improving the many unsafe roadways.)

With the possible exception of licensing (and bicycle paths, especially later in the decade), no cycling issue provoked as much passionate debate as a speed limit for cyclists. Fast riding was often disparagingly called "scorching," loosely defined as a combination of speeding and recklessness. The older cycling clubs, probably to distinguish themselves from the newer, apparently less cultivated, ranks of cyclists, rebuked scorchers. In fact, since 1892 the Toronto Bicycle Club had a rule: "No scorching on Club runs."

The CWA agreed with Chief Constable Grasett that a bicycle speed limit was needed – but agreeing on a specific number was more challenging. Addressing a City Hall committee, Dr. Doolittle lamented possible restrictions on speed. "A business man can walk four miles. The trolley is very much faster than eight miles, and wheelmen would be very much dissatisfied if we could not go as fast as the cars." Cycling clubs were willing to accept a 10 mph (16 km/h) limit.

In February 1895, councillors compromised by amending an existing road by-law to prohibit cyclists from travelling at an "immoderate" speed. The by-law already applied to horses and horse-drawn conveyances. "Immoderate" – sometimes called "furious" driving or "furious" riding when relating to horses – wasn't defined by a specific numerical limit but was left up to the judgment of individual officers. At an October 1895 city council meeting, it was noted that the City of Buffalo had a 10 mph (16 km/h) limit and a requirement for bells, but no further action was considered necessary – one alderman suggesting that city residents would complain about the noise from 10,000 bells.

The subjective interpretation required for "immoderate" meant that the biases of officers might be applied to the detriment of riders of a lower class. The clubs already looked down upon scorchers, or what the Toronto Bicycle Club's president, E.B. Ryckman, described as "hoodlums showing off new-found cycling skills on asphalt pavements." Certain streets were specifically exempted, during specific hours, from the prohibition, with fast riding (or driving in the case of horse-drawn conveyances) allowed on sections of Palmerston Boulevard and Eastern Avenue. The by-law prohibition remained in effect decades later when it was also applied to motorcars, even after numeric speed limits were established. Police in the 1890s could measure speed, much as race officials did, by measuring elapsed time to cover a specific distance, but they were far more likely to rely on observation, using known speeds, such as foot or horse travel, as a reference.

In April 1896, the *Evening Star* again raised the issue of cyclists' speed, asking readers to comment on a 5 or 6 mph (8 or 9 km/h) limit, and 8 mph (12 km/h) for outlying streets. A coroner's jury reviewing the death in early 1896 of a young cyclist, racing a friend on Roxborough Avenue, recommended an 8 mph (12 km/h) limit, and 6 mph (9 km/h) for intersections. Alderman Boustead supported a "reasonable rate" as a fair return for cyclists' call for good roads, and as a way to protect children from other road vehicles. Both cyclists and drivers of horse-drawn vehicles provoked public complaints. "And while all these little people are enjoying themselves [on Upper Jarvis], all at once, zip ! comes a horse and buggy ... or flash ! will come two or three scorchers."

In October 1897, when Alderman Preston proposed an 8 mph (12 km/h) limit, Ryckman "chortled" in the course of a "truculent" deputation at City Hall. The political influence of organized cyclists was evident, the *Evening Star* even commended Preston for his courage in raising a matter other councillors would avoid for fear of offending the city's "sporting contingent" of 2,000 CWA members, among about 25,000 cyclists.

The province made its first foray into the regulation of cyclists in early 1895, motivated by an apparent increase in collisions between cyclists and pedestrians. Peterborough MPP James Stratton introduced a bill to amend the *Municipal Act* to allow for the licensing and regulation of cyclists. Toronto MPP Oliver Howland, later a mayor of the city, introduced a similar bill. An influential delegation from the bicycle clubs and bicycle trade appeared before the Municipal Committee at Queen's Park, as did a number of pedestrians who had been injured in crashes involving cyclists. It was quickly clear where the committee's sympathies lay. When Mr. Beverley Jones presented himself as a victim of a crash, the committee chair jocularly remarked, "You don't look badly injured." A speaker at the same hearing pointed out that many of the injured parties present were lawyers to which MPP Howland joked that "a bicycle cannot go astray in Toronto without hitting a lawyer."

Ryckman, on behalf of the CWA, again reminded MPPs on the Municipal Committee about the significant economic contribution of the bicycle industry and the estimated 35,000 cyclists in the province, warning that any interference with such an interest should be undertaken with caution. MPP Stratton must have taken note, attempting to withdraw his bill's provision on licensing. The bill was nonetheless put to a vote. The *Globe* joyfully reported that it met "a violent death."

A general *Municipal Act* provision "for regulating and governing (but not licensing) persons using bicycles" was, however, adopted, applicable to cities with a population of over 100,000 – a short list that began and ended with Toronto. The regulation of cyclists in other cities was deferred to a future date.

In 1897 and again in 1898, Queen's Park passed new laws, including a bill by MPP Stratton as well as changes called for by cycling groups. Cyclists would, for instance, be obliged to give an audible signal before passing another road vehicle, while slower vehicles were required to keep to the right. An early opportunity to interpret the new rules involved a Law Society bencher knocked off his bicycle by a boy driving a butcher cart. The boy and the lawyer, travelling in opposite directions, each kept to the right, but the boy suddenly turned his cart across the road to enter a gate, knocking the lawyer off his bicycle. The boy was found to be at fault, and fined.

In June 1898, Toronto City Council adopted – after consulting with local cycling groups – By-law 3596, *To regulate bicycle traffic*, articulating rights and obligations within the new regulatory powers granted by the province. Carrying children on a bicycle and the practice of riding two abreast were banned. Cyclists were obliged to proceed slowly through intersections, and to control their vehicles at all times by keeping their feet on the pedals and hands on the handlebars. (The *Globe* poked fun at the provision: what was a cyclist to do, "if his nose itches or his hat threatens to resign and join the rush to the Klondike.") Drivers of vehicles were obliged, when meeting cyclists, to leave sufficient room on the right. Other proposals failed, including an obligation to dismount and walk across busy intersections on Yonge Street, and to reduce speed on portions of Yonge and King Streets with heavy pedestrian traffic. Lamps and bells also escaped regulation. Lamps at the time were unreliable acetylene devices that cycling groups had good reason to oppose, while the successful opposition to bells mostly reflected the influence of cyclists.

"A Veritable Wheelman's Paradise" – a City Cycling Circuit

In his inaugural address in January 1896 as Toronto's new mayor, Robert Fleming promised road improvements for the benefit of cyclists. Fleming, sometimes known as "the People's Bob," said that part of each street should be paved with the most suitable material for cycling, adding that "strips" on streets "where asphalt or brick does not now exist, should be put in first-class shape for bicycle riders." He added that parts of the street should be graded and paved with special attention to "the comfort of those using wheels." The *Globe*, in commenting on the speech observed, "The bicyclist feels that he is becoming a power in the land just now." News of Fleming's speech even crossed the Atlantic where a commentator in London's *Lady's Pictorial* wrote (exaggerating the mayor's words) that "Toronto – that city of telephones and blonde beauties – is going ahead in the matter of bicycling. News is to hand that the Mayor-elect intends to put down a cycling track in every new street that is constructed."

In mid-February 1896, cycling groups, at a meeting held at the Athenaeum Bicycle Club, proposed a 10-mile (16-kilometre) cycling circuit, to be created by combining paved roads with other roads that were either to be improved or upon which bicycle strips were to be added. The proposed circuit included Bloor Street along the top and Richmond and Adelaide Streets along the bottom, with parallel Bathurst and Jarvis Streets as north–south connections. Bicycle strips were also recommended for Teraulay (now Bay) and Victoria Streets, providing an alternative to Yonge. (Meanwhile, James Lochrie, manufacturer of the Antelope – which he promoted as embodying "the most significant improvements known in the art of Cycle building" – promised to build a bicycle path along Bloor near his factory in the city's west end, near Lansdowne Avenue.) The *Globe* beamed that the proposals, if implemented, "will make Toronto a veritable wheelman's paradise, exceeding in that respect even Buffalo."

The cost of the work was a key concern. Even Alderman Boustead, a member of City Council's Special Committee on Cycling Matters, at a subsequent meeting on the issue suggested that a tax on bicyclists would allow the city to improve roads, rationalizing to cyclists that a $1 annual fee would save $4 in bicycle repairs. In cases where City Hall acknowledged that road improvements were necessary, local property owners were, however, not necessarily willing to shoulder the cost, according to the normal process for improving roads.

Despite the *Globe*'s excitement, the issue of bike paths was complicated. For starters, Ontario's *Municipal Act* conferred no authority on cities to create bicycle paths, which may explain why city officials usually talked about bicycle strips that could be framed as road repairs. The CWA and most cycling advocates considered bicycle paths a distraction from the broader objective of improving roads for all users, with cyclists as an obvious beneficiary. In fact, the CWA's 1895 membership cards were emblazoned with "WE WANT GOOD ROADS." A.W. Campbell characterized bicycle paths as "but a protest against bad roads." The slow pace in improving roads, however, frustrated many cycling advocates, who, as well-to-do citizens, were not accustomed to being denied, fuelling the demand for bicycle strips and paths.

At a meeting with city officials in March 1896, cycling groups reiterated that their first priority was for roads to be kept in good repair, while Dr. Doolittle confirmed that cyclists did not want special treatment. The proposed cycling circuit was not approved, although in his report for 1896, City Engineer Keating listed a number of proposed and installed bicycle strips, including one on Spadina Avenue.

In addition to bicycle strips on city roads, bicycle paths, often known as cinder or side-paths, connecting the city to outlying areas, including along routes with no roads, or in parks, had strong support among cycling groups for recreational and sporting purposes. Chief Constable Grasett had called for a bike path on Toronto Island to get cyclists off foot paths. By 1896, a number of bicycle paths had been built in and around the city, including a cinder path along the Lakeshore Road, from Sunnyside (near the foot of Roncesvalles Avenue) to the Humber River, with ambitions to extend it to Mimico and beyond. Other paths, subject to financing, were planned, including one (installed in 1897) running up Kingston Road from Queen Street East to the top of Norway Hill – to make a difficult uphill ride easier for cyclists on their way out of the city along the popular cycling route.

A priority of the Inter-Club Association of Toronto wheelmen, formed in 1894 and succeeded by the Toronto Cyclists' Association, was the building of cinder paths. The club's secretary, lawyer George Kingston, could be very persuasive, publicly reprimanding cyclists and bicycle retailers for failing to contribute financially to the cause. In 1895, he complained about the waterfront bike path. "Is it fair that 9,700 wheelmen stand by and make use of a road for which 300 others have put up the money?" The *Mail & Empire* launched its own campaign for cinder paths, including among its initiatives the Massey Hall concert in the spring of 1896. It was no surprise that innkeepers on the Humber River that catered to cyclists were among the more enthusiastic contributors.

Once in place, intrusions on bike paths were taken seriously, especially given the damage caused by wagon wheels. After three men in a rig drunkenly rode along the lakeshore cinder path, and were each fined $5, the *Evening Star* declared that the "rights of wheelmen must be observed in the good city of Toronto." At the time, the legal basis for the by-law was unclear, although a provincial law in 1897 gave clear authority to prohibit such bike path incursions. Cycling groups were quick to push for enforcement, especially on the popular Kingston Road cinder path where farmers often parked their wagons, before going to nearby hotels. One intruder, a well-known Queen Street broker, was fined $1 for the offence in 1899, then made amends by contributing $5 to the cinder path fund.

Bicycle paths or bicycle strips were, however, opposed by some members of the public, who argued that if cyclists wanted special treatment, they should pay for it. In fact, in terms of cinder paths, this was precisely what the Inter-Club Association had aimed to do, while its successor, the Toronto Cyclists' Association, sometimes appeared ready to accede to a fee or tax on cyclists if revenues were directed to road improvements or cinder paths.

Some residents considered dedicated bikeways as a needed protection for pedestrians – *from* cyclists, instead of a benefit to cyclists. Beverley Jones pointed to his own injury in a collision with a cyclist, as well as the death of another resident, killed by a cyclist who fled the scene, as grounds for imposing a $1 fee on cyclists, which he suggested would raise $6,000, to be leveraged with municipal debentures, for the construction of 80 to 100 miles (128 to 160 kilometres) of bike paths in the Toronto area, similar to ones already in place in Brooklyn, New York. The issue of a bicycle tax came up on a number of subsequent occasions, rationalized on various grounds, including as a part of a registration system to reduce bicycle thefts – but always failed.

Some individuals were intent on making cycling more expensive in other ways by targeting a particular weakness of the bicycle: tires that were easily punctured. City police were instructed to better enforce a by-law that prohibited throwing glass, tacks, and other objects on the road.

Bicyclists Divided – the Pros and Cons of Bicycle Strips and Paths

The tension between cycling groups who saw bicycle paths as a way forward and other cycling groups who considered them a distraction in the fight for better roads might have ended peacefully enough, but for developments after 1896.

First, although not controversially, Queen's Park in April 1897, spurred by a delegation of the Toronto Cyclists' Association and CWA, amended the *Municipal Act* to articulate a municipal

The Ruling Passion Strong in Death.

" Poor Dick is gone ; he was a devoted cyclist, wasn't he?"
" Yes, indeed ; he left a will stating that he was to be cremated and used to help out our new cinder-path."

Image 7: "The Ruling Passion Strong in Death." Enthusiasm for cinder bicycle paths among some cyclists is depicted in this cartoon in *Saturday Night*, May 23, 1896. The male companion recalls the devotion of the woman's late husband to cycling. "Yes, indeed," she says, "he left a will stating that he wished to be cremated and used to help out our new cinder-path." (Courtesy of Toronto Public Library)

authority to set aside "so much of a highway, road or street as the council deemed necessary" for bicycle paths. Up to that point, municipal power to create such paths had been ambiguous, even if sometimes assumed.

In early 1899, tensions between the CWA and its own Toronto District, which called for bicycle paths to deal with the slow pace of road improvements, surfaced into an awkward public spat. (The fight had similarities to the conflict between bike lane proponents and so-called "vehicular cyclists" eighty years later.) At the centre of the controversy was MPP James Stratton's "side-paths bill," which sought to create a direct government role in building bicycle paths. The bill, drafted by the CWA's Toronto District, which by then had largely supplanted the Toronto Cyclists' Association in the city, envisioned bicycle paths connecting towns and cities, to be financed by a licence for path users, a system to be overseen by appointed commissioners.

Hal B. Howson rationalized, on behalf of the CWA's Toronto District, that the move was necessary given the poor quality of roads, pointing to shortcomings in the Statute Labour System, by which rural roads were built and maintained. The system depended on local farmers who contributed their time or resources, usually with poor results. (Farmers' interest in road-building had waned after railways proliferated.) Howson suggested that, at the existing pace, "the present generation will have passed away" before good roads become a reality. The CWA's secretary publicly rebuked Howson, reminding him that the side-paths bill was inconsistent with CWA goals, noting that an active provincial role risked separating cyclists and the general public in the "crusade" for better roads. The *Globe*'s headline about the Stratton-Howson initiative, "Obnoxious Bike Bill," left no doubt that it backed the official CWA position: "Agitation or legislation for sidepaths must necessarily detract from the strength of the good roads movement."

Stratton withdrew his bill in late March 1899, even after it had passed second reading, citing a lack of opportunity for full debate. It was clear, however, that dissension among cycling groups had dulled the political appeal of his initiative.

WHAT'S NEW, WHAT'S NOT

Women Awheel

The safety made cycling appealing to women, for the same reason that it made cycling more appealing to all. And once pneumatic tires were added to the safety, the vehicle offered not only efficient movement from a lower altitude but also a smooth ride. "What a wondrous advance in the march of progress has been the adaptation of the bicycle to its present use!" exclaimed the *Globe* in 1892, suggesting that the pneumatic safety might in time "be succeeded by something more nearly perfect, if that were possible."

Although the bicycle was accessible to women, the looser fitting, shorter clothing that made cycling more comfortable resulted in attacks based on morality. Women were quick to push back: How could cycling be immoral, asked one commentator, when the daughters of prominent families and matrons, as well as the clergy, counted themselves among cyclists? By 1896, cycling as fashion appeared to have gained the upper hand over cycling as immoral, at least among the class of women who could afford bicycles.

"Can you fancy it, my sisters?" asked writer Grace Denison, noting that before 1890 there had been no women cyclists in the country, but since then "we have learned a new enthusiasm, gone through the Battle of the Bloomer, taken into our life a new pleasure, the like of which we never before experienced or even in our dreams imagined." The Comet Cycle Co. displayed its Ladies Comet, featuring a dropped crossbar, at Toronto's Industrial Exhibition in 1890. In fact, in recognizing Florence Creed as the "Pioneer Canadian lady rider" for being the first to pedal a safety (a Ladies Comet) in 1889, *Cycling* offered a slight adjustment to Denison's date. Creed was the daughter of Thomas Fane, an owner of Comet Cycle which operated a five-storey bicycle-making factory on Temperance Street.

Outfits designed for cycling added to the appeal of the activity. At her Yonge Street shop, Rachael Wolfe, "The Leading Ladies' Tailor," sold cycling costumes from $10 to $12, touting them as without equal in the city "for style, fit and finish." Women likely influenced the trend away from uniforms – still popular for men in the established bicycle clubs – but with no sacrifice to fashion; indeed, the elegance of the dress of upper-class women on bikes may have added a substantial expense to women cyclists who believed they had to emulate them.

While bicycle accessories such as bells, lamps, odometers, repair kits, bike stands, saddles, as well as hats and shoes were popular, some "sundries" were specially designed for women, including skirt guards and "skirt lifters" to keep women's clothing out of spokes and chains. In the *Canadian Home Journal* in 1896, ads for bicycles and accessories competed with ads for beauty products and jewellery.

Advice on cycling etiquette was available from a variety of sources (including men, of course). The *Canadian Home Journal* offered advice on how to get on and off a bicycle (not from the back); whether to have a bell (yes, whistling and shouting were inappropriate) or a lamp (maybe, especially in the countryside); how to maintain a bicycle; and how to ride in a dignified manner. "The woman who looks vulgar is usually one who sits in a low saddle, rides immoderately." Some problems could easily be remedied by an adjustment to the height of the bike seat.

The popularity of cycling, even if it didn't drive the wider debate about women's dress, at least offered another opportunity to advance the cause of rational dress. Frances Willard, leader of the Woman's Christian Temperance Union and author of the best-selling *A Wheel Within a Wheel*, promoted cycling for women as a way towards rational dress, as well as good health, a Christian lifestyle, independence, and geographic exploration.

The *Canadian Home Journal* also noted the popularity of bicycles among older women at riding schools, where "[n]ot a few are white-haired, slender women, who look decidedly graceful when fear has left them." Kit Blake, author of the *Mail & Empire*'s popular "Woman's Kingdom," commented on a popular view held by young men about older women on bicycles, articulated by a city alderman as follows: "No girl over 39 should be allowed to wheel. It is immoral." She suggested that the same men considered bloomers acceptable for their sisters, but not for their sweethearts and wives, and certainly not their mothers. Blake added, probably to poke fun at the men, "Unfortunately, it is the old girls who are the ardent wheelers." Adding that the older women "love to cavort and career above the spokes, twirling and twisting in a manner that must remind them of long dead dancing days."

Saturday Night's "society expert" contributed a number of whimsical rules for the female cyclist or her companion. The unmarried woman should be chaperoned, "accompanied by her grandma or elderly maiden aunt on foot," while a male escort should "ride slightly in advance, so that he may run over any stray dogs and thus save his companion the trouble. By riding to the right, the gentleman could give a woman the benefit of his cigarette smoke. He ought also to do all the shouting at pedestrians to, 'Get out of the way there, you chump!'"

In addition to unwanted attention based on age, attire, and morality, there were claims that women were suffering an epidemic of injuries, including spinal damage from the strain of cycling. A *Globe* reporter, dispatched to local hospitals to investigate, could find no evidence for the claim. At Grace Hospital there was but a single patient who had suffered a bicycle-related injury – a badly sprained ankle caused not by the supposed strain of cycling but the result of a collision. The reporter likewise failed to uncover any cases of "bicycle hand" to which women were apparently more prone than men, the result of never releasing "the death-like grip" on the handlebars for fear that a moment's inattention would lead to catastrophe.

By 1896 there were even some bicycle clubs created by women, for women, although offering similar activities to the older clubs. At a May 1896 outing, the Guild Bicycle Club gathered on College Street, rode west to Bathurst Street, north to Davenport Road, then to the Town of Weston, before returning by way of The Junction. On a longer tour to Buffalo, the *New York Journal* reported that "[t]hey came clad in short bicycle skirts, and the conventional wheeling garb generally, but their captain, Miss Bennet, confessed that they had expected to find all the wheelwomen of the 'States' in bloomers and knickerbockers."

Cycling actually fit with then current ideas about the importance of regular exercise for muscle strength and well-being,

Respected His Memory.

He—Why did you buy black bloomers?
She—You know I'm in mourning for my first husband.

Image 8: "Respected His Memory." A male cyclist on this outing asks a woman why she is wearing "black bloomers." He is clearly focused on the woman's choice of clothing, while she, ignoring the questioner's intent, focuses on the colour. "You know I'm in mourning for my late husband." *Saturday Night*, May 9, 1896. (Courtesy of Toronto Public Library)

especially valuable given increasingly sedentary lifestyles, at least among the upper classes. In *The Canadian Practitioner*, Dr. Doolittle praised the therapeutic value of cycling for women's health. Indeed, he suggested that the brisk out-of-door activity of cycling would enhance, with a positive moral effect, a woman's association with a man, promoting "more muscular than erotic vigor."

There was some concern that the enthusiasm for cycling was diverting (upper-class) women from other leisure activities. The *Canadian Home Journal* complained that the "present bicycle mania is interfering with many summer sports [golfing, bowling, and tennis], but possibly the boat houses are suffering most." The writer offered the consolation that the "present condition of things will pass."

Women had not been completely shut out from muscle-powered conveyances before the arrival of the safety. Women could ride pedal tricycles and quadricycles, although the high cost and cumbersome size severely limited the potential market. The first issue of the *Canadian Wheelman* in 1883 carried a prominent ad for tricycles with women as a target audience. Subsequent editions carried ads for Victor tricycles, selling at $160. Tricycles, dating from the 1870s, were used by European royalty. Indeed, by purchasing one in 1881, Queen Victoria pushed back the boundaries of "acceptable female comportment," while prompting an adjustment to the name of the manufacturer's vehicle to "Royal Salvo." Technological advances developed for tricycles and quadricycles, including the chain drive, were later applied to the safety.

Québecoise Louise Armaindo had proven that women lacked none of the physical ability or courage to ride the high-wheel, although the dress of the day and etiquette made it virtually impossible. Armaindo, who visited Toronto for a high-wheel riding exhibition at the Horticultural Gardens Pavilion in 1882, enjoyed a successful high-wheel racing career in the United States, often in competitions with a select group of women, and sometimes men. The races involved a variety of distances, including six-day races, popular at the time. Her races could be characterized as spectacle, entertainment, or sport – often very much appreciated by women spectators, but ridiculed by male-dominated groups such as the League of American Wheelmen. Her costumes, many of them lacey and self-made, were practically suited to competition and athletics, and although sometimes considered scandalous, they were arguably boyish, and unlikely to influence the mainstream debate about women's dress.

Touring, Racing, Litigating, Accessorizing

For city residents, the most popular Sunday bicycle outing was High Park – "the one great Mecca," as the *Evening Star* called it. The waterfront path to the Humber River ranked second among popular cycle outings, followed by Weston Road to the town of that name. In a count of outbound cyclists on Sunday, May 10, 1896, there were a total of 5,600, among them 530 women, but the count excluded cyclists going to city parks or heading out of the city along Yonge Street and the Rosedale bridges. The numbers on that day would have been higher but for the threat of rain, air that was "sultry and oppressive," and high winds that raised dust clouds, and, as the reporter noted, challenged women by inflating their "voluminous skirts and abnormal sleeves that fashion has inflicted on them."

The Elysium Hotel and the Cycling Inn (both on the Humber River), the Eagle House in Weston, and the Half Way House Inn (the half way point between Toronto and the Town of Whitby) at Midland Road near Highland Creek were among the hotels and teahouses that served as rewards for a cyclist's exertion. Among longer rides, the road to the City of Kingston along the Kingston Road was popular, described by US *Outing* magazine as a cycling road "probably not excelled on this continent." The author suggested that it could "be scorched in one day, or ridden in two or thoroughly enjoyed in three days, according to taste and ambition of the rider."

Many cyclists, usually men, were often more preoccupied with the miles clicking off on their odometers, and the elapsed time, than enjoying the many ravines, rivers, farms, and forests that could be reached on the outskirts of the city. (The *Globe* wrote about the hundreds of places from which one could look out over "lake and stream and meadow too beautiful for the brush of any painter adequately to portray.") The serious wheelman, rising with the roosters, might have lunch at Whitby, Aurora, or Brampton, return home after dark, "dust-covered and weary, proudly telling his wife he had 'done seventy miles,' and that Bill What-You-Call-Him's wheel had broken down sixteen miles out, and he was walking in." In 1895, Dr. Doolittle still eclipsed all members of the Toronto Bicycle Club, riding 5,518½ miles (8,881.2 kilometres) – a statistic important enough to be precisely reported in the media. In that year, he also organized a ride from Toronto to Waterloo for the CWA's annual meeting. "Century" or 100-mile (160-kilometre) rides, completed within a day were celebrated measures of a wheelman's prowess.

The best roads might be identified by experience, newspaper reports, or guidebooks. *Ten Thousand Miles on a Wheel* by American Lyman Hotchkiss Bagg (published under the pseudonym Karl Kron) will likely never be matched for the meticulousness of its detail. The book, which included Bagg's 1883 travels on a high-wheel through Toronto, had 900 pages of dense text – a book so large that a touring cyclist might carry it only at the cost of other baggage. The tome included biographies, readable with a magnifying glass, of local cycling personalities. It would have been twice as long had the author used a larger font. (Bagg wheeled back into Toronto in June 1904, having added another 20,000 miles to his odometer, and, curiously, still riding a high-wheel.) Dr. Doolittle's

Wheel Outings in Canada published by the CWA was a more portable guide, which the organization, somewhat pretentiously, distributed to far-flung Australia, China, and Japan, even though the audience was almost certainly dominated by Americans.

The "Cyclists' Road Map for the County of York" covered an area radiating out 60 miles (96 kilometres) from Toronto, suggesting that this distance represented the maximum range for one-day or weekend trips originating in the city. The map prominently noted the many regional rail lines that offered an option in case of problems, such as fatigue, bad weather, or a broken wheel. Destinations near Lake Simcoe, including Jackson's Point, fell on the northern edge of the map, with the Town of Whitby to the east and Hurontario Street to the west. At many destinations, CWA members could rely on their local consul or the railway stationmaster for guidebooks and hotel information.

Cyclists had been world travellers even since the early days of the bicycle, although the high-wheel had made such adventures even more impressive. In July 1883, when the high-wheel was relatively new, forty Americans atop their high-wheels travelling through south-west Ontario were welcomed with great fanfare, in one town with a brass band. In Toronto, the Americans received a "magnificent" welcome that included a procession of 200 local, uniformed cyclists. The visitors were so well treated on their 400-mile (643-kilometre), ten-day journey that on their return home, they reported having gained weight.

The proliferation of railways was a boon to cyclists: a bicycle could be brought along and a cycling journey, both in the Toronto region or far beyond, could then begin. A local train station might also provide an alternative way home for a cyclist whose bicycle had broken down. The CWA's failure to convince the railways, or the federal government, which had jurisdiction over railways, to treat bicycles as free baggage remained a long-standing frustration for a group accustomed to getting its way.

In the early 1890s, electric streetcars, known as interurbans or "radials," because they radiated in various directions out of the city, were another way to extend the range of a trip into the region by bicycle. The radials at the time ran north along Yonge Street to York Mills, west to Mimico along the waterfront and east to Scarborough.

When bicycle club members weren't touring, they were often racing. The value of prizes and the size of trophies confirmed that the sport was lucrative. The Dunlop Cup, donated by the tire company and valued at $1,000, was almost as tall as the racers, so coveted that the outcome of the 1894 competition was first fought in the field, then in court, the matter hinging on whether the winner, T.B. McCarthy of the Athenaeum Bicycle Club, had gone around the barrel marking the halfway point. The Royal Canadian Bicycle Club (RCBC), which finished second, obtained a court injunction to halt the awarding of the trophy – but lost (again) at trial. In a ballad about the affair, the RCBC was characterized as a poor loser: "Take your medicine like others, who could not hold the pace." But the ballad underplayed how seriously all sides took the matter. The RCBC got its revenge, winning the race in 1895 and 1896, entitling it to take permanent ownership of the Dunlop Cup (and its successor, the silver-plated Dunlop Shield, because of consecutive wins in 1898 and 1899).

Among the multitude of races each summer across Ontario, the Toronto Bicycle Club's annual event, first held in 1881 at the Exhibition, was among the most popular. Race programs featured ads for hotels, diamonds, cameras, tailors, and, of course, bicycles, as well as more practical information such as cab fares and streetcar routes for out-of-town visitors.

By the mid-1890s the popularity of racing was already declin-ing – the "charm of novelty" diminished, as Dr. Doolittle put it. He would know – he had been one of the province's earliest racers, beginning with a May 1881 triumph in a high-wheel race, winning a napkin ring engraved with the word "Bicyycle." His only compet-itor fell at least three times on the poor roadway.

... and Clubbing

In Toronto newspapers, bicycle club events, including race com-petitions, touring, and social activities, usually dominated cycling news, typically reported on the sports pages under columns such as "The Wheel" or "Spokes" – even as cycling was transitioning into everyday transportation. The CWA's twice-monthly *Canadian Wheelman* similarly reported club activities, even adding a column for women in 1891. *Cycling*, first published in 1890 by the Toronto Bicycle Club, transitioned into serving a broader audience, using the tag line: "A Mirror of Wheeling Events – Devoted to the Inter-est of Cyclists in General." The Toronto-based *Wheeling Gazette* launched in 1897.

The costs associated with bicycle club membership had gener-ally sufficed to maintain exclusivity. The surge in cycling by the mid-1890s was, however, also accompanied by a surge in new, often less formal (and less expensive), clubs, with members drawn from a broader swath of the citizenry, more interested in the social side and enjoyment of cycling than with competitive racing. Of course, riding a bicycle didn't require a club at all but only the means to acquire a bicycle with the result that most cyclists were not club members.

The "craze for organizing bicycle clubs has at last reached the bank clerks," reported the *Evening Star* in March 1896. Church-based

Image 9: Members of the Toronto Bicycle Club in their club uniforms, posed in front of a banner for a September 1890 road race victory. At the time, high-wheel bicycles, in the background, were already starting to give way – even on the racetrack – to the safety bicycle. The club began holding its own annual race event at the Rosedale Lacrosse and Athletic Club, which had built a grandstand for 5,000 spectators. The grounds were accessible from the streetcar loop at the top of Sherbourne Street, or of course, by foot and bicycle. (Courtesy of Toronto Public Library, Image 960-7)

and employee groups, including at City Hall and Gooderham & Worts distillery, were among newcomers to the bicycle clubs. Even a few years earlier the question of whether married men should be members of clubs sparked debate. In the *Globe*'s "From a Woman's Standpoint," the columnist in July 1894 could find no satisfactory answer to the issue, saying that on the "yes" side, "If I say I think here married men should not belong to a club of the sort, almost the entire staff (with perhaps the exception of the elevator boy), being bicyclists and married men, might rise in their just wroth [*sic*] and smite me grievously."

The newer clubs helped temper the formality of the established clubs. The regimental look of the older clubs, including formal uniforms for rides, often with bugler and standard bearer, had been no accident. In 1879, American Charles E. Pratt, a civil war veteran of the Union Army, published *The American Bicycler: A Manual for the Observer, the Learner, and the Expert.* The executive officers of the Toronto Bicycle Club, like many other older clubs, had a captain, lieutenants, statistical secretary, reporter, bugler, and "club surgeon."

The Toronto Bicycle Club, which dated from April 1881, was later incorporated with $20,000 in capital. Only the Montreal Bicycle Club predated it in Canada. It was no surprise that the Torontos, as they were sometimes known, sent the largest delegation (227 members) to the 1896 CWA annual meeting, given that the club's home was in the same five-storey Toronto Athletic Club building (still standing today at 149 College Street, but used for other purposes) where the event took place. The building, designed by E.J. Lennox, included a bowling alley, gymnasium, dining rooms, and the city's first indoor swimming pool. The Torontos were rivalled in their influence, and the opulence of their home, by the Athenaeum

Bicycle Club, housed in an exotic Church Street building distinguished by its Moorish windows and "a magnificent wheel room," with space for 1,000 bicycles.

From the early 1890s, women began to play a small role in the bicycle clubs beyond that of companions for their husbands or brothers at club events. Women blunted the masculine, jocular character of the early clubs. In October 1890, *Cycling* reported that Margaret Eaton, youngest daughter of Timothy Eaton, the department store owner, had joined the Toronto Bicycle Club. A year later, an inaugural run of the ladies' section of the club took place. The men's bicycle runs, on weeknights and Saturdays (in 1896, there was even a New Year's Day run) soon included some women. Club events began to reflect the influence of women with teas, concerts, boat cruises, and even a bicycle gymkhana in Niagara-on-the-Lake, featuring an elaborate floral procession on decorated bikes, drawing many Toronto cyclists, arriving by ferry.

Many clubs, especially if racing was a central interest, were affiliated with the CWA, founded in St. Thomas, Ontario, in September 1882 as a national sporting organization. The CWA was so successful in fighting cycling restrictions that some members grumbled that while all wheelmen benefited from the association's advocacy, only members paid fees. The complaint had debatable merit given that membership in the CWA or local clubs was usually constrained by restrictive rules. At the end of 1896, the CWA had 8,700 members, largely through affiliated clubs, even exceeding the per capita membership of the older League of American Wheelmen. The CWA was also beginning to shed its Toronto-centric image, albeit not fast enough for some members in smaller cities.

FROM MILORD AND MILADY TO THE VALET AND THE MAID - WHAT NEXT?

The safety, an innovation centred on the chain drive, then supplemented by the comfort offered by pneumatic tires, had made the bicycle appealing to men and women of all ages, and to children. Dr. Doolittle was convinced that the bicycle had won a permanent place on city roads, not only for "the revellers in idleness and luxury, but also those who toil daily for their wants." He believed this trend would continue as bicycle prices dropped and roads improved, suggesting that the "practical, every-day utility of this vehicle has become ... patent to all."

Saturday Night's Sheppard suggested that bicycles were not a fad but had prompted permanent changes similar to other major changes such as the conversion from steam to electricity. Indeed, he suggested that the bicycle was spurring an egalitarian and democratic tendency in society. "If milord and milady ride bicycles ... followed by a valet and maid on wheels, no one will know which is the aristocrat and which the servant."

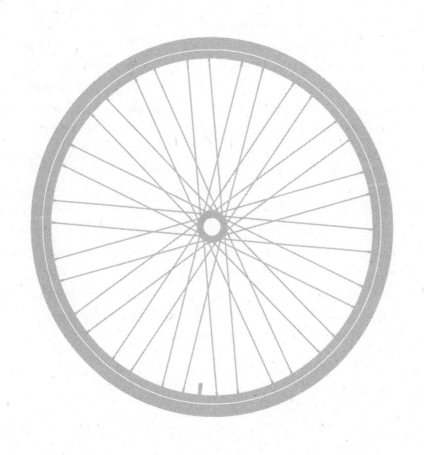

1910
From Fashion to Function

October 4, 1910 – A knight on his silent steed

A robust, elderly gentleman arrives in the early morning at the east doors of the provincial Parliament, parks his bicycle, adjusts his cap, and heads off to his second-floor office. The man, whose youthful vigour belies his sixty-seven years, has occupied his current post since 1905 – a precarious job dependent on the fickle affections of the public. At the moment, however, the man is liked well enough for today's Daily Star *to greet his return from England, with, "Sir James Whitney is on the job. Ontario is safe once more."*

Whitney is not only the premier, but a knight to his majesty King Henry VII, an honour bestowed on Whitney in 1908 soon after he won his second majority government. Today, this knight, on his silent steed, leads a province that has grown to a population of two and a half million. The Canadian Courier has called Whitney a man of the people who puts little stock in honours, adding that a "visitor to the Ontario Legislative

Buildings during the dog days, if the Premier chance to be in office, would probably find him in his accustomed shirt-sleeves killing a heap of work, and when he got done, riding home on his bicycle."

When Whitney bought a new bicycle in 1906, the matter was front page news, the Daily Star attributing the premier's youthfulness to his cycling, his sensible diet, and his willingness to stop and share a joke even on his busiest day. A reporter once wrote that "the premier is able to spin along on his wheel with a heart as light as the pneumatic tires which support his rather bulky frame," describing him as "scorching off like a merry schoolboy."

There are, however, occasions when the premier would rather not be noticed when he cycles. On his homeward ride to St. George Street he has been rebuked by the University of Toronto's groundskeeper for ignoring Stay Off The Grass signs. (Whitney may resent the reprimand, after all, his government has worked hard to put the university on a solid financial footing.) There have also been attempts, albeit inadvertent, to knock Whitney off his wheel. A young clerk recently ran into him under an archway at Queen's Park. On that occasion, it was the premier who issued the reprimand: "Why don't you watch where you're going."

Whitney continues to exceed expectations, much like the bicycle itself, which remains popular despite its fall from fashion before the turn of the century. When Whitney first became leader of the Conservative Party in 1896, the editor of the Toronto Telegram suggested derisively: "You could throw a brick through the window of any country lawyer in Ontario and hit a better man than Whitney." Today, there are few citizens who hold a similar opinion. So too the bicycle reliably serves city residents, but with little fanfare and with as little appeal to fashion as the unremarkable suits worn by the premier.

Image 10: "Oh mercy! They've got Sir James after us." Ontario Premier Whitney was often frustrated with the disregard by motorists for other road users. This 1905 *Toronto News* cartoon, "The Joy Riders," shows the premier on his bicycle pursuing a speeding motorist. (Archives of Ontario, Newton McConnell Fonds, C301-2-0-24)

THE NEW BICYCLE OF THE "REVIVAL"

What *Saturday Night* hadn't contemplated when it suggested a democratizing tendency of the bicycle was that when the master realized he was riding the same vehicle as the maid and valet, the bicycle would lose its appeal (to the master). "The mere fact that the simple people can ride makes riding unfashionable on the part of those who can afford luxuries. In short, the bicycle became too popular to be popular." In the American context, where the decline of cycling as fashion was deeper, *Scientific American* observed in 1905:

> When the fad became unfashionable its death-knell as a pastime of universal popularity was sounded. The bicycle was relegated to uses utilitarian. As a means of transportation, it will always fill a useful place in the economy of everyday life; but that bicycling will ever win back anything of its former position as one of the most fashionable and popular means of recreation is most improbable.

The bicycle in the new century was "no longer a fad of the idle and the excessively rich ... it receives its patronage to-day from those who use it because they need it, and have for it sensible appreciation and reasonable enthusiasm." The bicycle had graduated (or descended, as some might see it) from being merely a plaything for the rich to a useful tool for transportation. Many affluent citizens, including doctors, lawyers, businesspeople, and other professionals nonetheless continued to ride, even if in lesser numbers, and usually for more mundane activities such as getting to work. Even in March 1901, a few years after the end of the Bicycle Craze, the *Globe* observed that "the bicycle has become a necessity of our every-day business life," and the bicycle trade as stable as the staples of grocery and hardware stores, concluding that "there is little likelihood of the bicycle ever losing its hold in Toronto."

One prominent headline about the change from fashion to utility added the tagline, "FOR A BETTER PURPOSE." While in the early years of the craze, observed the writer, "eager cyclists, pleased with the novelty of being able to make long distances quickly and easily, raced and chased across the country," but as the novelty wore off, the practical use of the bicycle became clearer. The *Daily Star* offered a similar analysis, pointing to the reduction from thousands to hundreds the number of leisure cyclists in High Park. "Wheeling as a fad ... indulged in for the sake of wheeling has pretty well died out, and the bicycle has found its place as one of the great utilities of modern life." When a person is seen riding along a country road "it may be taken for granted that he is going somewhere. The bicycle has found its true sphere; it is the vehicle of the individual. It is incomparable in its place. It can never have a rival."

The lower price of bicycles gave a broader segment of the population access. Hyslop Brothers and Eaton's advertised bicycles at $25, comparable to a good quality men's suit. Credit arrangements helped: one local retailer offered new bikes for $10 down and $1 per month. Quality varied. Second-hand bicycles were another option. Liveries dwindled in number, consistent with the greater use of bicycles for everyday travel instead of as rentals for a weekend outing. Planet Cycle Works, originally the McLean and Bulley Company, offered a winter storage and cleaning service at its Queen Street East retail shop.

The bicycle had arrived as a toy, observed one commentator, then, as tends to happen with toys, it was spurned. But unlike other toys, the bicycle had obvious utlity and could now be likened to the wheelbarrow – useful and unpretentious. It was no surprise

(Overleaf) **Image 11:** Transportation Options. A man cycles north on Yonge Street near King Street alongside a stopped streetcar on October 18, 1911. City residents at the time had many transportation options in addition to walking: electric streetcars in the city and radials beyond, steam trains with suburban stops, and bicycles. The motorcar was still largely a plaything of the rich, as the bicycle had once been. (City of Toronto Archives, Series 372, Item 239)

that the media took far less interest in utilitarian cyclists. How could riding a bike to work – or *for* work – compete with the weekend jaunts to High Park or a country teahouse, the races and gatherings of the bicycle clubs, or a Rosedale bicycle soirée hosted by an heiress? Even if bicycle counts had been conducted, comparing cycling activity of the 1890s to the new century had challenges of quality and quantity. Sport and leisure played a more visible role in the 1890s, albeit with a transition to everyday use, while by 1910 utilitarian trips, including for commuting and for delivery services carried out during every hour and season, were more prominent.

From 1900 to 1910, *Saturday Night* didn't publish a single article about bicycles, unlike the 1890s when such articles, alongside beautiful illustrations, were common. Publishers presumably calculated that with a small audience among upper-class cyclists, or aspiring cyclists in that class, bicycle-makers and retailers would have little motivation to place ads. With the decline of the clubs, there were also fewer people writing about cycling, and fewer publications by and for cyclists. The *Wheeling Gazette* and *Cycling* barely lasted beyond the turn of the century. The *Canadian Wheelman* reinvented itself, briefly, as *Pastime and the Canadian Wheelman* to appeal to a broader sport and leisure crowd. Unlike club members of the past, everyday riders weren't likely to pay for, or be interested in, cycling publications dominated by racing and touring. Before their demise, cycling publications had started publishing articles about motorcars, which were of course the "latest thing," regardless of their limited popular appeal.

The bicycle had lost its big spenders. Tailor shops could no longer count on riders who wanted to flaunt their outfits, nor could retailers expect buyers who replaced their bicycles every year to keep up with the latest changes. (Even by 1897, Dr. Doolittle had observed that new bicycles were "barren of startling novelties," diminishing the appeal of an annual replacement.) The potential market for riding academies, country inns and teahouses, or accessories such as "anatomically correct" saddles or patented, self-adjusting "Safety" pants, had all declined, as had the associated advertising. After 1900, newspapers and bicycle-makers often suggested a "bicycle revival" was taking place, but the *revival* was usually a nostalgia for cycling for leisure or sport – and its big spenders.

The end of the bicycle fad was stark enough to be marked at the time, the decline of the cycling organizations providing a useful measure. The CWA had become a shadow of its former self. The Toronto Bicycle Club, like many other clubs, no longer even had a clubhouse. What could be the benefit of belonging to a social club based on an object that was neither novel, noteworthy, nor fashionable? Gone were the days when simply being seen on a bicycle was reward enough for the rider.

The return of bicycles to city streets nonetheless continued to mark the arrival of spring. On March 2, 1903, the *Globe* reported that the "early return of spring brought out such a swarm of bicycles on the streets of Toronto that it is evident wheeling will be no less popular this season. The repair-men are overrun with work." At its 1904 annual meeting, the CWA secretary acknowledged the demise of touring in the countryside but observed that cyclists remained so numerous in Toronto that "to stand at any prominent corner at noon, or at 6 p.m., it would seem almost impossible to regulate the traffic if many more appeared on our streets."

The high-wheel had drawn attention for its towering size and daring riders, the safety for its novelty and its place in fashion and sport, but by 1910 the bicycle had simply become a normal, unremarkable sight on city streets.

SAME WHEELS, NEW PURPOSE

The Speedy Messenger

The bicycle was a boon for deliveries, including for the telegraph system.

The telegraph, which dated from the 1850s in Toronto, dramatically sped up communication between people and businesses separated by hundreds, even thousands (after the laying of trans-Atlantic cables) of miles – but when the telegram arrived at its destination city, the message generally slowed to the pace of a person on foot. The bicycle offered a speedy upgrade, even though the message itself was not always welcome, including a telegram to the CWA's Racing Board Chair in 1894: "consider your appointment ... withdrawn pending investigation."

By 1902, Canadian Pacific (CP) Telegraphs had been relying on telegram delivery by bicycle for almost a decade, now employing forty-five boys and three men for the job. The city's four other telegraph companies likewise relied on bicycle messengers. The fact that "boys," sometimes as old as twenty-one, did the work ensured that wages could be kept low amidst an eager pool of prospective workers. There weren't many paying jobs that could combine the joy of cycling, often with a company-supplied bike and uniform, with the potential to contribute to the welfare of one's family or one's own pocket.

"The bicycle has revolutionized the messenger work," reported the *Daily Star* in 1902, "and the boys of today have what is colloquially known as a cinch, compared with those of 20 years ago. Then a boy had to hoof it wherever he went, unless he paid his own car fare." The reporter added that there "is probably no business where a boy may get a better general training than a messenger boy," estimating – presumably based on the employer's numbers – that a messenger could earn up to $50 per month.

"Messenger" work also included the delivery of a wide variety of other goods, often facilitated by sturdier bikes adapted by manufacturers to the task. Drug, hardware, optical, butcher, and produce shops, among many others, offered delivery by bicycle. The Robert Simpson department store provided same-day delivery: "Phone your order and it will go to you quickly by bicycle messenger." In fact, the bicycle department of the Richard Simpson Co. offered the service of a messenger to pick up a bike for repair, though the messenger presumably did part of the journey on foot or by streetcar. From at least 1899, there were professional delivery companies in the city, including the Queen City Bicycle Messenger Service (by 1910 known as the Queen City Auto Livery and Messenger Service), which provided day and night service for letters and parcels to any part of the city. Delivery by motorcar had also become an option. In fact, as early as 1901 Parker Dye Works was using an electric motorcar to deliver its goods in the city (and a gasoline-powered one for rural areas). But motorcars had a distinct cost disadvantage relative to bicycles – at least for smaller goods – given the initial cost and the need to employ adults, secure fuel, and pay for repairs as well as delays in the case of breakdowns.

Purchase credit arrangements for bicycles from retailers meant that boys or men of modest means could do delivery work. If all went well, the retailer would be paid from the messenger's anticipated earnings.

Image 12: Laundry shop, adjacent to bicycle shop, at 48 Elizabeth Street in 1912. Chinese-run hand-laundry shops often relied on bicycles for home delivery. By 1901 there were ninety-six such shops in a city with under 1,000 Chinese residents, a population artificially limited by a punitive head tax. The Toronto Bicycle Club, at the time trying to revive racing, included an event for Chinese boys at its 1908 and 1909 competitions at Scarboro Beach Amusement Park (in today's Beaches neighbourhood), describing the boys as "expert riders." (City of Toronto Archives, Series 372, sub-series 55, item 43)

Sadly, messenger boys' excitement and age weren't always suited to the dangers of the job, as the death in 1901 of a ten-year-old boy, attempting to squeeze between two horse-drawn carts, one heavily laden, made clear. "Tragedies of Toil," read a newspaper headline. The jury at the inquest recommended that no child under the age of fourteen be employed as a messenger.

Fourteen-year-old Ernest Preston, delivering fifty telegrams per day for CP Telegraph, fared better in his own crash in February 1905. The boy had been following a southbound streetcar on Yonge Street on his way to the CP office, likely looking forward to a respite from a temperature hovering around 16 degrees Fahrenheit (-9 degrees Celsius). As the car stopped, the boy found his path on the right blocked by a snowbank, then tried the other side only to see, as he reached the devil strip, a northbound car bearing down on him. He tried to throw himself out of the way but was hit by the car, which broke his leg. An appeal judge concluded that the conduct of the boy cycling within the rails of one track, then moving to the other on finding his way blocked, was not negligent. The boy had another advantage: lawyer J. Shirley Dennison, who routinely worked for the boy's giant corporate employer, Canadian Pacific.

The post office likewise appreciated the value of bicycles. Since 1898, it had been offering an express mail service anywhere in the city for an additional 10 cents per letter. Bicycles equipped with red boxes fore and aft were also used to rush mail that had missed the transfer wagons to the train station for out-of-town delivery.

With a bicycle, picking up one's own purchases was a free option. For over a decade, companies had been offering carriers, usually supported on the front axle and handlebars. The Quick Delivery Parcel Carrier Co. sold a steel wire basket, easily detachable for shopping. "Rapid Transportation Is a National Necessity" read an ad showing a well-dressed man carrying groceries in his new front carrier.

The Straphanger, the Police, and the Soldier

The frustrated streetcar straphanger, often standing shoulder-to-shoulder with other passengers, or instructed by a sign to "Sit

Closer, Please," was another potential customer for bicycle-makers and retailers. A reporter concisely summarized the competing appeal of the bicycle: "After waiting what seems an interminable time on the corner for a streetcar and then crowding on and standing all the way home, one certainly envies the cyclist. They go flitting by at whatever rate they wish."

One provocative bicycle ad, entitled "A Hold Up," suggested that streetcar fares were like bank robberies. The ad played well with a public that remained suspicious, if not hostile, towards William Mackenzie (no relation to Toronto's first mayor and the rebel leader of 1837) and Edward Mann, the wealthy railway barons whose holdings included the TRC, various radial lines running out of the city, and other streetcar lines (as far away as Brazil) and railways, including, by 1906, the Canadian Northern Railway, which was headquartered in Toronto.

Bicycles, especially if expensive repairs could be avoided, were comparable with streetcars in cost, even if the cyclist relied on the streetcar in the winter. The standard streetcar fare was 5 cents, but TRC patrons had to pay another fare for transfers for trips into the suburbs, including areas previously annexed by the city but into which the TRC had refused to expand. The company worried about its profitability should it expand into newly annexed areas of the city (beyond the terms of its 1891 franchise agreement) that remained sparsely populated. The TRC's uncertainty about the prospects of a renewal of its franchise in 1921, when its agreement with the city was set to expire, further dampened any incentive to expand.

In 1909, mayoral candidate Horatio Hocken proposed a $5 million expansion of the streetcar system, including underground electric lines that did not run afoul of the TRC franchise, which was limited to surface transit. Hocken campaigned on the slogan "Tubes for the People." (Almost exactly 100 years later, mayoral candidate Rob Ford campaigned on a "Subways, Subways, Subways" slogan, though Hocken had logic – and, more importantly, population density – more firmly on his side along his proposed routes.) A majority of voters in a 1909 election plebiscite supported the underground lines to relieve downtown traffic congestion, but the vote wasn't binding. Edward Geary, who defeated Hocken for the mayor's chair, didn't support the lines. (After 1910, the city began to make up for the shortfall in service by adding its own streetcar lines, under the name Toronto Civic Railways, into the city's suburbs.)

The police were among the groups that continued to appreciate the value of bicycles. By 1910, the police fleet of bicycles had grown to 120. Bicycles were even useful in police chases of horse-drawn vehicles. In one such example, a chase of a suspected thief escaping on a horse-drawn wagon began in the downtown, the first bike-riding officer turning over the chase to a second officer when he ran out of breath. The second officer in turn gave way to a third officer on horseback who steered the wagon off the road at Christie and Bloor Streets. (The accuser later withdrew her accusation as a misunderstanding.)

By 1910, police also had motorcycles, which, although superior in speed and power, also posed risks to other road users. Local papers appreciated the excitement of road chases by police of speeding motorists, but that excitement could be tempered by the outcome, summarized by front page headlines such as "Motor Cycle Constable Crashed into Cyclist." For the most part, however, the bicycle industry could promote cycling's health benefits, touting bikes as a "spring tonic," even a "gymnasium on wheels."

Dealing with the city's growing traffic congestion was among the tasks assigned the bicycle-riding officers. In 1909, Toronto police created a special traffic squad on bikes to ensure that operators of vehicles kept as far to the right as possible, slackened speed at crossings if pedestrians were present, and proceeded with caution or stopped when approaching a halted streetcar. The city, with its growing economy and over 350,000 residents, experienced increasing competition for road space.

With rumblings of war, it was no surprise that the bicycle, including a folding version (easier to transport and to carry, if necessary), was again being considered for military duty. Bicycles had already accompanied Dominion troops to the Boer War of 1899–1902 (and would soon do the same in the First World War). Bicycles didn't need to be fed or fuelled, nor did they recoil at the horrid bloodshed, although their role didn't include charging into battle.

Better Roads, the Cyclist Gains

With the increase in paved roads, the dispute that divided cyclists of the 1890s as between better roads and bicycle paths no longer sparked much passion. If a road wasn't good enough for bicycles, argued the *Daily Star* in 1906, then it wasn't good enough for other road traffic. "Bicycle paths on public streets … were advocated when bicycling was a fad and the streets bad. To-day wheeling is done for business, and streets ought to be good." The newspaper was willing to make a few exceptions, such as the bike path (or "track") around the east side of Queen's Park, given the ample space and small number of intersections, while calling a proposed bicycle path behind City Hall on Albert Street an "absurdity."

By 1910, Toronto had 275 miles of paved roads, almost half of them asphalted. Not all road users welcomed the progress: among police horses, "lameness is much more in evidence," lamented Chief Constable Grasett. But when Street Commissioner Harris received complaints about roads, it was usually about dust on unimproved roads. Motorists also benefited, although it quickly became clear that they needed not just better, but wider, roads.

The experience of a businessman cycling to a meeting suggested that the pace of road improvements fell short of public demands. Heading west to Clinton Street, the cyclist was forced to divert from his College Street route due to congestion caused by streetcars, motorcars, and wagons. After finding nearby streets in poor condition, he reached Bloor Street West, at which point he later explained, "I was obliged to dismount, not being able to turn by bicycle in a kind of swamp, with huge rotten cedar blocks rising out of it." He challenged the mayor and aldermen to traverse the city by roads where cyclists couldn't seek refuge along the streetcar tracks.

By 1909, when a *Daily Star* reporter accompanied a city official on a tour of the city's main thoroughfares, they found less than a dozen potholes. One of these holes appears, however, to have been found by the chief accountant of the Imperial Loan and Investment Company as he cycled along Yonge near Carlton Street. The cyclist got his tire caught in a rut beside the streetcar track when he was forced to swerve around a wagon. He was thrown into the path of another wagon that ran over him, causing severe bruising, and destroying his bicycle. He sued the city.

In and around the fringes of Toronto, a number of bicycle (cinder, or side-) paths survived, including the popular lakeshore

path to the Humber River, which had by then been extended to Mimico. The CWA still favoured good roads as the solution but showed some flexibility, supporting bike paths beyond the city and between towns if funded by cyclists.

Many roads outside cities remained particularly poor. When Karl Creelman set out on his round-the-world trip in May 1899 from his hometown in Truro, Nova Scotia, his bicycle barely survived the initial leg of his journey. Fortunately, he convinced Brantford's Goold Bicycle Co. to give him a new Red Bird, on the promise of promoting it in Australia. Creelman's trip was noteworthy, mostly for the scant attention it received, even on his passage through Toronto – very much unlike the exploits of gentleman bicycle adventurers of earlier years. Creelman completed his circumnavigation of the globe in 1901, after twenty-eight months abroad, covering over 15,000 miles (6,803 kilometres) on his bike, and thousands of miles more by ship or on foot.

Despite the arrival of motorcars, streetcars posed the greatest hazard to cyclists. In fact, by 1910, there had not been a single case of a cyclist killed in a crash with a motorist, despite a number of serious injuries. Of course, motorcars were few, and streetcars many.

(Opposite) **Image 13**: Poplar Plains Road in 1910. A steep incline leaves these two well-dressed cyclists pushing their bikes. The improvement in city roads benefited both cyclists and the small number of motorists. Sixty years later in 1979, Poplar Plains got Toronto's first bike lane – a welcome change not only for cyclists but for local residents who saw the roadway, which had come to be known as the Forest Hill Expressway for its heavy motor traffic, reduced to a single northbound car lane. (City of Toronto Archives, Fonds 1587, Series 409, Item 68)

Cyrus Rockwood, on the way to his job at *The Telegram*, was killed while cycling south on the devil strip on McCaul Street. A fast-moving streetcar failed to negotiate the turn at Queen, leaving the tracks and pinning Rockwood underneath. The motorman, a former horse-car driver, claimed it was the bicycle under the streetcar that had thrown the car off the tracks! The TRC was found negligent for defective equipment.

Cyclists and other road users also had to be cautious when crossing railways that traversed the city. At the time, there were only a few underground road passages at railway crossings in Toronto. Crashes between cyclists and horse-drawn carriages were also common, although less likely to be deadly. The driver of a carriage that hit a sixty-seven-year-old cyclist on College Street added insult to injury by claiming that the victim, the same age as Premier Whitney, was too old to be cycling on a road crowded with streetcars, motorcars, and carriages. The victim's lawsuit was successful, the matter reaching the Ontario Court of Appeal. The plaintiff also made it clear that he had every right to be on the road, pointing to his earnings of $3.50 per day. Of course, cyclists too could cause pain and suffering, even death, to pedestrians, but cyclists were more likely to frighten and annoy.

The early motorcars had far less capacity for harm than their successors: a 50-horsepower motorcar was considered powerful. (Today, passenger vehicles often exceed 300 horsepower and a weight of 2.5 tonnes.) In fact, many motorcars weighed less than a horse, while running on pneumatic tires that were only slightly wider and heavier than those of bicycles. Even when a motorist *ran over* a cyclist, the victim sometimes escaped injury. On one such occasion on Bay Street in June 1902, the victim got back on his feet, dusted off his clothes, and walked away after agreeing with the motorist that the poor road condition was to blame. In 1907, the car of the city engineer (there was no mention if he was driving) ran over a young "newsie" (newspaper vendor) with both its front and rear wheels, but the boy also apparently escaped injury.

The Bicycle Syndicate

While the city's social elite no longer valued being seen on a bicycle, they certainly appreciated the bicycle's money-making potential. The formation of the Canada Cycle & Motor Co., Ltd. in August 1899 was lucrative for the sellers of bicycle-manufacturing companies, the middlemen, and the principals of the new entity. (The abbreviation CCM is how the company later came to be known and will be used to refer to the company.) In fact, the new owners looked a lot like the old owners – as it turns out, many were the same people – with new roles, a new enterprise, and more money in their pockets. The press was certainly excited, the *Evening Star* called the combine "one of the biggest coups in Canadian finance," bringing together five of the country's biggest bicycle-makers. At the time, these companies had 85 per cent of the Canadian market, with an estimated 1,700 employees producing 38,500 bicycles each year.

By the mid-1890s a number of large-scale bicycle manufacturing operations had been established in the Toronto area, serving a market that had been accustomed to imported bicycles, or imported parts from the United States and the United Kingdom to be assembled locally. The H.A. Lozier Company, one of the five companies combined to create CCM, had been manufacturing virtually every part of its bicycles, save for the tubing for frames, at its Weston Road factory in The Junction. Another of the CCM companies, Massey-Harris, was a prominent farm implements manufacturer that in 1895 converted part of its King Street factory to bicycle-making to satisfy the growing demand. Rounding out the companies that became CCM were Welland-Vale Manufacturing in St. Catharines, the Goold Bicycle Company in Brantford, and Gendron Manufacturing in Toronto.

CCM's original management group was a *Who's Who* of Canadian finance and industry, including Walter Massey, president of Massey-Harris; Senator George Cox, president of the Bank of Commerce; and James Flavelle, the wealthy hog entrepreneur. CCM was soon touting Made in Canada bicycles by appealing to patriotic fervour stoked by the participation of Canadian troops, some of them on bicycles, in the Boer War. The appeal to patriotism was tempered by suspicions that the men who benefited from this and other monopolies were millionaires mainly concerned about themselves. Cox and Flavelle prayed at the Sherbourne Street Methodist, known as the "Millionaires' Church."

E.B. Ryckman, the son of a Methodist minister and a prominent member of the Toronto Bicycle Club, was among the middlemen who helped orchestrate the CCM combine, walking away (although not quite fast enough) with $75,000 and company shares for his part in the process. In a subsequent lawsuit, the plaintiff, Fred Evans, a principal in a company that made E&D Bicycles in Windsor, Ontario, proved that he had been cut out of the profits of a partnership set up to match-make sellers of bicycle-manufacturing companies and the investors in a new enterprise. In 1902, with this and another lawsuit against him not yet resolved, Ryckman began a long career in provincial and federal politics. (By 1926, Ryckman, who had a problematic fondness for gambling, was a federal cabinet minister, and in 1930 became the minister of national revenue.

When out of politics he was the president of the Dunlop Tire Company. His son Baird became a Toronto city councillor.)

The timing of CCM's birth was no accident. In early 1899, dozens of US bicycle-makers combined to form the American Bicycle Company (ABC). In October of that year, ABC announced that it would open a factory in Hamilton, to be run by its subsidiary National Cycle and Automobile Company (National). The formation of both National and CCM were motivated by the fact of too much bicycle production by too many bicycle-makers, amidst declining prices, declining demand, and a saturated market.

CCM opened a Toronto showroom in April 1900, copying its Hamilton-based rival National. In November 1900, CCM acquired National – a dubious decision given that National's parent, ABC, was bankrupt by 1901. The sale of bicycle parts comprised the greatest portion of CCM's early revenues, consistent with older bikes being kept in use by a utilitarian class of rider.

As the CCM name suggested, the new company intended to make and sell motorcars. "The union of cycle and motor is particularly happy," noted the *Daily Star*. "The one has reached its perichelion, the other is said to be the vehicle of the future."

CCM's original head office occupied an entire building at Bay and Front – a building that conveyed "an idea of the magnitude of this concern … befitting a company of their magnitude." Yes, it was big, but by 1902, continuing weak sales, and a weak economy, saw the company scale back production and close retail outlets, including one in London, England. CCM's head office and the operations of all the combined companies were moved to The Town of Toronto Junction, where CCM had taken over (and later expanded) the bicycle-making factory that once belonged to H.A. Lozier & Company.

Image 14: A 1905 postcard of Dundas Street suggests the importance of the bicycle to the Town of Toronto Junction. The giant Canada Cycle & Motor (CCM) factory sat on the edge of town, but it was moved north to the Town of Weston in 1917. The streetcar line, which connected directly to the TRC in the City of Toronto, was removed decades later. (Photo: Norman Attikin, Toronto Public Library Digital Archive)

The company's fortunes began to improve when Tommy Russell, then only twenty-four years old, became general manager in 1903. In 1904, CCM bicycle sales were back up to 1899 levels. In the meantime, CCM's competition included large department stores in the city that sold cheaper brands but advertised them under their store names. CCM expanded its bicycle factory in 1906 and in 1910.

CCM's automobile trade included the sale, as agents, of motor-car brands such as the Waverley electric and the Winton. CCM soon ranked among the top three automobile retailers in Ontario (while developing a popular line of ice skates – a welcome side-line for bicycle retailers in the slower winter months). In 1903, the company bought the defunct Canadian Motors, using the lat-ter's factory to make the Ivanhoe electric runabout. In 1905, spare capacity at The Junction factory was converted to making the lux-ury, gasoline-powered Russell Motor Car, named after Tommy Russell. The Russell was displayed at the city's first Automobile, Motorboat, and Sportsmen's Exhibition in 1908 where John C. Eaton bought a 50-horsepower model. (CCM's automobile-making business was later taken over by Willys-Overland and, by the 1920s, CCM's connection to automobiles was limited to retail-ing La Salles and Cadillacs.) CCM also marketed its "Gentleman's Motor Cycle," which at 85 pounds (38 kilograms) fell between a bicycle and a motorcycle in weight, with production at its factory in The Junction.

From its birth, CCM was a prominent advertiser, often display-ing motorcars side-by-side with bicycles. On an early fall day in 1908, however, a Russell motorcar and a bicycle found themselves in a less harmonious encounter. Marshall Rodman, a painter and decorator, had cycled south on Marguaretta Street from his home, then turned left to go east on Bloor Street. CCM's Tommy Russell was driving along Bloor in the opposite direction. In the ensuing crash, Rodman was thrown into the air, landing on the hood of the car, which Russell claimed he had been driving at a "moderate speed," even though his car only came to a stop when it crashed into a street pole on the far side of road. The *Globe* helpfully described Russell "as one of the most expert drivers in the district." A luxury Russell Motorcar was advertised in the same day's paper. Rodman survived his injuries but had no memory of the crash, which was at least convenient for Russell.

The Hyslop Bros. company, which dated from 1899 and was also selling Cadillac motorcars by 1910, and the Planet Cycle Works were among the few bicycle-makers beyond CCM that survived into the new century. James Lochrie was one of the others. His Antelope bicycle ads took direct aim at CCM, describing himself as free of any bicycle trust. By 1909, Lochrie's bicycle works was managed by his son Daniel, still at the same Bloor West location, although it is unclear if these works still included manufacturing. (Today, the site of Lochrie's factory and adjacent home are occupied by an auto-body repair shop. Planet and Hyslop carried on business into the early 1930s; in the case of Hyslop, carrying on business despite the death by the Spanish flu in 1919 of William Hyslop, the company's president.)

OLD PLAYERS, NEW PLAYERS

The Decline of the Bicycle Clubs and the CWA

As long as roads were being improved, utilitarian cyclists had little reason to worry (assuming they gave it any thought) about the decline of the bicycle clubs and the CWA, as well as the concurrent loss of influential cycling advocates.

With the fall from grace of the bicycle, the CWA had largely retreated to its original preoccupation with racing. The association's annual meetings were no longer the much-anticipated, lively events of years past. At the 1902 meeting, on the CWA's twentieth anniversary, invited politicians found reasons to decline, while delegates in attendance were so few (twenty-four), they were all named in the *Globe*'s account of the gathering. CWA membership across Canada had by then dwindled to 1,200; executive positions were filled by acclamation; and the choice for the host city for the annual race, a decision once fiercely contested, was at first overlooked. "The CWA is not a dead association ... and this year [it intends] making a strong effort to win back the support of the wheeling devotees," the *Globe* reported, adding that "[a]s a sport cycling has reached a low notch in Canada, but from a social and utilitarian viewpoint the possibilities are immense." Of course the CWA had little actual interest in utilitarian cycling.

At the same meeting, outgoing president Albert Walton, a leader of the RCBC and a prosperous drug store owner, reported that the association would revive its good roads work, "which has been one of our loudest battle cries from the inception of the association." The claim overstated the CWA's contributions, even in its heyday, especially outside of cities. Walton suggested that with better roads, the CWA "may look forward to the time when touring will again become popular and the bicycle and the automobile, the new means of travel, will carry its tourist along the country roads, enjoying the fresh air." Among notable accomplishments, Walton listed the CWA's return to full control over bicycle racing, having triumphed over a Montreal-based group, the Canadian Cyclists' Association, dubbed the "cycling insurgents" by Toronto papers. A committee was also established to investigate possible affiliation with motorcar groups.

At the 1904 meeting at the King Edward Hotel, Secretary Hal B. Howson, who had led the charge for the controversial side-paths bill in 1899, said that bicycle touring had almost entirely disappeared, offering poor country roads as the cause. He too sounded optimistic about a revival. The *Daily Star* charitably described the meeting, with forty members in attendance, as "enthusiastic." Subsequent accounts of CWA meetings simply confirmed the decline of the country's oldest athletic association, but unlike the League of American Wheelmen, which folded in 1902 (to be revived in 1939), the CWA survived.

The decline of the CWA simply reflected the demise of some clubs and the decline of others. Former club members pivoted towards other clubs – golfing, horse-racing, and yachting among them – suited to their upper-class tastes, and consistent with the appeal of cycling in the past as hobby and social networking activity. Percy McBride, president of the Toronto Bicycle Club in 1910, had the type of financial interest once considered uncouth for bicycle club officers: he owned a bicycle shop. The annual meeting was held on the second floor of the club manager's tailor shop. The club continued to hold its annual race, although at Scarboro Beach, an amusement park, with motorcycle racing and feats of daring (or folly) performed by cyclists among events that offered the greatest appeal to spectators. The Dunlop race was among the few races that maintained its popular appeal, drawing, despite rain, an estimated 20,000 spectators for the 1909 race that included stretches of Queen Street and Kingston Road.

The RCBC stood out among bicycle clubs for its continuing vitality, reflected in its new $12,000 home, completed in 1906, on Broadview Avenue, just north of its former, rented premises in Dingman Hall. On opening night, an orchestra entertained 100 couples at the new facility. Walton contributed significantly to the club, which by 1910 depended for its success, despite its name, on activities beyond cycling.

Defending the Detested Motorist

The founding meeting of the Toronto Automobile Club (TAC) on May 4, 1903, at the upscale Queen's Hotel, had twenty-six participants, a significant number given that there were only 178 motorcars in the city. George Gooderham of the distillery family, John Eaton, and CCM's Tommy Russell were among the attendees. Another participant had been at a similar meeting in 1882 for the founding of the CWA – Dr. Perry Doolittle.

Dr. Doolittle's role as the automobile club's first president helped explain why the club's structure, priorities, and activities resembled that of the earlier bicycle clubs. In fact, Dr. Doolittle and Hamilton's John Moodie Jr., a founder of the Hamilton Motor Club, had been among Canada's first high-wheel riders in 1878, and each of them among the first motorcar owners – in each case fitting the description of "trendsetters." The early bicycle and the early motorcar shared similar appeal: novelty, independence, and speed. Indeed, there was no apparent animosity between motorists and cyclists at the time, and for good reason given that many of the early motorists had been cyclists.

A Toronto automobile club had also been established in 1901, but it quickly floundered. The organizers of the 1903 club had an extra motivation: Queen's Park was proposing mandatory vehicle registration and speed restrictions. Both the $2 registration fee and speed limits, though lower than what had been initially proposed, became law later that year.

TAC's outings, advertised in the sports pages of newspapers, included destinations once popular with cyclists, including The Half Way House, reached along the Kingston Road. Among the early motorists was lawyer Thomas Rowan, victim of the 1896 crash on Spadina. He had given up his bicycle for a Canadian-made electric Victoria motorcar, which had room for his wife and child. Electric motorcars were cleaner, quieter, and initially more numerous in Toronto than gasoline- and steam-powered versions. They had the advantage of easy starting, unlike the troublesome hand crank for other vehicles, until the electric starter was popularized in 1912.

Despite the small number of motorcars in the city – fewer than 2,000 even by 1910, for a population of about 350,000 – motorists were influential, much like cyclists of the 1890s. The same influence, born of affluence, that had allowed cycling advocates to successfully resist restrictions and demand paths and improved roads, was at play. In fact, the demands by motorists were often made by the same people who had advocated for cyclists. What quickly became evident was the greater adverse impacts of motorcars.

Motorists would have drawn public and media notice merely for their upper-class standing and for the novelty of their machines – regardless of the noise, smell, and speed of the machines – but it was the sometime haughty, careless attitude of the motorists themselves that assured additional, typically negative, attention. "This is the kind of driver that makes automobilists so much detested," complained a citizen in April 1910 about a motorist who had almost forced two cyclists over a steep roadside incline in a park. The motorist, driving a Stoddard-Davis, was easily identified, partly owing to the small number of motorcars, as a clerk at the Traders' Bank Building.

Image 15: A family with a chauffeur at the wheel enjoy their motorcar in 1905. This family would, before buying a motorcar, likely have travelled the city with a horseman at the reins of a carriage. The importance of motorcars in the city was exaggerated by the amount of space they occupied, and the sometimes uppity attitudes of their occupants. The low horsepower and weight of early motorcars ensured that collisions with pedestrians and cyclists were far less likely to be deadly than later became the case. (City of Toronto Archives, Fonds 1587, Series 409, Item 68)

The ill-will against motorists prompted motor clubs to join forces in 1907 as the Ontario Motor League (OML), recognizing that the future of the "devil-wagon," as some called it, depended on resisting restrictions on vehicle power and speed, and motorists' use of public roads.

At City Hall, motorists were also starting to get more attention than cyclists. On the rare occasions when by-laws related to cycling were proposed – usually for lamps, bells, or reckless behaviour – they failed, suggesting either that cycling restrictions no longer stirred up much passion or that cyclists still had solid support on council. Bicycle rooms that had been in the plans for the impressive new City Hall, completed in 1899, had, however, already been converted to other functions. In 1908, cyclists also lost their right to bring their bicycles (after suffering a flat tire, for example) onto the streetcar on the payment of a second fare.

In March 1910, the OML opposed a by-law that would have obliged motorists to halt behind stopped streetcars, claiming that it would be of no benefit to streetcar patrons. Motorists attempting to squeeze past the doors of streetcars while passengers were about to board or exit was a known hazard. The OML sought to entice aldermen to its side by offering the use of members' vehicles to give distinguished visitors a tour of the city. The vote was deferred. In 1914, however, the province made it illegal for motorists to pass a stopped streetcar.

At the provincial level, Premier Whitney indicated a willingness to tolerate motorcars, but he despaired at being able to convince motorists about their low rank on the road, on occasion threatening, with popular political support, stiff regulation. "The pedestrians have the first right, after them come the drivers of vehicles," he told the Legislature at a March 9, 1910, debate: "[T]he chauffeur who thinks that when he has blown his horn to give warning he is entitled to the road is vastly mistaken. He comes after the pedestrian, and even the man on a bicycle." Whitney threatened to compel misbehaving motorists to attend instructional sessions: "By constant hammering it might be got into their heads what the rights of the pedestrian are." The Liberal opposition leader like-wise complained about the "tomfoolery of the motorman," who thinks that "when he toots his horn he is heralding the advent of the King's coming."

Many politicians, including the premier, expected the OML and the motor clubs to take responsibility for the conduct of motorists, consistent with a view of motoring as the sport or leisure activity of a small group. (The same sentiment was repeated in later dec-ades, especially after the Bicycle Revival of the 1970s, when it was common to hear people, mainly motorists, demand that cyclists address the misconduct of other cyclists, as if they were a similarly defined hobby group.) The motorist's leisure sometimes came after hard labour: OML members often spent weekends grading and otherwise improving roads.

The *Motor Vehicles Act* was amended on several occasions to impose new obligations, such as to slow down at intersections. In lawsuits by pedestrians and cyclists arising from road crashes, the burden to disprove negligence was placed on motorists. (This "reverse onus" is still in place today, despite the surge in status of the motorist.) In 1906, the offence of "reckless driving" was added, bearing similarities to the prohibition against immoderate cycling. The law was nonetheless slow to catch up to offending motorists; enforcement was even slower. In 1910, the province hired consta-bles to enforce road rules, but motorists had little to fear; there were but nine constables for the entire province.

Ads by the motor industry, like ads by the bicycle industry, touted its product as an opportunity to escape into the countryside from the crowded city and its foul air. Of course, motorists brought much of the din, danger, and smell of the city with them, and got a cold reception from rural inhabitants, exacerbating existing urban-rural tensions. Farmers complained, as they had about cyclists, but more vehemently, that they paid for or maintained the roads (albeit to a middling standard) and didn't want an "urban clique" engaged in an "urban amusement" racing along *their* roads, stirring up dust and frightening humans and animals. "Gas fiends," "reckless scorchers," and "motor maniacs" were among the labels ascribed to motorists, their weekend jaunts mocked as Sunday "pleasuring."

Motorists nonetheless had defenders at Queen's Park, including CCM's Tommy Russell, elected to the provincial Parliament in 1908 while he was also OML president. MPP E.B. Ryckman grumbled about the farmer who refused to get out of the way, "who consigned you to the ditch, who laughed and jeered at you, who gave you the merry ho ho." When the Province of Prince Edward Island instituted a ban on motorcars in 1909 (although there were only ten cars at the time), Ryckman called on OML members to boycott the province on their summer excursions. At its 1909 meeting, the OML, bending to public hostility, nonetheless updated its traditional slogan calling for good roads by adding the phrase "and sane use of them."

The Horseless Carriage – Filling a Gap or Creating One?

By 1910, the safety, the first version of which coincided with Karl Benz's 1885 motorcar invention, had already gone through a "craze" and the transition to everyday use. The motorcar, on the other hand, wasn't yet popular, nor were Toronto residents eagerly awaiting a chance to buy one. Leaving aside what a reporter had called the motorcar's "bad breath," there was the obvious problem of the high cost, especially in a context where most people already had good transportation: walking, cycling, and streetcars in the city, along with radials and railways into the suburbs and beyond. In fact, when the Messiah (as he proclaimed himself) visited Toronto in 1908, dressed in flowing robes and claiming a global following of two million, he went about the city on a bicycle to spread the good news and to cure the ill. At the time, household transportation costs ranked below shelter, food, and insurance (a ranking that would change in later decades once most households had at least one motorcar).

A strike by TRC employees in the summer of 1902 provided a snapshot of how city and suburban residents got around at the time. Among the alternatives for the 100,000 people who daily relied on streetcars, a reporter concluded that bicycles offered the best option, estimating that there were 20,000 to 30,000 in private hands in the city, including bicycles not in regular use. Other options included horse-drawn express wagons (used for freight), buses and wagons, horse-drawn cabs and hacks from local liveries, and the running of extra trains by the CPR and Grand Trunk to suburban stations, including Toronto Junction, the Don, and North and South Parkdale. Travel to and from the suburbs by train was common, although the failed Belt Line Railway, built in 1892, with its northern reach along Eglinton Avenue, targeted a suburban population that was at the time insufficient to turn a profit. (The radials continued to run, but they required passengers to transfer into the city's streetcars at the city boundary.) The motorcar barely merited mention. Once the strike, which was quickly resolved, got underway, on a rainy Saturday, most people did what came naturally – they walked.

In 1909, the streetcar system in the city carried over 98 million passengers, while the radial lines, also privately owned, had likewise prospered. The radials were popular enough for Toronto saloon keepers to complain that patrons of the radials as well as cyclists were bypassing their establishments on their way home each day, therefore calling for permission to move their enterprises to the suburbs. The radials took passengers west along the waterfront to Mimico and Port Credit; east to West Hill in Scarborough; and north along the Yonge line to Lake Simcoe. (The range of Toronto residents also benefited from TRC lines that connected to street-car lines in the Town of Weston and Toronto Junction. A radial line to Guelph was added in 1917.) The radials also brought fresh farm goods to the city each day. By 1907, a Toronto resident could travel to Lake Simcoe at Jackson's Point, 53 miles (86 kilometres) distant, where hotels, boarding houses, cottages, and bicycle liveries awaited. An energetic cyclist could cover the same distance in a day. (A cen-tury later, getting to Jackson's Point by mass transit, let alone bicycle, had become a demoralizing experience.)

When the first passenger train steamed out of Toronto in May 1853 to Matchell's Corners (now Aurora), a distance of 31 miles (50 kilometres), a person's overland travel options were few, and largely unappealing. Where waterways connected destinations, steamships were clearly preferable. A bumpy stagecoach trip for the 160-mile (260-kilometre) trip from Toronto to Kingston took three days; with the advent of rail service, the same trip was measured in hours. In fact, by the 1880s, an energetic cyclist could complete the same trip in a day. As early as 1887, two wheelmen had done just that, cycling from Toronto to Kingston in twenty-one hours, although they were quick to point out that the actual travel time was just seventeen hours, twenty-one minutes, once breaks were subtracted.

Horse-drawn carriages could be summoned from neighbour-hood liveries or flagged down as a cab on the street, although it was a luxury for most people. Wealthy families might have their own coach house. It was these residents that were most likely to be drawn to motorcars, which might actually offer a cost savings, at least in operation, given that horses had to be fed (even if idle), groomed, and stabled and, in most cases, a coachman paid to drive the carriage.

The notion today that everyone once had a horse confuses urban and rural life. Indeed, a common rebuke of advocates who challenge the car-dominated status quo is "Do you want to go back to the horse-and-buggy?" But horse-drawn carriages were mainly a vehicle for the upper classes, while most people went about on foot, by streetcar, or by bicycle.

A clerk at Eaton's or Simpson's, for example, wouldn't keep a horse in the back yard, then park it for ten hours on Yonge Street while at work. True, there were still many horses in the city, but they were largely used for commerce in the transport, by wagon or cart, of a large variety of heavy products and other materials such as refuse. Horses did remain a reference point for the newer means of locomotion: the electric streetcar was the "horseless trolley"; the bicycle the "iron (or silent) steed"; and the early motorcar the "horseless carriage."

Toronto's first horseless carriage was an electric automobile built in 1896 at Dixon Brothers Carriage Works at Bay and Temperance Streets. Local inventor John Still developed a 4-horsepower motor (generating a maximum speed of 15 mph [24 km/h]) that sat upon wheels with ball bearings and pneumatic tires from the Griffiths Cycle Corporation. The vehicle's battery was said to last up to five hours. Patent lawyer Frederick Fetherstonhaugh had invested in the battery-making operation, then bought the vehicle.

In 1900 several US companies with interests in electricity planned to bring electric automobiles to Toronto as a transportation service. A local newspaper predicted that city streets would quickly be filled with these electric vehicles for hire, drawing people from streetcars and horse-drawn carriages, while replacing much of the delivery and express cargo services. The absence of subsequent reports about the service suggests its lack of success. Some local enterprises, including Parker Dye, did begin using electric automobiles for their deliveries. Meanwhile, the post office also experimented with electric tricycles and quadricycles, but their power proved inadequate for the cargo weight, even when equipped with pedals, while performing poorly in cold weather.

The trend towards gasoline-powered motorcars in the city only became evident towards the end of the decade. In fact, in 1904, CCM's Tommy Russell was still singing the praises of the electric car, especially for urban use. "They are absolutely noiseless in running, free from vibration, and are so simple in operation that a child can drive them. With a radius of 35 to 40 miles [56 to 64 kilometres], they are the ideal city carriage." Gasoline motorcars, including ones described as "touring cars," however, offered greater range, which suited the upper-class owners for their recreational excursions into the countryside.

In the first decades of the twentieth century, the railways offered a far easier, and more reliable, way than motorcars to travel the region, the province, and the nation. Indeed, despite the vast expanse of Canada, a person could travel from coast to coast in a week, while the same trip by motorcar wasn't possible (even in the 1920s). An around-the-world motorcar race, launched with huge fanfare in New York City in February 1908, demonstrated the chasm between the celestial expectations of motorcars and the terrestrial reality. (The original plan included driving across the Bering Strait from Alaska to Russia!) It took the winning team thirteen days just to cover, pulled on occasion by animals, the 1,000-mile (1,609-kilometre) first stage of the race from New York City to Chicago, a journey that could easily be covered in eighteen hours in the comfort of a *20th Century Limited* train.

In 1908, Henry Ford, borrowing techniques from the bicycle-manufacturing industry, offered some hope for the future of motorcars by introducing assembly-line production at his plant outside Detroit, Michigan. The *Canadian Courier*, noting that motorcar prices had fallen from an average of US$2,100 to $1,500 (about $50,000 today) by 1910, predicted that if a downward price trajectory similar to that of bicycles ensued, "it will be easy for every ambitious Canadian to have a car in 1916." The underlying issue, however, was that travel by motorcar required roads, which were scarce beyond cities.

Provincial funding for road building had grown since the early days of the century, but even in 1908, rural road work still depended heavily on statute labour, a system ridiculed as "antiquated" by *Busy Man's Magazine* (later *Maclean's*). In 1909, the OML was still hiring men to repair more heavily travelled country roads, while the T. Eaton Company built and maintained a model road on a section of Dundas Street between Toronto and Hamilton. By 1910, the *Canadian Courier* noted, however, that provincial control of road-building was on its way, despite farmers' fear of their betrayal by government for the benefit of motorists. It nonetheless noted that "When the roads are good the farmers sing at their work, say 'Howdy' to everyone they meet." Motorists and farmers clearly had a mutual interest in better roads, similar to the shared interests of cyclists and farmers in earlier days, while the extent of those roads and the road traffic they might bring was not yet an issue.

WHAT OF THE BICYCLE IN THE NEXT TWENTY YEARS?

It wasn't motorcars that radically altered the speed, reach, and convenience of travel; it was electric streetcars and bicycles in the city, and the radials and railways (and steam ships on water) beyond. For the upper classes or social elite, for whom the bicycle had been as much – probably more – a status symbol, a fashion, and a novelty as it was a transportation device, it wasn't the motorcar that offered an obvious replacement – unless they perceived it as fitting the same role as status symbol, fashion, or novelty as the bicycle once had done. The upper classes were not on the lookout for a replacement transportation device, nor did most people consider the motorcar as filling a particular transportation gap.

Even by 1910, there was little reason to believe that motorcars were the way of the future, given public hostility towards motorists and the state of the road system. Patent lawyer Frederick Nelson, in his 1908 novella, nonetheless provided a somewhat prophetic view of the future, writing about the city of 1928 where motorcars would be as common "as bees in a hive" and accommodated in "great storehouses" at large factories. He predicted that by the end of the 1920s, the automobile, like the bicycle, would long ago have passed the period of exclusive possession by the wealthy or those who appeared wealthy. "The $20 a week man now had his own little automobile at the rear of his house and made a rapid transit to his work by means of the roads which had been especially reserved for vehicular traffic by the city." His work survived, probably not so much because his views were popular at the time, but because he was mostly right.

Nelson barely mentioned bicycles, although it was clear that he foresaw a further demise in the status of the cyclist when he wrote: "Yeah, not to own your own automobile was generally a sign that your salary must be a low one." The fact that even in 1910 Premier Whitney stood out, at least for a man of his status, for riding a bicycle – when an elegant horse and buggy would have seemed more suited to his position – already suggested the trend. The automobile marketers had, however, yet to assertively enter the scene to convince the public that a motorcar would bestow status and prestige. In fact, a few years before Premier Whitney's death in 1914, he was presented by his Conservative Party with a luxury motorcar. One newspaper attributed Whitney's subsequent decline to his having given up the healthy habit of cycling.

For inter-city travel Nelson foresaw competition between the Toronto and District Airship Company and express, electric rail service, which would by then have surpassed electric radials in speed. An electric power revolution was of course already under-way in Ontario. On October 11, 1910, Premier Whitney had vis-ited the industrial town of Berlin (now Kitchener) to ceremonially turn on the switch that allowed power from Niagara Falls – "the people's power" – to flow to the town. The same abundant "white coal" would soon reach, with publicly owned transmission lines, Toronto and other municipalities across south-western Ontario, suggesting a bright future, including for electric streetcars, radials, and trains.

A 1929 biography about the premier associated his custom of cycling with his simple, honest character: "Gruff and bluff, yet really a genial man ... not brilliant, yet capable of great accom-plishment; always honest, fearlessly honest, and so simple withal that apart from reading books his only hobby was that of riding a bicycle." By 1929 there would be good reasons to look back nostal-gically at the days when the bicycle played a more prominent role.

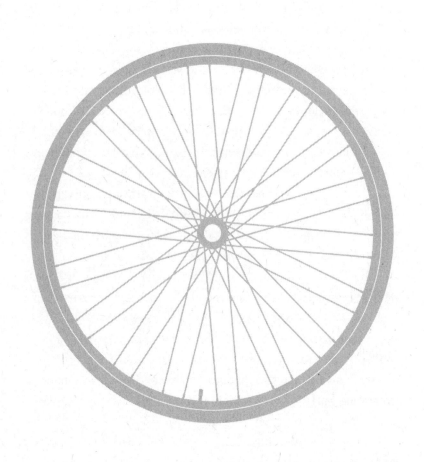

1929
Lethal Motorcars, Accidental Victims

December 14, 1929 – The motorcar gets its day in court

Magistrate Emerson Coatsworth, a former Toronto mayor, looks over the list of cases in his downtown courtroom, including charges against motorists. The docket for this Friday morning, December 14, is a typical one, but the list of the accused is not, among them a man the Globe *last year lauded for his zeal in promoting road safety, "deserving of the thanks of every person who is called upon to use the highways." The man, the country's best-known motor advocate, a founder of the Ontario Safety League, and current president of the Canadian Automobile Association, isn't likely to be thanked by his victims. Today it is Dr. Perry Doolittle who must answer to a charge of reckless driving that has added to the city's soaring road casualty toll.*

On November 22, late in the afternoon, Dr. Doolittle was driving behind a westbound streetcar on Bloor Street as it approached the Castle Frank stop, just beyond the Prince Edward Viaduct, which since 1918 spans the Don Valley. Speeding by motorists on the wide Viaduct is *common, but there was no mention of the doctor's speed as he approached the stop where patrons, bundled up against a chill wind, awaited the streetcar. Whatever his speed, Dr. Doolittle was unable to stop in time to avoid hitting three women waiting to board. When police arrived on the scene, they interviewed witnesses, then arrested Dr. Doolittle, taking him to the Dundas Street East station. The injured women were taken to hospital, while the doctor was charged with reckless driving, before being released on a $500 bail.*

Dr. Doolittle has tirelessly defended – amid increasing public outrage over the road carnage – the safety of the motorcar, at least when operated by a competent driver and rules are obeyed by other road users. The Automotive Industries Association has been so appreciative of the doctor's work that it recently presented him with a cheque for $5,000, "a token of its appreciation," albeit a sum sufficient to buy a small house in the city. But even an advocate as skilled as Dr. Doolittle has struggled to dissuade the public from the view that motorcars are inherently dangerous. The Mail & Empire *recently offered a telling commentary of the times, reporting that "[f]or the first time in several days, however, children were not included in the list of traffic accidents."*

Even constant vigilance on roads, or sidewalks, is no guarantee of refuge from the motor peril for cyclists and pedestrians. Crossing from the curb to the streetcar doors is best done with an eye on motorcars, despite a city by-law that obliges motorists to halt behind stopped cars. This year alone, hundreds of motorists have been charged for violating this law. The risky conduct of motorists has persisted despite highly-publicized tragedies, including the death of a "Great Citizen," the president of the Canadian National Exhibition, hit and killed as he alighted from a streetcar at Bloor and St. George Streets. *The motorist fled, and escaped capture, while another motorist, who similarly ignored the stopping of a streetcar and killed a cyclist riding along the curb, was convicted and sentenced to three months in jail.*

"Day by day," lamented one citizen, "the death cars crush our citizens ... The modern juggernaut speeds on its death-dealing course, and with but little effort to curb its murderous activities."

Cyclists too have moved beyond the sports page of local papers ... as road victims. In early November, a boy cycling home for supper from a music lesson became Toronto's eighty-first road fatality. "The neglected cycle once the fastest vehicle on the road, has paled before the automobile ... with its express-train speed and its tons of weight, has made wheeling both in streets and on roads more or less dangerous, even more dangerous than walking."

Among the three women injured by Dr. Doolittle last month was Mrs. John W. Marks. She and her husband move in the same social circles as Dr. Doolittle and his wife, Emily. In fact, both Mrs. Marks and Mrs. Doolittle are often mentioned on the same society pages. The Toronto Society Blue Book shows them belonging to the same clubs.

When the court clerk calls Dr. Doolittle's case, the Crown prosecutor announces that the charge is being withdrawn. "Why is this?" asks Magistrate Emerson. "The two women who were injured wrote and said it was their fault," the prosecutor answers, adding that they now say they had run suddenly into the street towards the streetcar doors. "I wanted to know why because I am a close friend of Dr. Doolittle and didn't want it to appear as if I was letting him off," explains the magistrate.

Image 16: The Bloor Viaduct on opening day. A cyclist enjoys an eastward ride across the Bloor Viaduct on October 18, 1918. The roadway would soon be overwhelmed with motorcars. The opening ceremony was restrained, not only because the war had yet to end but because a global flu pandemic was underway. The streetcar line, operated by the TTC after 1921, runs along the centre of the wide roadway. (In the 1960s, the streetcar was replaced by the Bloor-Danforth subway, running along a lower deck. Bike lanes were added in 1991.) (City of Toronto Archives, Series 372, Subseries 10, Item 868)

WHITHER THE CYCLIST AND THE PEDESTRIAN?

Automobiles didn't introduce danger to Toronto roads, but they changed the scale, magnitude, and geography of the danger. Pedestrians and cyclists still needed to pay careful attention to streetcars and steam trains at level crossings, but unlike motorcars, streetcars and trains had professional drivers, and ran on schedules – and on tracks.

The city's road casualty toll for 1929 was worse than 1928, and 1928 was worse than 1927, the year when Ontario's driver's licence was introduced to improve road safety – and coincidentally the last year of Prohibition. The number of laws governing motorcars had increased; so too had the danger of motorcars, as their numbers, weight, and power increased.

No one and no place was safe from the danger. Road casualties in 1929 included a pedestrian on the sidewalk, a toddler in a pram, a sergeant directing traffic, the driver of a hearse, even a monument to the poet Robert Burns. A boy was struck and seriously injured on Ossington Avenue; the motorist turned out to be the boy's shocked father. Frank Nelson's prediction in his 1908 novella about the proliferation of motorcars turned out to be accurate, but he didn't foresee, or didn't mention, the coming carnage.

The road hierarchy had become unrecognizable from the days when Premier Whitney said the motorist "must get out of the road of the pedestrian, even if he is standing still." The pedestrian's status had descended even since 1921 when a judge wrote, "The pedestrian has the right-of-way always." But whatever the legal road hierarchy, cyclists and pedestrians – including people at a streetcar stop – always lost in crashes with motorists.

The OML no longer claimed that motorcars were safer than other modes – comparisons that by 1929 could only provoke anger and ridicule. In 1909, the OML had pointed to the 111 fatalities involving streetcars – over a ten-year period – to support its argument about the relative safety of motorcars. But by the late 1920s automobile crashes were causing 100 deaths in little more than a year, not a decade. The OML pivoted to a new metric – the rate of death per automobile, claiming that cars were safer, even as the number of road deaths increased. As long as the number of automobiles increased at a faster pace than the number of deaths they caused, the *rate* of fatalities per 1,000 motorcars declined. Grieving families would find no solace in the metric (nor when it was changed in later decades to deaths per 10 million kilometres driven).

In 1910, deaths and injuries involving automobiles hadn't merited their own heading in the annual police report. They did by 1929. There was no mistaking the coincidence between the huge increase in motorcars, and driving, in the city, and the casualty toll. Toronto's motorcar population had grown from 2,000 in 1910 to 120,000 in 1929. The city's human population had grown far more slowly, from 350,000 in 1910 to 600,000 in 1929.

While adults did all the motoring, children did much of the dying. A letter-writer suggested that a plague would provoke a faster government response. In 1928 and 1929, fifty-four families suffered the death of a child in a road crash; other families were left to care for children that had suffered life-altering injuries. In November 1927, the Bureau of Municipal Research, a Toronto citizens' advocacy group, sounded the alarm about the casualty toll, saying it "should give pause to every citizen whether a motor owner or not."

After a deadly weekend in 1927 on Ontario's highways, the *Globe* asked how long it would take for the authorities to deal "in some effective way with the menace to human lives that hangs over the highways." In November 1929, the *Globe* again commented on the road danger, declaring: "An armistice is sadly needed." Less than a week later, after another deadly weekend, it could only repeat its lament: "Why does this tragedy go on from week to week." But the

Globe's grief had curious limits, deciding to not report Dr. Doolittle's crash into the women at the transit stop, the charges against him, and the outcome of the court case.

The Ontario Safety League (OSL), which the OML helped establish in 1913, used the death by misadventure in September 1929 of a telegram messenger on a bike (holding on to the back of a truck) as an opportunity to complain about all manner of cycling behaviour to explain the casualty toll. *Saturday Night*, which had resumed writing about cyclists, at least to complain about their conduct, called for stronger regulation and enforcement to "save many a young life and make the streets safer for all who travel them." But misadventure couldn't explain the great majority of cyclist and pedestrian fatalities among children, including the death in April 1929 of eleven-year-old Lewis Phillips, son of Alderman Nathan Phillips. (Phillips became the city's mayor in the 1950s. The public square in front of City Hall is named after him.) The boy, reaching up to post a letter for his father, was killed on the sidewalk by a motorist who lost control of his vehicle.

On weekends in the 1920s, there was "an endless procession" of motorists on the highways escaping "the turmoil of the city." Cyclists with similar ambitions could explore neighbouring towns and villages, and beyond. To the east was the Township of East York, the biggest of Toronto's suburbs with 25,000 inhabitants, and the Township of Scarborough; to the north-west was the Village of Fairbank, the second-largest suburb; and further out, the Town of Weston, home of CCM. The Township of North York lay to the north. These destinations were within easy reach by bicycle, including for boys seeking an afternoon adventure of exploration, but escape from the city didn't provide a refuge from the danger of motorcars. Monday's newspapers provided a long list of road tragedies in the city and its environs, presented to the reader in the manner of a roundup of weekend sports. It was the rare weekend that passed without new names added to the year's road fatalities.

SAME BICYCLE, NEW RULES

Regulation – for the Cyclist

The city's bicycle licensing regime, which took effect on June 1, 1929, served to confirm how far cyclists' influence had declined. In fact, the 1929 licensing by-law got scant media attention, unlike the comprehensive coverage given any bike licensing proposal in the 1890s. The annual licence fee was set at 50 cents, to be enforced with a $5 fine (later raised, bizarrely, to $50 before being cut back to $5 in 1936). The average value of a bicycle at the time, based on the reported value of stolen bikes, was $25. Unlike the bicycle licence, the Ontario driver's licence, and its associated testing provisions, at least suggested a timely public policy response to the rising road-casualty toll.

The potential for new revenues at City Hall, with a significant contribution from children (or their parents), offered a plausible motivation for the bike licence, which the *Globe* announced with the headline "30,000 Bicyclists to Pay City Licence," noting that "Toronto has found a new source of revenue amounting to $15,000 annually." These potential annual revenues would exceed the revenues from virtually every other licence at the time, including moving picture shows and dogs, and exceeded only by cigarette vendors.

The official rationale for the licence was to make it easier for police to return stolen bicycles to their rightful owners – a rationale that underlay some licensing proposals dating back to at least 1894 – but absent any contemporary outcry from cyclists about the matter, or a demand for a licence as the solution.

One news report mentioned the success of Winnipeg's bicycle licence in reducing thefts, although conflating the problem of theft with the ability of police to return recovered bikes to their rightful owners. The licence made it no more difficult for a thief to walk away with a bicycle. Winnipeg apparently achieved an 80–90 per cent recovery rate for stolen bicycles compared to 25 per cent in Toronto, but no research was offered to show a causal connection between the licensing regime and the number of recovered bicycles. Winnipeg police might simply have devoted more resources to the problem of catching bike thieves.

Bicycle thefts had been a problem in Toronto since the late 1860s during the brief popularity of the *vélocipède* (or "boneshaker"). The theft of high-wheels was likely a lesser problem given their conspicuous size and the challenge of riding off on one. The safety was an easier mark, its portability facilitating the thief's enterprise, aided by cyclists' habit of leaving their vehicles leaning, unlocked, against roadside curbs. Even in 1895, bicycle thefts had been described as an "epidemic." In 1899, the last year of the Bicycle Craze, 225 bicycles were stolen; by 1910 that number had ballooned to 1,100. But bike thefts had not risen so dramatically in the 1920s – in fact, bicycle thefts fell from 1,800 in 1921 to 1,600 in 1928 – to rationalize a cumbersome licensing regime. (Once the licence was in place, bicycle thefts actually increased, reaching 3,000 by 1934, an increase of 220 per cent over the previous year.)

One thing quickly became clear: it was easier to catch individuals, often children, for failing to obtain their bike licence than it was to catch thieves. Indeed, there was evidence that only the hapless bicycle thief need worry about detection. At his trial, sixty-six-year-old Sam Jones claimed that he didn't know how to ride a bike and was simply admiring what he believed to be a policeman's bike. The man's credibility was undermined by witness accounts that he picked up and walked off with a locked bicycle. The penalties meted out for bicycle theft – up to six months or more in Toronto's Central Prison, even for thieves who had fallen on hard times – suggested a sufficient deterrent. Jones escaped with a thirty-day sentence. While stolen bicycles were often not recovered, the same was not true of stolen cars, virtually all of which were recovered. Whether or not bicycles were licensed it was unlikely that police would devote as much effort to recovering a stolen bicycle as to a motorcar valued at hundreds, even thousands, of dollars.

It was no surprise that Toronto was the first city to take advantage of the authority granted by the province to require a bicycle licence. It was, after all, the city in 1928 that had asked for the necessary amendment to the *Municipal Act*. (By the mid-1930s, most of Toronto's neighbours had introduced their own bike licence, in many cases after Queen's Park rejected a call by police chiefs for a provincially run system, which would, if the rationale was the return of stolen bikes, be more effective given how easily thieves could move stolen bikes from city to city across Ontario.)

By the end of Toronto's first year of the bicycle licence in 1929, 13,500 licences were issued, but in the absence of regular enforcement, the scant publicity about the new licence, and the cost and effort to obtain a licence, the total number under-represented the actual numbers for bikes in use. In fact, under the initial by-law, it was impossible for police to identify a violator without stopping a cyclist and demanding to see paper proof of the licence. Only after a by-law amendment in the early fall of 1929 were cyclists obliged to affix a flexible city-issued metal disc, bearing only the words "Toronto Bicycle Licence" on the bicycle stem under the handlebars. The discs were soon replaced by metal licence plates.

City Hall may have been eager for the new revenues, but police were not eager for the extra work. In 1930, the number of issued bike licences actually dropped to 12,000, then surged to 30,000 in 1934, coincident with increased enforcement. In 1933, the police let it be known they wanted larger licence plates, and they might not enforce, and perhaps had not been enforcing, the by-law, consistent with the low number of licences for 1929–33. City Hall worried about the higher cost of larger plates. In 1934, the *Daily Star* dubiously attributed the increase in licences to the bright yellow colour of the new plates, reporting that "twelve queues of boys and girls, big brothers and sisters and a few older people" were at the City Hall paying wickets when the plates became available. The theory couldn't account for the equally large jump in dog licences.

It took several years to work out the kinks in the licensing system. Indeed, an early beneficiary of the bike licence was the bicycle thief. Initially, it was easy to apply for a licence using a fabricated serial number, then to resell a stolen bicycle with a City Hall–issued licence plate. Thieves from neighbouring municipalities could also bring stolen bicycles into Toronto to have them licensed. The by-law was later amended so that police would first verify that the serial number on the application matched the one on the bicycle. For cyclists, the result was to further complicate the process, ostensibly for their benefit, by adding a visit to the police station before obtaining the licence from City Hall.

On the day in 1929 when Toronto's Board of Control first approved the bike licence, the *Daily Star*'s 5 p.m. edition made no mention of it, while breathlessly announcing a "vast" plan for downtown road expansion: "City Planners' 15-Year Program $13,000,000." University Avenue was to be extended southward and two new diagonal streets built, including a 100-foot (30-metre) wide Passchendaele Road, cutting south-west through neighbourhoods from the new Vimy Circle at Queen Street and University Avenue. The plan naturally had the support of the OML, which suggested that downtown traffic congestion would be solved for the next fifty years. The image of the future roads showed luxury motorcars – but no bicycles.

The Bicycle and the Motorcar – Diverging Trajectories

In 1929, the city had a wide range of clubs, associations, and societies covering virtually every pastime, trade, and cause, including sheep breeders, yachtsmen, temperance supporters, and asphalters, but none that advocated for the everyday cyclist. The RCBC and the Queen City Bicycle Club were the only bicycle clubs listed in the 1929 city directory, but they saved their energy for battles on the racecourse, competing in the Dunlop Cup until the last road race in 1926, cancelled in part because of the inconvenience to motorists. In 1929, the RCBC added curling to its name, becoming the Royal Canadian Bicycle and Curling Club. (The Royal Canadian Curling Club still exists today, although its only connection to cycling and the Bicycle Craze is in a display case at its home, still at 131 Broadview Avenue, where the Dunlop Cup and Dunlop Shield trophies, fortuitously recovered from a repair shop some years ago, are housed.)

The CWA focused on its role overseeing bicycle racing. The *Globe*'s coverage of the CWA's 1929 meeting at the posh King

Image 17: A bicycle licence was adopted by the City of Toronto on March 11, 1929. Thirty years earlier the decision would have received great public attention, but on this day, the *Daily Star* was focused on a grand road development scheme for Toronto's downtown, including a new Vimy Circle near Queen Street and University Avenue. The drawing gave a prominent place to motorcars, showing but a single streetcar – and no bicycles. (Drawing: Earle Sheppard, *Daily Star*, Mar. 11, 1929, 2)

The New Vimy Circle

Edward Hotel was relatively prolific, if only to mourn the diminished place of the CWA and the bicycle. "The handful of enthusiasts who gathered here Saturday lacked nothing of the sporting spirit of the days of old, but their ranks have been depleted to an alarming extent."

Mount Carmel Catholic Church in Toronto invoked the aid of St. Christopher, patron saint of travellers, in a blessing of parishioners' vehicles – motorcars, trucks, lorries, motorcycles, and bicycles – but it was motorcars that dominated the queue. In defence of the divine, the road toll might have been worse without this intervention.

Children who expected sympathy from adults for the road peril would have been disappointed. "Motorcycles are a curse, and boys on bicycles are worse," complained one letter writer. "The sooner [they] are put in their proper place the better for all concerned," wrote another. For its part, the *Globe* launched a "Just Kids Safety Club," which was a great success, at least when measured by the number of badges distributed (300,000 by 1932). The club sought to educate children on how to recognize road dangers, but without advocating for road safety measures to reduce the danger. The Just Kids Safety Club, supported by the OSL, was dissolved in the early 1930s. Its existence amidst frequent child fatalities on the roads might only have dulled the appeal of car ads in the *Globe*. Newspapers were dubious champions for road safety – it was, after all, the ads of carmakers that fattened the publisher's wallet.

CCM couldn't be described as a cycling advocate, but it recognized that its children's market required making parents feel comfortable with the road risks faced by children. An anxious parent was a reluctant buyer. Its solution was in advertising. For one ad campaign, CCM interviewed 100 cyclists, including messenger boys, to convince potential buyers that cycling on city roads was safe. Several interviewees said bicycles offered nimbleness and agility, allowing cyclists to more easily escape crashes than pedestrians. The ads suggested that motorists were particularly careful around cyclists. Whatever the merit of the claims, CCM also worked with police and civic groups to conduct safety clinics, including rodeos to teach cycling skills. CCM's *Care and Operation of Your Bicycle* included ten cycling commandments, including "Ride straight, don't wobble" and "Don't 'cut in' in front of a moving car."

Both the bicycle and the motorcar were markers of socioeconomic class, but by the late 1920s, the bicycle was continuing its descent and the motorcar its ascent. The economy of the bicycle might have been celebrated, or facilitated, with improved road safety conditions, but it wasn't. In a society where consumption and material wealth served as measures of status, the affordability of the bicycle simply added to the reasons to deride, dismiss, or ignore the cyclist. The falling price of motorcars didn't prompt the same fall from fashion as had happened to the bicycle; upper-class motorists could always distinguish themselves with an expensive brand.

Despite public outrage about the road carnage, most motorists, many decision-makers, and even the media had begun treating bicycles, people on foot, and streetcars as impediments to motorists, even though motorists remained a minority among road users. In 1929, an estimated 20 per cent of city residents – or 60 per cent of households – owned motorcars. Mrs. Marks's affluent household, for example, likely owned a car, which was presumably used by her husband, while she relied on the streetcar.

A June 1929 decision by the Board of Control *against* widening Bloor Street, between Spadina and Sherbourne, in order to maintain – at the behest of merchants – wider sidewalks for shoppers stood out as an exception to the motorcar's upward trajectory. A *Daily Star* headline declared, "Wide Bloor Sidewalk Is 'Colossal Mistake,'" while a letter writer sarcastically linked the decision to bygone days: "And bicycle paths! Surely the city should install a few of those to take care of people who are taking up that new craze, the bicycle." On this particular occasion, the mayor resisted pleas from councillors and motor advocates to reopen the debate, while admitting that "the people are demanding wider pavements," in this case meaning wider roads. He didn't define who he meant by "the people."

While cyclists of the Bicycle Craze couldn't have dreamed of the extent and quality of roads in Toronto by 1929, including 525 miles (844 kilometres) of paved roads, most of them asphalted to a scientific standard, they wouldn't have foreseen that they would be worse off because of the danger of sharing roads with motorists.

By the 1920s, the business of road building had become the business of government, both municipally and provincially. In 1929, Queen's Park spent almost $25 million on roads, amounting to over 30 per cent of its overall spending, and over thirty times as much as it spent on roads in 1910. In fact, the fortunes of motorists had improved to such a degree that the OML was transitioning into a service organization for its members, able to rely, except for the most ambitious projects (such as the trans-Canada highway initiative pushed by Dr. Doolittle), on the motorists' political champions and its allies entrenched in government bureaucracies to plan and build new or improved roads.

At his inaugural address in January 1929, Mayor Sam McBride highlighted the importance of new thoroughfares into the city to cope with motor traffic. Several weeks later, at the OML's annual meeting, attended by government leaders with the enthusiasm they once showed cycling groups, the OML president observed that a "very happy relationship has existed between the Government and the league." The president nonetheless reminded politicians of the increasing need for wider highways into Toronto.

In built-up areas of the city, road widenings were often accomplished at the expense of trees, greenery, and even transit users. The wide median of the St. Clair Avenue West streetcar line was among the victims. (It would take until 2005 for the city to begin restoring the median for the new light rail transit [LRT] line.) The irony of improving streets for motorists, and thereby taking paying customers from streetcars was more obvious after 1921, the year the transit system was taken over by the city, and run by the

Toronto Transportation Commission (TTC). Public investment in roads to facilitate private car use drew patrons from the publicly funded transit service.

Government agencies responsible for road safety were usually the same ones responsible for road expansions and motorcar registrations. Ontario's Highway Safety Committee was chaired by the Minister of Highways and included the Registrar of Motor Vehicles, the OML, and the OSL. When the *Daily Star* in the 1890s proposed rules for pedestrians, it was with mischief in mind, but when the motor lobby made similar proposals in the 1920s, it wasn't joking. At a June 1929 road safety meeting at City Hall, the OML urged the adoption of a regulatory model from US cities, which included a ban on "jay walking." The OSL likewise asserted that pedestrians "must be made amenable to traffic regulations, must cross the street only at intersections, keep to the pedestrian right-of-way and obey the signals of traffic officers ... For humanity's sake, the sooner Toronto takes a similar stand the better." A *Globe* headline, "Safety Ideas Promulgated Lead to Greater Pleasure in Driving of Automobile," suggested the underlying objective. The pedestrian and the cyclist both ranked high on the OSL's list of road users whose conduct required reformation.

The motor lobby found an ally in Chief Constable S.J. Dickson, who in 1922 was quick to lay the blame for many road crashes at the feet of the pedestrian victims. "[I]n nearly all cases [72.3 per cent] there is a measurable element of contributory negligence on the part of the victims, and had reasonable care been exercised he or she would not have been injured." He concluded that "there is no reason why such pedestrians should not be held responsible for the accident." Police didn't, however, segregate children from adults in tabulating their numbers – and where the "unfortunate person" was dead, the motorist's story was often the only version available, further skewing the numbers towards blaming the victim given the likely bias of the motorist.

THE BICYCLE IN THE SHADOW OF THE MOTORCAR

Selling the Motorcar – Prestige, Power, and Speed

The first automobiles in the city were largely playthings of the rich. Carmakers' advertisements nonetheless focused on the utility of their products. When 90,000 visitors attended the 1913 Toronto Automobile Show, the numbers could not yet be equated with a desire to *own* a motorcar – in fact, there was still a strong belief that the motorcar was a passing fad. It was only after the marketers introduced sophisticated and manipulative campaigns, convincing many people, despite the on-road bloodletting, that car ownership bestowed the prestige associated with an upper-class lifestyle that car sales began to rise. By 1915, automakers surpassed the food industry as the biggest advertisers. Since many politicians became car owners, the problems most evident to them were the problems of the motorist, who was usually preoccupied with the need for more road space.

Year-over-year changes made by manufacturers, even if merely cosmetic, spurred demand based on the desire to keep up to date, as had once been the case for bicycles, while falling prices, deferred payments, and second-hand or rented vehicles made cars more accessible to more people. The automobile body or carriage offered greater potential for annual design changes than had been possible with the bicycle.

The capacity for speed was another obvious selling feature of the motorcar. The public, and many decision-makers, easily appreciated the greater danger posed by the capacity for speed of motorcars. The point was articulated in a newspaper headline in 1908: "Autos go much too quickly. Good for the tombstone men, but not for the general public." The public, after all, was already familiar with the greater danger posed by a speeding horse, bicycle, streetcar, or train – all of them constrained by physical or imposed limits on speed – compared to a slower moving animal or vehicle.

Ironically, the success of bicycle advocates in the 1890s in resisting speed limits worked against most cyclists in the new century, given the greater road danger from cars at higher speeds. In England, the speed of the earliest motorcars had been strictly limited; indeed, the *Red Flag Act* required a person on foot and carrying a red flag to walk in front of a motorcar. The repeal of the act touched off great excitement, especially with the motor lobby, which organized a London to Brighton motorcar race in the fall of 1896. Dr. Doolittle was there, amidst a contingent of cyclists in a "mad scramble after the motors … anxious to get a glimpse of the new means of locomotion." Three months before the race, England suffered its first pedestrian fatality involving a motorcar.

(Overleaf) **Image 18:** "An open air garage." By 1924, Yonge Street, looking north from King Street, was almost unrecognizable from a decade earlier. Chief Constable Dickson complained that streets had become "an open air garage," calling for the prohibition of car parking downtown for its interference with business. (After the Second World War, enormous amounts of public and private space were allocated to car parking. And in the fight for bike lanes decades later, it was the ferocious defence of curbside parking privileges that often thwarted advocates.) (City of Toronto Archives, Fonds 1244, Item 1113)

The motor lobby's first success in opposing speed limits was in 1903, when the newly formed TAC opposed a Queen's Park proposal for a 7 mph (11 km/h) limit. Queen's Park settled on a 10 mph (16 km/h) limit within cities and 15 mph (24 km/h) outside of cities.

It was no surprise that motorists didn't appreciate restrictions on speed, given that proposed limits fell far below the new technology's capacity. Many motorists had, after all, been lured by and paid handsomely for that capacity for speed. By 1910, half of all road infractions were for speeding by motorists. Daniel Lochrie, son of bicycle-maker James Lochrie – but like others of his social class drawn to motorcars – was among the motorists charged with speeding. At a court hearing, the magistrate, frustrated by the prevalence of speeding violations, threatened to raise fines to $20.

The lack of police enforcement capacity to catch speeding motorists sometimes prompted citizen action. Early in the century, an Oakville businessman who was thrown from his rig after his horse was frightened by a speeding motorist "declared war on the automobile." He arranged for the timing of cars belonging to members of the TAC as they drove along the Lake Shore Road on their run to Buffalo, then threatened to prosecute the speeders. In defence of its members, Mrs. Frank Baillie said that the club already had a resolution in place to prohibit fast driving – similar to the "no scorching" rule once passed by the Toronto Bicycle Club. Lakeshore Road would soon become notoriously dangerous for cyclists.

A contributor to *Maclean's* in 1914 who wrote that "the automobile had been invented in vain if it is to be forbidden to travel quickly" might have been forgiven for failing to foresee the coming carnage. But when advocates in the 1920s argued that the great motoring public was "held down" by the existing speed limit, attributing complaints to "cranks," they had plenty of evidence to know better.

In 1929 speed limits were raised to 20 mph (32 km/h) in cities and 35 mph (56 km/h) on highways, despite public concerns. In 1937 the speed limits were raised again to 30 mph (48 km/h) in cities (50 km/h remains the default urban speed today) and 50 mph (80 km/h) on highways. The voices of opponents proved to be too weak to stop the increases, while carmakers could generally count on others to do their bidding – even as they augmented the power, speed, and weight of their products to entice buyers. The Dodge Brothers promoted their 1927 sedan as the "Fastest Four in America" with the capacity to accelerate to 25 mph (40 km/h) in seven seconds.

The Canadian automobile industry, which was producing 200,000 motorcars annually by the mid-1920s, had itself become a powerful player. Automobile production in Canada and the United States exceeded bicycle production for the first time in the 1920s, although the cumulative number of bicycles in circulation remained significantly higher.

"Toys" for Business and Transportation

The popularity of bicycles among children could be no surprise. Children were simply enjoying the same attributes of the bicycle – freedom, independence, and adventure – that had made bikes so popular among adults during the Bicycle Craze. Among young people, "[t]he bicycle still holds much favour, and perhaps the rising generation may restore the wheel to its honoured place in the physical activities of the nation," observed a newspaper editorial.

The age of the average cyclist had continued to fall; so too had the socio-economic class of the average adult cyclist. As early as 1918, a newspaper article accompanying a full page of bicycle ads used the tag line "Rich Men Buy Them," suggesting that bikes were making a comeback among motorcar owners, at least for exercise – but this narrative only confirmed, at least implicitly, that bicycles were already being associated with lower-income groups. (The rich use them for exercise but they drive motorcars; the lower-income use them as a necessity for transportation.)

Although children were the most conspicuous users of bicycles by 1929, determining their actual proportion among cyclists was more difficult. Between the start and end of the decade, there had been a noticeable shift in advertising towards an audience dominated by children, or their parents. The *Globe* in 1928 contrasted local attitudes towards bicycles to those in Europe where "[a]n elderly person on a bicycle is not a ridiculous sight – he may be the prime minister, or a professor of logic, or a society leader." Whoever was buying them, bicycles remained big sellers across Canada in the 1920s, with special promotions such as the annual "Bicycle Week," organized by the national bicycle dealers' association and CCM.

The prominence of bicycles among children made it easier to characterize them as toys, and therefore to relieve City Hall from any obligation to accommodate cyclists on roads. But the fact that the bicycle was popularly used by children didn't make it a toy. (The irony was more obvious when parents later began driving their children, often to protect them from other motorists, to school – trips that has once been travelled independently by children on their bikes.)

In issuing bike licences, City Hall didn't attempt to distinguish adult cyclists from children, nor to make any effort towards

Image 19: CCM bicycles, including Joycycles (children's tricycles), had many admirers – and buyers. In 1918, the CCM factory, then recently relocated to the Town of Weston, reached a peak production of 900 bicycles per day. CCM was one of the Toronto area's most prominent manufacturers. The company, which employed thousands of workers into the 1970s, went bankrupt in 1983. (City of Toronto Archives, CCM Fonds 1488, Series 123, Item 1426)

estimating or counting their numbers. Children as cyclists were certainly more likely to be noticed, both because their inexperience ensured their over-representation in road casualties and because their propensity for folly, consistent with their age, made them easy subjects of complaint. Characterizing bicycles as toys suited automakers; indeed, their marketing further lowered the status of the bicycle and other modes of travel.

Treating bicycles as toys was nonetheless curious in the context of the era. In the 1920s bicycles had only recently gone to war with the Canadian Corps Cyclist Battalion (and returned to war with the infantry in the Second World War). Planet Cycle Works reminded prospective buyers about the war-tested sturdiness of its products, which it continued to display alongside motorcars at the CNE's Transportation Building until at least 1921. Police continued to use Planets, although it was unclear how many, and by 1929 it was clear that they were more enamoured, as were the suspects they chased, with "high-powered cars." At the tail end of the First World War and into 1920, this same "toy" offered a way to keep a healthy distance from the contagion of the Spanish flu. And if bicycles were truly toys, what sense could be made of City Hall's requirement for bicycle owners to obtain a licence, which was otherwise only required of adult enterprises (or dog owners).

The characterization of bicycles as toys also belied their value for adults going to work, among other everyday destinations. In fact, in its ads, CCM still encouraged employers to accommodate workers with special bicycle sheds and racks for parking. The bicycle likewise remained an invaluable tool for commerce in the delivery of goods from grocery, print, hardware, optical, and other businesses.

Bicycle-makers, however, generally reinforced the characterization of the bicycle as toys, to be given up on reaching adulthood: "Your boy will only be a boy once ... Let him know what it is to skim over the country roads on a CCM. He'll

Image 20: "To Avoid the 'Flu' Ride a CCM Bicycle." Bicycle-makers offered another reason to ride a bicycle when the Spanish flu began raging across the world in 1918. "Get away from the stuffy, over-crowded cars, with their danger of contagion" read the CCM advertisement. (CCM, Ad, *Globe*, Oct. 21, 1918, 9)

enjoy it just as you did – and more." In fact, manufacturers played into the bicycle-as-toy theme by adding *faux* motorcar features, even if the result was to make bicycles less practical by adding weight.

CCM started making a "Model T" bicycle and a motorbike-like "Model W," while Hyslop Bros. offered an "Auto-Bike" and a "Motobike." There was nothing unusual about children wanting to play at being adults, although bicycles as toys remained distinctly different from other toys. Toy guns, for example, served no purpose other than for role-playing, but even a bicycle with a toy gas tank could still get a child to school. Indeed, manufacturers didn't lose sight of the money-making potential of bikes, one ad noting, "There are heaps of stores, offices, factories that want bicycle messengers."

What constituted a toy in the transportation mix was an artificial construct; after all, cars might be used for a Sunday drive and have a variety of purely decorative features, yet not be considered a toy. And it wasn't children who were the targets of ads that sought (successfully) to convince adults that a car could magically transport them to a higher socio-economic status. (By the twenty-first century, during the worsening climate crisis, giant passenger vehicles that had little logic for utility were increasingly marketed as playthings, touting off-roading adventures that had no connection, except in imagination, to the average consumer's experience. Today, automakers often make little effort to disguise the toy-like nature of their products. Chrysler touts its 2023 Ram pickup truck with the pitch: You're never too old to play in the mud; "the only things that change are the toys."

From Utility to Amusement, and Back Again

During its history, the bicycle had already swung several times between being treated as an amusement or a toy and being treated as a device useful in reaching everyday destinations.

An early forerunner of the bicycle, the *Laufmaschine* ("running machine") was invented by German baron Karl von Drais to help speed him on his rounds of the forests he managed. The *Laufmaschine* put the rider on a seat with two wheels aligned one behind the other. (A modern version of this vehicle is today a child's toy, called a strider or balance bike.) The baron, astride the seat, propelled the vehicle by running with his feet on the ground; when he raised his feet to coast, the device miraculously stayed upright (a fact that still fascinates the novice rider today).

Once exported, the *Laufmaschine* largely became a vehicle of sport and leisure. In England it was known as the "hobby horse," borrowing the name from the children's toy, or "dandy horse" for the dandies who promenaded on it. In France, the *Laufmaschine* was known as a *vélocipède* (*vélo* for "fast" and *ped* for "foot").

The *Laufmaschine* or *vélocipède* re-emerged in the 1860s with an important innovation, a pedal crank affixed to the front axle, much the way a children's tricycle works today. This adaptation came to be known as the first "bicycle," though it was largely used for amusement, partly for the want of good roads, and was remembered as the "bone-shaker" for its bumpy ride, as a result of its iron or wooden wheels running over rough roads. In early 1869, this *vélocipède* arrived in Canadian cities creating a "[s]udden wave of euphoria" – except on sidewalks, where they were treated as a nuisance. A petition by *vélocipède* enthusiasts for the right to ride on sidewalks between 8 p.m. and 8 a.m. was rejected by city council. The *vélocipède* fared better indoors, as an amusement. The St. George's skating rink in the city was converted to a *vélocipède* academy that included a spectators' area and had thirty *vélocipèdes* on hand. Dixon Brothers Carriage Works, as well as artisans and amateur enthusiasts, built versions of the machine, but its popularity was fleeting. "It is always a wonder to us," wrote *The Canadian Illustrated News* in late 1876, "that the velocipede, which created such a fashionable fury in this country, only a few years ago, should have been entirely abandoned. We lately saw one solitary rider in this city." (The front-wheel drive *vélocipède* quickly re-emerged as a children's toy, sometimes with three wheels, but distinguished by the pedal crank on the front axle.)

The high-wheel rose to prominence in the 1870s as a logical next step for the *vélocipède*: if one turn of the pedal crank advanced the rider by a distance equal to the circumference of the front wheel, then making the front wheel bigger advanced the rider a proportionately greater distance. The pedal crank remained on the front wheel, which grew to an enormous size. The back wheel, needed only for balance, shrank. Ironically, when the high-wheel appeared at the 1876 Centennial Exposition, it was alongside items that would prove far more practical: the telephone and the typewriter. The potential for a "cropper," "header," or "crowning" on a high-wheel – the result of being pitched over the handlebars upon hitting a bump, rock, or stray chicken (all real and imminent dangers) – added to the drama and bravado of high-wheeling, while largely limiting its use to amusement and sport.

When the safety first appeared on Toronto streets in the late 1880s and early 1890s, high-wheel riders looked down, literally and figuratively, upon the upstart, dismissing it as suited to women and timid men. High-wheel riders had taken themselves very seriously, regardless of the fact that their vehicle was used as little more than a plaything. (Horses in cities had faced similarly distinctive uses as between utility and amusement, used until at least the late 1930s for commercial deliveries while at the same time, and to this day, central to a variety of sporting and leisure activities, including racing, show, and equestrian competitions that typically appeal to upper-class audiences.) Once the safety started beating the high-wheel in races, the risks no longer seemed worthwhile. It was the chain drive innovation that eliminated the need for the large front wheel while allowing riders to cover the same distance at the same (or greater) speed and with their feet close to the ground.

The Rail Not Taken

In the 1920s, while bicycle-makers and retailers still tried to poach customers from streetcars, it was often the automakers who had greater success. When streetcar passengers, especially ones stuck in a traffic jam, looked down onto the road, they were more likely to notice, with anger or envy, no doubt influenced by marketers, the comfortable motorist, not the rosy-cheeked cyclist.

Cyclists continued to have obvious reasons to support mass transit: any deterioration in streetcar, radial, and train service limited the bicycle's range, as part of combined trips, and usefulness, especially when snow, ice, or rain hampered travel. Good transit service was also a check on the proliferation of cars, which otherwise made roads more dangerous. The car was a one-size-fits-all transportation tool for travel and once the initial, heavy investment was made (including purchase and insurance), the motorist had little (or less) reason to be concerned about other modes, except insofar as those modes interfered with car travel. The non-motorist, on the other hand, chose among walking, cycling, transit, and trains based on the distance involved in a trip.

When the TTC took over transit service on August 31, 1921, streetcar patrons who hoped that years of frustration with William Mackenzie's monopoly were finally over soon found their forward motion slowed by motorists. The city hadn't actually waited for Mackenzie's thirty-year franchise to expire to get into the streetcar business, building lines, operated as the Toronto Civic Railways from 1912, where the TRC had refused to expand. The TTC also took over the radials operated by Mackenzie's companies, including the lines east and west out of the city along the waterfront, and north along Yonge.

In the competition between different modes of transportation, governments weren't neutral observers but heavy investors in roads, often competing directly with streetcars and radials owned by the public – thus, competing with itself. By the late 1920s, the radials were suffering significant declines with increasing competition from motorcars, and motorbuses, while overall TTC ridership remained strong. In May 1929, the TTC recommended taking the Yonge radial out of service, given the strong competition from automobiles on parallel highways, calculating it could run motorbuses at lesser expense. A TTC report concluded that the increase in "rubber-tired competition" had dramatically changed the economics of both local and long-distance transportation. The line escaped closure, although it was clearly running on borrowed time. Dr. Doolittle called for the removal of the Yonge interurban, freeing the road to become "a fine wide boulevard for miles to the north of the city." (A portion of the Yonge line survived until 1949.)

Image 21: "Certainly beats the crowded cars!" This 1929 CCM ad touts the advantages of the bicycle over the streetcar, while confirming an ongoing adult audience among buyers. "A wheel saves him from running to catch cars and waiting for transfers. A wheel saves him paying tribute for the privilege of standing in an aisle hanging on to a strap or handrail." (CCM, Ad, *Globe*, Apr. 11, 1929, 9)

The Mimico-Lakeshore and Scarborough radials survived to the end of the 1920s, but not much beyond. The Mimico line had suffered the biggest drop in ridership, although it was probably the awkward transfer point at the Toronto border that was the cause. Radial passengers hadn't simply moved into motorcars; many took to motorbuses, which were faster than the radials, at least until slowed by automobiles. The Toronto-Guelph radial suffered from motor traffic competition on nearby Highway 7. (The line was closed in 1931. Today, the Halton County Radial Rail Museum near Guelph celebrates the radial lines, but visitors arriving by transit must walk five kilometres along a highway from the nearest GO stop.)

By 1929, the political, social, and business forces behind the automobile were so powerful that changing course would have required a large public mobilization. Until the early 1920s, however, an alternate transportation future based on Sir Adam Beck's plan for a radial rail network across south-western Ontario appeared likely to succeed. As late as 1920, Might's (Telephone) Directory in Toronto, after listing radial services in the Toronto area, added, "It is expected that within a short time, the proposed Hydro Radials will be operating into Toronto, covering the western, central and eastern parts of the Province of Ontario."

Beck's reputation had been established by delivering affordable hydro power from Niagara Falls to Ontario cities and towns – first with provincially owned transmission lines, and then with its own production of "the people's power." In fact, the Hydro Electric Power Commission, which Beck headed while he was also a cabinet minister in Whitney's administration, initially produced so much power that there was a surplus for which consumers had to be found. His success was particularly noteworthy at the time in the context of utilities, including the TRC, that were usually operated by private monopolies.

Beck had actually been talking about electric trains to replace steam trains as early as 1906 when the hydro commission was established. Between 1912 and 1920, Beck's plan for a radial network was conceived, planned, and promoted with electric interurbans to cover south-western Ontario, connecting cities such as Niagara Falls, Guelph, London, and Whitby, most of which already had small regional systems, and points in between (greater even than today's provincial network of GO trains and buses).

Beck tirelessly promoted his radial plan, which had strong public support, even after his plan began to flounder. At one public meeting about the radial network, a speaker suggested that the then nascent Canadian National Railways would itself build electric lines, to which a person in the audience shouted, "Yes, in about a hundred years." (A prediction that turned out to be optimistic.)

By 1922, Beck's plan was effectively dead, having begun to unravel when the Conservative government was defeated and replaced in 1919 by the United Farmers of Ontario (UFO), which was antagonistic to his interurban plan. The new premier, Ernest Drury, was known to drive from Barrie to Toronto, despite his free government rail pass, while Drury's highways minister was an automobile enthusiast and energetic road builder. "Roads to the right of him; roads to the left of him, roads on all sides of him," a federal MP mocked him.

Drury obliged Beck to go back to municipalities for their (re)approval of his radial plan, but in the absence of guarantees from Queen's Park to back municipal investment. By early 1923, Beck had been reduced to fighting for a radial line from the Niagara region to Toronto, which included a high-speed waterfront route into the city and an underground connection to City Hall. He lost that battle as well. He died in 1925. (Today, a Regional Express Rail system remains years from completion, and still far short of Niagara Falls.)

WHAT FUTURE FOR THE BICYCLE IN TORONTO?

The reckless driving charge against Dr. Doolittle posed an obvious problem to the motor lobby beyond any damage to the reputation of its most prominent advocate. A conviction would suggest that if a motorcar could be dangerous even in the hands of a competent, cautious, respected motorist, then it could be dangerous in anyone's hands. The withdrawal of the charge, although obviously suspect, was the only acceptable outcome.

The automobile was already reshaping the city and government spending – albeit absent any specific political decision to adopt the automobile, as had once been the conscious decision of city residents with Sunday streetcar service. But by 1929 the motor lobby was so influential, automobile marketing was so effective, powerful corporations were making so much money, and governments were so heavily invested in the success of automobiles that the ascendancy of the motorcar appeared virtually unstoppable.

One commentator, adjusting the analysis of early twentieth-century anthropologist Edward Sapir, concluded that in harnessing the motorcar to the uses of society, the motorcar had harnessed society. Since cyclists' place on the road, their safety, and their future prospects were defined by the motorcar, the bicycle's and the bicyclist's prospects were dim.

The Roaring Twenties offered little space to anticipate, let alone inclination to plan for, the turbulent economic winds that had begun to blow in late 1929. The coming tough economic times and the war that followed would offer a temporary opening for the bicycle's return to higher esteem.

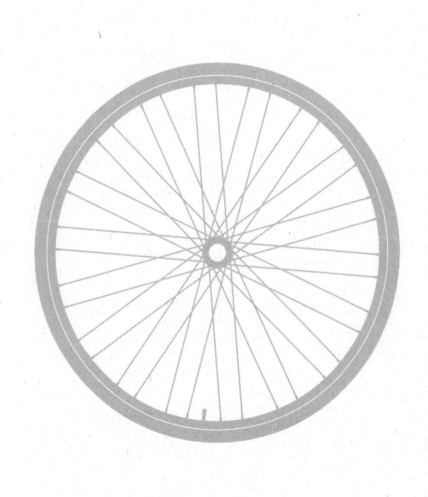

1953

The Bicycle Endures; the Cyclist Relies on Luck

April 10, 1953 – Public roads, but not for everyone

When a boy was hit last night riding his bicycle along the wide grass median of a recently completed stretch of Highway 401, the case quickly became a sensational story in this afternoon's papers, not because yet another child has died on the roads but because the victim was initially misidentified by family members. The death of a child on the roads is nothing new; the fact that a boy thought dead is alive – that's front-page news.

It's not likely that highway planners gave much thought to cyclists, even if this "dual-carriageway" creates a barrier for people on foot or bikes from its south side to the north side, where the boy lived in the Downsview neighbourhood of North York. Highway 401 and the Queen Elizabeth Way are designated as "controlled access" highways, although the concept of public roads that are limited to people in cars remains novel. The smooth pavement of the new highway, a direct route home late at night, and the new highway's sparse motor traffic must have been a temptation the boy found hard to resist.

When the highways department, responsible for the so-called Toronto By-pass, which runs east-west near Toronto's northern boundary, thinks about non-motorists, which isn't often, it's to find ways to discourage pedestrians from crossing the new highways. In fact, 80,000 thorny rose bushes have been planted along the By-pass. But cyclists can easily gain access from the on-ramps, and it's unclear if there were any signs to warn the boy from entering the highway on his bike. Each year, provincial highways, albeit not as ultra-modern as the 401, claim the lives of many adults and children on bikes, many of them on their way from one town to another.

The victim, fourteen-year-old Robert Gilchrist, was initially misidentified by police as Grant Wyldes, based on ticket stubs in the victim's pocket. The ambulance's speedy route from near Keele Street to the Humber Hospital in Weston, at the western terminus of the highway, wasn't enough to save the boy. Grant's elder sisters, summoned by police to the hospital, mistook the boy on the operating table, his face obscured by an oxygen mask, for their brother. The error was discovered when the boy's uncles were dispatched to convey the grim news to the "victim's" employer at the Pelmo Park pool. The supposed victim greeted them.

Once police learned of the mistake, it took several more hours to identify the actual victim. Reporters didn't expend any effort looking into the dead boy's background, or what might have brought him onto the highway. The large front carrier on the crumpled bicycle, shown in the Toronto Telegram's *photo, suggested that the bicycle was used for deliveries. By way of explanation for the tragedy, the* Daily Star *reporter pointed to an etching on the bicycle of a pair of dice showing sixes, a symbol of bad luck. The back fender had a metal plate with the words "Double-Trouble."*

Police from North York Township who attended the scene haven't offered an estimate of the motorist's speed when he hit the boy, nor clarified if the boy was travelling with or against motor traffic – an important issue given the motorist's claim that the boy's bike had no lights. The High-way Traffic Act doesn't require bicycles to have lights; compliance only requires a reflector (or a white or amber light) on the front, and a reflector and reflective stripes (or red light) at the rear.

The motorist who hit the boy is likely to be charged with some com-bination of manslaughter, or dangerous and careless driving, but it's just as likely that he will be acquitted, or the charge withdrawn before trial. The police routinely lay charges for road fatalities, perhaps to calm public anxiety or anger, but it's as much from habit as any hope of conviction. The criminal law has already proven itself unsuited to these tragedies, and, as in all such cases, the victim won't be able tell his side of the story, while police, judges, and the media who assess and determine blame will likely do so from the perspective of motorists.

THE BIRTH OF METRO TORONTO – A CIGAR FOR THE MOTORIST

In 1937, Sam McLaughlin, president of General Motors Canada, called for new motorways, including by-passes around cities, for the benefit of motorists – and of course for his company and its profits. "We shall probably need highways to accommodate 50 per cent more cars within twenty-five years," he said. The motor lobby had gotten accustomed to getting what it wanted; indeed, it had become difficult to distinguish the motor lobby's demands from the government's plans. McLaughlin was a descendant of the Bicy-cle Craze and the horse-and-buggy era; in his youth, he worked in his father's giant carriage works and often rode his beloved high-wheel from Oshawa to Toronto and back in a single day, a round trip of 80 miles (120 kilometres).

Toronto's 1943 Master Plan included five criss-crossing super-highways, identified with letters "A" to "E." At the time, the only highway in the province that could qualify as a "superhighway" was the Queen Elizabeth Way (QEW) along the lake between Toronto and Hamilton. City Council initially adopted the Master Plan "in principle," but later rejected it. The Regional Municipality of Metropolitan Toronto (or Metro) – a federation consisting of the City of Toronto and its twelve neighbours, among them fast-growing Etobicoke, North York, and Scarborough – was created by Queen's Park on April 15, 1953 (officially launched on January 1, 1954), and soon took up – with far greater enthusiasm – the planning of expressways and wider roads. A core function of Metro was to govern cross-boundary matters such as regional planning, parks, and sewage and water works – and major roads.

Frederick Gardiner, appointed by Queen's Park as the first Metro chair, previously led the Toronto and York Planning Board, which had identified the need for expressways to deal with the anticipated post-war surge in cars. After his appointment, the media quickly dubbed Gardiner the "super-mayor," although no one, except Premier Leslie Frost, actually voted for him. The media appeared to welcome the new strongman: "Is Super-Mayor a Superman Too?" asked one headline, sounding hopeful.

With Metro in charge, the A to E lettering that had been used in Toronto's Master Plan of expressways transitioned to names such as the Crosstown, Don Valley, Scarborough, Richview, Spadina, and the waterfront (renamed the Frederick G. Gardiner Expressway in 1957, while still under construction). There was no doubt that moving cars across the region was a top priority for Metro, which would have the borrowing power, size, and clout to make sure the job got done.

Image 22: Avenue Road in 1937, looking south from St. Clair Avenue. One of Metro Chair Fred Gardiner's priorities was to address motor traffic congestion, which he tackled with massive public resources, but without success. Avenue Road was among the roads slated for widening by Gardiner, ultimately achieved in the early 1960s at the expense of the sidewalk, roadside greenery, and the narrow utility strip (seen on the right of this image) which provided a buffer for pedestrians. Community groups in 2017 began a long fight for wider sidewalks and lower motor speeds on Avenue Road. (City of Toronto Archives, Fonds 1244, Item 1096)

On April 9, 1953, Gardiner told the *Toronto Telegram*, "Now we can cast off the shackles that have bound this city for 40 years. Now we can get to work and straighten out the kinks." (Eliminating "jogs" in major roads was a part of the plan to improve road capacity to move more cars, faster.) In fact, it was Gardiner who had decried York Township's failure to approve the northward extension of Spadina Road after the City of Toronto invested millions in widening it a few years earlier. There wasn't any doubt that people needed to travel around the Toronto region, but the notion that they were best served by cars on wide arterials and expressways – instead of by trains, streetcars, and buses, or even bikes – was the one that dominated Gardiner's approach.

At the time, the City of Toronto accounted for almost 70 per cent (714,000) of Metro's 1.17 million people, but the surging population of the suburban municipalities guaranteed that the balance of power would soon shift. North York's population, for example, had reached 120,000 by 1953, four times higher than it had been in 1945. The City of Toronto's human population was little changed from 1929, but the automobile population, which had largely stagnated during the Depression and the Second World War, was growing fast – more than *doubling* to 279,000 motor vehicles by 1952 from the end of the war. Car ownership was growing even faster in the suburbs, where planning was driven by people in cars. Pent up consumer demand, manufacturing capacity converted from wartime armies to peacetime consumers, and gasoline freed up from the war all helped fuel the car-buying binge.

For Gardiner, Metro's ravines and valleys were an untapped resource for arterial roads. Even the popular waterfront Sunnyside amusement park, "the poor man's Riviera," was getting in the way of the motorcar commuter. Sunnyside was demolished in 1955 to make way for the Lakeshore (now Gardiner) Expressway, its main offence that it sat "astride the most important traffic artery of the entire City." Although Metro's ravines were generally protected from development by assertive parks departments in Metro and the city, the Don Valley Ravine was not spared from the building of the Don Valley Parkway. In theory, expressways would protect cyclists and pedestrians by taking cars off local roads, except that motorists inevitably exited the expressways and filled city roads.

Arterial roads, over which Metro had authority, were widened, even if it meant pilfering space from front yards, green areas, and sidewalks. Gardiner declared, "I would cut five or six feet off many sidewalks, shove the poles back and create two new lanes for traffic." He added that "[t]here are millions of dollars invested in useless concrete in this city in sidewalks that are hardly used at all."

The City of Toronto at first tolerated Metro's enthusiasm for road building and widening, but later became increasingly resistant – it was, after all, city residents that would have to put up not only with the deluge of suburban motorists but also with the accompanying noise, danger, and tailpipe emissions. In the 1940s, police had been frustrated by enforcement problems posed by the influx of thousands of cyclists onto city roads each day, but the *hundreds of thousands* of motorists in the early 1950s presented problems on an unprecedented scale. The incoming motorists needed not only road space, which Gardiner was happy to secure for them, but also massive amounts of public space to park their idle vehicles, in part accomplished by turning over the curb lane for parking. (In later decades, the fight to rededicate curb space to bike lanes not only ran up against hostile motorists but also outraged shopowners who, unlike in the 1920s, had come to equate their success with curbside parking.)

The city's own approach to road building was tempered by the greater number of people who travelled on foot, bikes, and transit within its more densely populated borders. "I salute the authorities," wrote a local resident after Toronto council in March 1953 installed a new traffic light, an impediment for motorists, on Spadina Avenue. In his inaugural mayoral address in 1953, Allan Lamport proudly reported improvements to streetcar lines and the imminent completion of the Yonge subway line from Union Station to Eglinton Avenue. A Queen Street line, partially underground, between Trinity Park in the west to Broadview in the east, still awaited council approval. (Construction on this line, though extended in length, actually started seventy years later as the Ontario Line.) The underground lines had the added appeal to motorists of freeing up more road space.

As car ownership became *normal*, walking, cycling, and transit were further marginalized, although in the older parts of Metro, especially the City of Toronto, being a non-motorist didn't carry quite the same stigma as in suburban areas. But even where people might conveniently get around without a car, they might buy one anyway in order to "fit in" and to avoid being associated with lower-income groups. Post-war immigrants, arriving from nations where cycling was popular, were often the first to shun the bicycle and public transit even if they better suited their financial means.

Prior to the TTC taking on responsibility for transit across all of Metro in 1954, suburban residents were often left to rely on infrequent, sometimes privately run, buses. The problem, as the TTC would soon discover, was that low-density neighbourhoods made providing frequent bus service costly – and with less frequency, less appealing. When the TRC ran the city's streetcar system before 1921, it needed to be confident in the potential of profits based on related issues of population density and ridership numbers. This equation put a check on new, sprawling, sparsely populated suburban developments that later became the norm. But as automobiles became more common, developers were less constrained, provided governments were willing to build the necessary road infrastructure.

Fred Gardiner's dictatorial style helped suppress dissenting voices, creating the illusion of consensus. From a broader public perspective there was reason to doubt that the supposed love affair with cars was any more real than the fairy tales presented in car ads. There was certainly no consensus in favour of the many road widenings. When the widening of Spadina Avenue was proposed in the 1940s, a city plebiscite succeeded only with a small margin.

If Gardiner saw any place, let alone space, on roads for bicycles in Metro, he didn't mention it, even though his long-ago days as a bicycle messenger in Toronto for GNW Telegraph Co. might have suggested some empathy. For the cyclist, the increase in motor traffic made the road environment more hostile, while the longer travel distances in the sprawling suburbs effectively locked in reliance on private cars (or infrequent buses) for any place beyond the local neighbourhood, whether or not the resident's finances or age allowed for car travel. Car ownership could almost be seen as the price of admission to suburban living. The suburbs weren't a post–Second World War invention, but the new type of suburb was very much unlike the streetcar suburbs of earlier generations, now driven by an alliance of big developers, big banks, and big retail, and dominated by a dependence on cars. The forgotten bicyclist was left to navigate dangerous roads, then obliged to cross giant parking lots just to get to shops and other destinations.

THE URBAN AND SUBURBAN UPS AND DOWNS OF THE BICYCLE

The War and the Pre-war Depression

For most of the 1940s, the bicycle had been a valued element of the transportation system. Indeed, by the third year of the war in 1942, the demand for bicycles exceeded supply. At the time, bicycle-makers had to grapple with a lack of materials and shortage of labour (similar to the dynamic in play almost eighty years later during the global COVID-19 pandemic). The manufacture of bicycles, as other consumer goods, was regulated to prioritize the war effort, but the federal government's decision to allow the manufacture of 150,000 bikes recognized, as a reporter put it, "the new importance of the lowly two-wheeler in the transportation set-up."

Manufacturers restricted production to adult bicycles, a stark shift from pre-war years when the children's market ranked highest. In addition to second-hand bikes, many people restored little-or unused bicycles, and put aside their prejudices. Bicycle shops were overwhelmed with orders for repairs and refurbishments. "People are bringing in old models that have been buried in cellars for twenty or thirty years," reported one shop owner. Retailers voluntarily agreed to give priority to buyers who needed bicycles to earn their livelihood, including messengers, employees of public utilities, watchmen, police, and tax collectors. Bicycles offered an alternative not only to motorists dealing with gasoline rationing and related restrictions but also to TTC patrons having to travel on increasingly crowded buses and streetcars. Some car parking lots in the city were converted to bike parking.

A *Daily Star* story in April 1942 resembled the Massey-Harris catalogue cover of 1897, now including among cyclists a mom with her infant in the front basket, a well-dressed rider visiting friends, a church minister getting exercise, picknickers, two women on a Toronto to Brantford trip, and a woman fixing a flat tire. There was a modest comeback of bicycle touring in the countryside, aided by gear shifters that made uphill climbs easier. The Town of Weston, and more distant points for weekend outings, continued to appeal to Toronto residents for cycling excursions, as they had during the Bicycle Craze of the 1890s. Bicycle clubs saw a rise in membership. A bike path alongside the QEW was even suggested. The potential for cycling nonetheless remained constrained by concerns about the road danger.

While the bicycle enjoyed a resurgence during the war, largely born of necessity, bicycle usage had also been high during the 1930s, spurred at least in part by its low cost amidst difficult economic times. The number of bicycle licences issued in Toronto offered a good indication of bicycle usage, even though the numbers under-represented actual use given substantial non-compliance, as evidenced by the many charges laid by police under the licensing by-law.

Between 1934 and 1947, the number of bike licences issued by the City of Toronto ranged between 29,000 and 40,000 annually. In 1939, the 36,000 bike licences in Toronto constituted almost 20 per cent of all registered vehicles on city roads. Bicycle traffic in the city also included cyclists from surrounding municipalities, contributing to a police estimate in 1946 of 50,000 bicyclists on city streets each day. Among cyclists on the road, Mayor Robert Saunders, who held office from 1945 to 1948, was a common sight.

In the sheltered confines of indoor venues, including Maple Leaf Gardens, six-day bicycle racing reached its heyday in the 1930s, though disappearing by the 1950s (with a brief revival in the mid-1960s). The races were a happy union of professional sport and betting, with competitions that continued day and night, riders' skills tested on a wooden track with steeply banked ends and watched, according to a local sports reporter, by "as motley a collection of human bric-a-brac as sport is capable of presenting." "Girls and women, rouged and powdered; tinted in as many colors as Jacob's celebrated coat, cling to arms of lean, white-faced escorts. Men trying to look unconcerned carry babies on one arm … men sober and drunk, dolls, mobsters, business-men, walkers in every street of life in Toronto." The only connec-tion of these races to utilitarian cycling was in the marketing of particular bicycle brands leveraged by some of these professional riders, including Torchy Peden who had raced for Canada in the 1928 Olympics.

Post-war Decline

After the war, bicycles soon returned to their earlier, lowly status in the transportation hierarchy. When Toronto newspapers men-tioned adult cyclists, other than as crash victims, the portrayals were often of quirky or eccentric individuals, bizarre events, or long-distance adventures. A British couple planned to cycle across Canada on a tandem with their toddler in a sidecar. A "lean, bronzed man with bloodshot eyes" returned to the city after his eighth trip around the world. Cyclists who fell off bridges into the lake, and had to be rescued, were also treated as newsworthy. The police still had bicycles, although what they were using them for was unclear.

Weston's Basil Raynham, a veteran of the First World War, fit the definition of quirky, which may explain why the media often sought his opinion, and when they didn't, he volunteered it. Raynham's cycling mileage, which he meticulously documented and reported, reached 300,000 miles (500,000 kilometres) by 1950. Raynham considered cities too dangerous for cycling, to be avoided where possible.

After the Second World War, many adults continued to cycle for utilitarian purposes, although the attention they got was often limited to the list of road casualties in annual police reports. As in the past, the popular narrative was that only children cycled, although at least some advertising targeted adults, promoting bicycles as "dependable for transportation." Among adult cyclists, younger people were more common, including students commuting to school, university, or their first jobs. Cycling was often treated as a stage of life that came before car ownership.

The decline in cycling after the war was reflected, probably exaggerated, by the decline in the number of issued bike licences beginning in 1948. In that year, the licence fee was doubled to $1, prompting some grumbling, especially because low-paid delivery workers were prominent among riders. "I think it stinks," summed up one telegraph messenger. Diminished police interest in enforcement likely played a role, accounting for some of the decline in issued licences. In fact, there had been a far greater drop in bike licences between 1942 and 1943, when bicycle use had remained quite high. In 1953, however, less than 22,000 bike licences were issued (the number falling to 16,500 in 1955, the second-to-last year of the licensing regime).

Image 23: "Businessman riding a bicycle," c. 1945. During the war, bicycles were again popular, partly induced by rationing of gasoline, tires, and other materials. This smartly dressed cyclist has carefully secured his pant leg from the chain, although the health benefits of cycling may be diminished by the cigar dangling from his mouth. A bike licence appears to be affixed to the chain stay. During the 1930s and 1940s, the city issued as many as 40,000 bike licences annually. (Photo: Gordon W. Powley, Ref. C 5-1-0-82-7, Archives of Ontario, I0011219)

The Bike Licence and the "Juvenile Delinquent"

By 1953, the bicycle licence had been in place for nearly a quarter century, and despite the significant administrative and enforcement burden, only three things about it could be said with confidence: first, that it provided a useful historical record of bicycle usage; second, that it had contributed substantial revenues to city coffers; and third, that many children became "juvenile delinquents" on account of it.

The original goal of the licence – to identify the rightful owner of a stolen bike, once recovered – was rarely mentioned. Only when bicycle registrations – and revenues – dropped precipitously in 1948 did city officials begin to seriously consider the termination of the regime. In 1947, bicycle licence revenues still brought $18,000 into city coffers, comparable to the combined revenues from cab drivers, cabs, cartage vehicles, and cartage drivers, and exceeded only by revenues from licences for cigarette vendors and for dogs.

Some children undoubtedly enjoyed the adult-like formality of a bike licence, but for others, especially children who couldn't count on their parents to pay the annual fee, the failure to get a licence exposed them to police enforcement action. To make matters worse, a child found guilty of violating the by-law was labelled a juvenile delinquent under the *Juvenile Delinquents Act* (JDA), which applied to all offences – including municipal by-laws – committed by a person under the age of sixteen.

The bike licence was also different from most other municipal licences in that it wasn't evidence that the applicant had met a particular standard, only that a child (or adult) had visited a police station and paid a fee to City Hall. Ensuring that children had cycling skills was certainly not an element of the bicycle licence. Formalized cycling instruction could have been implemented in schools, to the benefit, and enjoyment, of children, but many commentators were just as happy to complain about cyclists instead

CITY OF TORONTO

WARNING TO BICYCLE OWNERS

1951 Bicycle Licenses Were Due on April 1st

LICENSE FEE — $1.00

ANY PERSON FOUND OPERATING A BICYCLE WITHOUT A 1951 LICENSE WILL BE SUBJECT TO A SUMMONS FROM THE POLICE DEPARTMENT. Your 1950 License Receipt or Police Approval Form MUST be presented when making application.

Obtain License by Mail

Send cheque payable to City Treasurer together with 1950 License and stamped, self-addressed envelope to License Office, City Hall, Toronto. Licenses may also be obtained in the Main Corridor, City Hall.

City Hall closed Saturdays, June, July, Aug. and Sept. Office Hours, 8:30 a.m.-4:30 p.m. Saturdays, 8:30 a.m.-11:30 a.m.

J. CHISHOLM,　　　　　　　　　　G. A. LASCELLES,
　Chief Constable.　　　　　　　　　　City Treasurer.

Image 24: "Warning to Bicycle Owners." Each spring cyclists were warned of the obligation to obtain a bicycle licence. Unlike most other city licences, this one also applied to children. The failure to obtain a licence, which carried a $5 fine, had particular consequences for children who, on conviction, were classified under federal law as "juvenile delinquents," allowing a judge to choose from a range of potential sentences. (City of Toronto, Ad, *Globe and Mail*, Apr. 13, 1951, 9)

of supporting an effective initiative. The licence, which might have discouraged some people from cycling altogether, also offered a pretext for police to stop anyone on a bike that did not appear to have a licence plate.

Some city magistrates showed compassion for the children who appeared before them for violating the licence by-law. "It would be a hardship to fine these boys as a great number of them can't afford to buy a license," Toronto Magistrate Arthur Tinker once told a reporter. Tinker routinely remanded bike licence cases to allow children to obtain a licence, thus disposing of the matter. Among the forty to 200 people in his court during the two days of each week set aside for by-law matters, the majority were street vendors without the requisite licence and children charged with cycling infractions, including the failure to obtain a licence.

In the early 1950s, twelve-year-old Roger Powley managed to avoid a court appearance, but not the anxiety that sometimes came from failing to obtain a licence. He didn't have the money for a bike licence, nor did he want to ask his father for help. A motorcycle-riding cop on Bloor Street West, after eyeing Powley's bike, made an abrupt U-turn. Powley, who mainly used his bike to ride in the area around High Park concluded it must be the absence of a bike licence that sparked his pursuer's interest. The boy swiftly turned up an alleyway, then, with the motorcycle's roar behind him, ducked into a used car lot. When he was confident at having evaded the police, he looped back onto Bloor. (Powley could vividly recall the event sixty-five years later, the passing years never tempering his opinion of the absurdity of the bike licence.)

Annual police reports didn't record how many children were actually summoned to court for failing to obtain a bike licence, or what dispositions were imposed, but the power conferred on judges merited a stern rebuke from child welfare experts (until a new act was passed in 1984). Judges hearing cases involving children had the authority to impose any penalty available under the JDA, including a sentence to a training school. Under the JDA, the judge's duty was to impose a penalty that guided the offender onto the "right path" – the penalty to be consistent with what a wise and kind, but stern and firm, parent would impose, regardless of the gravity of the offence.

Cycling violations by children were reported in the annual police report just before murders, both falling under the heading "Crime." Commentator J.V. McAree, sounding very much like a stern parent, suggested that young cyclists were getting away with violating road rules because police were probably "ashamed to be seen chasing boys who are breaking traffic rules." The number of licence violations alone, which reached as high as 2,300 in a single year, suggested that police weren't as ashamed as he supposed.

The bike licence did nothing to create better cycling conditions, and occasionally provoked public anger. "What does a bicycle owner get for his money? Absolutely nothing," wrote one city resident. Refusing to get a licence could itself be an act of defiance. In any case, a licence obtained from a City Hall wicket provided no greater protection from the road danger. A Toronto boy who had just picked up his 1952 bicycle licence was killed by a heavy truck on Queen Street. A coroner's jury judged the crash to be "accidental," while trucking industry officials promised to address the hazard of right-turning trucks. But nothing changed. (And the danger to cyclists and pedestrians from turning trucks persists unabated to this day.)

Police carried out safety checks on bicycles at schoolyard racks, inspections that also offered an opportunity to check for licence compliance. In April 1953, police teams "prowled racks of bicycles in five Toronto and suburban schoolyards ... tracking down unsafe machines," in the course of which they identified common defects such as loose spokes and missing or loose handlebar grips. The Kiwanis Club in North York offered a more benevolent approach, handing out reflective tape (to satisfy HTA requirements for bike lights) to several thousand young cyclists to ensure that their bikes would be illuminated by the headlights of approaching cars.

Charging children for bike licence infractions did little to reduce bicycle thefts; indeed, it may well have reduced police resources for catching thieves. Thefts remained high even into 1952 when bicycle use appeared to be declining. A decade earlier, in 1942, Toronto Mayor Frederick Conboy had complained about an "epidemic" of bike thefts, then asked the finance commissioner and Chief Constable Dennis Draper to report on the licensing system and, curiously, the control of cyclists' conduct. He didn't elaborate on the connection. Recovery rates for stolen bicycles fluctuated dramatically, the result of various factors, likely including police priorities.

There were alternatives to the bicycle licence as a way to recover stolen bikes, without imposing a burden on the city, police, or cyclists. Owners could simply retain the bill of sale, as they might for TVs, radios, and lawnmowers, or document the bicycle's serial number, then present it to police in the case of theft. Theft victims who hadn't taken these easy steps could be assumed to have accepted the risk of forfeiting the opportunity to have a bike recovered by police returned to them. Police could also hold events to display recovered bicycles and return those bikes for which individuals could demonstrate ownership.

Production of the licence plate was itself costly. When metal resources were in high demand during the war, women's groups pitched in by collecting the previous year's plates. York Township came up with an alternative solution, using a fibre material to replace the metal in dog tags and bike licences. Dogs often turned their own tags into a snack.

An Adult Solution to Children's Safety - a Ban from Roads

Bicycles remained popular with children even in Toronto's fast-growing suburbs, as long as they didn't stray beyond their own neighbourhoods onto arterials, which provided essential, but

Image 25: The bicycle licence in Toronto came to an end in 1956, as it did in all other Metro municipalities. During the quarter century that the city required a bike licence, thousands of children had been charged for failing to obtain one, while the original objective of the regime – the ability of police to return stolen bikes to their owners – had largely been forgotten. (Courtesy of City of Toronto, Item 2000.5.4349)

dangerous, connections to other neighbourhoods and commercial areas. Distances to children's everyday destinations – schools, playgrounds, community centres, and friends' homes – were still within a viable geographic range for children, but when a young person's job opportunities, or social and recreational interests, expanded beyond the local neighbourhood, the bicycle's utility quickly faded, except for those willing, or obliged by their circumstances, to risk travel on arterials. The sidewalk was an option, though illegal, but with few pedestrians to complain it often became a de facto bike path. The perceived safety of the sidewalk was, however, undermined when cyclists emerged, often unnoticed by motorists, onto the road to cross intersections. Ironically, while motorcars were celebrated for the freedom and independence that they gave adults, they took it away, without apology, from children and youth.

City Hall and other levels of government generally ignored children as road users, as if public road space had been officially ceded to adults. Educator Angelo Patri, author of the syndicated column *Our Children*, was one of the few public figures who took up the cause of young cyclists. Patri appreciated that bicycles were as important to children and young people as cars to adults, but that they were essentially powerless to effect change. Patri called for bicycle paths along new roads or on roads being reconstructed. "One child's life saved would be sufficient cause for the expenditure," he wrote.

Many anxious parents had decided it was better to voluntarily restrict their children from cycling than to risk harm. As long ago as the 1920s, Chief Constable Draper had called for greater restrictions on children playing in the streets, consistent with a road ban suggested by the coroner after yet another child fatality. The push for playgrounds dated from that time, but one question the chief and others didn't consider (as with off-road bike trails decades later) was how children were to get to those places, if not along dangerous roads. (Part of the answer was that parents would drive their children, adding to the road danger for others.)

It was only a matter of time before someone would propose banning children from cycling on roads altogether, precisely the solution offered by Mayor Nathan Phillips in 1958. Phillips, whose family tragedy gave him obvious credibility, although his son was killed on the sidewalk, nonetheless faced strong opposition, even from his own grandchildren.

Phillips's opponents, although generally supportive, questioned the enforceability of a ban. The objection of Alderman Fred Beavis was more comic, fearing the ban would threaten the manly activity of bicycle-riding. "We should be raising a bunch of sissies if we stopped boys going out on their bikes." Metro Chair Gardiner's frank comment in rejecting the proposal revealed the wobbly foundation of the transportation system. "It seems you are either going to be lucky and avoid an accident or you are not going to be lucky."

Newspaper columnist Scott Young also opposed the ban, but for different reasons, decrying a city where children were deprived of "one of life's early wonders." He added that "[we] would be better led if the mayor developed some positive ideas on how to make life safer for young bike riders." Young, father of twelve-year-old Neil (soon to be a rock star), proposed that dedicated space be set aside for cyclists, including bike paths along roads. He noted that many busy streets had shoulders or boulevards wide enough to accommodate such paths. He called for motorists to be taught to refrain from dangerous practices, such as brushing past cyclists. (In 2015, the province articulated in law an obligaton for motorists passing cyclists to leave, "as nearly as may be practicable," at least one metre of clearance. The law is, however, rarely enforced.)

Blaming children for acting like children – or blaming parents for failing to prevent their children from acting like children – was a safe bet for politicians, even if the absurdity only helped ensure more grief. Blaming parents merely added to the burden of guilt they were forced to carry for crashes involving their children, but at least comforted other parents with the illusion that their children would be safe. Constant vigilance by parents, however, was no more realistic than perfect behaviour by motorists.

In many accounts of fatal collisions involving young cyclists in and around Toronto, the motorist's version of events included a claim that the victim had swerved or veered in front of the oncoming car. After the death of a ten-year-old boy cycling home along

Highway 2 early in the school year in 1950, the *Daily Star* reported that the motorist "saw the youngster ahead, weaving from side to side, his head low over the handlebars, as if he were sick. When the car drew alongside, the bicycle lurched into its path." The driver, who had time to speculate about the child's health, apparently didn't have time to slow down. Motorists would be absolved as long as they, more or less, adhered to the rules of the road. The maximum speed was treated as a right, and then only as a baseline against which to measure the acceptability of any exceedance in a crash, as determined by enforcement personnel who were themselves motorists. On the other hand, the conduct of pedestrian and cyclist victims of crashes was meticulously scrutinized for fault. (When bike lanes were installed decades later, cyclists might also treat this space with the same "enter at your own risk" attitude towards pedestrians, albeit with lesser capacity to inflict harm in a crash.) Giving children extra room on roads for the errors they would inevitably make wasn't in the road planner's toolbox. (A concise solution to the danger for children was offered years later, ironically by a writer for the *Toronto Star*'s Auto World: "Give them room to make a mistake, drawing an imaginary line around them so that, no matter what they do – a sudden turn or stop or even a fall – you can avoid them." Vision Zero road safety plans that were to come in the new millennium were built on similar thinking: mistakes should be anticipated by road planners with good design, not punished with injury or death.)

Both Young and Patri, among others, proposed cycling instruction in schools. The instruction that was offered to children was typically limited to ad hoc programs run by police – and therefore grounded in what police knew best: road rules, perhaps, even likely, in the absence of actual utilitarian riding experience.

Civic officials and the police often conscripted animals, both real and imaginary, to educate children on road safety. In 1946, Mayor Robert Saunders brought Elmer the Safety Elephant to Toronto, after a visit to Detroit. At the beginning of the school year, a pennant with Elmer's image was run up the school's flagpole, but when a child injured in a crash was found to be at fault, Elmer was lowered during a student assembly, followed by a speech by a traffic officer. Another animal, a bespectacled terrier from the United States named Knee-High, was brought to the city by the *Daily Star*. The animals (a duck followed in the late 1970s) put a kind face on road danger, and although safety instruction was undoubtedly valuable, it also absolved planners, politicians, and automakers from the underlying problem of sharing roads with inherently dangerous cars.

BICYCLES AND MOTORCARS AT MIDDLE AGE

The Messenger at Work – No Place for Old Men

In the 1950s, bicycle messengers continued to contribute to commerce in the city, delivering a wide range of goods that still included telegrams, despite increasing competition from telephones and then teletype. Since the early 1930s, CCM also offered a light-weight bicycle for "speedy messenger service," as well as a delivery bicycle with a sturdy frame and basket for heavier items, resembling the basket on Robert Gilchrist's bike when he was killed on Highway 401. During the war, girls, generally between the ages of fourteen and eighteen, were also employed as telegraph messengers. For a brief period, from 1936 to 1940, CN Telegraphs' messengers were easily identified by their Flyte bicycles, CCM's unique, but short-lived, contribution to bicycle design, featuring curved front forks and rear seat guides – one of CCM's few true innovations.

Year-round messenger work remained popular in the city, as well as in neighbouring municipalities such as Scarborough, Etobicoke, East York, and Weston, but motor traffic, long hours, and thieves – the youngest messengers were the easiest marks – were common perils of the job. In the 1930s, gangs, then prevalent in the city, had made a business of preying on messengers.

The availability of messenger work for anyone who owned a bike, or could ride one, ensured there was always an eager, easily replaced workforce, despite common tragedies. In 1938, a nineteen-year-old CP messenger was celebrated for his bravery when he remained preoccupied with the telegrams he was carrying, despite being pinned under a streetcar after a crash. The reality of his predicament, and the otherwise indifferent attitude to the boys, was encapsulated in his lament to by-standers: "I guess I'll have to go to the hospital, eh … It's too bad. I don't know who's going to pay. I haven't any money." The amputation of both his legs wasn't enough to save his life.

In 1937, some messengers worked up the nerve to complain, despite the risk to their jobs. A group calling itself the Toronto Bicycle Messenger Boys Association wrote to Ontario Premier William Hearst, demanding a minimum wage of $8 per week and a work week limited to sixty hours. The young leader of the group, Anthony Farentino, said the boys sometimes worked well past midnight on Saturday night, cleaning up and closing shop after finishing their deliveries: "[I]t is a wonder that more are not killed because they are so tired and sleepy by the time they go home." The absence of subsequent coverage of the boys' demands suggests they had little success.

Image 26: Winter cycling. Bicycle delivery work continued during all months of the year. The perils faced by messenger boys included snow, ice, thieves, and motorcars. Drug stores relied heavily on messengers, including for late-night cigarette orders. This January 1938 photo, looking north on Bathurst Street near Dupont Street, shows four bikes (each of them clearly being used in some capacity), including one parked in front of Moore's Drugs. (City of Toronto Archives, Fonds 1231, Item 0872)

The Toronto Welfare Council bulletin in 1940 included a call for better working conditions for messenger boys. Among the challenges faced by the boys were "[c]old, dark winter nights, icy poorly lighted streets and lanes, orders late at night, too heavy loads." Columnist Judith Robinson wrote poetically about the boys who carried large loads of groceries, delivered with speed and little fuss: "The fire and daring of youth are in his unbelievable gamble with time, space and motor vehicles." She added that for many motorists, the messenger is not "a small appealing symbol of mankind's unconquerable will to live. He is a menace and a pest."

In 1940, City Council urged the public to order goods earlier in the day – a fair request, similar to that of the Welfare Council, given that late-night orders often included cigarettes. Council also appealed to drug store owners to ensure that deliveries after 9 p.m. were given only to boys who were at least age sixteen, but the responsibility was often left to parents themselves. Legislative initiatives at the provincial level with the same ends, including the regulation of delivery hours – and limits proposed in 1941 on the size of packages that could be carried – ultimately failed. Elected officials faced an obvious dilemma: merchants, especially druggists, profited handsomely from late-night delivery; the public enjoyed the convenience and nominal cost of such home deliveries; and messenger boys were eager for the extra income upon which their families often depended.

Thieves had continued to rely on a proven technique to rob messengers: telephoning a retailer with a false delivery request for a specific address, thus luring a messenger, and his cash, to a location suited to the thief. On arrival, the resident, ignorant of the request, sent the boy away. The thief lay in wait. The robbers could expect resistance from their victims, who had both their bikes and their employer's cash (and faith) at stake. The fact that the assailants were often as young as, or younger than, their targets, sometimes offered a measure of comedy, at least in the recounting of a frightening tale. In a 1952 case, the younger of two thieves, estimated to be about age eight, delivered a gangster-like threat: "Remember, you don't know what we look like." The victim nevertheless told his story to police and the press. In another case, a messenger was forced to deliver the robber, sitting on his handlebars, to the Don River, where the robber fled. Messengers usually avoided physical harm in encounters with thieves, but weren't as fortunate in interactions with motorists.

Car doors were a hazard, and more so with the increase in curbside car parking. A *Daily Star* account of a 1953 crash reported that a boy was thrown into the path of an oncoming vehicle after he "rode into a car door." From the vantage point of his bicycle seat, the boy, who suffered a concussion and burns from a bleach container in his carrier, would almost certainly have given a different account of the cause of the crash.

Newspaper delivery by bicycle was also common. The *Globe and Mail* even formed a bicycle club, but unlike the *Mail* and the *Globe* bicycle clubs of an earlier era, this club's aim was to increase subscriptions by rewarding boys with the offer of a new bicycle. "It's a swell bike, and it couldn't be easier to get one," said one winner, featured prominently in the paper. But while there was a happy connection between newspaper delivery and bikes, the same newspapers routinely carried accounts of road casualties, sometimes involving carriers, followed by ads for powerful cars. (By the 1990s, most mainstream newspapers were delivered by adults in cars.)

The Myth of the Safe Motorcar

By 1953, there was abundant evidence to demonstrate that the "safe motorcar" was a myth, and that calls to greater care, courtesy, and law-abiding conduct would not eliminate road casualties. For decades, civic leaders had repeated exhortations to motorists, pedestrians, and cyclists for more careful conduct on the roads, and when these pleas inevitably failed, simply repeated them with greater fervour, much like preachers admonishing their flock to "sin no more."

At the beginning of each new year, the casualty clock could be turned back to zero, suggesting a fresh start and salvation from the carnage – an opportunity denied to those who had already perished. It didn't matter that every preceding (and subsequent) generation since the rise to popularity of automobiles had heard the very same message.

Why did the focus on road users' conduct as the solution to road danger matter to cyclists? First, while pleas to better conduct, or stricter enforcement and penalties, couldn't hurt, they diverted attention from the inevitability of human mistakes by motorists or other road users, which would, given the inherent danger of motorcars, result in predictable injuries and deaths. And second, because as long as the myth of the safe car persisted, a car-based system didn't have to face the scrutiny (and blame) it merited, thus pre-empting consideration of strategies to reduce car use, or to make suitable accommodation for bikes on roads.

Some commentators challenged leaders for the futility of their focus on conduct, instead of the underlying dangers. Soon after the Ontario highway speed was increased to 35 mph (56 km/h) in 1929, journalist Victor Lauriston, mischievously calling himself a charter, and sole, member of the Canadian Speed Limit Club, wrote in *Maclean's*, under the title "Motor Murder," that "in spite of widespread and diligent preachments on the subject of Care, Courtesy and Common Sense ... in spite of loud threats and gentle pats on the wrist from law-enforcement authorities, we have not yet struck at the root of the evil," namely, "the menace of the high-powered car."

The approach of blaming road users and appealing for better conduct – for what were essentially sins of the automobile – had changed little from previous decades. In establishing the Safe Drivers' Club in 1921, the OSL said that it was only right to ask "every member of the community to exercise more thoughtfulness and care in an effort to cut down these accidents." "Try courtesy," urged the provincial minister of highways in a 1937 ad aimed at reducing crashes. In 1938, Chief Constable Draper chastized motorists who "will not, or cannot, be taught to drive safely." The *Globe* conceded that the chief had little or nothing new to say about preventing accidents but lauded him for "precepts that cannot be too often repeated." Three years later, in 1941, road deaths in Toronto exceeded 100 for the first time. In early April 1953, Ontario Highways Minister George Doucett attributed most traffic collisions to "rudeness, arrogance, lack of good manners, failure to display ordinary decency and common sense." The *Toronto Telegram*'s headline read, "Bad Manners, Not the Auto, Cause Most Traffic Accidents." It made perfect sense for the motor lobby to deflect attention from the inherent danger of cars, but not for public officials charged with keeping the public safe to do the same.

The pause in the rise of car-dominated transportation during the Depression and the Second World War could have been an opportunity for critical reflection, but pent up consumer demand, ubiquitous advertising, and the profits to be made in manufacturing, retailing, fixing, fuelling, accessorizing, polishing, and insuring cars, as well as in constructing and paving roads and refining and retailing fuel, ensured that contrary voices were difficult to hear. The motorcar was a perfect consumer product, at least for corporate manufacturers, retailers, the fossil fuel industry, and related industries.

In the half century since Lenton Williams became the first person killed by a motorcar on a city road – rushing, with lunch pail in hand, to catch the College streetcar in June 1905 – many hundreds of city residents had met a similar fate. A coroner had assessed Williams's death as "accidental"; similar conclusions followed pedestrian fatalities in 1906 and 1907. But how could the same finding of "accident" still be plausibly rationalized, or, more importantly, accepted by planners, bureaucrats, the media, politicians, and much of the public once the annual death and injury toll from motorcars became a predictable, constantly repeated reality?

In 1909, the OML could still credibly defend motorcars as safe by noting that from 1898 to 1908 even bicycles had claimed more lives (thirteen) than motorcars. Of course, bicycle numbers during that period overwhelmed cars, but the OML's point couldn't yet be dismissed as comic. In fact, only after 1910 did police reports separately list deaths involving motorcars. Previously, police had used the generic category "vehicle," which included horse-drawn conveyances. By the 1920s, motorcar deaths dominated every other mode, and by the 1950s, the motor lobby did well to avoid any comparisons between modes.

After the Second World War, the general excitement for motorcar ownership dulled the public outrage once common for road casualties. With the horrors of the war still fresh in people's memory, Royd Beamish, under the title "Death on Wheels," wrote that Canadian road deaths and injuries for 1939–45 actually exceeded war casualties by Canadian troops (although deaths accounted for more of the war total). Beamish suggested that road crashes often resulted from "a failure to realize the tremendous power that is so smoothly controlled by a finger tip when everything goes right, but that bursts its bonds to become a diabolic enemy at the first slip." Reporter Phil Jones dubbed 1952 "The Black Year" for its high toll of road deaths, a year that "will be remembered for tragedy and violence." But the memorableness of 1952's tragedy and violence quickly faded with the start of 1953.

Courts, Cops, and Motorists

The motorist who killed Robert Gilchrist was charged with dangerous driving, and acquitted three weeks after the crash, an outcome that barely merited attention in local papers. The fact that the boy's bike had no lights – the actual provisions of the HTA weren't mentioned – was enough to put the matter to rest, but the acquittal was just one of hundreds of circumstances in which motorists had escaped criminal conviction. (Ironically, thirty years after Robert Gilchrist's death, his mother was also killed by a motorcar, in her case in the apparent safety of her home, poisoned by carbon monoxide from a car left running in the garage. She lies buried in a westside Toronto cemetery beside her son from whom she had been separated at some point after his birth.)

Accidental death was the "general verdict in cases of the motorcar," concluded a citizen in 1929. Little had changed by the 1950s, except to confirm that the criminal law was unsuited to dealing with the road carnage. In many cases, there were no charges, in others, the accused pleaded guilty to a lesser (included) offence; the prosecutor withdrew charges because the evidence failed to satisfy the legal burden of proof; or the case failed at trial. In a society where most people were motorists or motorcar passengers, and motorists were over-represented among police, prosecutors, judges, coroners, and juries, the accused motorist could expect a sympathetic ear. In one case an observer reported that, "the Coroner was so moved with sympathy for the driver of the death car that it would not have been surprising if the jury had passed a vote of condolence to the man-slayer.'"

The motorist killed easily and often in Toronto, certainly more often than the murderer. The motorist, however, didn't start the day intending to cause harm, even if the victim was dead all the same. Many motorists who were charged had no record of violations, consistent with the commission of a mistake, instead of a pattern of criminal conduct. The motorist might have been blinded by an oncoming car's headlights, the rising sun or the setting sun; veered off course when a foot slipped from the brake onto the accelerator (as happened in the death of Nathan Philips's son); or run into a cyclist who "came out of nowhere." The common denominator was the automobile. Streetcar patrons too dozed off, cyclists were distracted, and pedestrians hurried, sometimes carelessly, along a crowded sidewalk, but the harm that resulted could be a missed transit stop, the jolt of a pothole, or the jostling of a fellow pedestrian, not the death of a child reaching up to post a letter at a street corner mailbox.

The rogue motorist – the person who drove too fast, drank too much, or cared too little – was an easy target of blame. Indeed, when the OML came around in 1927 to supporting the driver's licence for motorists, the motivation was as a check on reckless driving. Of course, every driver was one mistake from being a rogue driver, unless the victim could be blamed. Drinking and driving was an obvious problem, so common that collecting empty liquor bottles along highways was a lucrative enterprise for children, but attention on the rogue driver also diverted attention from the inherent danger of cars (beyond vehicle defects such as bad brakes that were then common). Blaming the "reckless and criminal minority," the rogue driver, or the "blackguard," was a convenient way to absolve the automobile, and the automaker – a narrative that suited the motor industry. The president of General Motors in 1937 claimed impressive advances in the safety of cars, while safe highways were slow to catch up. "We need education to reform traffic and to banish the witless driver," he wrote in a *Globe* article. He called for a devoted public effort.

The courts, at least before the casualty toll mounted, rejected the idea of automobiles as inherently dangerous. In a 1912 Canadian case involving a suit against a motorist, the court decided that Canadian and American courts "do not consider the motor vehicle an outlaw, or as dangerous *per se*, or that it should be placed in the same category as locomotives, gunpowder, dynamite and similar dangerous machines." Instead, harm was the result of reckless and negligent conduct by the driver upon whom fell the duty to exercise care consistent with the nature of a machine of "great power and speed." The obvious irony was that in the coming decades death by automobile outpaced each of the other listed dangers cited by the court, even death by gun (except in the US).

At the time of the court ruling in 1912, locomotives were regularly killing people in Toronto, but there was a solution: separating roads from rails with underpasses. The same solution to protect cyclists from motorists with separated bicycle paths had also been proposed by the 1950s – but got little traction.

Enforcing motor traffic laws kept police occupied, and when enforcement failed to make streets safer, the problem could be attributed to insufficient enforcement capacity. Toronto's police force had ballooned in size, much of its work dominated by driving violations. Toronto police could probably have devoted all their time and resources to enforcing traffic laws – and still not managed to make a significant difference. Police resources were devoured by dealing with the thousands of crashes that required investigations and led to *Criminal Code* charges. The enforcement of traffic by-laws and the HTA, directing motor traffic, and inspecting vehicles for defects further depleted resources. Parking infractions were another common problem. In the mid-1920s, Chief Constable Dickson complained that city streets had become "an open air garage." In 1929 Toronto police laid over 30,000 charges against motorists for infractions under municipal, provincial, and federal laws; by the 1950s, the number had risen to over 400,000.

Road violations were so common that the motorist suffered little stigma, except in the case of criminal charges, although drinking and driving might still be laughed off. Speeding by drivers was an offence often excused as a "heavy foot" or with a smirk, at least by motorists, even though each increment in a driver's speed increased the risk of serious injury or death for a person hit by the vehicle. The motorist remained fascinated with speed, despite its obvious harms. Even Metro Chair Gardiner, reacting to a record $10,000 in fines imposed on local motorists in a single day in April 1953, suggested that "traffic regulations are such you can't avoid getting a ticket" – but his insinuation was that the rules were the problem.

Simply keeping track of the rising number of collisions became a job in itself, leading police to establish a traffic accident bureau and a new record-keeping process. In 1934 a chapter for (motor) "traffic" was added to the annual police report. Governments and the private sector collaborated to deal with road crashes, creating an army of professionals and experts, among them police, ambulance, and fire officials; investigators and tow truck drivers; nurses, doctors, surgeons, and physical therapists; insurance adjusters and actuaries; lawyers, judges, and file clerks; auto body repairmen;

and jailers. The proficiency of the army that managed the mayhem masked the underlying problem of dangerous automobiles.

Highways Minister George Doucett was lauded for his tough attitude towards reckless and irresponsible drivers. "If we're going to clean up this menace on the highways, we got to be tough," he said. That toughness didn't spare Doucett, in his chauffeur-driven car, from head injuries suffered in a 1951 highway crash.

IS THERE STILL A PLACE FOR THE BICYCLIST IN TORONTO?

The public outrage of the 1920s at the road carnage had subsided by the 1950s, replaced by complacency, or resignation, as the cost of *modern* transportation. There was little room for cyclists on the road, even less room for compassion for the victim, regardless of age and vulnerability. There was virtually no effort to address the inherent danger of the automobile – the preferred, futile, preoccupation was with the behaviour of road users as if repeated pleas for caution might eventually achieve perfection in conduct. And once a person made the heavy investment needed for a car, they were likely to become its greatest proponent.

The city's roads of 1953 bore little resemblance to those of forty years earlier when streetcars, pedestrians, horse-drawn vehicles, people on foot, and cyclists dominated. The City of Toronto's compact urban form, unlike large parts of its Metro neighbours, still made the bicycle practical, even appealing, although greatly diminished in public esteem. The automobile was the new normal, even a "necessity." Creating a road system that best served the greatest number of people was not a priority; indeed, the question of how to accomplish such a goal was rarely even considered. Today, even seven decades after Robert Gilchrist's death on Highway 401, advocates are still fighting for safe places for pedestrians and cyclists to get across the barrier created by the 401, and to reduce the danger from cars to pedestrians and cyclists along roads with on and off ramps to the 401 and the other highways that traverse the city.

The bicycle had endured, while a reckoning with the many destructive impacts of automobiles to the city and its residents, and to the air and nature, was desperately needed.

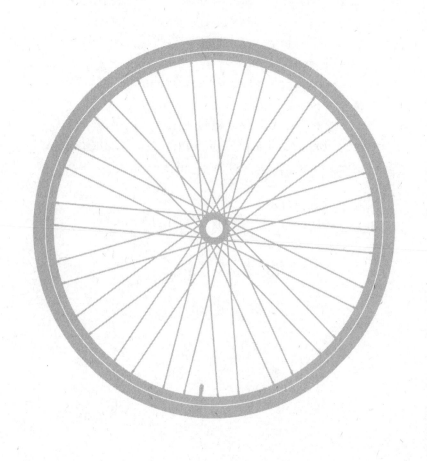

1979
The Bicycle Revival

December 20, 1979 – The new messengers

*Hilda Tiessen doesn't have much in common with the bicycle messenger
boys who rode city streets during most of the last century, except for her
bicycle, and, at about five feet, two inches, probably her height. At
thirty-seven she is twice the age of the messenger girls of the 1940s who
considered themselves too old for the work. As co-owner of Sunwheel
Bicycle Couriers, Tiessen is reviving the era of long-ago enterprises that
relied solely on bicycles for deliveries.*

*Sunwheel is preparing for its first winter on the road. Six months ago,
Tiessen and her partner, Barbara Wiener, set up Sunwheel with $65,
an adding machine, three summer students (funded with a government
grant), and a firm belief in the bicycle's place on city roads. Tiessen is part
of a broader environmental movement in Western countries that has come
to understand the limits, and consequences, of transportation centred on
private cars and dependent on oil, much of it imported. Metro, like many
other urban areas, is often engulfed in a toxic smog, to which the tailpipes*

of hundreds of thousands of automobiles contribute heavily. The Toronto region's vast network of high-speed arterial roads and expressways is evidence that Metro Chair Fred Gardiner achieved his road-building ambitions, even though he never actually succeeded – despite colossal public spending – in solving the very issue at the core of his mission: traffic congestion.

Running their own company allows the two women, who are in an openly romantic relationship, to create a welcoming work environment. The success of their enterprise, which faces stiff competition from established car-based companies, will require all of their determination and courage.

Sunwheel intends to exploit the fact that motorists in the central city often can't match the speed of cyclists (or even pedestrians) – an obvious advantage for the delivery of commercial documents. Cheap gasoline is a thing of the past, further favouring bicycle delivery. It's good, however, that Tiessen isn't in the courier business just to make money, given that profits remain a distant prospect, even as she turns away business that could be handled with cars. In fact, Sunwheel's raison d'être looks as much like an advocacy agenda as it does a business plan. But pairing her love of cycling with her interest in business has given her a sense of purpose that her previous social work career had failed to deliver.

For Tiessen's small band of couriers, pushing on bicycle pedals instead of a gas pedal is also in synch with the fitness craze that has motivated many people to get off (or to think about getting off) the couch. Federal ParticipAction ads taunt viewers with research that the average sixty-year-old Swede is as fit as the average thirty-year-old Canadian. Prime Minister Pierre Trudeau is himself known for his dedication to fitness. His eldest son, Justin, was born in 1971, the year usually cited as the start of the Bicycle Revival in Toronto.

"Bicycling is back – not for kids, but for adults," declared reporter Edna Hampton in August 1969, an early hint of the bicycle's coming revival. In July 1979, a newspaper confirmed the new place of the bicycle in the city,

*and the optimism for its future prospects: "The rediscovery of the bicycle –
based on more than just a nostalgic yearning to see messenger boys on
Toronto streets again – could prove to be one of the happier consequences
of the energy crisis."*

"THE BICYCLE FIGHTS BACK"

By the early 1970s the bicycle
revival was in full swing, with
tens of thousands of adult cyclists on city streets, many for
the first time, or for the first
time since childhood. In fact, so
many years had passed from the
days when bicycles were treated
as normal transportation for
adults that it wasn't clear which
era of the bicycle was actually
being revived.

After decades in the shadow
of the automobile, the bicycle's
return was cheered by many
Toronto residents, sometimes
as a challenge to the privileged
status of motorists. "It is ridiculous for one great big car to
take up space to carry one lone
person downtown," wrote one

Image 27: Hilda Tiessen and her team at
Sunwheel Couriers drew a lot of attention in
1979, and in subsequent years (including this
1980 news photo), for the novelty of their
enterprise, and the challenges of their work.
Tiessen's initiative fit nicely with the Bicycle
Revival, increasing environmental awareness,
and an appreciation of the destructive
impacts of car-centric urban transportation.
(Photo: Reg Innel/Getty Images)

resident; another added that "[t]he automobile already rules our life far too much and it is time we realized that the bicycle is an excellent form of transportation." A drawing in the *Globe and Mail* with the title "All Power to the Pedal" noted, "We all know that we have too many cars, too little fuel, too much air pollution and too little exercise. And we all know that a lot of people are turning to bicycles in a four-fold solution." A 1978 editorial entitled "The Bicycle Fights Back" in the same paper summed up the heavy price of automobile dependence:

> Toronto has paid in a great many unpleasant ways for granting the automobile lordship over its streets, with permission to pollute, make noise, occupy huge tracts of land, divide neighbourhoods, and inflict injury upon people. One of the unhappier consequences was to banish the bicycle through a process of intimidation or official unconcern.
>
> There are, however, stirrings that may not be denied.

S.S. Wilson's assessment of the bicycle in *Scientific American* in 1972 as "the most benevolent of machines" offered an obvious contrast to the reality of the car-first road system. Wilson ranked the bicycle as the most efficient form of transportation among machines (and animals) based on energy consumption per distance travelled. The automobile ranked poorly, which was no surprise, given that most of its energy had to be devoted to moving the machine itself instead of the relatively light-weight occupant(s).

Bicycle retailers in the Toronto area, both new and old, tried to keep up with skyrocketing demand. Between 1970 and 1975, Bloor Cycle, a major retailer, reported a sales increase of 400 per cent. The price of popular bicycle models made them easily affordable to a wide audience, many models ranging from $65 to $110 – prices similar to 1896, when these sums entailed a substantial outlay. The same surge in bicycle sales was happening across the country.

Estimates about cycling in the city varied widely, which was no surprise, given that for many decades cyclists hadn't been important enough to count. When bicycles started showing up on the road again, especially on arterials where they "got in the way," motorists took notice, and when motorists noticed, so did their political champions.

Police estimated that there were 500,000 bicycles in Metro Toronto, extrapolating the number from the 100,000 bikes that owners (mainly children) had voluntarily registered. A 1974 consultant's report for Metro put the number at 650,000 bikes, based on a survey of Metro households. There had also been a substantial decade-by-decade increase since 1950 in the number of cyclists – based, in the absence of local figures, on "typical" cycling numbers in Canadian and American cities – with an estimated 230 cyclists per 1,000 residents in 1950, 350 cyclists per 1,000 in 1960, and 480 per 1,000 in 1970. These figures did not distinguish between recreational and utilitarian cycling, though it was the latter that was responsible for the "revival."

The ten-speed bicycle model helped spur the resurgence. The ten-speed's profile, including drop handlebars, differed little from racing models of the past, albeit now converted to everyday use – and, of course, with ten gears. The ten-speed made the bicycle sporty and fashionable again, easily distinguished from the standard, functional bike with its chain guard, single gear, and fenders or mud guards (and sometimes with coaster brakes) – little different from bicycles of one's grandparents' generation. The buyer's test of quality now typically involved little more than a one-handed assessment of a bicycle's weight: lighter was better, consistent with a vehicle designed for speed and sport, even if intended for daily trips. It didn't matter that the ten-speed had obvious disadvantages on city roads, including the risk of getting skinny tires caught in sewer grates, or that on rainy days the lack of fenders (to reduce weight) guaranteed a skunk-like streak down a rider's back from water thrown up by the rear tire. Fashion came with a price, eagerly paid.

The ten-speed made the bicycle sexy and cool. "I am thinking of having my face lifted and buying a bicycle and a white straw hat with a red band … so that I may join the bicycle age," wrote the *Toronto Star*'s Scott Young. (It was Young who had called for bike paths two decades earlier.) He added that "the bike as a status symbol is more important than the principle itself," playfully suggesting that some downtown workers were merely posing as cyclists, driving to work, removing their bike from the trunk prior to arrival, then feigning exertion. Even Mayor William Dennison acknowledged the excitement, declaring September 16, 1972, as Bicyclists' Day in recognition of a community cycling event.

Maclean's, which had largely ignored the bicycle for seven decades, now published, as *Saturday Night* had done long ago, its own (less tongue-in-cheek) rules of etiquette, referring to cycling as "a sport of social etiquette and pleasure," requiring a man riding with a woman to remain on the outside, or behind her if riding single file.

Local shops, including ones selling meat and produce, continued to engage young people for deliveries by bike. It was nonetheless clear that some uses of the bicycle would not be revived.

Telegram delivery by bicycle had declined, the telegram itself slowly becoming redundant with long-distance communication by telephone and fax machine – and when telegrams arrived at their destination city, they were usually communicated to the recipient by telephone. (Physical delivery of the telegram was available for an extra fee.) In the early 1970s, a reporter described telegram messengers as "outcasts of the Phone and Mail System" – not yet gone but a remnant of their past glory. One stubble-faced messenger, years removed from a uniform or his youth, explained how much he enjoyed his job, especially the task of delivering wedding telegrams: "The poorer the immigrants, the more generous they are. They invite you in with your telegram and pour the booze into you. After, you gotta look out for the cops because if they catch you drinking on the job you've had it."

Meanwhile, one of the oldest players in the bicycle trade in Toronto was floundering. The CCM name was certainly no longer regarded by Canadians "with a feeling of personal affection and even proprietary pride," as a company history had suggested in 1946, just before its fiftieth anniversary. By 1979 the end was nigh for CCM. (The company, with its factory on Lawrence Avenue in the Town of Weston, went bankrupt in 1983, its demise largely due to the preoccupation of its owners in the 1960s and 1970s with extracting profits, instead of investing in the quality of its product, although stiff overseas competition and poor relations with its labour union dating from the 1950s were contributing factors.)

CYCLISTS LONG RIDE TO REGAINING THEIR VOICE

Before the Revival: The Bicycle's Darkest Days

In the 1960s, the bicycle had continued along a rut in its history that started in the 1950s, not unused, but generally unloved, especially by civic leaders. In the minutes of Toronto City Council during the 1960s, the bicycle was mentioned a mere three times:

once to approve an application by Maple Leaf Gardens' vice president Harold Ballard to hold indoor bicycle races on Sundays; the second to accept a communication from a citizen who wanted cyclists licensed and banned from sidewalks; and the third to debate a cyclist's claim for damages from an injury suffered in colliding with a device that counted cars.

The bicycle was similarly ignored at Metro Hall, except to restrict access to the Toronto Islands ferry; to prohibit cyclists from riding side-by-side or carrying packages that prevented gripping the handlebars; and to ban cyclists from riding on the Don Valley Parkway and the Gardiner Expressway. (A comprehensive 400-page textbook about planning in Metro and Toronto for the period 1940–80 mentions the bicycle precisely once, in the caption for a photo.)

The adults who still appreciated the convenience and enjoyment of everyday cycling, or had no other options, had to be willing to stand out. Indeed, riding a bike was a good way to *attract* attention, perhaps the motivation of a tandem-riding, downtown NDP candidate, along with his wife, in a 1965 election. The couple ran as candidates in a combined six elections – but never won. Elections weren't going to be won with the votes of people who rode bikes. Cyclists could still be dismissed as either too young, too poor, too odd, or destined in any case to become motorists. (More than twenty years later, local politicians Jack Layton and Olivia Chow, who were married in 1988, often rode their own tandem.)

A "bike boom" that occurred in the mid-1960s wasn't about pedal bicycles at all. This boom involved gasoline-powered, motorized bikes, also known as "mopeds." In popular perception, especially among teenagers, these vehicles could be comfortably distinguished from bicycles, while filling a gap between childhood

Image 28: The sheer joy of cycling is evident on the faces of these children in Scarborough. But Metro roads, including Ellesmere Road and Warden Avenue, made no space for their safety. The Bicycle Revival brought adults back to cycling for everyday travel, though most children had never given it up. Organized bike rides, such as this 1975 Bike-A-Thon, were (and remain) popular for advocacy or fundraising purposes. One popular fundraising initiative, the Ride for Heart on the Don Valley Parkway, draws up to 15,000 cyclists, demonstrating the appeal of cycling – at least when riders feel safe on roads. (Photo: Peter Mykusz, City of Toronto Archives, Series 1762, File 43, Item 17)

travel modes and adult motoring. The eligibility for a driver's licence at age sixteen had become a rite of passage to adulthood, even if it typically depended on a parent's car keys for actual driving. Children essentially went from being vulnerable pedestrians and cyclists – often banned by anxious parents from roads altogether – to being vulnerable motorists due to their inexperience and tendency to risk-taking behaviour, which left them over-represented in crash and casualty statistics among motorists.

Bicycles retained their place among children, although receiving little public attention for their road safety needs, let alone compassion, even in tragedy. A nine-year-old Scarborough boy on his bike who hit a man walking along a road with no sidewalk got more interest from the media than many young victims who were killed by cars. (The man was treated and released from hospital.)

As in the previous era, bike racks at schools or community centres, even in suburban areas, were often crammed, including with the popular "high-rise" model, known by names such as Mustang, a big seller for CCM in the 1960s, and Schwinn's Stingray. The high-rise design allowed children to make believe they were operating a motorcycle or "chopper": long handlebars slung back towards the rider (sometimes called monkey bars), thick tires on twenty-inch (fifty-centimetre) wheels, and an elongated "banana seat," viable for two people. Some models featured oversized gear shifters to resemble those on cars or motorcycles, until they were prohibited because of the risk of injury.

Bicycle clubs, which had never completely disappeared, saw a resurgence in the 1960s, animated by post-war immigrants who brought cycling traditions of touring and racing with them. The bicycle clubs that were formed, some affiliated with the CWA, had names such as Britannia, Italia, and Berolina, competing against

Image 29: The chopper motorcycle, a version of which was used in the iconic movie *Easy Rider*, provided design inspiration for the popular children's high-rise bicycle. The high-rise had features such as the banana seat and monkey handle bars. On their high-rise bicycle children had the opportunity for make believe, but whether toy or not, the high-rise got children to school, the community centre, and friends' homes. (Photo: Alamy)

more homespun groups, including the Don Mills Bicycle Club. Immigrants among club cyclists could safely distance their bicycle riding for sport from everyday cycling for utility. Once Toronto cyclists reached the countryside (an objective that was then more easily accomplished than today), they had to be wary of a small element of the rural population that, like farmers of long ago, didn't appreciate the urban interlopers, sometimes brushing dangerously past cyclists with their cars or pickups to intimidate them or as a reminder that motorists were the lords of the road.

The Automobile Juggernaut: A Few Bumps in the Road

New expressways, and a confident belief that more were yet to come, were an obvious reflection of the post-war dominance of automobiles. From 1951 to 1971, Metro watched or financed the building of a slate of expressways: the provincial Highway 401 was soon paralleled by the Gardiner Expressway along the waterfront, while the Don Valley Parkway ran along the city's east side and Highway 427 along the west. These motorways were intended as a ring around the city, to be bisected by the Spadina Expressway and the east-west Crosstown Expressway, themselves to be augmented by the Scarborough and Richview Expressways.

The futility of expanding the road system as the solution to congestion was already clear, even if transportation planners and decision-makers continued to use congestion as a cue to redouble their road-building efforts. Almost immediately after a street had been widened or an expressway opened, "the new traffic artery is jam packed with crawling flivvers," commented journalist Bruce West, "moving so slowly that any brisk walker could pass them with ease and anyone on a bicycle can go zipping by like a

Batmobile out of hell." The 401 had already been widened to eight lanes by 1979 (and today flares out to to as many as eighteen lanes, each successive increment of lanes rationalized based on growing motor traffic, itself induced by the extra lanes.)

Until Ontario Premier Bill Davis cancelled the southward extension of the Spadina Expressway on April 1, 1971, it appeared that Toronto would obediently follow the American transportation model: more roads to move more cars, faster, while giving free rein to planners who planned for cars. The Spadina Expressway was just one of ten expressways in Metro's master transportation plan that would, if built, leave Toronto looking like Los Angeles, an outcome that Metro Roads Commissioner Sam Cass apparently considered ideal. The cancellation was a landmark victory over the automobile juggernaut.

Davis signalled the possibility for a new direction: "If we are building a city for the car, the Spadina Expressway is a good place to start, but if we are building a city for people then the Spadina Expressway is a good place to stop."

That victory was just one of many reasons that made Toronto in the 1970s an exciting city to live in, and to believe that a new path was possible. Once the Spadina Expressway was cancelled, other planned expressways floundered, including various iterations of the Crosstown Expressway. Only a southward extension of Highway 400 was still being debated by the end of the decade. The Arab Oil Embargo in 1973 made the premier look all the wiser for his decision, further invigorating the push for alternative modes of transportation.

Community activism against the Spadina Expressway was quickly followed by a successful campaign to convince the TTC to abandon its plan to eliminate all streetcars by 1980. William

Allen, who succeeded Fred Gardiner as Metro chair in 1961 (and for whom the truncated Spadina Expressway was later named), once called streetcars "as obsolete as the horse and buggy." But Toronto's network of subways, streetcars, and buses, including electric trolley buses (until 1993), was the envy of many US transit agencies. For cyclists, the TTC remained a vital ally, although by the 1970s, some streetcar lines had already been removed.

By 1979, the TTC had 55 kilometres of subways in place. The Yonge subway, between Union Station and Eglinton Avenue, was the first to be completed in 1954, followed by a parallel University Avenue line in 1963. Both lines were subsequently extended into North York. The Bloor-Danforth subway followed in 1966, later extended east and west. At the regional level, provincial GO trains and buses offered the cyclist options for escape into the country-side, although schedules were designed for weekday commuters, and bicycles weren't initially welcome on trains. Since GO's founding in 1967, its trains radiated out from Union Station into the region, increasingly resembling Sir Adam Beck's long ago radial vision, but unlike Beck's electric plan, GO trains were still powered by diesel, leaving a trail of exhaust. Passenger rail travel across Ontario and Canada had declined since the end of the Second World War, largely consistent with the increase in car travel.

Toronto City Hall didn't always obediently accept the many thousands of cars arriving daily from the suburbs. In his 1973 inaugural address, Mayor David Crombie said that the city would not be widening roads or cutting down trees to make way for more cars (precisely the opposite of what Gardiner once proposed). "Sure, everyone has the right to come downtown – but he doesn't necessarily have the right to bring a ton of steel with him." In fact, the *Toronto Official Plan* once envisioned that upon arriving at the terminus of a regional expressway, motorists would park their cars and transfer to the TTC to get to the city core. The words "post-car era" were sometimes uttered in polite conversation in the city. From 1971 to 1974, downtown Yonge Street was turned into a pedestrian mall on summer weekends, an initiative that ended largely because the province refused to provide the city with statutory protection from potential lawsuits by businesses. An organized parade of cyclists rode to the opening in May 1971, then enjoyed a free pancake breakfast. Little did they know that pancakes, instead of new cycling facilities, would become a staple on City Hall menus for cycling events. (Subsequently, the non-profit Sierra Club organized an annual car-free day in the city. One such event along Yonge was held in an adjacent public square to avoid interfering with cars.)

In the 1970s, even automobile companies sometimes sounded like they might contribute to the environmental priorities of the day. In 1976, GM Canada said the major automakers were committed to programs to reduce the size and weight of the vehicles they produced. An industry commentator suggested that automakers "not only accepted the small car, but embraced it. They see it as the car of the future."

Sewell and the City, and the New Advocates

When John Sewell became Toronto's mayor on December 1, 1978, some residents expected him to give up riding his bicycle as undignified to his office. Sewell had actually given up his car years earlier as ill-suited to city life, in stark contrast to his predecessors, including William Dennison, supporter of the Spadina Expressway, who had relied on a chauffeur-driven Cadillac for city business. Unlike most politicians, Sewell didn't blame traffic congestion on too few roads, but on the absurd number of cars. He continued to ride his bike to City Hall, which since 1965 was in an award-winning structure that appeared to welcome the public with open arms. But it was city staff with free parking permits who still got the warmest welcome. On the two-lane-wide Bay Street entrance into the parking garage, motorists cut dangerously across southbound cyclists.

Sewell, a community lawyer, didn't much care for convention; in fact, he considered the business-as-usual workings of City Hall as a serious problem. Sewell's habit as alderman of dressing in blue jeans and a casual jacket was another minor act of rebellion in a historically staid and conservative city. He even eschewed the ten-speed bicycle fashion, preferring an upright model with wide tires better suited to dealing with on-road hazards, including sewer grates.

The bicycle wasn't high on Sewell's crowded reform agenda, but his choice of two wheels over four was as strong a statement about the bicycle's legitimacy on city roads as any city policy.

In 1975, City Council had established the City Cycling Committee, with cycling advocates appointed from the community (later including Hilda Tiessen). A year later council adopted a policy declaring the bicycle "an integral and efficient form of transportation." The cycling committee was officially an advisory body but, given the dearth of grassroots groups, it quickly became a focal point for cycling advocacy. Prior to the committee's formation, Pollution Probe, formed in 1969, had been one of the few groups in Metro advocating for cycling. Among its initiatives, Pollution Probe organized advocacy rides, including one during what was called "Cycling Week" in 1976. Torchy Peden, the 1930s bicycle racing star, was a featured guest. Another group, Urban Bikeways Inc., an incorporated non-profit group supported by retailer Bloor

Image 30: John Sewell, elected mayor in 1978, was City Hall's best-known cyclist in the 1970s, but he was far from being the only one. The caption for this City of Toronto photo for Bike to Work Week in 1980 read, "pedalling what they preach." (*Left to right*) Alderman Patrick Sheppard, Dan Leckie and Lynn Spink (assistants to the mayor), Mayor John Sewell, and Alderman David White (chair of the City Cycling Committee). Sewell lost his bid for re-election later that year. (Photo: City of Toronto, "Toronto City News," June 1980, vol. 3, no. 2)

Cycle, was often quoted in the media on cycling issues. One larger group, although of national reach, also took an interest in cycling in Toronto: the Canadian Cycling Association (CCA), previously known as the Canadian Wheelmen's Association (CWA). The CCA remained an organization focused on cycling as sport – but given the scarcity of other organized or experienced groups, it was often a default commentator on local cycling matters. (Even fifty years later, neither the CCA nor sport cycling clubs had become engaged, with some exceptions, in advocacy for utilitarian cycling, even if most sport cyclists no longer saw any need to distinguish their sport from cycling for utility; indeed, many members might do both, cycle for sport then cycle to work, typically on different bikes. When sport cyclists riding in packs through stop signs in High Park in 2022 drew the ire of park users and some local residents, a police ticketing blitz also entangled utilitarian cyclists, provoking a High Park rally of hundreds of cyclists of all stripes – but whether the rally actually benefited utilitarian cyclists remained an open question, especially in view of the divisions it created in that case with other road users, including people on foot, who were otherwise allies in the fight for safe roads.)

The *City Cyclist*, the first significant publication dedicated to Toronto cyclists since the *Wheeling Gazette* and *Cycling* folded eighty years earlier, was the cycling committee's instrument for disseminating information. (The long-ago *Canadian Wheelman*, although it had lots of Toronto content, was a national publication.) Unlike its predecessors, this city-funded publication focused on utilitarian cycling. Its first issue in June 1978 encouraged cyclists to "get your bicycle in gear in time for International Cyclists' Day," a highlight of the committee's first Bike to Work Week. Hundreds of cyclists heeded the call, turning out to ride from Queen's Park to City Hall in an event billed "Bike for a Better City."

The mainstream media returned to reporting on cycling, beyond stories of sport, oddities, or tragedy. Decades after abandoning its column, "The Wheel," the *Globe and Mail* in 1975 assigned Michael Moore to write about cycling on its recreation page, at the time dominated by fishing and hunting. The young reporter's passion for cycling extended beyond commuting to feats of endurance that would have impressed bicycle club members of the 1890s. Once each year, he helped organize, and participated in, a single-day, return ride from Toronto to Niagara Falls, covering 320 kilometres, a distance that would have qualified as a double "century" or 200 miles in the earlier era. The column (which ran until the mid-1980s) sometimes made it to the front page, at least when a reallocation of road space from motorists to cyclists was proposed.

REALITY CHECK

Transportation Planners, and the Evil that Lurks Below

The young men and women on the cycling committee quickly learned that nothing would come easily – but pushed forward all the same. "Nothing could cloud our view," recalled one advocate. The committee worked largely unnoticed in an institution where the motorcar still ranked first, second, and third. Early in the decade, one columnist had remarked that "there are hard-headed transportation planners who now regard the bicycle as a legitimate transportation option under certain circumstances. None of these planners, unfortunately, has anything to do with transportation policy in Toronto." For motorists, cyclists were a "nightmare." Alderman Allan Sparrow, an early member of the cycling committee, told a reporter that "we're still regarded as one of those nuisance committees – a good cause, perhaps, but definitely peripheral." The chair of the committee in 1978, Alderman David White, still held the same opinion.

Even when Toronto City Council could be convinced to take action, it was constrained by the fact that Metro had control over all arterial roads, officially designated as Metro roads, which were often the most useful roads to bicycle commuters, as they were to motorists. Metro Council was dominated by politicians eager to prevent any hardship to motorists. By the 1970s, after years of fast growth, Toronto's suburban neighbours – Etobicoke, North York, East York, York, and Scarborough – had two-thirds of the population and a majority of the seats on Metro Council. The suburbs also had most of the cars. Between 1953 and 1979, Metro's motor vehicle population had continued to grow faster than its human population, tripling to over 1.1 million vehicles.

On the roads, curbside sewer grates (catch basins) were among the hazards faced by cyclists. The slats or openings on the grates were designed to allow rainwater to drain without becoming clogged with leaves and debris, but they were also wide enough to snag the skinny tires of a ten-speed. These "wheel traps" or "tire eaters" were equally dangerous to cyclists who tried to skirt around them, risking the blast of a car horn, or worse. "Pollution Control and Population Control, Too?" was the macabre title given a letter to the editor. The problem was especially urgent on heavily used cycling routes on Bloor, Danforth, and Yonge.

By 1972, Toronto's works department had developed a safe herring-bone design for grates, but at $60 each, the cost to replace tens of thousands of grates was unpalatable for the city and Metro, except on a gradual basis. In 1973, Toronto and Metro, combined, replaced 1,500 grates – a pace that, if maintained, would

Image 31: Sewer grates posed a hazard to skinny-tired ten-speed bikes popular in the 1970s. Cyclists either had to skirt around the grates, or take their chances riding over them. A safer herring-bone grate had already been designed at the time, but the cost of replacing thousands of such grates across the city and Metro ensured that the replacement process would be slow. (Photos: Albert Koehl)

see all 40,000 grates replaced by 2013. When Toronto City Hall announced that it would replace grates that wore out or when major road work took place with the safer design, advocates weren't fooled – major road work took place on a timeline measured in decades, and the life expectancy of the average cast iron grate exceeded that of the average cyclist.

"A Curse on Sweaty, Unwanted Cyclists"

Public excitement about the cycling revival usually ended abruptly when cyclists demanded space on public roads. "A curse on sweaty, unwanted cyclists," read the headline for an article by *Toronto Star* columnist Christie Blatchford. She characterized cyclists as either academics, students, or the unemployed, adding that the "truth is cyclists no longer know their place, which is not on city streets." Blatchford's vitriol encapsulated a popular sentiment about cycling, namely, a "nice" activity – perhaps spoken with a condescending "good for you" pat on the back – engaged in by the idle and others who were going nowhere in particular. Driving, on the other hand, was serious business.

Blatchford's tirade was provoked by the city's Bike to Work Week, during which parts of a few roads, for a few hours, were turned over to cyclists. She derided Joan Doiron, an assistant to Councillor Allan Sparrow and a key member of the cycling committee, as a "militant cyclist" after Doiron, in an obvious bit of hyperbole, encouraged cyclists to "clog" city streets during bike week. The fact that the soft-spoken, kindly Doiron, known to bake cookies for advocacy meetings, could be portrayed as a militant reflected the level of outrage towards anyone who dared to demand a share of the *public* road. Blatchford also complained about "self-righteous" cyclists, which, given the title of her article, was at least amusing.

The massive amount of road space needed for driving and parking ensured that motorists were zealous guardians of that space. A letter writer in 1972 summarized the looming "war," observing that although the cyclist was "first regarded with that astonished smile of pity and derision that is usually inspired by an unfortunate creature talking loudly to himself on the street, now I receive many looks of baleful hatred, combined with angry tyre squeals and unnecessary horn blowing." Even lower-income segments of the population could be counted among defenders of the car-first model, despite the obvious financial hardship of buying and operating a car. Owning a car was evidence of having "made it" – as defined by the slick marketing of carmakers – within the reigning societal model. For many in this group, taking the bus, or riding a bicycle, was not an acceptable option.

Former war correspondent Arnold Brunner wrote that bicycles brought out the worst in Toronto drivers. "I have been scared – in a war zone, you know … But from the perspective of a thin, muscle-powered bicycle, Toronto becomes a noisy jungle teeming with four-wheeled beasts with human – although not necessarily intelligent – heads. I was scared, horrified and harried all at once." Brunner had particular criticism for TTC drivers who "would whiz around and cut me off at bus stops … Being overtaken by a bus or going around a bus is dangerous. So a cyclist must stop behind the brute and risk asphyxiation from its exhaust."

It quickly became clear that the political response to the bicycle revival would not match the manic response in the post–Second World War period for motorcars, despite the modest investment that would be needed. Even the media, despite the profits it reaped from car ads, sometimes complained about the slow pace of government action to accommodate cyclists. The *Globe and Mail* lamented in 1973 that "[d]espite the enormous publicity which heralded the bicycle craze, Toronto is far from a cyclist's paradise." A year later, it called for on-road bike paths, declaring "we want the bicycle; we want a city for bicycles." In 1976, Toronto was again chastized as "abysmally slow to act," while the call for on-road bike paths (except on arterials) was reiterated: "So far, the few bicycle paths that exist in Toronto are strictly for recreational use – fit for pleasant Sunday afternoons in the Humber Valley, but not worth a twig for getting downtown on a bike." In 1978, a *Globe* editorial lamented that North American thinking had yet to accept that cyclists "merit decent accommodation on our streets," instead obliging cyclists to "cope, on a take-it-or-leave-it basis, with a road system designed for the free flow of cars and trucks."

For its part, the *Toronto Star* called for off-road paths and sidewalk-level paths along roads with wide allowances, pointing out in 1972 that even "car worshipper" Sam Cass "realizes the need for arterial bicycle paths, and some are planned in the suburbs. But how about downtown, too?" The *Toronto Star,* which opposed bike lanes on roads, didn't elaborate where space for such paths, aside from the waterfront, might be found.

Demands for bikeways often descended into lengthy debates about cyclists' conduct, perhaps ironic, given that the number of charges against motorists for road infractions had risen to 800,000 annually, while the road casualty toll remained disturbingly high, counting 20,000 injuries – a fourfold increase compared to twenty years earlier – from 50,000 road collisions within Metro in 1979. Cyclists and pedestrians remained over-represented in the numbers. The only road safety victories that might be celebrated were in the context of continuing grim numbers. There were 135 road deaths in Metro in 1964 compared to ninety in 1979. (By comparison, road deaths in the 2010s, with a far larger population, averaged about sixty per year.)

On Trial - *Just Kids*

The power imbalance on roads between automobiles and people on foot and bikes, especially children, was obvious – at least to an outside observer. One might have expected city authorities to eagerly concede the need for change to protect those at risk; instead, they were more likely to vigorously defend the status quo, which commonly made victims of the most vulnerable.

Jurors at a July 1976 coroner's inquest into a Scarborough crash that claimed the lives of two boys had an opportunity to show that a transportation model that so wantonly took lives was no longer acceptable. But after reporting that they were "unable to determine the exact cause of the accident," the jurors set out a long list of recommendations that sounded very much like a stern lecture of the victims – two boys, ages eleven and twelve, who would have been too young to make their case, even had they survived.

The boys, Glenn McNickle and his classmate Nat McNulty, were returning home from a local arcade, with Nat on the back of the banana seat of Glenn's high-rise bicycle. They cycled north on Brimley Road, a four-lane arterial with a posted 60 km/h speed limit – despite being lined by parks and working-class homes – then crossed the broad intersection at Lawrence Avenue. A TTC bus, also northbound, crossed Lawrence at virtually the same time, encountering the boys where the roadway narrows from its wider mouth at the intersection. (In crossing the intersection, the boys likely followed the edge of the crosswalk, which, in the normal configuration, would be set back from the north-south flow of cars.) The bus driver, according to reports of the inquest, left only 0.9 metres (36 inches) of space between his large vehicle and the curb when he passed the boys. Glenn died instantly under the rear wheels, his friend Nat was rushed to hospital.

Within hours of the tragedy, the media rendered its judgment, focusing on the fact that the two boys were on the same bike. There was, however, no evidence that "riding double" in any way contributed to the crash. Even a skilled adult cyclist brushed so closely by a multi-ton vehicle would be frightened and would struggle to maintain their balance. The boys were experienced cyclists, often riding with neighbourhood children on local streets. Glenn's siblings and father enjoyed cycling on nearby trails, including the Birkdale Ravine bike path built by Scarborough students in 1972. (After the one-metre passing rule became Ontario law in 2015, one inventive cyclist claimed his newly defined entitlement to space on the road by strapping a $2 pool noodle to the back rack of his bicycle and letting it extend into the roadway. His pool noodle was the *Toronto Star*'s story of the year, but everyday road perils remained less newsworthy.)

When Nat died two days later, city newspapers gave him a few curt paragraphs. The *Toronto Sun*'s report appeared beneath a more prominent headline: "Cop Warns Cyclists on Shunning Safety," with a photo of two boys on a bike similar to Glenn's, and the caption: "RIDING Double like These Two Youngsters Is Not Only Illegal, It's Dangerous." The narrative was tidy and convenient, perhaps even comforting to other parents, while ignoring, let alone addressing, the actual danger.

The jury's recommendations targeted children, calling for a ban on cycling on arterials during rush hour; stricter enforcement against cyclists; instruction about road rules; and the confiscation of bikes for road infractions. A call for bicycle licensing for all riders was tacked onto the list, with associated revenues to be directed to "new safety standards and public awareness of existing bicycle laws." The jury also recommended a study about bicycle "safety features," presumably based on a suggestion by the TTC lawyer that narrower handlebars on high-rise bikes could have made a difference. The lawyer presumably took his cue from provincial road safety experts and Metro officials who in 1969 made high-rise handlebars and banana seats a suspect for the increase in cyclist deaths from 1967 to 1968. But reducing the disturbing five-decades-old tragedy of cyclist deaths on roads to these two design features and a single-year fluctuation in deaths could only be described as darkly quaint.

Indeed, a provincial Department of Transportation report made no causal connection between road deaths and the features of high-rise bikes.

While calling for young cyclists to be punished, educated, banned from roads, and their bikes confiscated, the jury had little to say about the speed limit, TTC driver training, cycling instruction in schools, dedicated bike lanes for cyclists, and the risks posed by sewer grates. (The *Toronto Sun*'s front page had a photo indicating the final resting place of the bike and victims, with chalk marks directly over a sewer grate, a known hazard.) The outcome only reinforced the bias that journalist Victor Lauriston had noted four decades earlier in the context of a trial involving a driving tragedy: "[E]veryone, except in the most flagrant cases, loves the motorist and hates to be hard on him. Particularly is this true of his fellow motorist in the jury box. The juror, contemplating the prisoner in the dock, thinks, 'There, but for the grace of God, goes myself.'" The bus driver got much of the public sympathy. Only one juror was willing to consider the crash from the boys' perspective: "A driver of a car should be aware that legally he has to give a bike-rider a lane ... We (the jury) weren't all in agreement that the bus driver should have passed at that time."

The outcome was consistent with a public sentiment that cyclists got what they deserved for flaunting road rules, regardless, apparently, of the age of the victims – or even if their conduct actually caused the crash. Blaming parents of child road victims was another preferred option, even if it simply heaped guilt upon grief. Civic officials entrusted with protecting vulnerable road users had little to offer that was new. "There's no doubt cities like this are not for the children," said Sam Cass in 1972. "But it's also a fact. We have to live in this urban world." Life lessons for children, such as independence, were submerged by the needs of the motorist.

Image 32: A comforting narrative. This front-page photo in the *Toronto Star* on June 21, 1972, repeated a comforting message for parents, namely that young cyclists were safe if they had proper equipment and obeyed road rules. Here a police officer places an "approved" sticker on a ten-year-old boy's bicycle. The photo appeared under the headline: "Metro Traffic Kills a Soaring Number of 'Carefree' Children." But while every bend in the road was expertly engineered for motorists, the state's responsibility did not extend to creating safe roads for cyclists. (Photo: Keith Beatty/Getty Images)

A city that was dependent on cars required sacrifices, even when those called upon to make sacrifices had no voice in the matter.

A 1970 study for Metro by the Ontario Department of Transportation, about the increasing number of road injuries suffered by young cyclists, identified a number of common factors, including arterial roads, signalized intersections, locations near home, and heavy, after-school motor traffic – circumstances that summarized the Scarborough tragedy, but neither the province nor the municipality had done anything to address the identified problems.

A small newspaper headline, "Boys Killed on Bikeway Route" offered an alternative narrative. The first phase of an off-road network of bike trails adopted by Metro in 1974 included a hydro corridor near the deadly intersection, but the path wasn't yet in place (nor completed forty years later). "We just can't go on letting children get killed on roadways like this," lamented Leonard Steele of Urban Bikeways. The "only real solution to bicycle safety problems is providing a safe place to ride a bike." Fortunately, both the city and Metro had community activists willing to step into the breach to kick-start the building of those safe places to ride.

MAKING SPACE FOR THE BICYCLE

Safe Places to Ride - Gallop to the Rescue

By the late 1970s, cycling was at a crossroads: many daily trips could easily be cycled (research showed that 40 per cent of all trips in the city were under four kilometres in length) – but most adults who had taken up cycling, or were considering it, weren't likely to remain cyclists or shift from cars or transit to bikes without safe places to ride.

The surge in adult cyclists on city roads forced governments to respond, not necessarily out of a concern for cyclists but rather out of a concern about the inconvenience it entailed for motorists. The matter even rekindled, in a starkly new context, long-ago debates among cycling groups about whether to advocate for better roads or for dedicated bike paths. Contemporary roads were superb compared to those of the 1890s, but for most cyclists, or prospective cyclists, increased motor traffic had sabotaged any advantage.

As early as 1971, Toronto's public works department had considered testing, in collaboration with Metro, a bike lane. But it appears that nothing came of the initiative. The cycling committee's 1975 Statement of Policy, later updated, contemplated a wide range of bikeways, while listing the best cycling route as one that "is an exclusive and physically-separated bicycle-only lane." (The term "bikeway" encompasses both on- and off-road cycling facilities such as bike lanes, bicycle trails, and signed routes that guide cyclists along quieter streets.) In terms of the desirable types of infrastructure, the committee's policy was broad, including, "if at all possible," cycling routes on arteries that provide access to major attractors such as workplaces and shopping areas. Cycling advocates were in no position to dictate.

For Winona Gallop riding a bicycle was a normal childhood activity, at least when she was a child in the 1930s. As a parent in the late 1960s, with daughter Virginia perched atop a pillow on the back rack of her bike, Gallop had begun cycling with her own children along the waterfront boardwalk in the city's Beaches neighbourhood. There was one problem: a motorbike-riding park warden with a stern message, "No bicycle riding on the boardwalk."

Gallop wasn't defeated by the warden's edict, but motivated to action, backed by individuals with an important stake in the outcome: her son and his grade-school classmates. To Gallop's surprise, Toronto's Parks and Recreation Committee quickly approved, in the spring of 1970, her proposed bike path alongside the boardwalk. By the summertime the bike path was in place, stretching more than two kilometres from Balmy Beach west almost to

Ashbridges Bay. In all of Metro at the time, there was only one similar path that ran along Mimico Creek in Etobicoke – a path, albeit shared with pedestrians, that was the only tangible evidence of a 160-kilometre network of bike "freeways" proposed by that municipality's chief planner in the 1960s.

Gallop was soon working on a westward extension of the Beaches bike path along Lakeshore Boulevard and Leslie Street to Cherry Beach, a project that proved more challenging given the various governments and agencies with jurisdiction over the area. Gallop's eldest son, by then a teenager, and other students hired with government grants, mapped out the route, then wielded pick-axes and shovels to clear the waterfront portion of the trail, while city-contracted crews with heavy equipment cleared other segments. With the path nearly complete in 1978, the city showed its appreciation by requiring Gallop and the students to sign waivers accepting liability for any injuries suffered by users.

By 1979, cyclists could ride the eight-kilometre route between Balmy and Cherry Beaches, interrupted only by a 780-metre gap near the bottom of Leslie Street. (The gap was finally closed in 2019, although no one at City Hall thought to invite Gallop, then aged eighty-five and still living in the area, to the ribbon-cutting ceremony.) Gallop then pushed City Hall to extend the bike path downtown along Queen's Quay, recognizing that direct, dedicated cycling routes were the next step, likely to be achieved in small steps, given the prevailing political attitudes. She was nonetheless already thinking bigger. In a letter to the City Cycling Committee, she pushed for the development of a network of bikeways. "As a group, *we must come to a decision for Toronto cyclists, on the choice of a core route*, and actively pursue the achievement of that goal" (emphasis in original).

Meanwhile, in Scarborough, a group of students was similarly engaged in pioneering work to encourage cycling. After starting a local chapter of the recently founded Pollution Probe and securing substantial government funding, students at the University of Toronto's local campus mapped out a bike path plan anchored by a 15-kilometre route from the Warden subway station to the Metro Zoo, then under construction, offering access to destinations along the way, including schools and shopping.

In April 1972, Norm Hawirko, a leader of the student group, stood before Scarborough's Board of Control to present the proposal, noting that an arrangement had already been worked out with the hydro authority for the path, most of which ran along the Gatineau Hydro Corridor. The plan devised by the students would involve no cost to the local municipality. Unfortunately, the controllers didn't share the students' enthusiasm, instead fretting that visitors from beyond Scarborough might benefit from the bikeway and that tax revenues from the hydro authority might be lost. The Parks Commissioner proposed a modest five-kilometre parkland route along a western branch of Highland Creek, which Hawirko complained went nowhere. "Well, you've got to start small," Scarborough's mayor told him.

The students took their setback in stride, quickly getting to work on a 1.6-kilometre route within Birkdale Ravine Park. A landscape design student did the mapping while another student with construction experience used a borrowed backhoe to clear the trail, confirming that the project was both figuratively and literally groundbreaking. In early June 1972, politicians happily attended the opening ceremony, while city officials contributed more aggravation, refusing to issue tax receipts for in-kind donations of road materials for the path. "[T]his is the thanks you get," one of the students complained.

The city must nonetheless have appreciated the value of the path, subsequently extending it by three kilometres south-east through another park, albeit without a safe road crossing. (The student proposal remains incomplete, fifty years later, although an initiative in 2018 along the Gatineau Hydro Corridor, now renamed the Meadoway, is progressing, with support from a wealthy corporation. A neighbourhood group is today campaigning for the installation of a walking and cycling trail from Warden to Kennedy subway stations, along an abandoned railway spur, to complete the first portion of the long-ago student proposal to connect Warden Station to the zoo.)

On the other side of Metro, a bi-directional bike path running alongside a wide stretch of Eglinton Avenue West was approved by Metro Council in 1972. The path, along a route once earmarked for the Richview Expressway, had the obvious benefit, as with the other off-road paths, of not encroaching on motorists' coveted road space. A similar bike path was proposed in another remote part of Metro (in north-east Scarborough), but how a cyclist would get there could only be a mystery, and the path was ultimately never built.

BIKE-A-THON

SATURDAY, SEPT. 16 (IF IT RAINS– SEPT. 23)

Bike-A-Thon in support of Bikeway construction.
Sponsor forms available at most bike shops, schools and libraries, and Pollution Probe Scarborough.
Come with or without sponsors.
Donations are appreciated.
50¢ admission to Ontario Place for participants.
Draw for CCM Bicycles.
Evening Concert.

POLLUTION PROBE SCARBOROUGH
For information phone 284 3346/284 3358
Address 1265 Military Trail, West Hill, Ontario.

Image 33: Bicyclists' Day. A Scarborough student wing of Pollution Probe, after installing the Birkdale Ravine bike path, organized a Bike-A-Thon to call for more bikeways across Metro. Hundreds of riders turned out, in part due to newspaper ads, including this one in the *Toronto Star* on September 14, 1972. The ride had eight starting points around Metro, converging at Ontario Place. Toronto Mayor Dennison declared September 16, 1972, "Bicyclists' Day." (Courtesy of Pollution Probe.)

The 2.25-kilometre Eglinton path (later extended east and west) was impressive: paved, separated from motor traffic by a grass buffer, and pleasantly landscaped, albeit located in a sparsely populated area of Metro, straddling Royal York Road, that could draw few cyclists. The *Toronto Star* claimed that the work demonstrated that Sam Cass had become a "convert to the Bicycle Revolution," joining Metro Parks Commissioner Tommy Thompson, who had for years "toiled alone as the cyclist's friend." Thompson had proposed a system of bike trails connecting the Humber and Don Rivers via a waterfront trail to form an arc – a proposal that was soon taken up by Metro. (Thompson's proposal resembled what eventually became the 85-kilometre Pan Am Path, an initiative for the 2015 Pan Am Games hosted by Toronto, albeit with gaps in the trail that still exist today.)

The reports of Cass's conversion proved premature. The Eglinton bike path, which had been envisioned as the first of several experimental Dutch-style *bicycle tracks* that would include Sheppard Avenue, Keele Street, and Finch Avenue, was the only path actually installed.

Metro Recognizes the Value of Bicycles – On Trails, Not Roads

In early June 1974, Metro Council appeared ready to respond to the Bicycle Revival, approving the first stage of a plan for "arterial" bike trails. "Long Overdue Bicycle System Finds Beginning," read one headline. The Plan was described as "excellent, imaginative" – and the report so popular far beyond Metro that a second printing was required – while council was urged to "not sit on it." By June 1979, Metro was to have 124 kilometres of bike trails, stage one of a 425-kilometre trail network.

At the time, the list of trails suitable for cycling, most of them *not* designated as cycling paths, within the vast area of Metro, whether under Metro or local jurisdiction, was miniscule, amounting to about 32 kilometres, essentially trails within parks, including vestiges of the bicycle's first hoorah in the 1890s along rivers and ravines. Cyclable trails along the Humber River were partly attributable to Hurricane Hazel, which had turned the river into a raging torrent in the spring of 1954, motivating the conversion of the river banks into parkland. Trails along the Don River, first proposed in the early 1960s, but segments dating back much further, had become Metro's longest, amounting to about nine kilometres at the time (although lacking convenient access points). Knowledgeable city residents could also string together trails and quiet roads for a pleasant outing by bike, perhaps relying on "Bicycle Routes in Toronto," written by Esther Kaplan and her husband Robert (later a federal cabinet minister), published by *Toronto Life* in 1972.

The Bicycle Revival also provoked some *reductions* in paths available to cyclists. When the number of cyclists in parks was small and children predominated, cyclists might be tolerated but when their numbers increased, and included adults, Metro intervened with a ban on cycling in some of its parks. Cyclists arriving from paths along the Don River, skirting the grounds of the Ontario Science Centre, through Wilket Creek and Sunnybrook Parks, were barred from entering Edwards Gardens, adjacent to an upper-class North York neighbourhood.

Metro's bike plan had an obvious catch, namely, that cyclists were to be moved off roads where many were cycling, onto trails, ostensibly for cyclists' safety. This approach had not, however, been a fait accompli when the issue was first considered. In October 1972, the Metro Transportation Committee had instructed Sam

Cass to "report on the feasibility and desirability of introducing a network of bicycle paths as part of the Metropolitan Road System." Cass was clearly not eager for an intrusion of bicycle paths on roads, noting in his letter the need to study "alternative systems of routes," which later found expression in the Strok & Associates' recommendations for bike trails. Cass recommended the hiring of a consultant, suggesting a staff report would take longer. It was noteworthy, however, that Metro staff appeared sympathetic to the idea of bike paths on roads.

In March 1973, Metro's Parks Department and its Roads and Traffic Department had released "A Metropolitan Toronto Bicycle Route System," to be anchored by a 110-kilometre "Initial Trial Bikeway System." The trial or *pilot* was to have park trails *and* bike paths – including "designated paths on road surfaces" (as articulated on maps) – offering cyclists safe access to common destinations. The trial included a closed circuit, incorporating paths along the Don and Humber Rivers, connected to each other along the waterfront in the south and Eglinton Avenue in the north. By the time the report was presented, and before the pilot was initiated, Metro had already hired consultants Strok & Associates to undertake a new study.

Wojciech ("Walter") Strok's definition of the bicycle suggested his intended audience was unfamiliar with the device, described as requiring "effort and a forward motion at speeds in excess of 5 m.p.h. to maintain the degree of stability necessary for transportation of persons." This fact had been evident to Baron von Drais in 1817. Strok brought to his task the perspective of an occasional cyclist, his recent cycling experience limited to borrowing his daughter's bike from time to time. His challenge was to devise a plan to serve all of Metro even though cycling numbers, use, and potential growth differed greatly between sparsely populated suburbs and the older, denser neighbourhoods of Toronto and East York.

In his report, Strok presented what looked like a parallel cycling universe with a network of bike paths that were to be lit, landscaped, and paved (in a dark cherry colour), supplemented by amenities such as water fountains, washrooms, and newspaper kiosks, and perhaps to be policed by motorcycle-riding cops, because "only an exceptionally physically conditioned policeman" on a bike could catch a fit cyclist on a ten-speed. A bicycle licence was to be implemented as part of a complex regulatory regime that created a special court and granted police authority to confiscate bikes, suspend licences, assess demerit points, and order training sessions, while classifying riders in terms of their experience and where they could ride.

Strok's trails were to be located in parks, hydro corridors, ravines, and other public rights of way. He acknowledged that cyclists needed safe routes to get to the trails, therefore proposing that local municipalities install bikeways along secondary roads – although no municipality had expressed any such intention – and, controversially, that "each residential sidewalk can become a highway," excluding sidewalks with heavy traffic, to allow safe and convenient access to the trails. But in the absence of safe access, Strok's trails would, as one advocate put it, be "like an expressway without ramps."

Strok didn't anticipate much growth in bike commuting for adults, citing the climate as a deterrent. In fact, he concluded that a great majority of bike trips in Metro were by children, predominantly for school, shopping, and exercise. In phase one, he nonetheless included some trails leading to commercial, recreational, employment, and educational centres in the central city for the purpose of being able to assess the potential growth in cycling among adults.

The public at large might be inclined to see Strok's plan as a solution to "the bicycle problem" (referenced in Metro Council debates), given that their own experience of cyclists was likely from behind the wheel of a car, from which vantage point cyclists made driving more difficult. Alternatively, the public's experience with cycling might be as recreational riders, arriving at parks with a bike strapped to the bumper. As motorists, it was more difficult to see the real issue as the "car problem." Cycling advocates understood Metro's underlying message: roads were for motorists.

Some cycling advocates derided Strok's report as too child-oriented, which could be no surprise given his view of the dominant place of children among Metro cyclists. For its part, the CCA dismissed Strok's approach for his reliance on off-road bike paths, fearing that cyclists would be limited to those paths, while constraining the potential growth of cycling among adults. "If bikeway designers regard bikes as playthings, the bikeways' only users will be people who come to play." The CCA, however, also generally opposed bike lanes, albeit showing some flexibility in terms of paths for novice riders, asserting that bike lanes wouldn't provide a significant safety benefit, especially when cyclists emerged at intersections. (Its position was consistent with a "vehicular cycling" approach, which was emerging in the United States.) The City of Toronto's Planning Department likewise scoffed at the report's "overwhelming bias in favour of recreational usage of bicycles."

Whatever the merit of bike trails as the solution, their value depended on actual installation, especially if planners were to assess the uptake by adult cyclists. And yet, even after the expiration of the stage one timeline – and despite the political appeal of getting cyclists off roads – by December 1979 there were only 80 kilometres of bike trails – of the phase one plan for 124 kilometres – in place across Metro, including trails that pre-existed the plan. (The Metro plan for bike trails was officially abandoned on April 16, 1982, ostensibly due to concerns for sensitive natural areas and construction challenges – concerns and challenges that hadn't slowed Metro's construction of the colossal Don Valley Parkway, for which hills were flattened, swaths of forest cleared, and a river course altered.)

The Metro plan floundered despite a promising start. "1975 Is the Year of the Bike in Metro," proclaimed a *Toronto Star* headline, adding that in Metro, "almost everybody loves a bike." According to the reporter, 1975 was "the year when the cheapest form of transport has finally emerged from an uphill battle against prejudice to become a boon to commuters as well as those who cycle for recreation." In 1975 alone, Metro approved 26 kilometres of bike trails, with the result of almost doubling the trails then in place. A Metro roads department official enthused that by 1980, "we could go on to complete a recommendation that every resident in Metro should be within one mile of a bikeway."

By the end of the decade, the trails installed were ultimately too few, too scattered, or too remote, for anything other than local recreation – "splendid for the weekend leisure cyclist but of little help to the commuting cyclist unless he works in Etienne Brulé Park [on the Humber River]."

Road Space for Cyclists?

Toronto City Hall, unlike its Metro counterpart, was far more receptive to the idea that bicycles belonged on roads, reflecting the "philosophical split between those who see the bicycle as a means of transportation and those who see it as recreation." The compact urban form of the city, much of it shaped by the pre-car era, contributed to the obvious difference in thinking. By the end of the decade, the differences in approach did not, however, amount to significantly different outcomes when measured by accomplishments.

The first proposals in Toronto for on-street bikeways generally focused on cycling routes designated by signs – usually termed "discretionary" bikeways – instead of demarcated or dedicated space. The City Cycling Committee quickly took up the call for discretionary bikeways, including a 10-kilometre, north-south route from the waterfront to Lawrence Avenue, the city's northern border at the time, a route the city soon approved. A similar east-west bikeway was abandoned. Later in the decade, a more direct north-south route along Yonge Street was rejected for fear of exposing the city to liability for cyclists' injuries.

In late 1976, Toronto City Council went a step further by approving a series of bike lanes, largely along the discretionary routes already in place. The installations were slated for spring 1977, subject to budget approval and the anxiety of the city's Public Works Commissioner, Ray Bremner, who predicted "serious consequences" for motorists. Bremner was conveniently aided by the city solicitor, who suggested council only had power to install *exclusive* bike lanes that would even prohibit emergency and transit vehicles from incursion. Whatever the merit of the opinion, the bike lanes were stalled pending an amendment to Ontario's *Municipal Act*. In the meantime, the city hired consultant Barton-Aschman Limited to undertake a comprehensive study of on-road cycling facilities.

By the time Queen's Park amended the *Municipal Act* in 1978, the bike lanes approved in 1976 had largely been forgotten while the consultant's study drained the meagre time and resources of the cycling committee's volunteers.

The profile of the Toronto cyclist, as reported by the consultant, differed significantly from the Metro cyclist. In Toronto more people cycled, more of those cyclists were adults, and more of those adults cycled for utilitarian purposes. Almost 190,000 people in a city population of 640,000 cycled at least once per year, while a majority of bike trips were to specific destinations, including work and school. The growing downtown population, the fitness boom, high energy prices, environmental awareness, and greater acceptance of bicycles as transportation all contributed to the increasing interest in cycling. Safe cycling infrastructure, therefore, offered the potential for more people to take up cycling for utilitarian ends. The consultant observed that since "bicycling into the downtown is a relatively 'hazardous' experience, it follows that there is considerable potential ... for increased numbers of bicycle trips into this area, particularly for work-related travel."

Barton-Aschman Limited reported that cyclists and motorists used the same roads for the same purposes – and at the same time of day. This observation, which explained the growing conflict over road space, was significant; indeed, had subsequent decision-makers, especially those preoccupied with keeping cyclists off arterials, paid attention, a lot of time squandered in futile debates about putting bike lanes where they "make sense" – usually in places out of the way of motorists and typically of little value to cyclists – could have been avoided.

Bloor Street ranked at the top among ten "corridors" assessed for cycling facilities. The consultant nonetheless recommended parallel Harbord and Wellesley Streets as the preferred east-west route, despite an obvious gap in continuity at Queen's Park and potential conflicts with buses along the route. The proposal was rationalized by a desire to maintain Bloor's arterial function for cars and to "ensure the continuing viability" of local businesses. (One more obvious barrier was that Bloor, as an arterial road, was actually under the authority of Metro Council.) The loss of on-street parking was assumed to put local shops at risk, although no supporting research was offered. (A study decades later arrived at precisely the opposite conclusion, showing that only 10 per cent to 20 per cent of customers at Bloor shops arrived by car.)

Many cyclists had another good reason to be disappointed with the consultant's final report, "Planning for Urban Cycling," because it recommended wider curb lanes instead of bike lanes. The wider curb lanes were generally to be created by restriping, narrowing the centre lanes, leaving extra space for cyclists in the curb lane. As to bike lanes, only Yonge Street, between Bloor and Queen Streets, which had also ranked among the best cycling corridors, was recommended, but only as one of three options for an ongoing study about a pedestrian mall. The consultant characterized the wider curb lanes as a "major re-allocation of space within the existing road surface." These "reallocations," although falling short of demarcated space, would, however, take more debate. Public Works Commissioner Bremner remained cranky about the initiative, complaining that the wider curb lanes on Harbord and Wellesley would adversely affect "traffic." (The wider curb lanes were not installed until the summer of 1981.)

In explaining the choice of wider curb lanes over bike lanes, Barton-Aschman pointed to a "significant disagreement about the value of on-street bike lanes in improving cycling safety." The consultant wasn't convinced that bike lanes could be justified as a safety advantage, or that they would increase cycling numbers. In fact, the consultant concluded that the city's narrow streets and small building setbacks meant that "the complete physical separation of bicycles and motor vehicles is, for practical purposes, impossible to achieve in downtown Toronto." The consultant had almost certainly been influenced by the heated debate in the United States, where the "integration" of cyclists into the flow of cars and trucks (soon to be known as vehicular cycling) was gaining support. The consultant concluded that cyclists were best accommodated when integrated with motor traffic, noting that "the road system should be designed to accommodate the legal operation of both bicycles and motor vehicles, providing safety and efficiency for both modes." The bicycle should not be given a "unique status."

Vehicular cycling soon came to be best known by its association with American John Forester, son of English writer C.S. Forester. In 1979, John Forester was the president of the League of American Wheelmen (before a subsequent falling out). His "Effective Cycling" skills-training program, which was published as a book in 1976, became the basis of many cycling education courses, including CAN-Bike and Toronto's "City Cycling Skills" booklet in the 1980s.

Sam the Safety Duck, a character created by the Ontario Ministry of Transportation and Communications, was likely an early admirer of the vehicular cycling approach. In public service announcements, Sam instructed young cyclists that "you don't ride a bike, you drive a bike." Sam's teaching encapsulated the vehicular cycling approach, articulated by Forester as, "Cyclists fare best when they act and are treated like drivers of vehicles." The ministry's public service message was that young cyclists are safe when they abide by the rules of the road and follow the advice in its bicyclists' handbook. Many parents watching Sam, wearing a construction helmet (bike helmets were not yet mandatory), riding a bike alongside heavy vehicles and amidst heavy tailpipe exhaust, would likely cringe at the sight.

Toronto's First Bike Lane – "Another Devastating Attack of the Anti-Car Blues"

In the late summer of 1979, the city installed its very first bike lane. The bike lane on Poplar Plains Road cost $2,000, measured about 600 metres in length, and ran up the ancient shore of Lake Iroquois, on a one-way street. The enabling by-law allowed motorists to use the bike lane to drop off and pick up passengers. Residents in the South Hill neighbourhood were likely the main beneficiaries of the new bikeway, which required the narrowing of the roadway from two lanes to one, thus taming the so-called Forest Hill Expressway, which got its name from motorists racing two abreast up the hill, then, upon arriving at St. Clair Avenue, following the guidance of a police officer to first turn right then left into wealthy Forest Hill.

Toronto's first bike lane, modest by virtually every measure, traumatized the *Toronto Star*. "There's a limit to bicycle lanes," declared an editorial, adding that it would "only exacerbate already intolerable traffic jams and pose a serious safety hazard." (The hazard at issue was that frustrated motorists might use the bike lane to skirt around other cars.) Indeed, the city was apparently suffering "yet another devastating attack of the anti-car blues." Of course, there were no other bike lanes, and little more than talk about future projects.

A GOOD START OR A LOST OPPORTUNITY

In 1979, cycling advocates were in a catch-22: to get bikeways, they had to show high cycling numbers, but to get such numbers, they needed safe roads. Governments might have accommodated cyclists with dedicated space as a way to capitalize on the potential benefits to the community of more cycling; instead, even politicians who sounded sympathetic to cycling were happy to find excuses for inaction, fearing the reaction of motorists to any tinkering with roads.

"I just hope it's not too late," Peter Kent of Bloor Cycle cautioned in 1974, referring to studies about cycling paths. Comparing Toronto to Europe, he added, "[W]e have fat reports and no bikeways." By the end of the decade, cyclists, whether they lived in Toronto or elsewhere in Metro, had more fat reports, but only a marginal increase in bikeways of any kind.

There were reasons to believe that the public was ahead of its politicians in the desire for safe roads for cycling. Even if it took the city a decade to build a functioning cycling system, wrote Rabbi W. Gunter Plaut, "10 years is a short time in the life of a city."

If progress towards a cycling-friendly city was measured in symbolic terms, there was more to celebrate: cycling had been revived among adults for everyday transportation; cycling activists had emerged across the city and Metro; there was some political and media support for safe bikeways; and the city, thanks to Hilda Tiessen, now had a delivery business that (again) relied solely on bikes. The bicycle was also generally accepted as part of the solution to urgent problems of smog, poor fitness, and dependence on foreign energy supplies.

The fight *against* the Spadina Expressway and the fight *for* streetcars and bicycles showed that the "traffic" planners' vision of a city with criss-crossing motorways wasn't the city of the people. The question was whether car-centred planning had become so deeply entrenched in government bureaucracies, corporate interests so deeply invested in the status quo, and social attitudes in the car-first narrative so ingrained that transforming the city into a place for people instead of cars, as Premier Davis had declared, was still possible – or whether inertia would continue to be confused with action.

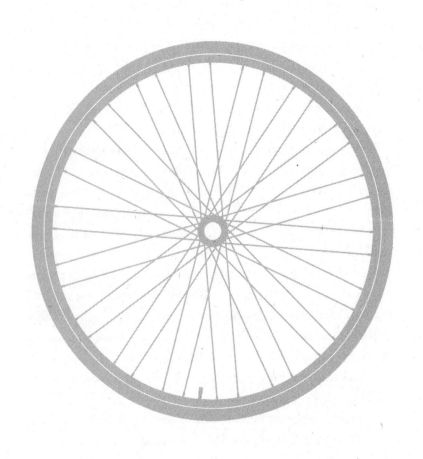

2019
A Changing City

October 7, 2019 – The cyclist and the climate crisis

The Bloor Viaduct is eerily deserted this morning but for a silent stream of westbound commuters on bikes heading downtown. The riders keep to the bike lane as if fearing a sudden return of the motor traffic that is usually roaring past, as it has for the past 100 years. A few cyclists, among them Lyn Adamson, are riding in the opposite direction to join a human barrier of climate activists blocking access to cars and trucks – part of a peaceful, coordinated global protest demanding action on the crisis. A year ago, the United Nations issued its most dire warning yet: without large cuts to greenhouse gas (GHG) emissions, eco-systems will begin collapsing in twelve, now eleven, years.

Adamson, a sixty-eight-year-old grandmother, can't be considered a radical anymore – even if her mane of untamed, grey-streaked hair suggests the part. Heat waves, floods, and ice storms are recent, collective experiences of climate change in the city. But if there is a way to rouse political leaders and the public from the current, somnambulant approach to the worsening situation, which has already turned millions of people around the world into refugees, it is by interfering with the apparently inalienable right to drive anywhere, anytime. Toronto's 1.3 million cars and trucks, and other vehicles entering from outside, are responsible for one-third of the city's GHG emissions – a burden that doesn't even include emissions from producing, refining, and transporting the fossil fuels that fill automobile tanks.

Adamson has been lending a helping hand to good causes for longer than some of her comrades at the barricades today have been alive. In fact, in the summer of 1980, she pitched in to help Hilda Tiessen's fledgling courier enterprise, before its run of success. But it was to a specific moment in 1994 that Adamson attributes her dedication to community activism and social justice. At a downtown intersection, the driver of a heavy truck started to turn right with Adamson, who was stopped on her bike, caught between the vehicle and a street pole. It was likely the sound of her bicycle basket being crushed that alerted the driver, sparing her from the long list of victims of turning trucks.

The persistence Adamson brings to her activism is reflected in the way she rides her bike. It was her stubborn determination to ride, instead of walk, her bike up one of the city's steepest inclines on her way home each day that resulted in a diagnosed case of knee strain that hobbled her for several months. Her only concession to the hill was to replace her heavy Dutch-style bike with a sportier, multi-geared model, purchased at a police auction. Her new bike, like the old one, is weighed down with panniers stuffed with the tools of the activist: flyers, petitions, a computer, and food provisions for volunteers.

Climate change has simply added to the reasons why Adamson rides a bicycle. As a child in the 1950s, her bicycle served as liberator from the spread-out distances of (then) small-town Pickering. In the 1970s, as a newcomer to Toronto, her bicycle offered a clean alternative to a city *often choked by smog; and as a single mother of two young children in the 1980s, her bike, with a trailer in tow, became an economical family travel option, hindered only by the disapproving looks of some adults.*

Lamenting what might have been had governments heeded early calls to climate action doesn't occupy much of Adamson's time. Her own band of ClimateFast volunteers won't give up or give in, despite often poorly attended events that might discourage less committed individuals. Two weeks ago, however, she helped organize the city's biggest-ever climate rally, inspired by sixteen-year-old Greta Thunberg whose lonely vigil on the steps of the Swedish Parliament has become a global movement. The rally easily counted 25,000 people, the crowd stretching from the steps of the Legislature to College Street.

Adamson doesn't have to call herself a cycling activist to support safer cycling conditions, just as cycling, pedestrian, transit, or other social justice advocates don't have to be climate activists to demand road safety and other improvements that will reduce GHG emissions. The city's, indeed, the planet's, problems are increasingly intertwined: solutions to one serving as solutions to the other.

A CITY *OF* CYCLISTS, NOT *FOR* CYCLISTS

By 2019, Toronto was (again) becoming a city *of* cyclists, even if it was still a long way from being a city *for* cyclists. In most parts of Toronto, which since amalgamation in January 1998 included all the former Metro municipalities, cycling had increased – not because of new infrastructure but despite its absence, or dubious quality where it did exist.

North of midtown Eglinton Avenue, there was an area the size of Guelph with no cycling infrastructure. Even the southern end of the Poplar Plains bike lane still lacked any direct connection to the St. George Street bike lane; instead, cyclists were directed by a small sign atop a utility pole to turn right and proceed 80 metres, where they were left stranded – four chaotic motor traffic lanes between them and the top of the bike lane. An alternate southbound bike lane route was often blocked by motorists queuing for a car wash.

The greatest number of cyclists, given the absence of safe infrastructure, remained in the category of potential riders, despite distances that were easily cycled. The implementation of bike lanes remained piecemeal; studies masqueraded as action.

By the end of 2019, Toronto's inventory of bike lanes (including cycle tracks, boulevard level paths, and contra-flow lanes) had barely surpassed 150 kilometres, covering less than 2 per cent of the city's 5,600-kilometre road network. In the almost half century since the beginning of the Bicycle Revival, as many cyclists had died on Toronto roads as the kilometres of bike lanes installed. City councillors in 2019 who had been in office since the days when slavish devotion to motorists was considered a prerequisite to electoral success could treat the failure of the bike plan as a win for motorists, and, therefore, for themselves.

A University of Toronto report in 2019 characterized the city's safe cycling routes as "isolated and disconnected islands." In the city's road hierarchy, cycling safety still ranked somewhere below motorist travel times, left-turn lanes, right-turn lanes, and car parking, despite a Vision Zero road safety plan, first adopted in 2016, that prioritized human life "over all other objectives within all aspects of the transportation system." The Vision Zero approach at least ended the long-standing myth of the safe car, conceding that exhortations to care, courtesy, and law-abiding behaviour were insufficient; instead, planners now needed to anticipate mistakes by road users with good road design, including measures such as separated bike lanes. Carmakers themselves implicitly acknowledged that cars were inherently dangerous, promising a new panacea: driverless cars that were infallible – a promise that came too late for the 300,000 people who had died in automobile crashes on Canadian roads.

In the four decades since 1979, utilitarian cycling had increased fairly steadily both in real numbers and in the share of road traffic. By 2019, a Nanos Research survey – the newest of the cycling surveys conducted for the city every decade since 1999 – confirmed the growing number of cyclists, with city-wide cycling activity now resembling numbers reported by Barton-Aschman in the 1970s for the old city. Seventy per cent of respondents to the 2019 survey reported being either utilitarian or recreational cyclists, compared to 54 per cent in 2009, and 48 per cent in 1999. Overall in the city, the number of utilitarian cyclists – those who used their bikes for at least some trips to go to work, school, shop, or visit – had jumped to 44 per cent in 2019, or about one million adults (age fifteen and over), from 20 per cent or 388,000 people in 1999. By comparison, one of the earliest bicycle surveys in the city, conducted in 1986 by Ryerson Polytechnic Institute (now Toronto Metropolitan University), showed numbers for utilitarian cycling at far lower levels, estimating that the former Metro Toronto had 100,000 utilitarian cyclists, among which 40,000 were in the (old) City of Toronto.

The 2019 survey confirmed a city-wide change, reporting that suburban residents were only marginally less likely to be utilitarian cyclists than residents of the older parts of the city – ranging from a low of 40 per cent in North York to 49 per cent for the Old City and East York. Safety on roads, however, remained a top concern for cyclists and would-be cyclists. But the number of residents who would never consider cycling even with bike lanes in place had dropped to 20 per cent.

Surveys in Toronto showed majority support – even among motorists and even in the former suburban municipalities – for improved cycling infrastructure and better road safety, although City Hall remained slow to catch on, or to catch up. Council incumbents generally retained their seats as long as they wished, instead of as long as their ideas remained current and in tune with the changing city.

In the downtown, where the population had surged, walking and cycling accounted for more than 40 per cent of trips to work. In some suburban areas, condo building booms were increasing population density, ensuring that the utility of the bicycle – and walking and transit – was no longer a downtown phenomenon. Since 2016, the Etobicoke-Lakeshore ward, including Humber Bay Shores, saw the city's third-highest population growth. The growth was in residential towers, instead of single-family homes in sprawling neighbourhoods where travel by car dominated. It was likely no coincidence that in the October 2022 municipal election, a young candidate, for whom road safety trumped traditional concerns about the convenience of motorists, defeated an incumbent of twenty years.

The mode share (the breakdown of travel by the means used, namely, walking, cycling, driving, or transit) for cycling across the mega-city had risen to 2.7 per cent by 2016 – a substantial increase over 2011, a mere five years earlier, and more than double the number in 1991 for what was then Metro. (The absence of safe cycling infrastructure in most of the city served as the backdrop for the numbers.) In some neighbourhoods, the mode share for commuters showed that the bicycle had come to rival the car. In Cabbagetown, cycling accounted for 34 per cent of trips, and 26 to 33 per cent in other central city neighbourhoods. Downtown streets where bike lanes had been installed saw the biggest increases in cycling – by 50 per cent on Bloor Street West, and by 1,000 per cent on Richmond-Adelaide.

By 2019, a Ministry of Transportation analysis for Toronto estimated that 55 per cent of trips to work and to school – by persons over the age of fifteen for work, and over the age of eleven for school – were made on foot, by bike, and on transit. An Ekos Research survey in 2019 reported that 59 per cent of city residents identified walking, cycling, and transit as their main mode of transportation, reflecting an ongoing trend away from cars, distinguishing Toronto from the rest of Ontario where car trips outnumbered other modes by 4 to 1. Twenty-eight per cent of Toronto households didn't own a car at all. The human population in the city was again growing faster than the car population, reversing a post–Second World War trend that saw the number of people per car consistently drop (or the number of cars per capita increase). And when some business leaders proposed yet another expansion to Highway 401 in 2018 – to add a second deck – the idea was quickly ridiculed in public debate.

The transportation priorities, preferences, and values of the people of the amalgamated megacity were starting to resemble those of the pre-amalgamated old City of Toronto.

Slowly, even minimum car parking requirements became the subject of scrutiny. For years, minimum parking requirements devoured public and private space and disfigured the city to serve the car. In some new buildings, the requirements were relaxed in return for additional bicycle parking or bike-sharing stations. (In 2021, the city eliminated minimum parking requirements for new residential developments.)

The story of bike lanes on Bloor Street – which had become a virtual rallying cry for cyclists – made the frustrating pace of action to accommodate cyclists starkly obvious. When other advocates and I formed Bells on Bloor (now part of the Community Bikeways coalition) in 2007, our aim was to demonstrate the strength of the demand for bike lanes – and a glimpse of what our city would look like with more cyclists on Bloor and other roads. We organized family-oriented, "pedal-powered" parades which quickly grew from 500 riders in 2007 to 2,000 in 2009, but what our "nice" approach didn't achieve – except for a brief moment in 2009, when the chair of the cycling committee prematurely announced installation – was bike lanes. We augmented our parades with a variety of community initiatives that ranged from building community alliances to court actions. In October 2013, recognizing that the city lacked the vision or ambiton needed for a complete east-west bikeway – despite its vital place in a true cycling network – we proposed a pilot bike lane along a particularly heavily cycled stretch of Bloor Street adjacent to the University of Toronto. Who could possibly oppose such a short bike lane?

Approval of the pilot as permanent came in November 2017, but only after an exhausting community mobilization, the expenditure of significant political capital by a second generation of Laytons (Mike) and Cressys (Joe) on council, and what the city's transportation manager agreed was the most comprehensively studied road project in North America. (By the end of 2023, a complete cross-town bikeway was within sight, while several installed or approved extensions made Bloor-Danforth the city's longest bike lane at 21 kilometres.)

The same attributes that made bicycles well suited to cities – quiet, clean, and small – also made them easy to ignore. In fact, thirty-five years after consultant Barton-Aschman emphasized the importance of bike counts (reiterated in the city's 2001 bike plan), the city's efforts had merely improved to mediocre, from lethargic. If "what you count is what you care [about]" was true, cyclists understood their place. Cycling groups did their own counts, although not always convincing politicians. After a week-long, video-recorded count on Bloor Street in 2017 showed a daily average of over 6,000 cyclists, one councillor suggested it might just be cyclists circling the block.

FOUR DECADES SINCE THE BICYCLE REVIVAL - WHAT HAPPENED?

Macho Militants and the 1980s

Despite City Hall's adoption of wider curb lanes as the preferred option over bike lanes, as recommended in the final Barton-Aschman report, and consistent with the vehicular cycling approach, it took until mid-1981 simply to install the wider curb lanes recommended for the east-west Harbord-Wellesley route. In fact, the installation left a short gap between Queen's Park Circle and a car parking lot on Tower Road at the University of Toronto. The gap was considered necessary so as not to interfere with university staff driving to the lot. To connect to Wellesley Street (located further south), eastbound cyclists were obliged to use Tower Road, passing behind its diagonal parking slots, then, at the Hart House Soldier's Tower, navigating their way through students rushing to class. (In 2023, Tower Road was turned into a pedestrian walkway.) Public Works Commissioner Bremner still found reasons to oppose, for evolving reasons, wider curb lanes, including the fact that some motorists on Harbord treated them as an opportunity to try to pass slower motorists. One cycling committee member suggested that "the poor design was intended to demonstrate that cyclists couldn't be accommodated," while another rider described the poor pavement near the curb as "a veritable death trap." Most cyclists still preferred parallel Bloor Street.

While Toronto's first bike lane in 1979 had suggested the city was ready to accommodate its cycling residents, that notion ended as abruptly as the Poplar Plains bike lane. In fact, there were no bike lanes built in Toronto during the 1980s, nor, of course, on any arterial road under Metro authority or on any secondary road in the other Metro municipalities.

By the early 1980s, the lack of progress was partly due to cycling advocates, including most members of the City Cycling Committee, who were opposed to bike lanes. The influence of the vehicular cycling (or integration) approach imported from the United States in the 1970s had continued to grow in Toronto, drowning out other cycling voices. Who could be more effective advocating against bike lanes than cycling advocates themselves? The vehicular cycling approach was also the preferred approach of many planners, while pro-cycling politicians were spared from having to take unpopular positions calling for the reallocation of road space.

The city's second bike planner, David McCluskey, hired in 1984, was a vehicular cyclist, as was his successor Dan Egan – until his conversion to bike lane proponent later in the decade. When the *City Cyclist* published articles about bike lanes, which wasn't often, it was by contributors who dismissed them, content with the "prevailing view among North American bicycle planners ... that cyclists can be safely integrated with traffic."

John Forester, the American engineer who was the most prominent champion of vehicular cycling, continued, with increasing evangelical zeal, his teachings against bike lanes, declaring that cyclists were equals to motorists, and, with proper skills, safe amidst motor traffic. He exhorted cyclists to avoid submitting to a "cyclist-inferiority phobia" or seeking refuge on bikeways, promoted by motorist-dominated institutions and leading to "incompetent, childish and fearful cycling." Forester's arguments were especially appealing to the most skilled and experienced cyclists, who were also the most confident and convincing advocates. The fact that vehicular cyclists were predominantly male and generally young prompted the "macho militants" tag. Vehicular cycling recognized, even celebrated, how seasoned cyclists already rode – unapologetically and confidently alongside cars and trucks.

In Toronto, vehicular cycling had the added benefit of offering a concise rejection of Metro's policy of moving cyclists from arterial roads onto off-road trails. "Bicycles Belong" (on roads) was the title of a prominent cycling committee campaign. Vehicular cycling also offered an expedient way forward at a time when attempts to transform the road system for the benefit of cyclists posed a daunting challenge. But vehicular cyclists didn't consider their approach as a compromise or interim step – it was the end goal.

Forester's comprehensive *Effective Cycling*, including practices such as "taking the lane" or making left turns from the centre of the road – techniques still accepted (and legal) but unappealing to many riders – became the template for cycling skills courses developed at City Hall. There was an obvious benefit to learning these skills, whether the student supported vehicular cycling or not.

Bike lanes remained a preferred approach across much of Europe, and among many advocates in Montreal (perhaps because of the stronger European influence) – and on the tourism pages of local papers, where they were celebrated as attractions. Bike lanes also retained some, albeit less vocal, support in Toronto, as shown in a 1980 survey by Ryerson Polytechnic Institute for the Ontario

Ministry of Energy. Another Ryerson report, for the City Cycling Committee in 1986, similarly ranked the lack of bike lanes among the top concerns of utilitarian cyclists. But survey responses at least partly depended on how questions were framed. "Do you want bike lanes?" wasn't the type of question that a cycling committee survey at the time was likely to ask or emphasize, amidst "father knows best" attitudes among many vehicular cyclists. Another survey in 1989 reported that 64 per cent of respondents, among respondents who did not cycle to work, would be encouraged to commute by bike if there were bike lanes. By 1989, Toronto Public Health and council's Healthy City Office needed no more convincing about the need for bike lanes; the latter group urged council to "adopt as a high priority the development of a network of on-street bike lanes."

The vehicular cycling approach stifled the growth of cycling in the city. What appeal, especially among people interested in taking up cycling, was there in a rallying cry for the right to cycle alongside cars and trucks? Lyn Adamson concluded that vehicular cycling held back cycling in the city. "It's not about me ... it's about new people, it's about people who have just moved to the city, it's about families, it's about little kids feeling confident about getting to school safely in traffic."

There was nothing insincere about vehicular cyclists' commitment or passion for cycling, but the experience offered a cautionary tale about what can happen when those who speak for "cyclists" or the "cycling community" represent a particular type of rider, but not necessarily a broader audience of potential riders. The issue also highlighted a problem with using a cycling committee model, which remains in place in various Ontario cities. Cycling committee members, as city appointees, were assured of a platform and credibility for their views, even if those views were not validated in the broader community. Would applicants have been appointed to the committee at the time after an interview with committee leaders and associated city and political staff – or even bothered to apply – had they championed bike lanes?

A shift away from the vehicular cycling approach at City Hall began soon after Dan Egan, among others from the city, attended the 1989 Velo-City conference in Copenhagen. The trip was an awakening for Egan, convincing him that the type of urban trans-formation that he and other planners desired wasn't going to hap-pen by integrating cyclists with motor traffic. After Egan returned to Toronto, the city soon began to show, as it had with expressways and streetcars, that it could chart a course different from that dic-tated by thinking imported from the United States.

Most cycling committee initiatives during the 1980s were consist-ent with vehicular cycling: skills training programs, a "Safety Grid" of bicycle routes, the replacement of sewer grates, bike parking, and campaigns such as the "Road Warrior" to promote law-abid-ing conduct by cyclists to buttress their right to be treated as equal road partners. In January 1985, the committee held the "Confer-ence on Cycling and the Law" to further legitimize the cyclist's place on the road. Conference recommendations included changes, later implemented, to the HTA to recognize bikes as legal road vehicles (although this was likely already the law) and a legal obligation for cy-clists stopped by police for road infractions to identify themselves – a change that did not stop bike licensing proponents from continu-ing to assert that police had no way of identifying riders believed to have broken the law. Other conference recommendations included cycling instruction in schools (a matter of provincial jurisdiction), which was especially important in a context where many parents had little experience in utilitarian cycling. (As a twelve-year-old, I once had the clever idea of cycling against the flow of motor traffic on the busy arterial, Tecumseh Road, in Windsor, Ontario, where I grew up, on the assumption that I would be safer seeing approaching cars. I was quickly dissuaded by honking car horns.) But instead of acting on this and similar calls for cycling skills education, politicians were often more eager to lament the lack of skills and promote false solutions such as licensing regimes, which are almost uniformly devoid of any cycling-instruction component.

Sewer grates remained a cycling committee priority, while the city's replacement pace remained leisurely, with a spending plan that would see all grates replaced by 2041. In July 1984, Councillor Jack Layton asked council to approve painted warnings around grates as an interim measure. Despite a paltry $13,000 cost, councillors rejected his motion, worried about potential liability from acknowledging the danger. Days later, police reported the death (which occurred a number of days after the crash) of an eleven-year-old Parkdale boy, apparently after getting his tire stuck in a grate. Council reversed its earlier decision, after public pressure and an intervention by Ontario's Attorney General Roy McMurtry. Council also agreed to an accelerated replacement schedule. Ironically, and despite the danger of grates (the public works chair himself had been hit by a car while skirting around a grate), by the time of the inquest, the investigating officer revised his original report, concluding that the boy's fall was caused by his attempt to mount the curb, an opinion accepted by the jury. It would take another fifteen years to replace most sewer grates, by which time the fad for skinny-tired ten-speeds had passed.

Cyclists also got a made-in-Toronto curbside "ring-and-post" lock-up, which was so successful, increasing from a few dozen in

1984 to 6,800 by 2001, that it provoked a minor controversy about who should be credited for its invention. City Hall also distributed cycling maps, supplementing cycling guidebooks. Fred Gardiner's 1985 *Ten Bike Tours in and around Toronto* proved there were Fred Gardiners who loved bikes more than cars and expressways. To get from City Hall to the lake, this Gardiner cautioned that "if it is a weekday, and you are not an extremely experienced urban-cyclist, you'd better walk." (Walking remained the safer option even thirty years later.)

The 1990s - A Bike Lane Bounce

The cycling committee's position on bike lanes changed in tune with Egan's conversion, although some of its members remained loyal to vehicular cycling. American cycling advocates were among the most fervent disciples of this approach; one visitor to Toronto in the 1990s derided a local advocate as a "murderer" for her group's support of bike lanes, given the asserted danger to cyclists. Forester (who died in 2020 at the age of ninety) himself never wavered, although he acknowledged in the seventh edition of *Effective Cycling* in 2012 that the vehicular cyclist was "alone in the world."

In the 1990s until amalgamation, the City of Toronto saw a bike lane–building spurt not again matched in terms of useful routes (until the pandemic), spurred by dynamic public servants, bike-friendly councillors, and a relatively supportive council, all invigorated by a blossoming grassroots movement. A 1993 petition for bike lanes, when petitions still required a pen and paper, garnered almost 28,000 signatures. In 1993 alone, Toronto City Council approved nine kilometres of bike lanes. Between 1993 and the end of 1997, the city (then one-sixth of its current size) installed over

20 kilometres of new bike lanes, on secondary streets over which it had jurisdiction, including College-Gerrard, St. George-Beverley, Sherbourne, Harbord, and Davenport (the longest of the bike lanes at 3.4 km, including its extension under the CPR tracks at Dupont, despite vigorous opposition to the narrowed passage for cars). Cycling staff might still have felt like "a mouse in the room" – as manager Dan Egan had once considered his unit within the giant transportation bureaucracy – but the mouse was now energized. Even a decade earlier, when the city's first bike planner was hired, Joan Doiron had remarked, "There are about 1,000 people down here (at City Hall) serving the automobile, so why not one for cyclists as well?"

In March 1994, *Cyclometer* suggested that cyclists might "expect to see two or three new bike lane routes in the City every year for the next decade." (*Cyclometer*, soon to be distributed by a new medium, the internet, replaced the *City Cyclist* as the City Cycling Committee's publication in November 1989.)

After a number of cyclist fatalities in 1996, Councillor Jack Layton, who had run unsuccessfully for mayor in 1991, called for 1,000 kilometres of new bikeways, declaring he would "not rest until we have bike lanes on a complete grid of Metro arterial roads." His declaration found voice, but not action, in the post-amalgamation city's 2001 bike plan.

Ironically, the first bike lane installed within the boundaries of the city was on a Metro road despite Metro's "policy," based loosely on the Strok & Associates report, of moving cyclists onto trails. The installation was the result of fortuitous circumstances. In 1990, after the City of Toronto hired a consultant to identify "spines" for a bike network, staff saw an immediate opportunity in a Metro road project on the Prince Edward Viaduct. The consultant's data convinced Metro that the crossing was wide enough for a bike lane with no loss of motor vehicle capacity. (The width of the Viaduct induced many motorists to speed, increasing the danger to cyclists.) By early 1991, a 1.6-kilometre bike lane on Bloor Street from the east side of the Viaduct at Broadview Avenue to Sherbourne Street was in place. Cycling numbers surged, reaching 2,200 per day, more than doubling pre-installation figures and reaching 3,100 daily in 1993. The phrase "Build it, and they will come" was born, generally repeated as a *eureka* moment, despite its predictablility, after each subsequent installation.

The consultant then returned to the task at hand, recommending a number of bike lanes on roads over which the city had jurisdiction, but also recommending that Metro install, by 1993, a Bloor-Danforth bike lane, describing it as "an ideal east-west route spanning the entire city," which, at the time, meant from Victoria Park Road in the east to the Humber River in the west. The proposal wasn't just wishful thinking; the consultant had interpreted Metro's installation of the Viaduct bike lane and its engagement in the consultant's study as evidence of a willingness to rethink old ways. The cross-town bike lane envisioned by the consultant would take another three decades.

Toronto City Hall proved to be a more receptive audience than Metro Hall for the consultant's recommendations. In 1990, Queen's Quay got a short bike lane (to close a gap in the waterfront trail), followed by a southbound, downhill bike lane corollary for Poplar Plains. The latter installation might have been more noteworthy had the local councillor's proposal for a protected bike lane, akin to ones in European cities, been accepted. Ironically, the councillor, Howard Levine, had never ridden a bicycle, the result of a childhood ban imposed by his parents, who were fearful of the road danger in 1950s Toronto.

A novel clearway on Bay Street was also created, with the curb lane restricted to buses, taxis and bikes, but undermined by motorists' routine incursions. In August 1997, even Harbord got a bike lane despite the local Business Improvement Area's opposition articulated as "no bike lanes, period." The city's new bike lanes quickly saw increases in cycling traffic as high as 42 per cent, with little impact on motor traffic volumes. A manager in the city's transportation department wrote, "Perhaps for the first time in North America since the invention of the automobile, road space for motor vehicles is being reallocated to bicycles." He presumably put little stock in the wider curb lanes created in the 1980s.

Sue Zielinski, hired as the city's bicycle commuter coordinator, launched a dizzying array of cycling initiatives while helping to create, fund (with monies from other levels of government), and support a variety of community groups. In 1993, Transportation Options, a non-profit she helped to create (and that still exists today, though focused on other objectives), organized the second annual international Auto-Free Cities Conference that was held in Toronto. In 1995, Transportation Options established Detour Publications (a viable enterprise until Amazon appeared) to publish and distribute sustainable transportation materials, including its own journal, *Trans-Mission*, and the newsletter *Bikes Mean Business*. Zielinski likely brushed up against the boundaries of her official role with what resembled community activism and advocacy, although her job description of building community capacity for cycling insulated her. Toronto was also still brave enough to be different, not as much as in the 1970s under Crombie and Sewell, but still willing to lead, unlike the post-amalgamation period when leadership came to mean following the lead of other cities.

By 1995, a program was needed, literally, to distinguish the long list of sustainable transportation groups – the number likely stretching the strength of the underlying grassroots movement. Song Cycles, led by a skilled choir master, was among the new groups, its advocacy including adapting lyrics, such as those of a Macedonian folk song, to explain how to change a flat tire. In 1995, when *Bicycling Magazine* recognized Toronto as North America's "Number 1 Cycling City" for its "impressive blend of programs, ridership and natural amenities" and its dynamic and diverse cycling community, the award reflected Zielinski's contributions.

Where bike lanes were installed, cyclists were, however, reminded of their subordinate rank in the transportation hierarchy. A section of one bike lane was converted each evening to car parking for patrons at an upscale restaurant, while a section of the northbound St. George Street lane was moved to a parallel (less direct) route. The Carlton Street bike lane, along the College-Carlton route, was removed and placed on parallel Gerrard Street despite a musical entreaty by the bicycle choir at City Hall and one commentator's summary of merchants' complaints: "Business sucked then [before the installation] and it still sucks now." The merchants succeeded despite evidence that their petition included false names added by an employee motivated by a cash prize.

Prior to amalgamation in January 1998, the only other Metro municipality that installed a bike lane (the Eglinton bikeway was a Metro initiative) was the City of Etobicoke, under Mayor Doug Holyday, on a stretch of Royal York Road, between Dundas Street and Lawrence Avenue. The installation was likely motivated as a traffic-calming measure demanded by local residents. Holyday was later elected to the newly amalgamated City Council (then succeeded in 2014 by his son Stephen, a vehement opponent of most bike lanes).

By 1993, even Metro Hall acknowledged that "the public attitude towards the bicycle as a mode of transportation has changed
dramatically." There had always been a lot of bicycles in Metro: a
1993 study estimated that there were 1.46 million adult bicycles
in Metro, exceeding the number of cars, and approaching the per
capita number of bikes in (West) Germany. But the road danger
kept most bicycles in storage lockers, garages, and basements, or
on balconies, except for recreation.

In July of that year, Metro Councillor Olivia Chow convinced
Metro to establish its own Pedestrian and Cycling Committee (su-
perceding the grassroots Metro by Cycle). A staff report, "Review
of Bicycle Facilities in Metro Toronto," then proposed a network
of bikeways, including bike trails, bike lanes (subject to sufficient
road width), and wider curb lanes, the latter estimated to be feasible with re-striping on 69 per cent of arterial roads. The report
offered the assurance that bikeways would not be created "at the
expense of other users of the road," namely, motorists. Metro's
transportation commissioner, Doug Floyd (who cycling activists nicknamed Pink Floyd, after the rock band, to chide him for
his conservative views) nonetheless had reservations, ominously
warning that more bike lanes would mean less car lanes and concluding, "I don't have to tell you the implications of that."

It soon became clear that Metro Council's idea of accommodat-
ing cyclists was to copy the City of Toronto's wider curb lane approach of the early 1980s, despite the absence of evidence of actual
safety benefits for cyclists. At a committee debate for the report,
a cycling advocate mocked council's preference as "a wide curb
lane in every pot." Councillors reacted angrily to the ridicule of
their apparently well-meaning initiative. Some councillors threatened to do nothing with the budgeted funds; another councillor

proposed that cyclists should be licensed. A compromise was nonetheless worked out by which the input of cycling advocates would be sought before any monies were spent. Little came of the report, or the compromise, save for a segment of Danforth Avenue from Broadview Avenue to Pape Avenue that did get a wider curb lane in 1995.

During the rest of the 1990s until amalgamation, Metro installed a number of truncated bike lanes, largely on bridges that had surplus motor traffic capacity (as had been the case with the Viaduct). A short bike lane installed at Metro's north-eastern frontier on Steeles Avenue in the course of road widening-work was notable only for its absurdity: the area was (and is) dominated by farms. Road signs (still) warn motorists about deer crossings.

Queen's Park, which had jurisdiction over road safety and education, took little interest in cycling (even for education in schools), and when it did, it was usually to focus on cyclists' heads, instead of the safety of the roads. When *Maclean's* in 1993 suggested that the province was "taking the bicycle more seriously," it was for a proposed helmet law, which did nothing to actually prevent crashes. The question "Was the cyclist wearing a helmet?" became a convenient explanation – disguised as a question – for a road crash that injured a cyclist. Helmets later became mandatory for cyclists under the age of eighteen – and subsequently for riders of electric bikes. (One of the province's greatest contributions to cycling came years later, when the last of Ontario's coal-fired power plants was closed. Smog had long been among city cyclists' top complaints, and a deterrent to cycling.)

While cyclists in the city saw improvements in the 1990s, the cyclist's old friend, the TTC, started the decade with a bang, but went out with a whimper. In 1993, Queen's Park, under NDP

Premier Bob Rae, announced $3 billion in funding to build new transit lines at a time when the TTC was experiencing declines in ridership across Metro. The automobile mode share had reached 68 per cent. Subways were to be built along Eglinton, Lawrence, and Sheppard Avenues; in fact, excavation along Eglinton (west of Allen Road) started in the fall of 1993, then came to an abrupt end after the election of Conservative Premier Mike Harris in 1995. The excavation was filled in, and $100 million in spending along with it. (The project started again sixteen years later, as the Eglinton Crosstown LRT, much of it underground, but, after long delays, still not operational by the end of 2023.)

Post-Amalgamation 1998 - Plans, Platitudes, and Pancakes

There could be no doubt that amalgamation in January 1998, which had been imposed on Metro's constituent municipalities by Queen's Park under Premier Mike Harris, was part of an effort to temper the influence of the City of Toronto. One of the things that the premier certainly wanted to temper – as did Premier Doug Ford after his election in 2018 – was the higher priority the city gave to people on foot, bikes, and transit at the expense of the motorist. Amalgamation would ensure the watering down of political influence of the city with the more car-centric politics – and greater populations – of the suburban municipalities. This was bad news for the person on a bicycle at the very time when the old city had begun embracing bike lanes as a necessary safety measure.

In this context, it was perhaps a surprise that in July 2001, the new city – with former North York mayor Mel Lastman in the mayor's chair – got an ambitious bike plan, "Shifting Gears." The impressive document setting out the plan was the product of two years of study involving city staff, consulting firms, and public consultations, laying out a network of precisely 1,004 kilometres of bikeways, including 460 kilometres of new bike lanes. The numbers had a striking resemblance to those proposed by Jack Layton in 1996. It quickly became clear, however, that the city had no plan to implement the plan – or the vision of creating "*a safe, comfortable, and bicycle friendly environment in Toronto*" (italics in original). At the time, the vast new mega-city had 166 kilometres of bikeways, comprised of 46 kilometres of bike lanes, largely located in the former City of Toronto, plus signed "bike routes," and 110 kilometres of off-road bike trails.

Council was careful to qualify its approval as "in principle," which meant that virtually every planned bike lane would return to council for further debate prior to installation. The plan offered a "pragmatic approach" – with "minimal impacts on other road users" – to avoid drawn out battles over bike lanes on arterial roads. All parts of the amalgamated city were treated as equally deserving of bikeways, an approach accomplished by overlaying a grid of bikeways on the city, satisfying political objectives of fairness but ignoring potential demand and patterns of usage. Many cycling advocates recognized the plan's shortcomings, but were willing to trade their reservations for action.

The plan's first phase focused on creating bike lane "spines," spaced at four kilometres (to become two kilometres in the second phase) and linked to major trails. The plan, to run from 2002 to 2011, included phase two bikeways to bridge barriers such as Highway 400. The plan addressed a wide range of issues, including cycling education, lower motor speeds, separation of pedestrians from cyclists on trails, improved road lighting, and snow clearing on bikeways. The practice of terminating bike lanes prior to intersections was to be reviewed. Even climate change got attention.

While the scope of the plan was grand, the post-amalgamation Pedestrian and Cycling Infrastructure Unit was not – in fact, it counted only four staff, including Egan as manager, to implement cycling *and* pedestrian projects and programs across the vast city. The plan's implementation was further undermined by a lack of money, and minimal support within the bureaucracy and among politicians outside the city core. In 2002, year one of the plan, zero bike lanes were installed – and over the following five years, barely five kilometres per year, far short of the 46 kilometres per year envisioned in the plan.

The election of David Miller as successor to Mel Lastman in November 2003 suggested the bike plan might get a jolt of energy, but Miller's credentials as a downtown intellectual and environmentalist likely constrained action for fear of arousing suburban suspicions, especially among motorists anxious about their exulted place on *public* roads. Miller generally avoided policies that might provoke motorists, although his $60 motor vehicle tax was an exception that assured him of lasting enemies. He blamed the lack of progress on the bike plan on councillors who fought every proposal, but he also had to deal with a post-amalgamation bureaucracy still populated by the same Metro transportation planners that Councillor Jack Layton once mocked as "expressway crazy, addicted to the car."

Decisions about where to install bike lanes were usually reached by a process of elimination: once useful routes along arterials were eliminated from consideration to avoid enraging motorists, cyclists got what was left over. Public opposition, typically from motorists, was often framed as "we're not against cycling," consistent with its obvious benefits, "but not here." The *right* place, if actually identified, was usually a place where the bike lane had little value for cyclists. In theory, the bike lane stubs, or orphaned lanes, that were built would make sense when connections were added, but the connections rarely materialized. The plan's execution resembled a paint-by-numbers kit – first the blues, then the yellows, and someday, depending on the diligence of the painter (City Hall), the final image would emerge. The new lanes could not even be characterized as better than nothing, because little-used bike lanes were easy targets for frustrated motorists stuck in traffic jams of their own making.

While cyclists didn't get bike lanes where they needed them, they got them in curious places, such as Esther Shiner Boulevard. At the opening ceremony for this road, the late Esther Shiner's convertible – made famous by a photo of her and then North York mayor Mel Lastman celebrating the opening of a short portion of the Spadina Expressway in 1978 – was parked directly on the bike lane. The new 350-metre-long bike lane was interrupted by dangerous car and truck turning channels into a giant IKEA parking lot. By 2019 much of the bike lane had simply faded away. On parallel high-speed Sheppard Avenue, which offered a superior route, the only nod to cyclists was a warning to keep off the sidewalk.

In early 2009, during Miller's second term, City Council appeared ready to make up for lost time by pushing a cross-town Bloor-Danforth bikeway. (To that point the notable successes had largely been limited to off-road bike trails on the Finch and Gatineau Hydro Corridors.) The imminent release of a feasibility study led the cycling committee chair, Councillor Adrian Heaps, to announce that the project would proceed, with portions of Danforth, given its ample width, potentially in place by year's end. Cyclists celebrated, only to see Heaps back down after pressure from local councillors, incited by local merchants. Instead of action, a new study was announced, later converted into a $500,000 environmental assessment (EA) – a cumbersome process that was soon to become a de facto prerequisite for bike lanes on arterial roads, despite the dubious legal foundation and comic implications of studying the environmental impacts of a bike lane.

The planned transformation of Bloor in Yorkville, along the posh Mink Mile shopping district, offered another opportunity to move forward on Bloor-Danforth bike lanes. Cycling advocates demanded that the city reclassify the project to require scrutiny under EA provisions, including the failure to address cyclists' safety. The city's refusal provoked advocates to intervene in a court challenge against the project. The city again prevailed. The absurd result was that the city didn't have to assess the environmental impacts of a road project without a bike lane, but it would assess the environmental impacts of a road project with a bike lane.

The years 2008 and 2009 were noteworthy for the bike plan, at least in padding installation numbers. Little used bike lanes, undermined by the absence of useful connections, on two Scarborough arterials, Birchmount Road and Pharmacy Avenue, became a flash point for motorists' anger, even though staff reports showed little increase in driving travel times. The Scarborough lanes were a sobering experience for both Scarborough councillor Adrian Heaps, then chair of the cycling advisory committee, and city cycling staff, prompting a new approach, articulated in the 2009 report, *Changing Gears*, that shifted the planning focus to creating a connected network of bike lanes built outward from the downtown.

The new approach had little benefit for Heaps. The challenger for his Scarborough council seat made the controversial bike lanes

Image 34: "Good fences make good neighbors." In 2008, the Safe Cycling Coalition challenged the city's failure to consider a bike lane, pursuant to provincial direction, in its rebuilding of Bloor Street in Yorkville,. The court dismissed the case. Precisely a year later, a stand-off between a cyclist and the province's former attorney general turned deadly. It's impossible to know if the tragedy would have been averted had a bike lane been in place, but poet Robert Frost's line was worth noting. From left to right: the author (pro bono lawyer for the group), Martin Reis (ARC), Margaret Hastings James, and Take the Tooker's Angela Bischoff and Hamish Wilson. (Photo: Martin Reis)

a wedge issue, her campaign literature shouting, "NO MORE BIKE LANES on Busy Streets in Scarborough."

When Miller's term concluded at the end of 2010, there were only 84 kilometres of new bike lanes, less than 20 per cent of the original target, to show for the 2001 bike plan. While the bike plan had achieved little to improve cycling, it had served politicians well, providing them with a plausible response when residents demanded bike lanes along popular cycling routes: "It's not in the bike plan." The ten-year time frame of the plan also ensured there was little political accountability: by the time the plan's failure was undeniable, the original committee chairs, even the mayor, would have moved on. Cyclists in the city could nonetheless continue to count on City Hall for platitudes about the value of cycling, official maps of bikeways, and a steady supply of pancakes at the end of the annual Bike to Work ride.

While there was little to celebrate in terms of cycling improvements, the city was celebrated for a particularly notorious bicycle thief, dubbed by a *New York Times* journalist as the "unofficial world champion of bike thieves." By 2008, Igor Kenk, owner of a Queen Street bike repair shop, had amassed 2,800 stolen bikes, warehoused (and individually numbered) in various locations. At the time, the actual number of bike thefts in the city could only be guessed; most people did not bother reporting them, relying on a lock as the first and last line of defence. Recovery rates for stolen bikes were dismal, despite creative programs, including a 2007 campaign that handed out stickers reading, "Don't Steal My Bike, Goof." Kenk's actual motivation remained largely incomprehensible, once telling police he was preparing for a fossil fuel apocalypse.

Swimming with the Sharks ... and with Mayor Tory

"Starting small" – as the Scarborough students had been instructed in the 1970s – remained the reigning approach to cycling at City Hall, even before the election of Rob Ford as Toronto mayor in late 2010. Ford simply gave the term a new meaning. The assertion "I have to drive" had remained effective in thwarting almost every demand for a share of the public road, even though other road users could say with equal or greater credibility that "I have to cycle (walk, or take transit)."

As a city councillor for an Etobicoke ward, Rob Ford had blamed cyclists for their own injuries and deaths, suggesting that cycling on city roads was like swimming with sharks: sooner or later you would get bitten because "roads are built for buses, cars and trucks, not for people on bikes." He added, "my heart bleeds for them when I hear someone gets killed but it's their own fault at the end of the day." Many motorists shared Rob Ford's view of cyclists: they were not fellow residents deserving accommodation on city roads but risk-seekers engaged in extreme sports akin to mountain climbing, bungee jumping, or skydiving.

With Rob Ford as mayor, most cycling, transit, and pedestrian initiatives that threatened to take space from motorists, or to add costs to driving, were attacked as a "War on the Car." Cycling advocates who attempted to distance their own proposals as *not* being part of the war further legitimized the bizarre notion of a War on the Car. The meme reflected an obvious insecurity among motor enthusiasts, whose privilege in the city was increasingly being questioned. Even piddling reallocatations of public space were interpreted, and angrily attacked, as an affront and indignity. The meme wasn't new, but it found an eager audience among motorists, contributing to Ford's victory among a weak slate of candidates in the 2010 election. (Incumbent David Miller did not seek re-election.) As a speaker at Ford's inauguration, brash hockey commentator Don Cherry curiously derided cyclists as "pinkos" – an opening post-electon salvo in a mayoralty that would make the city the punch line for jokes far beyond Canada.

Early in Rob Ford's tenure, a recently installed bike lane on Jarvis Street (as well as the Scarborough lanes) was removed, even though traffic counts showed an overall increase in numbers.

Jarvis no longer resembled the smooth, tree-lined darling of cyclists in the 1890s, but had become an intimidating five-lane mo-
torway, including a reversible centre lane alternating between
morning and evening rush hours. Removing the bike lane became
a *cause célèbre* for politicians who fancied themselves foot soldiers
in the defence of the car. When it came to cycling, City Hall finally
showed that it was capable of speed, at least in eliminating a bike
lane, despite the cost and an otherwise penny-pinching leadership.

Rob Ford's bombast on cycling provided cover for councillors
who might otherwise have needed coherent arguments to rationalize their opposition to bike lanes. "Don't send us any more
activists, don't send us any more unionists, don't send us any
more cyclists," Deputy Mayor Doug Holyday peevishly urged city
residents after losing an unrelated vote in 2012. Councillors were
less willing to hitch their wagons to Rob Ford once the circus-like
atmosphere at City Hall made any association with him politically
awkward.

During Rob Ford's tenure, City Hall also revived the delusion
that off-road bike trails were a viable substitute for bike lanes. A
ten-year, 77-kilometre Bikeway Trails Implementation Plan was
approved. The shortcomings of off-road trails to get to everyday
destinations had long been known: meandering trails that increased distances, the absence of lighting or snow clearing, insufficient access points, the danger of collisions with pedestrians (since
virtually all trails were shared), sweat-inducing ascents back onto
roads from ravine trails, and the danger involved in getting to the
trails along busy roads. Despite the far higher cost of construction
for bike trails relative to most bike lanes, they provided local recreational opportunities and didn't take space from motorists. By
2016, 37 kilometres of new trails were in place.

Image 35: Bells on Bloor annual ride. While City Hall during the mayoralty of Rob Ford was generally hostile to bike lanes, the annual Bells on Bloor ride continued into its fouth year in 2010. Bloor Street had become the Holy Grail of bike lanes and the longest, hardest-fought battle for cycling infrastructure in the city's history. (Photo: Martin Reis)

At the time, the total length of bike trails exceeded bike lanes by a large margin, a gap that remained equally large in 2019. Among the trails in Rob Ford's plan was the Finch Hydro Corridor, which Strok & Associates had listed under "long-term" projects, almost certainly not imagining that the long-term would stretch into a new millennium. Another trail that was finally on the verge of completion was the waterfront path, renamed in memory of the *Toronto Star*'s past president and editor-in-chief Martin Goodman on the city's 150th anniversary in 1984. By 2019, the waterfront trail, which was equally useful to recreational and utilitarian cyclists, stretched almost 25 kilometres from the eastern beaches to Mimico, fully meriting its title, "Jewel in the Crown" of Toronto's bikeways, even though its eastern terminus at Balmy Beach still fell 21 kilometres short of the city's eastern border. The good news story of the trail was tainted by the slow pace of action and avoidable tragedies, including a five-year-old boy on his bike who fell from the trail onto the adjacent six lane, high-speed Lakeshore Boulevard in 2017.

When Toronto's medical officer of health in 2012 recommended the lowering of speed limits (coincident with similar recommendations by Ontario's chief coroner), the chair of the city's Public Works and Infrastructure Committee told him to "stick to his knitting." It turned out, however, that it was the chair who was out of touch. Many city residents wanted, and soon got, lower limits for their own neighbourhoods. (Studies showed that a pedestrian hit by a car at 30 km/h was almost assured of surviving, but at 50 km/h the same person would likely die.)

Toronto's public health agency had for years called for motor traffic reductions to address lethal air pollution but framing road safety as a health issue attacked the problem from a different angle.

Sedentary lifestyles, to which car dependence contributed, were leading to chronic illnesses that cost the health care system billions of dollars – but how were people to follow a doctor's advice to be more active by walking and cycling for their daily commutes if they had to worry about their safety on roads?

Another irony of Ford's mayoralty was that although the city flirted with the ignominy of shrinking its modest system of bike lanes, his administration initiated, and succeeded in installing – or securing council approval for – a 14-kilometre, downtown cycling circuit that included Toronto's first physically protected bike lanes. The circuit, which included new bike lanes on Richmond-Adelaide and upgraded ones on other streets, included a short link along Queen's Park Crescent that had first been proposed for study by the city's consultant Barton-Aschman in 1979. Installation of the circuit was guided by the same public works chair who opposed reductions in speed limits. In this case he was likely motived by the prospect of showing up former Mayor David Miller's bike-friendly council, which had talked about protected bike lanes but had never managed to install one. The new circuit closely resembled (albeit excluding Bloor Street) the circuit proposed by the city's wheelmen in 1896. It would have merited greater recognition had the city not grown in the intervening 120 years.

(Overleaf) **Image 36:** BIKESTOCK rally at City Hall in September 2014. In the run up to the municipal election, a rally featuring musicians brought together cycling groups demanding bike lanes on Yonge, Bloor, and Danforth. In the election John Tory defeated Doug Ford, who later became provincial premier. Toronto's Old City Hall, completed in 1899, is in the background. (Photo: Robert Zaichkowski)

On transportation matters, Mayor Ford spent much of his energy derailing his predecessor's initiatives, including Transit City's five provincially funded LRT lines spanning 120 kilometres, concentrated on underserved, marginalized suburban neighbourhoods. The LRT lines could have been a boon to cyclists, especially for combined bike-transit trips – but Ford's fight for "the little guy," whose cause he claimed to champion, could only be understood in the context of a little guy who never took transit, walked, or cycled. Rob Ford relied on a "subways, subways, subways" mantra, which, at an enormous projected cost, put transit underground and out of the way of motorists. Horatio Hocken's "Tubes for the People" slogan a century earlier had a stronger claim to common sense. By the end of his term, Ford only had ballooning cost projections to show for his subway plans.

Rob Ford launched his campaign for re-election in 2014 but withdrew after being diagnosed with cancer. (He died in March 2016.) His elder brother, Doug, who replaced him in the campaign, lost to John Tory. Then in March 2018, thanks to good luck and shrewd tactics, Doug became Conservative Party leader, and, several months later, Ontario premier. His campaign included promises for a Buck-a-Beer and the cancellation of the province's Cap-and-Trade climate program, which, among other things, had funded cycling infrastructure in Ontario's cities. The province continued to pay little attention to cyclists and the small strides made by the previous Liberal government, including updated provincial planning laws, were weakened or targeted for revisions. A simple change to the provincial HTA would at least have shown that Doug Ford's Conservative government was willing to treat road safety as a non-partisan issue. But despite the calls of a coalition of community groups over a period of five years, both the Ford government and the previous Liberal one rejected a "Vulnerable Road User Law." The initiative, organized by Bike Law Canada founder Pat Brown, simply called for meaningful penalties, including licence suspensions, for motorists convicted in HTA cases involving the death or serious injury of a pedestrian or cyclist. In practice, fines under the HTA, even in cases involving a fatality, often did not (and do not) exceed several hundred dollars, foisting another indignity onto victims or their families. The new law would also have required convicted motorists to attend court to listen to the victim impact statements of grieving families.

John Tory, who became mayor in December 2014, usually couched his position on bike lanes in language about balancing competing demands on the city's roadways, despite a road system that was dramatically out of balance. His approach lowered the temperature of the "War on the Car" rhetoric, while largely preserving the status quo on the roads. A 2018 proposal, "REimagining Yonge," to convert a chaotic, motor traffic–clogged stretch of Yonge Street in North York into a people-friendly street was at first opposed by Tory in favour of an alternative, at a projected additional cost of $20 million, that included moving the planned bike lane onto a parallel street dominated by a cemetery. The alternative proposal confirmed that in the forty years since the Barton-Aschman report, many city leaders had yet to accept that cyclists used the same roads as motorists, at the same times of day, because they were going to the same places. This area of Yonge had seen a condo building boom that converted it from a car-oriented strip mall to one where most people walked, cycled, or took transit. Tory later changed his position on the Yonge proposal, and swayed enough councillors to vote in favour, but at the cost of another two years, and significant additional effort by community advocates and city staff.

Tory had inherited a low bar for success from Rob Ford on cycling – and most other matters. In his first years in office, Tory mainly needed to show that he wasn't Rob Ford. (The irony was that Tory himself abruptly resigned in February 2023 for his own misbehaviour.) In five years under Tory, from 2014 to 2019, the average annual bike lane installations barely exceeded those of Rob Ford's mayoralty (even though Ford had removed lanes), and barely matched the annual numbers of the failed 2001 bike plan.

The failure of the 2001 bike plan didn't dampen City's Hall's enthusiasm for a new bike plan: the "Ten-Year Cycling Network Plan," adopted by council in June 2016, cost $250,000 in consultant's fees, and occupied city staff for eighteen months. In the meantime, bike lane installations again came almost to a full stop, as they had in the lead up to the 2001 plan. The suggestion that the new plan was "building on" the 2001 plan offered a pleasant euphemism.

In the council debate to approve the 2016 bike plan, Tory reassured council that the plan set "a target that has a level of ambition to it, but is achievable, is to be funded, and will be achieved. And will be achieved." He added that "I want to be able to stand in front of people and say we approved that plan, and we went out and did it." By the end of 2019, the plan was on pace to meet its 2025 targets by 2050. Tory didn't stand in front of anyone to explain the failure.

In the July 2019 "update" of the bike plan, city staff, perhaps anticipating that the poor results would provoke tough questions, presented a long list of justifications, including that staff resources had been depleted in preparing the lengthy update, three times as long as the 2016 plan itself. In fact, instead of providing an actual update, staff essentially rewrote the plan, while eliminating the ten-year timeline (although introducing three-year segments that offered the potential for greater accountability). Staff needn't have worried about any scrutiny – if any members of the oversight committee had read the revised plan, it wasn't evident. Advocates nonetheless urged the city to redouble its efforts at improving cycling conditions. One long-time cycling activist summed up the frustration: "It takes forever to get nothing done."

City residents advocating for cycling no longer needed to look to Amsterdam or Copenhagen for inspiration. Between 2016 and 2018, the smaller city of Montreal added 90 kilometres of new bike lanes to a network that was already double that of Toronto. Toronto's poor performance was noteworthy in the context of strong public support for cycling; the growing number of cyclists; the adoption of a Vision Zero road safety plan; a cycling staff contingent that had grown to seventeen (and to twenty-eight by 2022); a TransformTO goal of converting 75 per cent of trips under five kilometres to walking, cycling, and transit; and the city's 2019 declaration of a climate emergency. The city's Complete Street Guidelines offered another path to road safety based on a more balanced sharing of public roads, under which bike lanes were simply part of a holistic approach to road safety. Indeed, bike lanes did not simply protect cyclists but also created a safety buffer for sidewalks, restoring the margin of error that pedestrians had lost when Fred Gardiner widened roads.

City Hall's unprecedented levels of funding from the federal and provincial governments (prior to Doug Ford's election) at least confirmed advocates' suspicions that the fight for safe cycling conditions wasn't about money, it was about road space. In 2018, less than 12 per cent of the city's cycling capital budget was actually spent on new bike lanes – the remainder was either not spent or spent on peripheral items, including $500,000 on new bike lane guidelines (never released) about how to install bike lanes. "A bike budget that pays for everything except bike lanes," summarized a *dandyhorse* headline.

The greatest single increase in bike lanes in Toronto's history actually occurred in 2015, although it was little more than a sleight of hand. City Hall began *double-counting* bike lanes: a bike lane on each side of a one kilometre stretch of road suddenly became two kilometres of bike lanes. (The practice was slowly phased out after 2019.) The city remained content with shortcuts. In fact, although it was sluggish in building, but creative in counting, bike lanes, it had at least over the years proven itself eager to chase every alternative scheme, no matter how fanciful, as long as motoring space was preserved. Laneways, rail paths, and off-road trails had all found attentive City Hall audiences, despite their marginal utility for everyday cyclists. In the early 1990s, an engineer's proposed system of elevated, glass-enclosed tubes for cyclists also enjoyed time in the city's political and media limelight, despite a $2 billion price tag.

While Toronto lagged in its implementation of bike lanes and trails, it never wanted for reports, studies, and plans for cycling facilities – a list to which "prioritization metrics," "enhanced methodologies," and "pre-feasibility studies" were later added. In the decades since Mayor Dennison declared Bicyclists' Day on September 16, 1972 – followed in subsequent years by Bike to Work Week, then Bike Month – there was one thing that cyclists had never gotten: a bike lane to City Hall.

RIDE ON

Fashion and Function in the New Millennium

From its elitist origins, and despite its more recent treatment by City Hall, the bicycle had proven itself well suited to city life: to commerce and leisure, to rich and poor, and in the era of climate change, to the planet. The bicycle was even proving to be useful to people for whom age or disability made walking difficult. "It's my wheelchair," commented one senior. "It's easier than walking," added a ninety-two-year-old cyclist. A bicycle was as useful to a businessperson on the way to work as to a student on the way to school, and similary useful to a homeless person living in an encampment. A coroner's jury in June 2018 recommended an expansion of the bike share system in a case involving a homeless man. Curiously, while cyclists had often been dismissed as being too poor or too radical (or too sweaty), they might now be derided for being too rich and as latté-sipping elites. Attacks on cyclists based on their class status had become a confusing business.

More women were riding bikes, including women over forty-five, without any politician daring to suggest it was inappropriate. City councillors or federal and provincial cabinet ministers who cycled to work no longer had to worry about being criticized for diminishing their office. The media now included many journalists who got to work by bicycle, including Matt Galloway, the host (at that time) of CBC's popular morning show, *Metro Morning*. He sometimes supplemented the typically grim traffic report with anecdotes from his own invigorating commute.

In some newer residential towers, bicycles were no longer always relegated to dark, dank corners of parking garages. One condo on King Street was built with a bicycle room on every floor. City Hall had a bicycle room in its underground garage, complete with a $21-per-month shower-and-towel service, and space for 170 vehicles. The $2.5 million cost of the City Hall bike room was perhaps ironic given that the city had yet to complete a cycling network. Union Station also added a bicycle room (for 240 vehicles) for GO train commuters.

Bicycle shops, easily integrated on main streets in the central city, proliferated. On a 10-kilometre stretch of Bloor Street, bicycle shops outnumbered Tim Hortons doughnut shops. Curbside Cycle was among the shops on Bloor, but now in a bricks-and-mortar shop integrated into the commercial strip, replacing owner Don Watterson's curbside operation that dated from 1991 (a date Watterson recalled by association with the catastrophic eruption of Mount Pinatubo). The original enterprise was housed in a small tent beside the Brunswick House pub – an ideal location to catch the notice of two-wheeled commuters, but less ideal in avoiding the attention of by-law enforcement officers. A vacant candy shop across the road offered slightly less visibility but greater legality. Over the following years, Curbside figured out, by trial and error,

(Opposite) **Image 37:** Olivia Chow and Jack Layton, at the time both federal members of Parliament (Layton as leader of the NDP), ride a tandem at the city's popular Pride parade in 2008. Being seen on a tandem had become a "thing" for politicians, but Chow and Layton were also everyday cyclists. Chow was the chair of the Toronto Cycling Committee when council adopted the 2001 bike plan. (She became Toronto's 66th mayor in June 2023.) (Photo: Frank Yang, flickr)

which bicycles were best suited to Toronto's terrain, streetcar tracks, and road salt. It then focused on persuading buyers that a bicycle for everyday use required an investment larger than a department-store special built for once-in-a-while recreation.

The popularity of ten-speed bikes had continued to decline since the 1970s, replaced by mountain, hybrid, folding, and city bikes. Former mayor John Sewell had been riding a traditional Dutch-style bike in the city for so long that it was finally in fashion. Bicycle retailers offered choices suited to city riding, beginning with models that allowed riders to maintain an upright posture, instead of the hunched over one for ten-speeds, and including among their offerings brightly painted bikes, outfitted with mud guards, reliable lights, multiple (but not a flamboyant number of) gears, panniers, carrying racks, and baskets.

Retailers were again providing options for the urban cyclist's attire. Winter cyclists could find high-tech, lightweight gear – although long-johns, mittens, and a tuque worked almost as well. One shop actually designed and sold cycling outfits for men and women, reminiscent of an earlier era. *Courier chic* was available for riders who wanted to be associated with the edgy non-conformism of the document couriers.

Cargo "bikes," even with three or four wheels, were gaining popularity with a new generation of parents taking their children to school, at least in the central city. These parents were now more likely to be celebrated on social media than disparaged for poor parenting.

In 2008, when *dandyhorse* magazine was launched, its objective was to reach a new cycling audience of women and people in the arts. As founding editor Tammy Thorne explained, "It struck me that we were really preaching to the converted and I wanted to reach beyond the enthusiasts." In an age of declining print media, she managed to keep the publication going, online in its later years, for a decade, on a shoestring budget, largely with passionate volunteers, including herself, working "off the side of my desk." Over a decade earlier, cycling advocate Garry Wice had relied on similar passion to write a column for the *Toronto Star*, convincing the paper that the potential audience for cycling far surpassed that of the paper's coin and stamp collecting column.

By the new millennium, the *Toronto Star*'s conversion from shrill opponent of bike lanes to solid supporter, even on arterials such as Bloor Street, was almost complete, no doubt influenced by a growing number of bike commuters among its readers. Norris Macdonald, former editor of the *Toronto Star*'s substantial "Wheels" sections (dedicated to cars, not bikes), complained that when his articles were *perceived* to be critical of cycling, the number of angry letters could fill two full pages of the paper.

Bike Cops, Bike Share, and Food by Bike

Toronto Police rediscovered bicycles in 1991, beginning with a contingent of twenty officers, which grew to 100 officers by 2019, most of them happily liberated from the unhealthy confines of patrol cars. Some parking enforcement officers (PEOs), a division of the police service, also turned to bikes to perform their duties.

In mid-2017, PEO Kyle Ashley attained virtual folk hero status simply by enforcing the no-parking-in-the-bike-lane by-law and shaming the perpetrators on social media (with faces obscured). Ashley first came to public attention with a "selfie" standing beside an illegally parked motorist who agreed to play along. "Parking in the bike lane costs $150" was the caption for a photo that showed both the motorist and Ashley frowning. The tweet travelled the globe.

Image 38: "Heels on Wheels." Opera star Wallis Giunta, posing with her bicycle, was featured in *dandyhorse* magazine in October 2011. The beautiful scene is reminiscent of photographs of club cyclists in the 1880s, who often posed with their high-wheels in front of faux landscapes. Tammy Thorne, *dandyhorse* founding editor, had set out to broaden the audience for cycling publications by appealing to women and the arts community. (Photo: Molly Miksa)

The cavalier attitudes of some motorists parked in bike lanes had long been on display. A bike lane installed in 1991 on a short stretch of Bloor Street East was routinely blocked by motorists attending Sunday worship. Stopping in the bike lane was often shrugged off with "I'll just be a minute," or more creative excuses. Ashley even ticketed courier companies, Uber and Lyft, tourist buses, city officials, and Canada Post, which soon announced it would stop parking in bike lanes.

Ashley lasted only one year in his new position, but nonetheless showed that City Hall could sometimes be in the cyclists' corner. He made clear that whatever the merit of the motorist's excuse, it was the cyclist that suffered the risk, and the consequences. The same three-officer bicycle patrol unit that Ashley convinced his superiors to establish continued to ticket offenders and to publicize its work on social media, albeit less theatrically – but only until 6 p.m. each weekday, after which Uber and Lyft could again treat the bike lane as their private domain.

Bike liveries had made a comeback, although in an unrecognizable form and without the need for an attendant or cash – a credit card or smartphone sufficed. In 2019, Bike Share, by then run by the city's parking authority, recorded over two million rides on bikes rented from hundreds of stations across Toronto, solving the "last kilometer" problem of daily commutes. Bike Share had replaced the defunct Bixi in 2014, which had itself stepped in for a more modest initiative, the Community Bicycle Network's BikeShare program that started in 2004, lending out bicycles from community hubs or local shops, including cafés.

Some of the potential for expanding bicycle-transit trips, which in 1985 stood around 12 per cent, had been tapped. In 1984, the TTC started allowing bikes on the subway (but not during rush hour), while buses outfitted with bike racks on the front bumper slowly became the norm. The TTC also added bike parking at subway stations, and, later, do-it-yourself repair stations. New, low-floor streetcars, introduced in 2014, not only included rear-door access for cyclists but also a designated interior space. By 2016, the number of people who occasionally or regularly combined cycling and transit trips had reached 45 per cent.

Image 39: Illegal parking in bike lanes. Motorists routinely blocked bike lanes, forcing cyclists to skirt around them, sometimes dangerously into the path of other motor traffic. Illegal bike lane parking has sometimes led to confrontations between cyclists and motorists, as in this winter 2021 photo where the CyclingVigilante (as he called himself on Twitter) confronts a bike lane violator. (Photo: Albert Koehl)

The number of bicycle couriers had continued to grow, now predominantly delivering food instead of business materials, and easily identified by their large insulated backpacks. These couriers were engaged by "digital platforms" in the "gig economy," directed by computer-generated algorithms via smartphones instead of by dispatchers via pagers. Carrying cash was no longer among their worries; a thief might now do no better than eating someone's sushi dinner.

By 2018, Foodora alone had a roster of 500 riders in Toronto, equal to the estimated number of document couriers on bikes in the entire city in 1998. (By 2022, there were possibly as many as 15,000 food couriers on bikes in the city.) Document couriers had been in a slow decline since the 1990s when newer technologies, including email and electronic storage devices, began replacing the need for door-to-door service. The 1980s heyday of Sunwheel Couriers was still remembered by some couriers. In those years, Sunwheel employed as many as fifty bicycle couriers, although the enterprise didn't survive – in part a victim of competition from companies that copied its model. The last straw was a large, unexpected bill from the Workplace Safety and Insurance Board (WSIB) in 1990, which treated Tiessen's venture as a cartage company instead of a taxi service. In the new millennium, the remaining document couriers at least offered a stark contrast to the large cube vans, which doubled as temporary storage depots, of multinational corporations that now dominated letter and parcel delivery, often blocking sidewalks and bike lanes.

Long-standing grievances by bike couriers about working conditions and compensation outlived the changes in technology. In 2019, Foodora couriers went to court for the right to unionize. (The couriers won a precedent-setting case in early 2020 in which the Labour Relations Tribunal classified them as "dependent," instead of "independent," contractors. But Foodora, which boasted a family-like work environment, promptly announced its departure from Canada.)

The New Cycling Advocacy

By 2019, what had been a modest cycling advocacy movement in 1979, centred around the City Cycling Committee, had come to include a far broader range of groups, including at least some organizations with paid staff. The voice of the grassroots and non-profit groups was strengthened by alliances with pedestrian, transit, climate, and social justice organizations built on a growing appreciaton of shared objectives – a recognition of the importance of cycling to better transportation and a healthier community, instead of a perk or reward for "cycling enthusiasts." When Bloor Street finally got a pilot bike lane in 2016, it was with the unanimous support of all six local residents' associations.

Emerging cycling groups reflected the diversity of a city where more than half of residents were born outside Canada. The Women's Cycling Network, based in the Flemingdon and Thorncliffe Park neighbourhoods, was founded by refugees from war-torn Afghanistan. Hijabs and Helmets provided the security of group rides for women whose headscarves might draw unwanted attention, not unlike the problems of women cyclists in the 1890s for their "rational dress." (The pandemic further increased the diversity and range of cycling groups in the city for both utilitarian and recreational riders.)

It had been a long road from the 1970s City Cycling Committee (known after amalgamation as the Toronto Cycling Committee, and then the Cycling Advisory Committee) to the lively advocacy scene of 2019, which included the membership-based Cycle Toronto, among many other groups.

When the city's cycling committee was dissolved in 2011 during Rob Ford's mayoralty, there was little mourning, given the committee's waning influence. Its dissolution confirmed one of the problems with a city-appointed-committee-as-advocate model, namely, that it existed at the pleasure of council. The committee's official role was always that of advisor to City Hall, but by drawing from the city's small pool of cycling advocates, the committee's advocacy role was clear, if unstated, and originally, at least in part, by default.

By 1980, Hilda Tiessen and Joan Doiron had recognized the need for a community-based voice for cyclists to push for political action, arguing that the cycling committee was an inadequate substitute. With the maturing of cycling advocacy, the committee model was more likely to constrain community organizing, both by drawing the most effective advocates and by giving the impression to other cyclists that their interests were being taken care of. The institutional setting of the committee within City Hall would also have dampened the enthusiasm of some members to challenge councillors and staff about inaction on cycling matters for fear of causing them embarrassment – and betraying a presumed trust of the very city officials who appointed them and under whose authority (and roof) they met and worked. This constraint would be exacerbated by an understandable inclination to defer to city staff, upon whom the volunteers depended for resources, expertise, information, and support.

In Montreal, which did not have a cycling committee, Le Monde à Bicyclette was formed by a loose-knit group of activists who made up for their lack of resources with creative stunts that amplified their voice. It was perhaps no coincidence that Montreal began seriously building bike lanes in the 1980s, instead of in the 1990s.

Tiessen and Doiron collaborated to create The Bicycle Works! – a community group they envisioned as leading various cycling initiatives, operating from a central hub, and supported by thousands of members. The first meetings drew about fifty people, but the initiative didn't progress much further, although many of its ideas were later revived by other groups. (By 1988, Doiron was a school trustee, a position she leveraged, with the help of assistant Lyn Adamson, to promote sustainable transportation initiatives.)

Another community group, the Toronto Bicycle Network, launched in the fall of 1982, might have filled the advocacy gap given founder Richard Aaron's original objectives, including the promotion of utilitarian cycling. The group (which still thrives today) eventually settled upon organizing recreational rides for every skill level, from novice upward, at the price of a modest annual membership fee. Another group, the Community Bicycle Network, formed in 1993, employed four staff at its peak, but it was mainly focused on promoting cycling, including among its many offerings the cheekily named Wenches with Wrenches to teach repair skills, as well as a bicycle lending program.

It took until 1998 for another advocacy initiative, the Bicycle League of Toronto (BLT), to be launched. Founder Nick Gamble, a local cycling activist and UK émigré, hoped that other advocates would step forward to help, recognizing that a successful membership-based group required more time and energy than he had to offer. The support he ultimately received was largely limited to encouragement. The BLT was short-lived.

A decade later, in September 2008, with the launch of the Toronto Cyclists Union, later renamed Cycle Toronto, the city got its first membership-based cycling advocacy group since the demise of the Toronto Cyclists' Association in the late 1890s. Unlike the appointed cycling committee, the legitimacy of the Cyclists Union, to be funded by members and donors, would be rooted in the community. Organizer Dave Meslin, after a year-long fact-finding mission, brought together local cycling leaders to gauge popular support for an organized voice for the city's cyclists, finding an eager audience. He carefully avoided supplanting existing grassroots groups, instead articulating the role of the new group as filling a gap between cycling groups that did advocacy work but had no funding and other groups that did no advocacy work but had stable funding.

Meslin set aside a year to prepare for the launch, supporting himself with a quirky initiative that he called "The Professional Guest," exchanging his skills in fields such as baking, sock darning, and dog-walking for a couch and pillow at a host's home. Before the official launch, Meslin was able to confirm that Gamble hadn't exaggerated the commitment required to set up such a group, suffering a heavy toll on his mental health. He had to rely on other advocates to step in, including for the position of executive director, which he had envisioned for himself.

By the time of its tenth anniversary in 2018, Cycle Toronto and its then executive director Jared Kolb had achieved an organizational longevity that had eluded many other groups, including the Toronto Cyclists' Association, the leaders of which, including Dr. Doolittle, were ultimately drawn to the brighter lights of the motorcar.

"Critical Mass" rides, based on a US model, became a popular grassroots cycling event in Toronto. The rides, beginning in the mid-1990s in Toronto, had no official organizer or leader, nor a planned route – or even an articulated objective, except to assert cyclists' right to be on the road and to reject the car-clogged, polluted status quo. Toronto's first Critical Mass rides counted a few dozen participants, most of them couriers, and started in front of Bread Spreads, a popular courier gathering spot on Temperance

Image 40: Critical Mass rides, with no pre-determined route, were a monthly event in Toronto beginning in the mid-1990s. In May 2008, the once-per-month rides, sometimes drawing hundreds of riders, controversially ended up on the Gardiner Expressway, an oft-debated piece of infrastructure for its heavy drain on municipal resources and its barrier to the waterfront. (Photo: Martin Reis)

Street downtown. Aggressive motorists unwilling to cede any part of the road were assured of an equally (or more) aggressive response from the seasoned riders. On one occasion two couriers lept onto the roof of a car (with open sunroof) with a view to sharing their perspective with a driver who had been harassing the group. In subsequent years, the rides grew in numbers, sometimes including parents with children, and starting from the corner of Spadina Avenue and Bloor Street. The cyclists were jeered or cheered by onlookers and sometimes interrupted by police who issued tickets for red light violations, although this actually undermined the safety of the group, which depended on a safety-in-numbers approach and maintaining a single group, without infiltration of cars. By 2019, Critical Mass rides had largely disappeared, replaced with myriad other rides.

The Bicycle's (Accidental) Advocates

Most cycling advocacy work continued to rely on volunteers whose only assurance was that their effort would get little fanfare. "The prototypical Toronto cycling activist," wrote historian Steve Brearton in 2008, "is a determined dreamer who remains largely unknown and unrecognized."

For most cycling advocates, generally self-appointed, a devotion to the cause of cycling was only a starting point. Turning this conviction into action often required a willingness to stand out for one's views, especially in the first decades after the Bicycle Revival of the 1970s. For other advocates, while enjoyment had drawn them to the bicycle, it was the injustice of a crash or, worse, the unbearable grief of losing a loved one that diverted them into activism and advocacy. For many other cyclists, the obvious power imbalance on the roads, and societal or institutional biases in favour of the more powerful, dangerous, and destructive motorcar, shaped political values and political consciousness.

In 1992, the city's wider curb lanes finally started paying dividends for cyclists, not for any discernible safety benefit but for contributing to the conversion of Nancy Smith Lea into a lifelong road safety advocate. Smith Lea had been thrown from her bicycle in a crash with a motorist who was turning into a channelized exit – a road design feature that allows motorists to maintain their speed on a turn – from Harbord Street onto St. George Street in the heart of the University of Toronto. The configuration of the roadway was particularly telling in a location where people on foot and bikes dominated, and for which the City had been given previous warnings about the danger. The failure of the police officer to attend court for the motorist's careless driving charge further fuelled Smith Lea's conversion.

Smith Lea joined Spirit of Spadina, which pressed, but failed to convince, Metro Hall to install a bike lane on Spadina Avenue as part of the planned restoration of the streetcar line, removed in 1948. For its part, City of Toronto staff actually drew up plans for a protected bike lane, but Metro took no interest. ("Edge lines" less than a half metre wide were later painted in the curb lane, eventually replaced by "sharrows" – directional arrows painted on the road indicating a notional, shared space for cyclists – neither providing safety for cyclists.) In 1996 Smith Lea was a founder of Advocacy for Respect for Cyclists (ARC) after the deaths of two women in road crashes a week apart. ARC persuaded the regional coroner to undertake a broader review of cycling deaths. An earlier group, Cycle Watch, formed in 1987 by Tony Boston after the death of his wife, Adrienne, who was killed while cycling on Bathurst Street, had similarly sought to bring attention to road tragedies, and specifically the bias by institutions in favour of motorists. The motorist in Adrienne's case was acquitted, despite the investigating officer's belief that the driver's view of Adrienne was likely obscured by fuzzy dice hanging from the car's rear-view mirror.

In 2006, Smith Lea was a founder (then director until 2021) of the Toronto Coalition for Active Transportation (TCAT), a road safety research group.

After the death of her husband in November 2012, Kasia Briegmann-Samson took on a role she wouldn't have wished on anyone. Tom Samson was killed by a hit-and-run driver, a tragedy that police initially blamed on Tom, reporting that he had gone through a red light – a narrative that conveniently resolved the matter, but that made no sense for a cautious man who told his children, "the car will always win. Don't take chances." The Samson family fought back, hiring a lawyer to challenge the police conclusion. A later collision reconstruction report showed that Tom had come to a full stop, or very close to it, consistent with making a legal left turn from the centre of the road when he was hit. The original police account of Tom's death begged the question: if police could be so wrong in this case, in how many other fatal crashes when their reports went unchallenged – because the victim could not speak – had they made similar errors, which then (mis)informed public perceptions and understanding? In 2016, Briegmann-Samson helped found Friends and Families for Safe Streets (FFSS), a group that revived the type of event common to earlier eras, including a World Day of Remembrance for Road Traffic Victims, which demonstrated public anger and resistance to the carnage on the roads.

For several decades, Wayne Scott was among the city's best known cycling advocates, his baritone voice, boundless energy, and shaved head all commanding attention. Scott never owned a car – convinced they were ill-suited to urban life – except for a pedal ("kitty") car during his childhood, once riding it to a local shop where he helped himself to handful of candy, then, forgetting his vehicle, running home to show his windfall to his surprised

(Overleaf) **Image 41:** "Streets for People" reads the banner at this November 1992 "die-in" by Spirit of Spadina activists, including Lyn Adamson and Nancy Smith Lea, to protest Metro's refusal to add bike lanes in the reconstruction of the roadway. (I am standing at the top, far left in the photo, document in hand, supportive but not yet ready to jump fully into the fray.) (Photo: Keith Beatty/ Getty Images)

mother. Years later, in the 1980s, Scott became a courier, by chance, while searching for work as a graphic artist. After answering a "Bike Messengers Wanted" sign, he moved from the smoke-filled bar rooms of his rock 'n roll days to the city's smog-filled roads. He was well liked by his fellow couriers despite a quirky conviction (to their way of thinking) that couriers should obey all rules of the road. An on-the-job injury that left Scott unable to work for a number of weeks quickly revealed the injustice of compensation regimes that denied benefits to bike couriers as "independent contractors."

In 1982, Scott embarked on a sixteen-year-long battle against the Canada Revenue Agency that ended in victory at one of the country's highest courts. The precedent-setting "food-for-fuel" ruling would allow both foot and bicycle couriers to deduct the cost of the extra food they had to consume in the course of their work. The case made international news, one local courier marvelling, "The little guy finally won one." The decision highlighted an obvious injustice: couriers in cars could deduct the cost of gasoline – and businesspeople deduct the cost of lunches and drinks – while couriers, who toiled on streets amidst those cars to make deliveries to businesses, were deprived of a similar benefit. "Justice is not served by remaining wedded to concepts which are outdated and in need of change," read the judgement.

In 1998, the city recognized Scott for his long food-for-fuel fight. A year earlier, Scott and other advocates had adroitly steered the city and Metro councils into declaring October 9 as "Messenger Appreciation Day" (the date reflects the 10-9 courier parlance for "say again") to celebrate the positive contributions of couriers to air quality, greenhouse gas reductions, and commerce in the city. The recognition might have turned out differently. At the time, one city councillor, characterizing bicycle couriers as "kamikazes," had called for couriers to be licenced by the city. (Ironically, that councillor, after his later appointment as an immigration judge, was sentenced to jail for soliciting a bribe.)

In the last years of his life, Scott continued to fight for another "little guy," bicycle courier Darcy Allan Sheppard, whose image Scott displayed on the heavy cargo bike he rode around the city, even when cancer had begun sapping his strength. Sheppard, a thirty-three-year-old man of Métis heritage with a troubled history of addiction, was killed in an August 2009 crash along a posh retail strip of Bloor Street known as the Mink Mile. The motorist, with his own troubled history of addiction, was Ontario's former attorney general, Michael Bryant, and at the time a leading contender for the Liberal Party leadership and provincial premier. Bryant was charged with criminal negligence and dangerous driving causing death.

Public sympathy turned against Sheppard soon after Bryant hired a legal, media relations, and investigative team in the run-up to an anticipated trial. Nine months after Sheppard's death, a special prosecutor withdrew all charges against Bryant – saying that there was no reasonable prospect of conviction – in a case that had exposed simmering tensions between motorists and cyclists, but with obvious undertones of class and privilege. Scott persisted in his fight for Sheppard, long after the case was closed, demanding a public inquiry into the prosecutor's handling of key pieces of evidence. Ironically, in the last moments of Sheppard's life, in the midst of a stand-off with Bryant, the courier, astride his bicycle in front of Bryant's convertible, called out to onlookers: "You are my witnesses." One witness, metres from the scene, watched Bryant, whom she didn't recognize, sitting stone-faced in his car, then phoned 911 to report that the motorist "was like out to kill this guy." Sheppard died seconds later, dislodged by a roadside fire hydrant and mailbox from Bryant's car door, onto which he was holding as Bryant drove off.

Hamish Wilson's activism might not have been prompted by a particular injustice, but it endured for over thirty years, a span during which he ensured that he was well known to city officials and politicians, even if with little fondness. His single-spaced correspondence, usually laden with puns such as "City Clowncil," "Caronto," and "votorist" typically arrived in home mailboxes in the dead of night, useful insights often buried beyond the reader's interest or patience. Wilson ensured that every cycling issue, and many broader transportation matters, debated by a City Hall committee had at least one speaker (himself), although his summons to speak was often followed by an exodus of his council audience, or used by them as an opportunity to email, text, or chat. Wilson frustrated friend and foe, his quixotic "tilting at windshields" (as he called it) a reflection of the eclectic mix of individuals that make up a movement, his contribution especially valuable in the early decades of the bicycle revival when standing up for the cause required a devil-may-care attitude.

A long list of other volunteers organized parades and rallies, lobbied for specific bikeways, ran do-it-yourself (DIY) repair shops such as Bike Pirates, matched donors of bikes to recipients, or even carried out guerilla-style actions, such as painting new bike lanes under the cover of darkness. This army was supplemented by other volunteers that produced blogs, newsletters, zines, photo essays, videos – or undertook myriad other advocacy works.

Image 42: Persistence is central to good advocacy, as courier Wayne Scott (*left*) demonstrated in his work. His "food-for-fuel" battle for foot and bike couriers lasted sixteen years. Most advocacy work is also distinctly unglamorous. In this case, with brooms and dust pans in hand (I'm in the centre), we swept up treacherously slippery micro beads left behind in the painting of the Bloor pilot bike lanes in August 2016. It was our way to say "thank you" to the city for the installation. Jun Nogami (*right*) is another long-time advocate – a prolific photo essayist and a leader of ARC. (Photo: Jun Nogami)

THE LASTING JOY OF BICYCLING

During most of the seven decades since the Second World War, governments had manically expanded, extended, and enlarged roads and highways, and for all this effort and spectacular expenditure, by 2019 motorists often managed to travel only a bit faster than the bicyclist, sometimes slower than the pedestrian.

The simple joy of riding the "most benevolent of machines" continued to provoke the hostility and indifference of many decision-makers. Politicians were still catching up, often reluctantly, with a public in the new City of Toronto that now wanted safe roads, lower speed limits, bike lanes, and action on climate change.

It was a testament to the grace, economy, and utility of the bicycle that it had endured, and, despite the odds – and powerful corporate, political, and cultural forces – was enjoying a steady resurgence in Toronto and many other cities. Cars still dominated the air waves with billions of dollars in advertising and demanded, despite – perhaps because of – their inefficiency, a disproportionate share of public space and public resources. Indeed, it was easy to mistake the poor value of cars to transportation given their overwhelming of human senses: sight, sound, and smell. It was this illusion of importance that had continued to thwart real progress towards a model that included a place for the bicycle, the pedestrian, and the transit user – despite the obvious logic and urgency of such a transition.

Two hundred years after Baron von Drais raised his feet from the ground on his *Laufmaschine* and marvelled at how the bicycle remained upright, the same joy was still being experienced by novice riders of all ages, at least in safe spaces. It was still possible to be fascinated with the efficiency of the technology: a vehicle that could carry a person across the city or be hoisted upon the shoulder of that same person. The cyclist could believe that it was the motorist and the motorist's political champions, frustrated by the high cost of buying and operating a car and motor traffic bottlenecks, who were being conned.

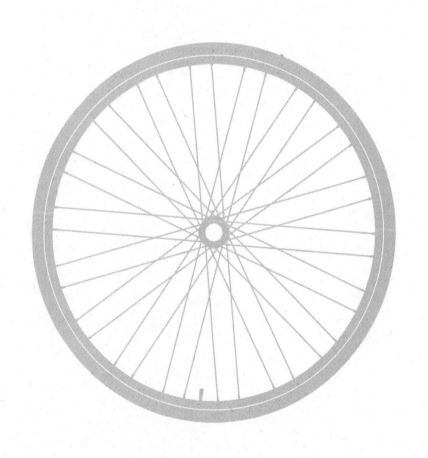

2020-2023
Pandemic - and a Familiar Friend

The COVID-19 pandemic kept Toronto in its deadly grip for the better part of three years, forcing upon the city's political leadership new priorities for public space. If "we are all in this together" – as a popular pandemic rallying cry suggested – then public roads would now have to be shared like they belonged to everyone, including residents who cycled, or wanted to cycle, to get around the city.

"Do your part, stay apart" had an ironic ring in a city where an estimated one million people had crowded downtown streets in June 2019 to celebrate the city's first National Basketball Association championship. With the pandemic's official arrival in March 2020, people encountering neighbours on local streets might cross to the opposite side of the road, while the city closed entrances to some parks and playgrounds – before slowly judging outdoor activities, including cycling, to be safe from virus-spreading. Mayor Tory's original edict to "stay home" quickly ran up against the reality that virtually everyone had to go out at some point – to buy food and medicine, get a breath of fresh air, or, if they were employed in essential services, go to work.

The appreciation of the bicycle grew rapidly, as it had during the world wars and the Depression. The bicycle once again proved itself to be a trustworthy friend. "In times of crisis, their nature serves us well," observed one advocate. The city's list of designated essential services included bike shops, which were quickly inundated with orders for repairs and demand for new bikes. In June 2020, sales at Curbside Cycle on Bloor Street exceeded those of the previous June by 130 per cent.

The mayor, responding to public pressure, quickly pivoted to talking about temporary bikeways to mirror busy transit routes as an option for the many transit users who had abandoned the TTC for fear of the virus. The major decline in motor traffic, given the closure of most workplaces, reassured politicians that any backlash from motorists for reducing *their* road space could be put off to another day. Of course, City Hall was simply following the lead of London, Paris, Milan, Montreal, and other major cities in embracing the bicycle for its value in moving people.

By the end of May 2020, city council, which typically debated almost every bike lane as if its installation might upset a road balance achieved at the pinnacle of human ingenuity, approved, with little dissent, a slate of new bike lanes. A City Hall press release announced that the moribund bike plan would be "accelerated" with 40 kilometres of bike lanes to be installed by the end of the year, describing the initiative as "the largest expansion of Toronto's on-street bike network ever in one year." The plan turned out to be historic for another reason: unlike the 2001 and 2016 plans, most of the promised lanes were *actually* implemented. By the end of 2020, the city had almost 30 kilometres of new bike lanes.

Ironically, new, "temporary" bike lanes (created with cement curb-stones, paint, and bollards) were superior in quality to most of the city's existing cycling infrastructure. A bike lane on University Avenue, a decade after a councillor's miscast vote doomed a previous initiative, was installed literally overnight, confirming what advocates had long asserted: building bike lanes was easy, cheap, and didn't require delays measured in years, dictated by road reconstruction schedules.

In the summer of 2020, Bloor-Danforth finally got much of the cross-town bike lane identified as a vital east-west spine thirty years earlier. (In October 2023, the Bloor bike lane was extended again, this time deep into Etobicoke, leaving only a short gap to the city's western border, where the City of Mississauga was planning its own Bloor Street bike lanes.) On Danforth Avenue, the bike lane ran alongside new patios and planters approved under the city's CaféTO program, proving that usually staid Toronto could be bold, and beautiful. "Can't make that European trip this year? No problem. Visit the Danforth," suggested one letter to the editor.

The reallocation of public road space went far beyond new cycling infrastructure. Curbside parking was not only converted to outdoor cafés but also converted to queuing areas (given the need for "social distancing") for patrons at liquor, grocery, and drug stores. Some roads were closed to cars to be enjoyed on foot or by bike, reintroducing children to spaces from which they had long been excluded, at least in practice. Dedicated bus lanes were established along some arterials. But the cyclist was the most visible beneficiary, and later in the pandemic bike lanes (even when part of Complete Streets plans) again became a convenient target for the wrath of motorists opposed to any reallocation of road space when temporary lanes were to be made permanent. Indeed, after the initial shock of the pandemic, the cyclist (and bike lanes) soon reverted to the preferred scapegoat for all manner of ills: increased tailpipe emissions from cars idled by road congestion (apparently) caused by bike lanes, (claimed) delays to emergency vehicles, and (imagined) interference with TTC shuttle buses, all of which were more logically attributed to motorists, many of whom would never contemplate car-pooling, cycling, walking, taking transit – or even using a smaller vehicle. It was of course the cyclist at an intersection, not the car, SUV, or pickup truck driver, who could easily lift their vehicle onto the sidewalk to clear the way for an ambulance.

Roadway space that was reallocated from cars to people was very much a reclamation of the public space that Fred Gardiner had seized for the motorist in the 1950s. Indeed, it was pedestrians, including parents pushing baby strollers and the elderly, that benefited most from new bike lanes, which assured them of a wider margin of error. A misstep or stumble off the sidewalk would now land the pedestrian in the bikeway, instead of in the path of a two-tonne motor vehicle.

Motorists could no longer assume – consistent with trends pre-pandemic – that their longstanding privilege and apparent dominion over public roads would be respected. A local residents' association along midtown Yonge Street, where a Complete Street, including bike lane, was installed as a pandemic pilot in June 2021, claimed, to an attentive Mayor Tory, that their tony, "landlocked" (or limited access) neighbourhood would be prejudiced by a reduction of motor lanes on Yonge. In early 2023, Tory urged council to further delay the conversion of the pilot to a permanent fixture to allow for yet more study. A majority of councillors ignored the mayor and approved the project. The vote turned out to be Tory's last on cycling matters: he resigned days later (the result of an unrelated matter).

Council even approved the planned revitalization, with pedestrian and cycling priority, of downtown Yonge. In adopting "yongeTOmorrow," Council ignored the opposition of the Downtown Yonge Business Improvement Area (BIA), which predicted "catastrophic" impacts on business. Such opposition had at least partly become an anomaly: the days when merchants could be counted on to do the bidding of motorists against bike lanes were gone. Whenever the Bloor bike lane in the central city was undermined by intrusions from illegal parking or construction, the first to complain was often the general manager of the Bloor Annex BIA.

Food delivery by bike, thriving before the pandemic, surged, as did the use of electric bicycles for the task. Many couriers were new to the city and new to the country, hailing from warmer nations such as India, Bangladesh, and Pakistan, their hands now kept warm during winter months by *pogies* affixed to handlebars while masks played the dual role of face warmer and contagion protection. Deliveries by car similarly surged, despite the absurdity of delivering 500-gram burritos or burgers in 1,500-kilogram cars.

The dramatic decline in Toronto's car and truck traffic in the first months of the pandemic was accompanied by an equally dramatic decline in road casualties. When motor traffic levels began returning to "normal" in the last months of 2020, the casualty toll increased, including the deaths of four cyclists. Speed cameras that became operational on city streets in July 2020, after years of debate, quickly confirmed that speeding by motorists was almost as common as driving. In their first months, the cameras, limited to school zones in fifty publicized locations, detected tens of thousands of infractions, and hundreds of thousands of violations annually thereafter. The numbers should have chastened motorists in the habit of calling out cyclists for disobeying rules of the road.

Image 43: Food delivery by bicycle surges. Food delivery by bicycle during the pandemic allowed many city residents to shelter at home, safe from the virus. Delivery workers, including this one on Spadina Avenue, still toiled on dangerous streets. Thirty years after the Spirit of Spadina "die-in" near this very spot, painted sharrows offer dubious protection for cyclists on a road that balloons to as many as six lanes, exclusive of the streetcar line, at intersections. (Photo: Albert Koehl)

For automakers the pandemic offered a new opportunity to promote the sheltered passenger cabin of its products, including oversized pickups that were aggressively marketed despite their greater danger to pedestrians and cyclists. Electric vehicles – 130 years after an electric car was first built in Toronto – had become the industry's new, subsidy-seeking, saviour. Driverless cars remained, as in previous decades, imminent, while existing cars had yet to learn the simple task of reading a posted speed limit.

Several months into the pandemic in 2020, the police killing, captured on video, of a Black man in the United States accused of a minor offence provoked mass protests about racial prejudice and inequality. The fact that the pandemic was taking a heavier toll on marginalized and racialized communities in Toronto, as elsewhere, while making greater demands of them as workers, exposed existing fault lines between rich and poor, and between the white population and First Nations, Black, and other racialized groups. The inequitable distribution of bike lanes across the city itself got attention, with demands for improved infrastructure in lower-income suburbs.

The (former) Town of Weston in the city's northwest fit the definition of a marginalized, racialized community hit particularly hard by the pandemic. For many motor commuters, the town was little more than a conduit to and from highways into and out of the city, prejudicing the safety of local residents, many of whom had few options beyond riding on crowded TTC buses. The Weston Road streetcar was long gone. A short but dangerous gap in the nearby Humber bike trail was, after years of study, including a municipal environmental assessment (EA), about to be closed when the province ordered a full provincial EA, likely motivated

Image 44: "Home of the Bicycle." The Town of Weston, since 1998 part of the amalgamated City of Toronto, still greets visitors with signs that highlight its proud bicycle-making heritage. The town had been a favourite excursion destination for Toronto cyclists in the 1890s. Today, the absence of bike lanes and the fact of heavy motor traffic ensure that many local cyclists take refuge on the sidewalk. (Photos: Wikimedia and Albert Koehl)

by a desire to appease golfers at an adjacent golf course. The intervention had all the hallmarks of Premier Ford's petty meddling in municipal affairs. In fact, the provincial order was so curious that city councillors voted overwhelmingly to authorize its legal department to file an application for judicial review. The province relented only after the city's legal challenge was about to go to court in late 2023.

In 2021, bike lane installations in the city started bending back towards the pre-pandemic pace, with an average of 18 kilometres per year installed in the three years to the end of 2023 – despite a 33-kilometre annual target that was central to the city's climate plan. A full retreat to the listless pre-pandemic performance was, however, improbable, no matter that public consultations still gave inordinate, outdated attention to the question: "What about (motor) traffic?" The question about delays to motorists continued to slow progress, but no longer thwarted road safety projects.

Opponents to bike lanes during the 2022 mayoral election – "the hopeful heirs to Ford Nation," as one commentator called them – sounded increasingly irrational, churlish, and even desperate. During public consultations for the Bloor Street bike lane extension in the spring of 2023, some opponents claimed that the bike lane would interfere with the loading of hearses for funerals at a local church. It was not the first time that the dead had been conscripted to the anti-bike lane cause.

The tragedy of the climate crisis was not just that the consequences of inaction had long ago been predicted, but that the necessary transition to clean transportation offered improved air quality, healthier communities, and safer neighbourhoods. Any slack in the timelines for climate action had been squandered, while the potential of the bicycle to contribute to reducing the

Image 45: A new hazard for cyclists. A cyclist wears a protective mask in June 2023 as out-of-control wildfires in Northern Ontario and Quebec blanketed Toronto with smoke. The irony of the advice from health officials to wear masks was that cyclists had escaped masking recommendations during the pandemic. The clean air benefits of closing the last of the province's dirty coal-fired power plants a decade earler were now being lost to new hazards. (Photo: Albert Koehl)

city's five million tonnes of GHG emissions from transportation remained largely untapped.

In June 2021, the Town of Lytton, British Columbia, suffered the highest-ever temperature recorded in Canada, reaching 49.6 degrees Celsius. Days later, most of the town burned to the ground. Wildfires raged across that province; floods followed. The terms "heat dome" and "atmospheric river" entered everyday discourse. In fact, although the outdoors had been a safe refuge from the pandemic, in June 2023, when wildfires raged across Eastern Canada, engulfing Toronto and other cities in a haze of smoke, cyclists were advised to wear masks to protect their lungs. On some days, Toronto's air quality was among the worst in the world. Canada was driving from the pandemic into the frying pan.

For his part, Premier Doug Ford, after the 2022 provincial election, eliminated, despite the absence of public demands, motor vehicle registration fees, even returning fees already paid, with an annual cost to the treasury of $1 billion. In most of the province, the motorist could still sit back, alone, in the comfort of a car, confident that bureaucrats and politicians were monitoring "traffic," ready to reward the motorist with new or widened roads when the old ones filled up.

The election of Olivia Chow as Toronto's 66th mayor in June 2023, however, again brought to the city's highest public office a leader who was a committed promoter of cycling, walking, and mass transit. And while Chow's victory was aided by her name recognition, other developments offered evidence that the city's politicians were finally catching up to the public on issues of road safety and climate action. Weeks before Chow's election, council approved by a vote of 21 to 1 a westward extension of the Bloor bike lane deep into suburban Etobicoke. The local councillor listened politely to

Image 46: Parking for bikes, not cars. In this downtown development (as in many others) four times more bike parking spots were proposed than car parking. Even a decade earlier the notion that minimum parking requirements for cars would be abolished – as they were in 2021 for new residential buildings – was about as likely as the legalization of marijuana. Many developers no longer wanted to front costs of up to $160,000 per spot for underground parking stalls that many residents did not want. (Photo: Albert Koehl)

the howls of indignation from some residents about the loss of two motor lanes – despite the obvious safety advantage to pedestrians – then repeated her commitment to the Complete Street project, while taking aim at the lone council dissenter from Etobicoke. "It's an irresponsible, short sighted and out-of-touch position to suggest that we don't need safe cycling infrastructure in our city."

Since the 1890s, the bicycle's fundamental design and operation – despite major technological advances in other fields – had remained surprisingly similar, and so simple that it could be operated safely by a child. In fact, a writer's predictions in 1893 about the bicycle in a distant future had in many respects turned out to be accurate: a bicycle "little changed" but for lighter materials and lesser friction in movement, folding bikes among popular models, and electric bikes that could be easily recharged. He predicted that bicycles would no longer be used in wars – not for lack of utility, but because people would be so healthy and well-humoured that there would be no reasons for conflict. Whether or not he was right about the populace's happy, cycling-induced disposition, his prediction provided a contrast to the reality of wars fought in the ensuing decades in conflicts over energy resources.

The bicycle had endured for reasons starkly different from the car. As one advocate put it: "No Bravado. No Celebrities. No Big Budget. No Stunts. Some things just sell themselves." Indeed, after an initial small investment (perhaps for a second-hand vehicle), a bicycle could take the rider across the city (or far beyond), with inputs often involving little more than oil for the chain and air for one's tires and lungs.

The attacks against cycling infrastructure were not so much about the bicycle or its rider as about satisfying the automobile's voracious appetite for space, both for driving and for parking. (Advocates for busways and LRT lines or wider sidewalks faced precisely the same predicament.) The underlying problem was not the inherent nature of the bicycle, but the inherent nature of the car.

During the pandemic, the bicycle had again proven itself to be a loyal and valuable friend. In the fight to save the deteriorating climate, it continued to offer part of the solution, and hope for the future.

Acknowledgments

With the fall from fashion of the bicycle at the turn of the century, the craze for writing about bicycles also ended, at least for several generations. As a result, for the period from 1900 to 1970, my research largely depended on primary sources, which often required the expert guidance of staff at various public institutions, including the City of Toronto, provincial, and national archives, specific departments of Toronto City Hall, Sharon Babaian at the Museum of Science and Technology, and the Toronto Reference Library. I owe a special word of thanks to Lorne Shields who provided generous access to his impressive cycling collection.

I am grateful to a number of people who agreed to be interviewed for this work, including Lyn Adamson, Mike Barry, Norm Hawirko, John Beckwith, Bicycle Bob (Silverman), Steve Beiko, Marty Collier, Kyle Ashley, Joan Doiron, Dan Egan, Stephen Fisher, Nick Gamble, Adrian Heaps, Sarah Hood, Bill Humber, Tom Koch, Howard Levine, Kevin Montgomery, Robin Mautner, Marvin Macaraig, Darnel Harris, Dianne Denhart, Alex Paterson,

Marilyn McNickle, Dave Meslin, Michael Moore, Phil Piltch, Roger Powley, Jim Jacobs, Martin Reis, Jim (Jammr) Rooney, Uri Samson, John Sewell, Harvey Shaul, Nancy Smith Lea, Ted Suddon, John Swaigen, Siva Vijenthira, David White, Li Yu, Sue Zielinski, David Warren, Will Wallace, Tammy Thorne, Wayne Scott, Don Watterson, and Winona Gallop.

I am thankful for the additional insights, advice, and assistance provided by a number of individuals, among them Joe Hendry, Michael Black, Jonathan Schmidt, Monica Campbell, Lynn Spink, H.V. Nelles, Arthur Klimowicz, Adrian Currie, Julia Morgan, Evan Ferrari, Pat Brown, Gideon Foreman, Glen Norcliffe, Janet Joy Wilson, Hamish Wilson, Michael Schabas, David Andrews, Mary Pearson, Garry Wice, Brice Sopher, Sean Marshall, James McKenty, John Taranu, Dave Richardson, Robert Zaichkowski, Eric Kamphoff, Aaron Enchin, Kasia Briegmann-Samson, Nicholas Kovats, freelance editor Tilman Lewis, and Peter Middleton. A special word of thanks is due to the anonymous reviewers for their constructive feedback and insights on the manuscript, to copyeditor Beth McAuley, and to Jodi Lewchuk, Leah Connor, and other staff at University of Toronto Press for their interest in this work and for their patience and good humour throughout the publishing process.

A book requiring such a commitment of time and effort would of course not be possible without the support of family and friends, no one more than my wife, Emily.

Abbreviations

ARC	Advocacy for Respect for Cyclists
CCC	City Cycling Committee
CCM	Canada Cycle & Motor Co., Ltd.
CoT	City of Toronto
CP	Canadian Pacific
CTA	City of Toronto Archives
CWA	Canadian Wheelmen's Association
DVP	Don Valley Parkway
HTA	*Highway Traffic Act*
LAW	League of American Wheelmen
LRT	Light Rail Transit
MTO	Ministry of Transportation (Ontario)
OML	Ontario Motor League
OSL	Ontario Safety League
PWIC	Public Works and Infrastructure Committee
TBC	Toronto Bicycle Club
TCA	Toronto Cyclists' Association
TCAT	The Centre for Active Transportation (originally Toronto Coalition for Active Transportation)
TRC	Toronto Railway Company
TTC	Toronto Transit Commission (formerly Toronto Transportation Commission)
TTS	Transportation Tomorrow Survey

Notes

Preface

xi *"Killer at the Wheel"* ... "Killers at the Wheel," *Globe*, May 20, 1929, 4.

xi *"slaughter of innocents"* ... "The Slaughter of the Innocents," *Globe*, June 1, 1929, 4.

1896 – The Bicycle Craze

1 *Toronto's "pooh-bah ..."* "Toronto Cyclists' Association," *Globe*, May 15, 1896, 8.

1 *"silver-tongued orators ..."* "Rock City Wins," *Evening Star*, Apr. 4, 1896, 8; "Quebec's Meet: The Ancient City Carries Off the Prize," *Globe*, Apr. 4, 1896, 24.

2 *accounts of the meeting* ... See, for example, "Canadian Wheelmen Meet," *New York Daily Tribune*, Apr. 4, 1896, 4.

2 *top post of the Toronto Cyclists' Association* ... "The Toronto Cyclists' Assoc," *Globe*, May 15, 1896, 8 – TCA collaborated with CWA. TCA member applications available from *Globe*'s cycling dept. See "A Broader Field, the Inter-Club Assoc to Take in All Wheelmen," *Globe*, Apr. 28, 1896, 8; "A Cyclers' Union," *Evening Star*, May 15, 1896, 4.

2 *to themselves on the Sabbath* ... See, generally, Armstrong and Nelles, *Revenge of the Methodist Bicycle Company*.

2 *Tutti-Frutti* ... Ad, Adams' Tutti Frutti, TBC, 1892 Program for 11th Annual Meet, p 18.

2 *speeding or amusement* … "The Goold Bicycle Company, Brantford," *Globe*, Mar. 18, 1893, 17 – "the professional man and messenger alike find it most convenient and economical."

2 *standard use of pneumatic tires* … Doolittle, "Cycling of To-day," 407, comparing the new reality to bygone days when club outings might involve a ride into the country, a supper, and game of ball. (Mrs. Doolittle was rarely mentioned.) "… she challenges us to a sprint along some secluded by-way, and flying after her happy, throbbing, pedalling form, we realize in her our equal, and when, with a spurt up the hillside and a dismount under the shade of the old oak, she breathlessly taunts us with our inability to catch up, we feel that the sweet, lovable girl of a decade ago, has given place to the still sweeter, more lovable and healthy new woman of to-day."

2 *"out-of-date aristocratic mount …"* Doolittle, "Cycling of To-day," 407 – "unwillingly and regretfully we climbed down from our lofty perch to the realm of comfort and safety which we now occupy." See Norcliffe, *The Ride*, 74, 252: Rover Safety of 1885 often regarded as final dev't of safety: chain drive, early version of diamond frame for strength, wheels with tangential or crisscrossing wire spokes threaded to hub, hollow rims, lighter, stronger (steel-tubed) frames, and ball bearings.

2 *"carriage of the patrician …"* Doolittle, "Cycling of To-day," 407.

3 *elegant east-end home on Sherbourne* … By 1910, Dr. Doolittle had his office and home at 150 Bloor Street East after moving from 180 Sherbourne Street, at Shuter. He later moved to 619 Sherbourne. See *Might's Directory*, 1910, vol. 2, 562. As to departure date: Ad, *Globe*, Aug. 4, 1896, 5 – Ship leaves Sat, Aug. 15, thus likely left Toronto, Aug. 13 (to allow for travel time of at least 10 hrs to Montreal).

3 *"[E]verybody's talking about cycling …"* "Around Town," *Saturday Night*, May 9, 1896, vol. 9, no. 25, 1.

3 *dreaming bicycle* … "In Town," *Globe*, Mar. 14, 1896, 9.

3 *a window overlooking the street* … "Town Bicycle Traffic," *Mail & Empire*, Oct. 11, 1895, 5, TPL, Microfiche Collection – Bike count: 9am, 117 … noon, 267; 12:30, 284 … 5pm, 226; 5:30, 343; 6pm, 395. High cycling volumes at noon hr suggests trips to lunch (perhaps home). Day of week not specified. Total 3,500, over 9.5hr period.

5 *busiest cycling routes even today* … For comparison to the popular Bloor Street bike lane today, see Jnyyz, "How Many Cyclists Are Using the Bloor Bike Lanes?," Biking in a Big City, Sept. 28, 2017, https://jnyyz.wordpress.com/2017/09/28/how-many-cyclists-are-using-the-bloor-bike-lanes/.

5 *"they're going to try to put us down …"* "Town Bicycle Traffic," *Mail & Empire*, Oct. 11, 1895, 5. One bystander was less charitable: "I'm going to break up the wheel of any fellow that tries to ride over me."

5 *"on top of you at once..."* "A Bicycle Suggestion," *Daily Star*, Oct. 30, 1894, 2 –
   hills also to be flattened for cyclists, and horse-drawn vehicles to be banned
   from Jarvis to clear way for cyclists.

7 *Fleming had his business office ...* "Thousands Cheer," *Globe*, Jan. 7, 1896, 6;
   "Music and the Drama," *Globe*, Oct. 1, 1897, 10; "General News of the City,"
   Globe, Aug. 11, 1897, 10; "Bicycles in Baggage Cars," *Globe,* May 4, 1896, 10;
   Norcliffe, *The Ride,* 215, citing *Cycling,* Apr. 14, 1892 – opera house could
   accommodate 250 bikes.

7 *two bicycle rooms ...* "Chit Chat," *Globe*, Oct. 10, 1898, 6 – large bike rooms
   (measuring 80 feet long) "indicate plainly that in the opinion of the architect at
   least the wheel is a factor worth noting ..."

7 *room for 100 bicycles ...* "Bike Room," *Globe*, Oct. 31, 1896, 28.

7 *repaired and cleaned ...* "The Temple Building," *Globe*, Oct. 22, 1898, 9 (home of
   the International Order of Foresters; the building was demolished in 1970).

7 *counted 196,000 people ...* "Re Police Census," App C, CC 1896, 61. See also
   Humber, *Freewheeling,* 50; Norcliffe, *The Ride,* 269n34; and Mackintosh,
   Newspaper City, 137, quoted in Mackintosh, "A Bourgeois Geography," which
   suggests, based on CWA estimates of 30,000 bikes in Toronto in 1898, that 16
   per cent of Torontonians would have bikes in 1898, assuming a population of
   200,000, and one bike per person (although some cyclists had more than one).

7 *growing demand ...* Might's Directory, 1896, 1485–6, approximately eighty listings for bike-related products and services – lubricators, tires, manufacturing,
   repairs, rentals, and storage. By comparison, only five such listings in 1890 (at
   1374), including T Fane & Co., 33 Adelaide.

7 *bikes for $70 ...* Griffiths Cycle Corporation, Ad, *Globe*, Mar. 27, 1896, 8;
   T. Eaton Co., Ad, *Evening Star*, Apr. 24, 1896, 1; T. Eaton Co, Ad, *Evening Star,*
   Apr. 8, 1896, 2; Griffiths Cycle Corporation, Ad, *Globe*, May 17, 1898, 10.

7 *exchange with an older model ...* Might's Directory, 1896, Part 1, 1486–8.

8 *guitar lessons, for a bicycle ...* "Articles for Sale," *Evening Star,* Oct. 17, 1896, 3.

8 *"spin in the country ..."* "The Interclub Concert Is All the Rage," *Globe*, Apr. 24,
   1896, 8.

8 *"but almost a necessity ..."* John Griffiths Cycle Corporation, Ad, "A Bicycle Is
   No Longer a Luxury," *Globe*, Feb. 17, 1896, 6.

8 *The Toronto World*, Aug. 15, 1893, 3.

8 *"the novel experience ..."* In Chief Constable Annual Report, 1897, Grasett
   suggested that "every class of society" now rides a bicycle.

8 *125 bicycles for rent ...* Bikes could be rented for $1 on Saturday night,
   returned on Monday. By comparison, rent for boarding house room $3–$4/
   week – Might's Directory, 1896, 1489.

8 *outstripped that for horses ...* Doolittle, "Cycling of To-day," citing *Massey's Magazine*, 409.

8 *claimed one newspaper report ...* "By the Way," *Globe*, July 16, 1896, 9.

9 *"its perfect appointments ..."* "The Cycling Craze," *Evening Star*, Feb. 19, 1896, 4 – "The great hold which bicycling has upon the public is strikingly shown in the widespread interest which has been taken in the Remington Cycle School."

9 *offer cycling lessons ...* H.A. Lozier, Ad, *Canadian Home Journal*, May 1896, vol. 6, no. 5, 20; "Making Bicycles," *Globe*, Apr. 18, 1896, 8.

9 *visits beyond the city ...* "The Toronto Bicycle Club," *Globe*, Oct. 22, 1892, 1.

9 *"undoubtedly appreciated by cyclists ..."* "Around Town," *Saturday Night*, May 9, 1896, vol. 9, no. 25, 1.

9 *useful conveyance for the faithful ...* Once Sunday TRC service was legalized, cyclists were sometimes accommodated, indeed, encouraged, with free carriage of bicycles on trailers hitched to streetcars serving recreational destinations such as Munro Park. See, for example, CTA, Fonds 16, Series 71, Item 11469 – photo of "free" carriage of bikes in TRC trailer. As to bicycles on radials, see "Toronto District Council," *Globe*, May 2, 1899, 9, noting CWA's negotiations to allow for cyclists to bring their bicycles on payment of a fee.

9 *used by its detectives ...* Chief Constable, 1894 Annual Report, 25, describing bicycle use by police as "distinct success."

9 *"severe test upon them ..."* Letter "re New Rapids bicycles for police," Dec. 24, 1896, reproduced in "The Tangent Cycle Co.," Ad, *Evening Star*, Apr. 10, 1897, 3.

11 *poisoning of strays ...* "The Dogs: Catching and Killing Unlicensed Canines," *Globe*, Feb. 4, 1880, 2.

11 *the seizure of dogs ...* "Make War on Dogs," *Globe*, July 6, 1894, 7.

11 *Keating, they found a supporter ...* Mackintosh, "A Bourgeois Geography," 144 – Under the TRC agreement, the city was obliged to install quality pavements along the street railway. Cyclists advocated for improvements to devil strips – "Cinder Paths for Cyclists," *Evening Star*, June 18, 1897, 8.

11 *replaced by electric cars ...* Readers will notice that imperial measurements are accompanied by metric equivalents in chapters leading up to 1979. In 1979 Canada switched completely to metric. All conversions are approximate.

11 *longest continuous route ...* Toronto Railway Co, "Toronto As Seen From The Streetcars," 7.

11 *good reason for caution ...* In fact, the *Globe* suggested that the streetcar danger was dissuading many people from cycling, therefore supporting special strips for cyclists. This was not, however, a common view, perhaps because wheelmen might not want to admit such a fear, or because the bigger push was for good roads. "The Wheel," *Globe*, Feb. 18, 1896, 8.

11 *albeit only for Toronto* ... An Act to amend the Act to Regulate Travelling on *Public Highways and Bridges*, 1897, 60 Vict, c 56, subs 1(d).

12 *"as gracefully as possible ..."* "Etiquette for Cyclers," *Saturday Night*, Oct. 19, 1895, vol. 8, no. 48, 7.

12 *ensure a safe route* ... From Spadina, the northbound BELT Line cars turned east on Bloor, then south towards downtown along Sherbourne. Rowan's residence was at 206 Bloor Street West.

13 *right to ride within the tracks* ... *Rowan v. Toronto Railway*, 1899 CarswellOnt 18, 29 S.C.R. 717; Judgment: Oct. 3, 1899. Another northbound cyclist, following a short distance behind, veered off tracks on hearing the car's gong.

13 *great source of dust* ... The irony of the city's poor roads was its strategic location as a transportation hub, offering the shortest overland route between Lake Ontario and Lakes Simcoe and Huron (at Georgian Bay) for access to natural resources of the hinterland. By 1854, Ontario & Erie Railway connected Lakes Huron and Ontario, replacing some ships that had used the Welland Canal, completed in 1829.

13 *slippery pavement for cyclists* ... "Cyclists at the City Hall," *Globe*, Mar. 7, 1896, 16. A CWA delegation in 1896 called for an end to morning and evening watering (likely by both the TRC and the city). City Hall appeared sympathetic. "General News, Bicycle Accidents," *Globe*, July 31, 1897, 28 – visitor, not anticipating watering, narrowly avoided serious injury.

13 *city's many butcher shops* ... Mackintosh, *Newspaper City*, 97–100; by the 1890s emptying of privies into alleyways had decreased. Much of the filth entered local waterways.

14 *asphalt, macadam, or brick* ... Engineer's Report, Table 3, 101, CoT Council Minutes, 1909 – in 1896, 257 miles of roads, 80 miles unpaved. Among paved roads cedar block had a large lead at 109 miles; macadam, 40 miles; and asphalt, less than 15. In 1896, a total of only 3.6 miles of road were paved. Cited in Chief Constable Annual Report, 1896, App C, 583, TA.

14 *compared to less than 14 miles in Toronto* ... Mackintosh, *Newspaper City*, 113.

14 *newspapers favoured asphalt* ... Mackintosh, *Newspaper City*, 114, citing Keating, 1896 Engineer's Report, noting popularity of asphalt roads with city cyclists.

14 *aesthetics, and propriety* ... Mackintosh, *Newspaper City*, 27–31, 110. Liberal yearning for asphalt over wood, dirt, stone. Doolittle, *Wheel Outings*, 33, describes "Toronto the Good": "Of her churches, she is justly proud, for Sunday in Toronto is, indeed a day of rest; no beer, no streetcars, no excursions."

14 *chaperones, riding down Jarvis* ... "A Symposium on Bicycling," *Evening Star*, Apr. 21, 1896, 1.

14 *"select swell street of the city..."* Mackintosh, *Newspaper City*, 85, until the start of the 1890s, three loads of manure were being carted off from Jarvis Street each day. CoT Council Minutes, 1895, Works Department, App C, 464 – 2,360 dead cats and 780 dogs removed from city streets. "By the City Only," *Evening Star*, Apr. 24, 1896, 1; Doolittle, *Wheel Outings*, 42.

14 *wasn't slippery when wet ...* A.W. Campbell, "Best Roads for Cyclers," *Evening Star*, Feb. 27, 1897, 1. Among other qualities, Campbell noted that macadam didn't reflect heat like asphalt and was easier on horses. His article was part of the paper's front page devoted to cycling. Campbell had been a founder of the Good Roads Association in 1894, then became Ontario's first Highways Commissioner (part of the agriculture department) in 1896.

15 *water absorption and rot ...* Mackintosh, *Newspaper City*, 98. Warring Kennedy, Inaugural Address, App C, 8, CoT Council Minutes, 1895, lamenting dangerous conditions of many cedar block roads, once considered *de rigueur* road surfaces, popularity aided abundance of cedar and low cost, but with a reputation undermined by experience.

15 *water led to deterioration ...* Mackintosh, *Newspaper City*, 120. The *Daily Star* lampooned the practice in "A Gum Game on the Aldermen," July 11, 1901, 1.

15 *sully one's reputation ...* "Fines for Cyclists," *Evening Star*, May 3, 1894, 3. Three cyclists were fined $1 in Toronto Junction. In 1892, sidewalk cycling was not yet illegal under by-laws. CofT Minutes, 1892, Minute 629, 206.

15 *"has fallen from grace ..."* "The Wheel," *Globe*, May 18, 1895, 18. See also Communication from Inter-Club Association, Minute 770, Oct. 28, CoT Minutes, 1895 – in 1895, some advocates called, unsuccessfully, for City Hall to grant cyclists right to ride on some sidewalks between midnight and 5 am.

15 *who didn't go to school ...* Mackintosh, *Newspaper City*, 173, 182, 198, 211–12; "The Peddlers," *Evening Star*, Oct. 2, 1895, 20.

15 *doctors making house calls, failed ...* "Use of sidewalks by bicyclists," CoT Minutes, 1896, App A, 696. The city solicitor agreed that the city had authority but advised against it. In the new century, sidewalks continued to offer a refuge for cyclists, especially in the suburbs, despite a hefty $1 fine, where road improvements were slower. "West Toronto Cyclists Avoid Sidewalks," *Daily Star*, Mar. 10, 1910, 11; "A Justice of Peace Fined in Toronto Junction," *Globe*, Sept. 10, 1904, 28. A Justice of the Peace who was visiting The Junction discovered that his status didn't exempt him from the fine. He acknowledged the transgression but was indignant at having been charged by an officer who was a fellow member of Orange Lodge. "When we meet in the lodge room I'll thank you in another way," he threatened on exiting the courtroom.

15 *strong support from farmers ...* Norcliffe, *The Ride*, 153; "Good Roads Work," *Canadian Wheelman*, Nov. 16, 1896, 6–7; Davies, "Ontario and the Automobile," 303 – the good roads movement in Ontario was a rural movement dating from the 1890s.

16 *"all prevailing desire ..."* Rush, "The Bicycle Boom," para. 10, citing a "Toronto correspondent" in Red Bird, "Spokes from Toronto's Wheel," *Canadian Wheelman,* Sept. 6, 1897, complaining about "the apathy of the vast body of cyclists who could control any and every Municipal, Provincial and Dominion legislative body if they would unite and work harmoniously." In 1896, Pattullo had called on CWA members to contribute financially to rural road work but got a feeble response until Doolittle approached Canadian bicycle business-es and American ones operating in Canada, "Good Roads Work," *Canadian Wheelman*, Nov. 16, 1896, 8.

16 *"a lot of dude wheelmen ..."* "Good Roads Work," *Canadian Wheelman*, Nov. 16, 1896, 6–7.

16 *"anyone with an axe..."* Doolittle, "Cycling of To-day," 409. The *Municipal Act* was amended in 1896, 59V, c 51, s 39 to grant the CWA authority to erect the signs at its own expense.

16 *favourite slogan of Dr. Doolittle ...* Humber, *Freewheeling*, 11.

16 *granted by the province until 1895 ...* CoT Procceedings, 1890, Oct. 27, 1890, Minute 1189.

16 *authority to pass cycling by-laws ...* Waters, "Rebirth of Bicycling Law?," citing *R. v Justin* (1894), 24 OR 327 at 329 (CA), involving sidewalk-riding by a cyclist.

17 *"anything obnoxious to the wheelmen..."* "Cyclists at the City Hall," *Globe*, Mar. 7, 1896. See also Meeting notes for "Subcommittee re Bicycle Paths," Board of Works, Mar. 6, 1896, CTA, Series 583. At the time, lamps were cumbersome acetylene devices.

17 *existing brakes on the market ...* Norcliffe, *The Ride*, 53, 56. See Reynolds, "Technological Innovation," 35–6, who states that it was bought by an English syndicate in late 1896. Doolittle promoted the brake (also anticipating its use on cars) at bike shows in Sydenham, England, and in Paris, France, before it be-came popular in Canada. See also "The Doolittle Brake," *Canadian Wheelman*, Feb. 15, 1897 – "The only correct and perfect coaster brake."

17 *"danger of being run down..."* CoT Council Minutes, 1894, Exec Committee, Report no. 10, App A, Apr. 6, 113, also recommending speed limits.

18 *"glow-worm in our electric-light streets ..."* "The Board of Works – No Bicycle Regulations," *Globe*, Apr. 17, 1894, 3. A speed limit was also proposed. The *Canadian Home Journal* counselled pedestrians to stand still and wait for an

approaching cyclist to pass, assuming the pedestrian could actually see the unlit cyclist approaching. "Women's Sports," *Canadian Home Journal*, Jan. 1896, 15.

18 *to address reckless cycling* ... CC, 1894 Annual Report, 25.

18 *improving the many unsafe roadways* ... "In the Stretch," *Globe*, Apr. 14, 1897, 8.

18 *"No scorching on Club runs ..."* Norcliffe, *The Ride*, 186, citing *Cycling*, 1892. The *Evening Star*, however, blamed CWA-affiliated members, alleging they used the streets to train for races – "Ald. Preston Is Right," *Evening Star*, Oct. 12, 1897, 1.

18 *"go as fast as the cars ..."* "The Board of Works – No Bicycle Regulations," *Globe*, Apr. 17, 1894, 3.

19 *a 10 mph (16 km/h) limit* ... "Bicyclists Discuss the Proposed City By-law," *Evening Star*, Apr. 13, 1894, 4.

19 *travelling at an "immoderate" speed* ... CoT Council Minutes, 1895, App B, Feb. 4, By-law 3308, amending By-law 2464, "For the regulation of the Streets, and for the Preservation of Order." See also CoT Council Minutes, 1895, May 27, Minute 407.

19 *the noise from 10,000 bells* ... "Alderman Dunn Thinks Scorchers Should Be Put Down," *Globe*, Oct. 8, 1895, 5.

19 *"cycling skills on asphalt pavements ..."* "The Bicycle Bill, Mr. Stratton's Measure to Regulate Wheels Withdrawn," *Globe*, Apr. 3, 1895, 5; "The TBC Elections," *Globe*, Mar. 13, 1896, 6.

19 CoT Council Minutes, 1896, By-law 3428, June 8, App B. Fast riding allowed sunrise to 8am and 2-8pm.

19 *issue of cyclists' speed* ... "A Symposium for Bicycling," *Evening Star*, Apr. 21, 1896, 1. *Cycling* in 1892 suggested that a limit of 8 mph would be welcomed by cyclists, see "Regulations for Cyclists," *Cycling*, Oct 27, 1892, vol. 2. No 23, 419.

20 *6 mph (9 km/h) for intersections* ... "Crowley Inquest," *Globe*, Apr. 21, 1896, 8, 10 – Sampson Crowley (younger brother of well-known bike racer) collided at night with other cyclist, fell, hit his head. Jury also recommended lanterns and bells.

20 *two or three scorchers* ... "A Symposium for Bicycling," *Evening Star*, Apr. 21, 1896, 1.

20 *among about 25,000 cyclists* ... "Ald. Preston Is Right," *Evening Star*, Oct. 12, 1897, 1. Proposal to the Board of Works – 8mph speed, slowing at intersections, not carrying passenger, dismounting at busiest points, and having a bell – turned over to subcommittee.

20 *licensing and regulation of cyclists* ... "A Bicycle Bill," *Globe*, Mar. 23, 1895, 18; "Rights and Privileges" and "The Bicycle Bill," *Globe*, Mar. 27, 1895, 6. Howland's lesser-known bill was also considered. See "Municipal Committee Today," *Globe*, Apr. 2, 1895, 8; "The Legislature: Notes," *Globe*, Apr. 2, 1895, 7;

and "Notes and Comments," *Globe*, Apr. 2, 1895, 4. In opposing licensing, the *Globe* also noted that bikes caused little wear and tear on roads.

20 *"You don't look badly injured ..."* "The Bicycle Bill," *Globe*, Apr. 3, 1895, 5.

21 *"a violent death ..."* The Bicycle Bill," *Globe*, Apr. 3, 1895, 5.

21 *began and ended with Toronto ... Municipal Amendment Act*, 1895, c 42, s 24.

21 *required to keep to the right ... An Act to amend the Act to Regulate Travelling on Public Highways and Bridges*, 1897, 60 Vict, c 56. "In the Stretch" and "Jack at Play," *Globe*, Apr. 14, 1897, 8; and "The New Bicycle Bill Receives Its Finishing Touches," *Globe*, Apr. 3, 1897, 14.

21 *knocking the lawyer off his bicycle ...* "The Butcher Boy and the Bicycle," *Globe*, June 19, 1897, 24.

21 *pedals and hands on the handlebars ...* "It Is Now the Law – Provisions of the New Bicycle Regulations," *Globe*, July 13, 1898, 7; CoT Council Minutes, 1898, App B, cyclists also required to use caution when turning from one road to another.

22 *"rush to the Klondike ..."* The by-law reiterated the ban against immoderate speed, specifically for cyclists. The right of cyclists to ride in devil strip acknowledged, subject to conditions. "The Bicycle By-law," *Globe*, July 14, 1898, 4.

22 *an obligation to dismount and walk ...* CoT Council Minutes, 1898, By-law 3596, App B, and "By-Law to Regulate the Bicycle Traffic," Report 5, no. 5. Reception and Legislation Committee, App A, p 493. The by-law acknowledged the right of cyclists to use the devil strip, to be vacated upon the approach of a streetcar; see also "Bicycle By-law," *Globe*, June 15, 1898, 2; and "Can't Tax the Bicycles," *Globe*, Apr. 30, 1897, 4 – city solicitor advised city had no power to licence cyclists.

22 *"first-class shape for bicycle riders ..."* CoT Council Minutes, 1896, Mayor's Inaugural Address, App C, 6. See also "Streets for Bicycle Riding" *Globe*, Jan. 21, 1896; "Mayor Once More," *Globe*, Jan. 21, 1896, 6; and "For the Bicyclists," *Evening Star*, Jan. 20, 1896, 1.

22 *"a power in the land just now ..."* "The Wheel," *Globe*, Jan. 22, 1896, 8.

23 *"every new street that is constructed ..."* "Bicycle Costumes," *Canadian Home Journal*, Apr. 1896, 8, quoting *Lady's Pictorial*.

23 *near Lansdowne Avenue ...* James Lochrie, Ad, *Canada Lancet and Practitioner*, 1895 (canadiana.org). See also *Evening Star*, Feb. 27, 1897, 15 – opening Yonge Street showroom. Some evidence that Lochrie's Bloor Street cinder path (between Dundas Street and Lansdowne Avenue) was still in place in 1910 – see *Sims v. Grand Trunk R. W. Co.* 1905 CarswellOnt 274, 5 O.W.R. 664.

23 *"exceeding in that respect even Buffalo ..."* "For City Cycling Paths," *Globe*, Feb. 17, 1896, 6; *and* "For Better City Streets," *Globe*, Feb. 26, 1896, 8.

23 *save $4 in bicycle repairs* ... "Minutes of the subcommittee (re bicycle paths),"
    Board of Works, Mar. 6, 1896, 35, 37. CTA, Fonds 200, Series 582, file 1.

24 *"but a protest against bad roads ..."* "Best Roads for Cyclers," *Evening Star*,
    Feb. 27, 1897, 1 – "Cycle paths are a means of recreation, but good roads add to
    individual and national wealth."

24 *demand for bicycle strips and paths* ... Norcliffe, *The Ride*, 174.

24 *did not want special treatment* ... "Cyclists at the City Hall," *Globe*, Mar. 7, 1896, 16.

24 *including one on Spadina Avenue* ... "A Number of Bicycle Paths to Be Built,"
    Globe, Sept. 30, 1896, 8. An existing footpath along the east side of Queen's Park
    (along Queen's Street Avenue) was appropriated by cyclists, while the park's
    lawns and beaten paths were popular among beginners. Some bike strips still
    being planned with cedar blocks, a dubious choice. A proposed strip on Arthur
    Street, was superseded by an improved roadway. See "Mr. Keating's Budget,"
    Globe Feb. 1, 1897, 5.

24 *a difficult uphill ride* ... "Cinder Paths for Cyclists," *Globe*, June 18, 1897, 8.
    One-mile Kingston Road path approved by York Township, with private
    contributions after the 1897 *Municipal Act* amendment. By June 1897, the path
    was almost complete to the top of Norway Hill. A bike path also constructed
    on Eastern Avenue (GTR crossing to Pape). Lakeshore Road bike path ran to
    Church Road, Mimico. Bike groups sought improvements to devil strip along
    radial lines – "Cycle Paths," *Globe*, Feb. 7, 1899, 10. Chief Constable Grasett
    called for new bike paths on Toronto Island where cyclists rode on sidewalks,
    see CC Annual Report, 1895, 15.

25 *building of cinder paths* ... "City Inter-Club Association," *Mail & Empire*, Feb.
    23, 1895, 13.

25 *contribute financially to the cause* ... "A Cinder Path Boom," *Globe*, July 23, 1895, 6.

25 *"300 others have put up the money? ..."* George A. Kingston, "The Cinder Path
    Project," letter to the editor, *Globe*, Apr. 16, 1895, 8.

25 *Massey Hall concert in the spring of 1896* ... "The Cinder Path," *Evening Star*,
    Apr. 21, 1896, 1 – poor state of waterfront path given as reason to attend.
    Revenues fell short of expectations, the *Evening Star* suggested cyclists who
    bought tickets preferred a bike outing – "A Small Audience," *Evening Star*, Apr.
    24, 1896, 1.

25 *the more enthusiastic contributors* ... "The Wheel – About the Cinder Path,"
    Globe, May 2, 1895, 8. On a Sunday in early April 1896 a reported 750 cyclists
    were at the Humber River - "Truly all the world's awheel," see "Cycling News,"
    Evening Star, Apr. 8, 1896, 2.

25 *"in the good city of Toronto ..."* "Honour Cinder Path," *Evening Star*, June 29, 1896, 1.

25 *$5 to the cinder path fund* ... "In City Today," *Evening Star*, Mar. 15, 1899, 2; and "Blocking the Cinder Path," *Evening Star*, June 2, 1899, 5.

26 *ready to accede to a fee or tax* ... "Around Town," *Saturday Night*, Sept. 15, 1894, vol. 7, no. 43. *Saturday Night* supported a tax on cyclists, with revenues to improve roads. It suggested many young cyclists were not ratepayers but were benefiting from roads, and that 95 per cent of ratepayers/households made no personal use of roads, relying solely on transit and sidewalks.

26 *in place in Brooklyn, New York* ... Beverley Jones, letter to the editor, *Evening Star*, Mar. 29, 1895, 3. Inquest determined victim fell on road, then run over and killed by cyclist. See "Victim of the Bicycle," *Globe*, Sept. 10, 1894, 10.

26 *but always failed* ... "Bicycle License Tax," *Evening Star*, May 23, 1898, 1; "Taxation of Wheelman," *Globe*, Nov. 17, 1897, 6. Mayor proposed $1 tax to improve roads and build cinder paths, inviting bike groups to discuss it. They voted it down.

26 *prohibited throwing glass, tacks* ... "On a Wheel – Some Trials of a Beginner," *Globe*, Aug. 4, 1894, 13. City of Toronto Council Reports, Nov. 18, 1895, Minute 801 – $10 reward for apprehension and conviction for throwing dangerous items on roads.

28 *"deemed necessary" for bicycle paths* ... *Consolidated Municipal Act*, RSO 1897, c 223, s 640(1) as amended, c 57, *An Act relating to bicycle paths*. See also "Toronto Cyclists' Annual," *Globe*, Apr. 27, 1897, 10.

28 *ambiguous, even if sometimes assumed* ... Toronto By-law 3596, *To regulate bicycle traffic*, July 1898, based on *Municipal Act* amendment, prohibiting vehicles from encroaching on "strips" reserved for cyclists. Cyclists were given right of way over horsemen and horse-drawn vehicles, subject to cyclist's obligation to give audible warning of their approach.

28 *an awkward public spat* ... "Cycle Paths," *Globe*, Feb. 7, 1899, 10. Howson boasted that the CWA's Toronto District had been the most energetic group in Canada at installing paths. By 1899, the Toronto District had taken over TCA's work on cycle paths. Winnipeg also had a bike path regime, financed by a 50 cent tax on cyclists, producing 17 miles (27 kilometres) of path, 1901–4; see Lehr and Sellwood, "Two-Wheeled Workhorse," 6, and *Winnipeg Bicycle Paths Act*, SM 1901, c 53. In 1906, the Cycle Paths Board resigned when paved roads obviated need for paths.

28 *financed by a licence for path users* ... By 1897, TBC and others had withdrawn from TCA; only seven clubs remained. "Toronto Cyclist Association [*sic*]," *Evening Star*, Apr. 27, 1897, 2; "Want Good Roads – the Sidepaths Bill a Menace" *Globe*, Mar. 15, 1899, 10; and "The Bicycle Licence," *Globe*, Mar. 15, 1899, 6; and Howson, Chair, CWA Roads and Touring Committee.

28 *waned after railways proliferated* ... Davies, "Ontario and the Automobile," 349, 350.

28 *before good roads become a reality* ... "Want Good Roads – the Sidepaths Bill a Menace," *Globe*, Mar. 15, 1899, 10. Cyclists wanted "to be let alone in the matter of taxes, tags, licences, regulations and discrimination, and to take their chances with the users of other vehicles." CWA supportive of privately funded sidepaths. There were similar debates in the United States. See Friss, "The Path Not Taken," 68–72.

28 *"crusade" for better roads* ... "Want Good Roads – the Sidepaths Bill a Menace," *Globe*, Mar. 15, 1899, 10.

29 *strength of the good roads movement* ... "Obnoxious Bike Bill," *Globe*, Mar. 4, 1899, 24.

29 *dulled the political appeal of his initiative* ... "The Sidepaths Bill Withdrawn," *Globe*, Mar. 24, 1899, 10. In 1900, Howson reintroduced the bill with support from clubs in various towns, but by then the desire for paths had substantially waned – "Cycle Path Bill in Legislature Stratton Bill to Be Presented," *Evening Star*, Mar. 21, 1900, 6.

29 *but also a smooth ride* ... Norcliffe, *The Ride*, 25 – Dunlop popularized the pneumatic in 1888 (invented in 1848), also triggering developments in valves, puncture-proof tires, and improved rims. By 1892, most bikes, even high-wheels and tricycles, had pneumatic tires. In the early 1890s, Toronto bike shops were busy converting hard rubber tires to pneumatics.

29 *"if that were possible ..."* "The Toronto Bicycle Club," *Globe*, Oct. 22, 1892, 1.

29 *counted themselves among cyclists?* ... Helen Ward, "Women on the Wheel," *Canadian Home Journal*, Sept. 1896, 30; "The Latest Thing in Wheels Is a Bicycle Made for Ladies," *Globe*, Feb. 29, 1888, 2.

30 *"even in our dreams imagined ..."* Grace E. Denison, "The Evolution of the Lady Cyclist," *Massey's*, Apr. 1897, vol. 3, no. 4, 281.

30 *Toronto's Industrial Exhibition in 1890* ... "Fane's Bicycle Display," *Globe*, Sept. 13, 1890, 5.

30 *Florence Creed* ... "Miss Florence Creed," *Cycling*, July 28, 1892, vol. 2, no. 17, 277–78. *Cycling* noted her involvement with the Wanderers Bicycle Club, her participation in several invitational races, and her achievement of the first Century Club (100 miles) pin for a woman. *Cycling* wrote that she had "mastered the first ladies' safety" - phrasing that leaves open the possibility that a woman had ridden a man's safety at some earlier point.

30 *"for style, fit and finish ..."* R. Wolfe, Ad, *Evening Star*, Apr. 12, 1897, 2; Crawford Bros., Ad, *Evening Star*, July 6, 1895 – $9 cycling suits.

30 *spokes and chains* ... Norcliffe, *The Ride*, 55–8.

30 *beauty products and jewellery ...* See, for example, Ad, *Canadian Home Journal*, Apr. 1896, vol. 1, no. 12.

31 *"low saddle, rides immoderately ..." Canadian Home Journal*, Aug. 1896, vol. 2, no. 4, 22 – "The woman who looks well on her wheels is she who rides at an easy pace, and has her saddle at proper height." White underskirts were to be avoided.

31 *the cause of rational dress ...* Norcliffe, *The Ride*, 192–3, notes that bicycles are not just a mirror of society but also instruments that coincided with other changes. Rush "The Bicycle Boom," 1 – arguing bikes were "only a small part of a much larger concentration of forces that reshaped feminine garb." Beausaert, "'Young Rovers,'" 51 – most women's cycling wear, at least in small-town Ontario, was actually regressive in style. Cycling attire still presented the popular, highly-coveted "hourglass silhouette," consisting of belted, lighter-coloured shirtwaists and "skirts that were dark, or alpaca in typical outerwear fashion." *Saturday Night* suggested there was also an influence on men's dress, with knickerbockers gaining acceptance – "Around Town," May 9, 1896, vol. 9, no. 25, 1. Norcliffe, *The Ride*, 132, likewise notes waning popularity of uniforms for men in bike clubs, adding the "shift in clothing was not unique to bicyclists; but rather, it was part of a much larger transformation in social attitudes."

31 *independence, and geographic exploration ...* Willard, *A Wheel within a Wheel*. The *Canadian Home Journal*, Apr. 1896, vol. 1, no. 12 (illustration), 8, suggested, "The evolution of the bicycle costume will form an interesting history at some date not far distant; since the question of 'to be bloomers,' or 'not to be bloomers,' seems more nearly approaching settlement."

31 *"when fear has left them ..." Canadian Home Journal*, Apr. 1896, vol. 1, no. 12, 23. "From the little tot of five years to the elderly lad of three score."

31 *"It is immoral ..."* The cited quote is often, erroneously, attributed to Blake herself, but see "Woman's Kingdom," *Mail & Empire*, Aug. 17, 1895, 5. Kit Blake became Kit Coleman after her marriage in 1898. She wrote that "the bicycle demands bloomers. They are the safest. They are the coming fashion." She called bloomers "the most moral of garments" that, unlike lacey clothing, weren't likely to arouse male attention, describing them as the "finest chaperone in the world."

31 *long dead dancing days ...* "Woman's Kingdom," *Mail & Empire*, Aug. 17, 1895, 5.

32 *"you chump! ..."* "Etiquette for Cyclers," *Saturday Night*, Oct. 19, 1895, vol. 8, 7.

32 *the result of a collision ...* "General City News: False Rumors Exploded," *Globe*, July 23, 1896, 10. *Dominion Medical Monthly and Ontario Medical Journal*, 1896, 568, 570, suggested that a poor saddle could have detrimental physical

effects for women, but the article then promoted A.G. Spalding Co.'s Christie Anatomical Saddle, with an ad on a later page.

32 *would lead to catastrophe ...* "Bicycle Topics," *Evening Star*, July 4, 1896, 5. "It begins by a bulging out of the muscle on the side of the hand ... the fingers grow larger and harder ... until they are all out of shape." Some risks had a stronger basis in reality. See, for example, "Bicycling," *Canadian Home Journal*, June 1896, 22, about males who "amuse themselves by driving [vehicles] within close range of a woman's wheel, in order to enjoy the malicious pleasure of making her nervous," conceding that young boys at the helm may be oblivious to discomfort caused to wheelwomen and novice riders.

32 *by way of The Junction ...* "Bicycling," *Canadian Home Journal*, June 1896, 23. The Baptist Union Club, which included women cyclists, had its first run on May 22, 1896 starting from the Jarvis St. Baptist Church.

32 *in bloomers and knickerbockers ... New York Journal*, July 29, 1896, 11.

33 *at least among the upper classes ...* Rush, "The Bicycle Boom," 1.

33 *"more muscular than erotic ..."* Doolittle, "Cycling for Women," *The Canadian Practitioner*, May 1896, vol. 21, no. 5. He concluded: "An indolent life is more fruitful of sexual evils than is a busy, vigorous one." On another occasion, Doolittle cited a woman's complaint that afternoon teas had come to be monopolized by cycling topics, with conversations "entirely engrossed with the all-important subjects of the proper length of a cycling skirt, and the latest in golfers; while to hear them decant on the qualities of their favorite mounts, one would think that they were just past mistresses in the art of mechanics." Doolittle, "Cycling of To-day," 409.

34 *"boat houses are suffering ..." Canadian Home Journal*, July 1896, 21.

34 *selling at $160 ...* Pope Tricycle, Ad, *Canadian Wheelman*, 1883, vol. 1, no. 1, 8 – "For General Use by Ladies and Gentlemen." See, for example, Victor Tricycle, Ad, *Canadian Wheelman*, Mar. 1884, vol. 1, no. 7, 2. A related article in the same journal suggested that tricycles would not replace high-wheels (for men) but that "[t]ricycling is rapidly increasing ... gaining riders from among those who never for a moment thought of becoming bicyclists." "Tricycle Riding," Ad, *Canadian Wheelman*, Sept. 1883, vol. 1, no 1, 4 – "Tricycling is exceedingly popular in the States, and the ladies are beginning to follow the excellent advance set them by the fair sex of 'over the water.'" See also "Cycling and Cyclists," *Globe*, Feb. 24, 1885, 4, and "Woman's World, Tricycles," *Globe*, July 20, 1886, 6. Tricycles and bicycles were growing in favour in Toronto. Tricycles were often equipped with treadles.

34 *limited the potential market ...* Norcliffe, *The Ride*, 33. See also Babaian, *Most Benevolent Machine*, 19–22.

34 *etiquette made it virtually impossible* … Hall, *Muscle on Wheels*. By the late 1880s, competition from younger women had increased.

34 *high-wheel racing career* … "Bicycling," *Globe*, Mar. 28, 1882, 3; and "Bicycling," *Globe*, Apr. 1, 1882, 16. Armaindo once rode 1,000 miles in a six-day race.

35 *"fashion has inflicted on them …"* "Cyclists on the Sabbath," *Evening Star*, May 11, 1896, 1 – the bike count was conducted 6 a.m.–8 p.m. with "sentries" posted at western (Humber River) and eastern (the Woodbine) exits from the city.

35 *rewards for a cyclist's exertion* … Doolittle, *Wheel Outings*, 31–3 – "On any fine Sunday afternoon the hostelries at the Humber … or at the Half-Way, as far again in the other direction, or along any of the thoroughfares leading from the city, will be found to be alive with cyclers." A century later, CWA published a similar guide by Elliott Katz, *The Canadian Cycling Association's* [the CWA's new name] *Complete Guide to Bicycle Touring in Canada*. See also "Places Where Cyclers Rest," *Evening Star*, Feb. 27, 1897, 15 – full page about bike touring; and see also "On a Wheel – A Trip for Cyclists to the Eastern Suburbs," *Globe*, Aug. 2, 1894, 5.

35 *"taste and ambition of the rider …"* H. English, "Toronto Bicycle Club," *Outing*, Sept. 6, 1890, vol. 16, 490–1 – Toronto area roads "all fairly good," except Lakeshore Road. See also Doolittle, *Wheel Outings*, 33.

36 *"painter adequately to portray …"* "On a Wheel – A Trip for Cyclists to the Eastern Suburbs," *Globe*, Aug. 2, 1894, 5 – Kingston Rd lauded despite tough stretch from Woodbine to top of Norway Hill, before bike path installed. "Don and Danforth Rd." was also popular.

36 *"Bill What-You-Call-Him's …"* The quote is from an article that looks back at the mid-1890s craze: "The Late Bicycle Craze," *Daily Star*, Mar. 24, 1902, 6.

36 *precisely reported in the media* … "The Wheel," *Globe*, Jan. 22, 1896, 8.

36 *from Toronto to Waterloo* … George A. Kingston, letter to the editor, *Globe*, Apr. 16, 1895, 8.

36 *measures of a wheelman's prowess* … "Montreal," *Canadian Wheelman*, Sept. 1883, vol. 1, no. 1, 6, reported on such a ride; the article also reported (on p. 7) that a member of the Belleville Bicycle Club made a 105-mile (168-kilometre) return trip to Kingston in one day. The Century Road Club awarded a commemorative button to every cyclist that rode 62 miles (100 kilometres) in a single day. In 1896 the time limit for such rides was reduced to ten hours.

36 *Lyman Hotchkiss Bagg* … Kron, *Ten Thousand Miles*.

36 *still riding a high-wheel* … "Rode High Wheel 25,672 Miles," *Daily Star*, June 29, 1904, 2; "Bicycle Tours," *Globe*, Nov. 8, 1902, 13.

37 *dominated by Americans* … "The Wheel: Dr Doolittle's Wheel Outings," *Globe*, July 23, 1895, 6, lauding book's "high order of excellence." See also "The Quebec

Meet," *Globe*, Apr. 4, 1896, 24. A CWA priority in 1896, working with the League of American Wheelmen (LAW) was to end customs duties on visiting US cyclists.

37 *trips originating in the city* ... "Cyclists' Road Map for the County of York with Portions of Ontario, Peel, and Simcoe," in Hayes, *Historical Atlas of Toronto*. Victoria Park, Kleinburg, and Weston were among other destinations; more distant towns included Acton, Cooksville, and Newmarket. See "The Cyclists' Road Guide of Canada with Map," 74–5. The article, "Jackson's Point," *Globe*, Apr. 29, 1899, 7, listed for the cyclist the good quality roads near Jackson's Point, 55 miles (88 kilometres), from downtown Toronto.

37 *guidebooks and hotel information* ... CWA divided Ontario and other parts of Canada into districts, each overseen by "consuls" or chief consuls with specific responsibilities, including guidance to touring cyclists.

37 *world travellers* ... *Outing*, Sept. 1884, vol. 4, no. 6, 474. American Thomas Stephens's three-year 13,500-mile (21,750-kilometre) trip around the world ended in 1887 with much jubilation. Other adventurers met their demise along the way; see Norcliffe, *The Ride*, 232.

37 *reported having gained weight* ... Bates, "The Great Canada Bicycle Tour," *Outing*, July 2–12, 1883, describing the trip as "the most notable touring event on the wheel in any country since the bicycle was invented." Doolittle, then twenty-two years old, acted as the group's guide. City's ravines got positive review, but roads described as generally "abominable," albeit some good roads in the suburbs.

37 *whose bicycle had broken down* ... *The Varsity*, Nov. 13, 1895, vol. 15, no. 6, reported that a student was 17 miles (27 kilometres) into his country ride when a crash damaged his bike. He was able to walk to a train station half a mile away. The Town of Weston and York Township, for instance, could be reached on the Grand Trunk Railway from Union Station.

38 *accustomed to getting its way* ... "Toronto Cyclists' Association," *Globe*, May 15, 1896, 8. See "Good Roads Logic," *Canadian Wheelman*, Dec. 7, 1896, 5 – Parliament yet to decide in favour of cyclists; "Baggage Bill," *Canadian Wheelman*, Nov. 16, 1896, 7 – re private member's bills supporting cyclists. The railways worried about the number of bikes they would have to carry without charge. The CWA continued its fight with the federal government. See, for example, "The Bicycle Bill," *Globe*, June 9, 1897, 8. A bicycle bill to force railways to carry bikes as free baggage passed the House of Commons but was defeated in the Senate. The fight continued into the new century, see "CWA Annual," *Globe*, Mar. 29, 1902, 34.

38 *often racing* ... The Inter-Club Association wanted, but failed, to build a top-rate racetrack in a city suited to annual CWA competition. Toronto's bike racing

tracks included the Rosedale Lacrosse Grounds, Woodbine, Hanlan's Point, Dufferin, and the Exhibition.

38 *lost (again) at trial ...* Ross v. Orr, Ontario Reports, vol. 25, no. 76, 595, 1894. See "Made a Dead Heat," *Globe*, Oct. 1, 1894, 6. The court ruled that race trustees had the authority to decide the winner. After completing laps around the Woodbine track, competitors embarked on a 15-mile (24-kilometre) circuit along Kingston Road, watched by thousands of spectators.

38 *"could not hold the pace ..."* Merrill Denison, *CCM: The Story of the First Fifty Years*, 16–17. "Did McCarthy turn the Barrel?"

38 *Among the multitude of races ...* TBC/1892 Program for 11th Annual Meet.

38 *for out-of-town visitors ...* Many other races were less formal, including competitions at the annual police games and among bicycle messengers. "Successful Meet," *Globe*, Aug. 16, 1894, 8, including competitions "such for 'old men' over age forty-five. The civil service, among others, also held races. "Messenger Boys Get a Move On," *Globe*, July 16, 1896, 9; "CPR Messenger Meet," *Globe*, Aug. 24, 1897, 8.

39 *the "charm of novelty ..."* "The Rock Wins," *Evening Star*, Apr. 4, 1896, 8 – "only genuine lovers of the sport are now tempted to attend races." Some races held in 1895 had been financially disastrous, and racing had become the "least part" of CWA's work.

39 *the word "Bicyycle" ...* H. English, "Toronto Bicycle Club," *Outing*, Sept. 6, 1890, vol. 16, 490–1, described Doolittle as "the popular club surgeon, who in his day probably won more honors than any racer under amateur colors." See "First Cycle Race over Rough Route," *Globe*, June 29, 1931, 3 – first high-wheel race (in Ont) May 24, 1881, likely against Hamilton's John Moodie Jr.

39 *transitioning into everyday transportation ...* "The Wheel," *Globe*, Dec. 31, 1895, 8.

39 *a column for women in 1891 ...* *Canadian Wheelman*, funded by membership fees and ads, was preceded by *The Bicycle* as the official gazette of the CWA and the Cyclists' Touring Club in Canada (the latter group fell away). The original byline was "Journal of Cycling," but by Dec. 15, 1898, vol. 15, no. 3, it was "A Fortnightly for Young Men."

39 *"A Mirror of Wheeling Events ..."* The tagline was later changed to "Devoted to the Interests of Cyclists and the Cycling Trade of Canada."

39 *Wheeling Gazette ...* Cited in *Canadian Journal of Medicine and Surgery,* Jan-June 1998. The *Wheeling Gazette* also had articles for women cyclists, as noted in *Canadian Wheelman*, Jan. 4, 1897, 5. (No copies of this publication have been found.)

39 *sufficed to maintain exclusivity ...* Friss, *The Cycling City*, 53, writing in the American context, noted that membership helped distinguish individuals, especially urban elite, as social or recreational riders who were different from

utilitarian riders and scorchers who brought ill-repute to cyclists. TBC required
an applicant to be supported by at least two club members and to be judged for
upstanding character.

39 *didn't require a club* ... In 1892, *Cycling*, Apr. 14, 1892, vol. 2 no. 10, 135,
estimated that there were eight clubs with 500 to 600 members, which was a minority of all cyclists in the city. The trend to non-club members among cyclists
increased thereafter.

39 *Evening Star in March 1896* ... "A Cycler's Union," *Evening Star*, May 15, 1896, 4.

41 *newcomers to the bicycle clubs* ... For example, "Baptist Bicyclists," *Globe*, Aug.
27, 1895, 8 – 100 male and female members from local congregations. See also
"Epworth League Bicyclists," *Globe*, May 4, 1896, 10; "Bicycling," *Canadian
Home Journal*, June 1896, 23.

41 *smite me grievously* ... "A Woman's Standpoint," *Globe*, July 7, 1894, 7.

41 *formality of the established clubs* ...Norcliffe, *The Ride*, 181.

41 *regimental look of the older clubs* ... *Canadian Wheelman*, Nov. 16, 1896, 14.
Older clubs expected members to have three outfits: a formal uniform for
parading (cap, jacket, badge, and breeches), a casual touring outfit, and a light
cotton outfit for hot weather. Racers had additional outfits. See *Canadian
Wheelman*, Sept. 1883, vol. 1, no 1, 7–8.

41 *the Learner, and the Expert* ... Pratt, *The American Bicycler.*

41 *bugler, and "club surgeon"* ... Beausaert, "'Young Rovers,'" 50, quoting *Canadian
Wheelman*, April 1895, noted waning interest in uniforms, buglers, and standard bearers. See also "The Wheel," *Globe*, Feb. 14, 1889, 3. The previous TBC
clubhouse was at 416 Church Street. See "Big Membership," *Evening Star*, Mar.
18, 1896, 2; "The Wanderers, of Toronto, at Hamilton," *Canadian Wheelman*,
Sept. 1883, vol. 1, no 1, 3. An 1883 tour by the Wanderers' Bicycle Club to
Hamilton reflected the early days of bicycle. The wheelmen, dressed in grey
and black uniforms, arrived by ferry from Toronto, likely fancied themselves
conquering knights on their "iron steeds." The risk of being flung from their
mounts added adventure and opportunity for jocular ribbing (recounted in this
case as "graceful evolutions in the dust"). "[A] short run ... around the principal
streets, attracted considerable attention." Tour closed with a ball at the "magnificent" residence of the Hamilton club captain.

41 *five-storey Toronto Athletic Club* ... Doolittle, *Wheel Outings*, 37–8, has Doolittle's
description. An outdoor bicycle track, croquet lawn, and tennis court rounded
out amenities. "Big Membership," *Evening Star*, Mar. 18, 1896, 2, re 227 delegates.
TBC previously occupied an elegant house at 346 Jarvis Street, near Carlton.
"The Wheel," *Globe*, May 13, 1895, 6 – the Jarvis Street clubhouse had "elegantly-
appointed rooms, ready to receive the weary cyclist after a hard tussle on the road

with a worthy adversary" – smoking, billiard, card and committee rooms, plus offices, a basement restaurant, wheelhouse for members' bikes, and a "cosy parlor."

42 *with space for 1,000 bicycles* ... *Cycling,* Apr. 14, 1892, vol. 2, no. 10, 138, re size of the wheelhouse. H. English, "Toronto Bicycle Club," *Outing,* Sept. 6, 1890, vol. 16. TBC started with five members on Apr. 13, 1881, to encourage "cycling and the promotion of good fellowship." In 1884, the Wanderers Bicycle Club became the first incorporated bicycle association.

42 *husbands or brothers at club events* ... Doolittle, "Cycling of To-day," 407–11, noting popularity of cycling among women: "The bicycle run and the bicycle tea, and the bicycle moonlight and the bicycle smoker have almost entirely usurped the place of the old entertainment."

42 *jocular character of the early clubs* ... Beausaert, "'Young Rovers,'" 35, 37, 45, includes a review of women in small-town bicycle clubs, noting that women softened virulent masculinity that clubs had cultivated. With women on board, there was less focus on military, drills and racing and "more on designing social outings suitable for heterosexual groups." Fostering respectability, chivalry, and manliness were among the original purpose of the clubs. See Norcliffe, *The Ride,* 190.

42 *youngest daughter of Timothy Eaton* ... Norcliffe, *The Ride,* 188, citing *Cycling,* Oct. 1890, vol. 1.

42 *soon included some women* ... "Bicycling," *Canadian Home Journal,* June 23, 1896. The guild (reorganized from the YWC guild) had colours of white, pale blue, and navy. The committees included social events, membership, and bicycle runs. Miss A.S. Brown was the president. See "Sporting Intelligence – The Toronto Club," *Globe,* May 12, 1882, 3 – typical TBC run might meet at Queen's Park, followed by route along Vaughn Road to Village of Fairbank, then to Downsview and back (~18 miles). See also Norcliffe, *The Ride,* 192.

42 *arriving by ferry* ... By 1896, Toronto cyclists' calendars included bicycle "gymkhana" at Niagara-on-the-Lake with floral procession that contrasted with previous era. *Canadian Home Journal* reported 100 bicycles almost "all beautifully decorated ... preceded by the fire brigade in their bright uniforms and all mounted on decorated wheels." "Bicycling," *Canadian Home Journal,* Sept. 1896, 8. Beausaert, "'Young Rovers,'" 53, citing *Canadian Wheelman,* Oct. 1895, writing about small town Ontario, noted popular "bicycle teas" and trends away from races to concerts, garden parties, and carnivals.

42 *a national sporting organization* ... Cycling groups from across Canada had met earier in the month in Toronto to set the process in motion of establishing a national association. "Bicycling," *Globe,* Dec. 7, 1882, 8. James B. Boustead (at various points a Toronto alderman) and James S. Brierly were, respectively, the first CWA president and secretary-treasurer.

42 *constrained by restrictive rules ...* Admission largely focused on the applicant's "good character." *Canadian Wheelman*, Dec. 7, 1896, 1. Membership application, published in the *Canadian Wheelman*, had to be supported by two CWA members or three reputable citizens. Objections to be filed within two weeks to pre-empt "objectional person."

42 *CWA had 8,700 members ...* Cyclists usually joined CWA indirectly as members of affiliated clubs. Individuals could join independently. See Reynolds, "Technological Innovation," 17. See also *Canadian Wheelman*, Dec. 7, 1896, 8. CWA versus LAW membership: Canada – 1 in 600; US – 1 in 800 (71,650 total).

42 *members in smaller cities ...* "[W]e unsophisticated farmers," an Ottawa cyclist wrote sarcastically, "if we can trade off our wheat and sell our hogs are going to stand by the old concern even if it does take fifty cents a year." "Moss from an Old Log," *Canadian Wheelman*, Nov. 16, 1896, 18–19.

43 *"patent to all ..."* "Quebec's Meet," *Globe*, Apr. 4, 1896, 24 (verbatim speech). As to bike prices falling and improvements to roads, see Doolittle, "Cycling of To-day," 412 – "and with the smooth gliding motion and the general quiet of its tread ... will make us all echo the sentiment, 'God bless the man who first invented wheels.'"

43 *"a valet and maid on wheels ..."* "Around Town," *Saturday Night*, May 9, 1896, vol. 9, no. 29, 1 – "Aristocracy can hardly survive the time when they are not recognized and envied on the street."

1910 – From Fashion to Function

45 *"Ontario is safe once more ..."* "May Fix Date of S. Wellington Voting," *Daily Star*, Oct. 4, 1910, 6 – Whitney "arrived on his bicycle as usual in his office at an early hour this morning after his seven weeks' absence." *The News* likewise reported, Oct. 4, 1910, 6 – that the premier's administration "has a strong hold on the affections of the public."

45 *on his silent steed ...* "The Premier A-Wheel," *Daily Star*, May 18, 1906, 1 – Whitney is twenty-four years older than Confederation itself.

46 *killing a heap of work ...* *Canadian Courier*, Aug. 1, 1908, 5. Whitney lived at 113 St. George Street, south of Bloor Street, 1 kilometre from Queen's Park.

46 *like a merry schoolboy ...* "The Premier A-Wheel," *Daily Star*, May 18, 1906, 1.

46 *rather not be noticed ...* Schull, *Ontario since 1867*, 157, quoting Premier Whitney: "Ontario does not think that I am a great man. It does think I am honest. And honest I must be."

46 *Stay Off The Grass ...* Jeanneret, Marsh, *God and Mammon: Universities as Publishers* (Bloomington: University of Illinois Press, 1989), 83.

46 *"watch where you're going ..."* "Long-Time Employee Once Spilled Premier,"
Globe and Mail, July 30, 1964, 5. Whitney disliked patronage appointments.
Once when on his bike, a supplicant asked to be appointed to replace the
recently deceased Manitoulin Island sheriff (see "Sherriff Jackson Dead," *Globe*,
May 22, 1907, 14.) Whitney replied that it was all right with him, if the under-
taker didn't mind (namely, to take dead man's place in the grave). Anecdote,
recounted as a quote in scholarly works, but this is not confirmed in the earliest
source, Schindler, F.F., *Responsible Government in Ontario* (Toronto: University
of Toronto Press, 1969), 23n18.

46 *"a brick through the window ..."* Schull, *Ontario since 1867*, 124.

47 *same vehicle as the maid ...* See Norcliffe, *The Ride*, 28 – "When an innovation becomes commonplace in the later stages of a carrier wave, it ceases to
distinguish a privileged class of consumers and therefore rapidly loses its social
significance."

48 *"too popular to be popular ..."* "Blessing of the Bicycle," *Globe*, June 3, 1907, 6,
reprint from *Montreal Witness*, "The bicycle ... has now descended to the poorest
... though many bicycles are still in use both for business and pleasure, the riders
are for the most part boys of the working classes." "Madge Merton's Page for
Women," *Daily Star*, Aug. 11, 1906, 16, noted the "poor unfashionable bicycle."

48 *its death-knell as a pastime ...* "The Bicycle and the Automobile," *Scientific
American*, Sept. 23, 1905, vol. 93, no. 13, 234 – "The history of sports and
pastimes in this country furnishes no parallel to the rapid growth in popularity
of the bicycle, and its even more sudden decline as a means of recreation." As to
the deeper, swifter decline in the US, see Rubenson, "Missing Link," 79 –
Canadian bicycle use evolved as elsewhere in the world, i.e., unlike the US,
and 81 – although in Minneapolis, in the early 1900s bike counts also showed
increases. See also London, "Keeping a Respectable Distance."

48 *"receives its patronage to-day ..."* "A Common Mistake," *Globe*, Apr. 27, 1901, 17.

48 *"the bicycle has become a necessity ..."* "The Wheel," *Globe*, Mar. 19, 1901, 10,
contrasting contemporary use to pure amusement of past, suggesting that as a
"convenience for business the wheel appears to be used more than ever."

48 *"FOR A BETTER PURPOSE ..."* "Bicycle Craze," *Globe*, Sept. 30, 1899, 9 – apparent decrease in livery business, consistent with less leisure riding. There was
also a lower demand for light-weight bikes but greater demand for "substantially constructed" bikes.

49 *"found its true sphere ..."* "The Present Standing of the Bicycle," *Daily Star*, Apr.
29, 1901, 6. Bikes were largely renounced as playthings, and the early morning
rides along the lakeshore past Humber River had been replaced by trips to
shops or places of business.

49 *Hyslop Brothers and Eaton's ...* See, for example, Hyslop, Ad, *Daily Star*, May 10, 1910, 10; Hickey's Clothing & Haberdashery, Ad, *Daily Star*, Apr. 12, 1910, 12 – Men's suits advertised for $18–$25.

49 *"Quality varied ..."* "Bicycle Collapsed," *Daily Star*, July 14, 1906, 14 – "The rim of the rear wheel broke, the spokes were thrust outward and punctured the tire, and the wheel instantly a wreck."

49 *Second-hand bicycles ...* See, for example, *Daily Star*, Sept. 7, 1909, 5, with ads for Cleveland for $15; Lady's Planet for $15, Massey-Harris for $10. McLeod at 181 King Street offered to buy or sell used bikes. It's plausible that CCM under-estimated demand for lower-priced bicycles but appealed to a market of more affluent buyers rooted in 1890s concepts. See, for example, Ad, "Thoroughbred Bicycles," *Daily Star*, May 26, 1910, 12.

49 *winter storage and cleaning ...* Might's Directory, 1910, lists one bike livery, but Chief Constable Annual Report, 1910, 53, lists eight bike livery licences. By comparison, there were forty-four livery stables. Ad, Planet Bicycle, *Daily Star*, Jan. 17, 1910,

49 *bicycle had arrived as a toy ...* "Spirit of the Press," *Globe*, June 3, 1907, 6.

52 *media took far less interest ...* Rubenson, "Missing Link," 73–4 – bikes had transitioned from "bourgeois pastime into commonplace travel."

52 *soirée hosted by an heiress ...* "Ride after Social Evening at Rosedale Home Cancelled," *Globe*, June 19, 1899, 8.

52 *carried out during every hour and season ...* "Devotees of the Bicycle: Torontonians of Position, Substance and Accumulating Years Who Ride the Wheel for Pleasure and Convenience," *Daily Star*, May 12, 1900, 3.

52 *didn't publish a single article ...* For 1890–1900, twenty cycling articles; for 1901–10, zero.

52 *briefly, as Pastime ...* *Pastime* appears to have been replaced by a four-page CWA Bulletin in Apr. 1901; see "The Wheel," *Globe*, Apr. 2, 1901, 10. The Globe's cycling column, "The Wheel" lasted until 1909, but focused on racing, not everyday riding.

52 *flaunt their outfits ...* Cycling clothing still advertised, though more often by department stores instead of tailors, see, for example, Eaton's, Ad, *Daily Star*, May 7, 1904, 12 – for cycling skirts. Interest for bicycle rooms also waned, although a luxury building planned in May 1899 still included a bike room, see "Will Be Ornate," *Globe*, May 9, 1899, 3.

53 *"barren of startling novelties ..."* "What Dr. Doolittle Saw at the Chicago Show," *Canadian Wheelman*, Feb. 15, 1897, vol. 14, no. 7 – light-weight craze was then already dying. And see Oddy, "Cycling's Dark Age?," 82 – by 1908, only slight year-over-year differences.

53 *self-adjusting "Safety" pants* ... "Bicycling and the Attempts Made to Meet the Wants of Wheelmen," *Globe,* Jan. 25, 1896, 17.

53 *the revival was usually a nostalgia* ... See, for example, John Westren Dunlop, "An Open Letter to Old-Time Bicycle Enthusiasts," *Daily Star,* June 13, 1908, 18 – "The call of the open, the woods and the quiet countryside is making itself felt more strongly every year." See also "Bicycle Kingdom Revival," *Canadian Wheelman,* May 1903, vol. 21, no. 1 (this is likely an ad); Ad, "The 'Greater' Cleveland," *Globe,* Apr. 22, 1910, 4 – "It is in front today in the big bicycle revival." "To Revive Cycling," *Globe,* Apr. 21, 1909, 9.

53 *no longer even had a clubhouse* ... "Cycling – The Torontos' Meeting," *Mail & Empire,* Feb. 3, 1899.

53 *overrun with work* ... "Cycling Chat," *Globe,* Mar. 21, 1903, 29; "The Wheel – Will Be a Good Season," *Globe,* Mar. 19, 1901, 10 – dealers optimistic but focused on touring, distinguished from cycling used for "plodding to and from business."

53 *demise of touring in the countryside* ... He attributed the problem to poor roads, but the roads were presumably no better or worse when touring was popular. "Lacrosse Men in Session," *Globe,* Apr. 2, 1904, 26. In his deputation, the alderman estimated 3,000 cyclists in Toronto – "The Bicycle Bell Proposal Dropped," *Daily Star,* Dec. 9, 1908, 2. But see Lehr and Selwood, "The Two-Wheeled Workhorse," 6 – in Winnipeg (with one-quarter of Toronto's population) bike licence numbers showed a steady *increase* since at least 1902 with 6,500 registered bikes; by 1905, there was a 30 per cent increase to over 8,500; then levelling off.

54 *bicycle offered a speedy upgrade* ... "Your reply not satisfactory," read the CWA message to R.A. Robertson, on his handling of an eligibility issue. "R.A. Robertson Suspended," *Globe,* June 27, 1894, 6.

54 *now employing forty-five boys* ... "Lively Boys on the 'Go' Always," *Daily Star,* Aug. 2, 1902, 17. Other telegraph companies included Dominion, Great Northwestern (GNW), Canadian Northern, and CPR; see Might's Directory, 1910. CPR and GNW alone counted at least 100 bike messengers.

54 *"revolutionized the messenger work* ..." "Lively Boys on the 'Go' Always" and "Messengers of the Telegraph Service," *Daily Star,* Aug. 2, 1902, 17. "To-day a boy doesn't think twice about taking a message out to Strachan avenue or up to the head of Spadina road, but in those days, when shank's mare [walking] was the only available means of transportation, a boy did not welcome such a distance."

55 *could earn up to $50 per month* ... "Lively Boys on the 'Go' Always," *Daily Star,* Aug. 2, 1902, 17. In 1902, a messenger received 2 cents for the delivery of a telegram, and 3 cents for picking one up, often by call from one of the city's 2,500 call boxes. At 2 cents per message, a boy delivering 50 messages/day earned $1,

less whatever expenses the employer might charge for the bike and uniform. Working steadily for 25 days/month, he earned $25.

55 *adapted by manufacturers to the task* ... Cleveland, Ad, "Livery and Parcel Delivery," *Globe*, Apr. 14, 1897, 8.

55 *optical, butcher, and produce shops* ... Ad, *Daily Star*, July 6, 1902, 13. One company offered speedy delivery of cream by bike.

55 *same-day delivery* ... Robert Simpson Co., Ad, *Globe*, Aug. 26, 1898, 3.

55 *pick up a bike for repair* ... Richard Simpson Co., Ad, *Daily Star*, May 1, 1901; Might's Directory, 1910, 1384 – eight listings for "Messenger Service" but some may also have used motorcars.

55 *day and night service* ... CTA, Fonds 2, Series 1099, Item 49.

55 *motorcars had a distinct cost disadvantage* ... By 1927, CP alone (among four telegraph companies in the city) employed seventy bicycle messengers. CCM, Ad, "100 Boys Tell Why They Feel Safe on a Bicycle," *Daily Star*, Apr. 10, 1928, C11, citing same figures. "The Automobile in Business," *Daily Star*, July 27, 1901, 1

56 *a punitive head tax* ... Loucks and Valpy, *Modest Hopes*, 145–56, describe these hand-laundry shops. By the 1920s the number of these laundry shops had tripled; see also "A Chinese Cycle Race Is on Tap," *Daily Star*, Aug. 14, 1908, 17; "Cycling Racing Saturday Night," *Globe*, Aug. 17, 1909, 7. The one-mile race was limited to Chinese entrants (using a pejorative name), pointing out that "Nearly every China boy in town who delivers laundry uses a wheel, and they are all expert riders." In a 1929 court case ("Men's Police Court," *Daily Star*, June 21, 1929, 2), a judge suggested that stealing a bicycle from a Chinese person was like "taking Lindbergh's aeroplane away from him." Another cursory, early reference to Chinese immigrants on bikes was in "The Wheel – By the Way," *Globe*, Mar. 16, 1896, 8.

55 *messenger's anticipated earnings* ... A boy who bought an Antelope bicycle on credit from bicycle-maker Lochrie later decided messenger work didn't suit him. Lochrie refused a return, suing for non-payment but the judge told him the contract with a minor was not enforceable, then offered, likely in jest, to buy the bike if Lochrie refused its return. "Valuable Prizes ..." *Globe*, June 1, 1903, 10.

56 *a newspaper headline* ... "Tragedies of Toil," *Globe*, July 9, 1901, 10; "Harold Robinson's Death," *Globe*, July 10, 1901, 5. On his second day on the job, a boy, hired by the Toronto Messenger Co., confidently told his mom he would return with a dollar in his pocket. Cycling east on King Street he was blocked by a butcher cart and heavily laden wagon, travelling in the same direction. He lost his balance and fell beneath the rear wheel of the wagon.

57 *boy cycling within the rails ...* Judge ordered a new trial (or $1,000 in damages). Court of Appeal pointed to TRC motorman's failure to sound the gong, an established practice on encountering another car, as potential evidence of failure to take reasonable care. *Preston v. Toronto Railway.*

57 *an additional 10 cents per letter ...* "Mulock's Fast Mails, a Fast Scorcher in Grey," *Daily Star*, July 4, 1898, 1.

57 *transfer wagons to the train ...* "Postal Bicycle Brigade," *Globe*, May 28, 1909, 2; "Bicycle Mail Service," *Daily Star*, June 17, 1909, 1. University of Toronto had its mail delivered by bike five times/day from the post office. Early 1900s, postal service tested four-wheel, steam-driven locomobiles for special loads, but a failure.

57 *"National Necessity ..."* Ad, *Canadian Wheelman*, Feb. 15, 1897. In the stationary position, braces could also be swung on the ground to support the carrier, with a capacity of thirty pounds. Hampson's, with a shop on Parliament Street, offered a large box mounted on the rear of the "bicycle" outfitted with two back wheels. Ad, *Maclean's*, July 1, 1914, 104.

58 *"Sit Closer, Please ..."* Ad, *Daily Star*, Apr. 18, 1910, 6 (directed at men).

58 *"They go flitting by ..."* "Bicycle vs. Trolley," *Globe*, Apr. 21, 1903, 9.

58 *like bank robberies ...* CCM, Ad, *Globe*, Apr. 8, 1908, 7 – "A hold up ... call it car fare, if you like." See, for example, CCM, Ad, *Daily Star*, May 13, 1904, 2 – "save your time and your nickels"; CCM, Ad, "Prosperous Dawn," *Globe*, May 2, 1902, 10 – "it's a regular bank on saved car fares."

58 *the wealthy railway barons ...* Some of the frustration was because streetcars were blocked by horse-drawn carriages, freight wagons, and even motorcars. "TEAMSTERS give the motorman a chance," read one TRC plea. Ad, *Daily Star*, Apr. 2, 1910, 24. Many horse-drawn wagons still ran their wheels along trolley tracks.

58 *The TRC's uncertainty ...* The city unsuccessfully challenged TRC all the way to the Privy Council, then Canada's highest court, for its refusal to expand service into new areas of the city, including many the newly annexed areas between 1893 and 1914. The court interpreted the TRC franchise as applying to city boundaries in 1891. Levy, *Rapid Transit in Toronto*, 7–8.

59 *Edward Geary ...* Hocken's plan included 3.75 miles (6 kilometres) of underground lines, including under Yonge from Eglinton Avenue to Front Street, and 18 miles (28 kilometres) of surface lines. "Hocken's Subway Plan at $5,000,000," *Daily Star*, Nov. 17, 1909, 1.

59 *under the name Toronto Civic Railways ...* Levy, *Rapid Transit in Toronto*, 9. Three lines were built: St. Clair West (Yonge to Caledonia Road); Bloor St.

West (between Dundas and Runnymede Roads); and Danforth Road (between
Broadview and Luttrell Avenues) linked via Coxwell Avenue to Gerrard St. East.

59 *the police fleet of bicycles* ... Chief Constable Annual Report, 1910, 36.

59 *police chases* ... "Police Chased Man in Relays," *Daily Star*, Nov. 7, 1908, 1.

59 *"gymnasium on wheels ..."* CCM, Ad, *Daily Star,* Apr. 28, 1902, 2 – re "tonic";
"Cycling, the Joy of the Wheel," *Globe*, Apr. 14, 1903, 13 – re "gymnasium";
Ad, *Daily Star,* June 3, 1902, 4 – for pleasure and health, "no exercise that can
surpass bicycling."

60 *special traffic squad on bikes* ... "The New Traffic Squad on Bicycles to Regulate
Traffic," *Globe,* July 24, 1909, 24 – Amended city by-law.

60 "wheeling is done for business ..." "A Bicycle Path Not Needed," *Daily Star*, Aug.
21, 1906, 6.

61 *275 miles of paved roads* ... By 1910, asphalt had continued its ascendancy over
other pavements, including cedar blocks, of which little remained. Toronto
Municipal Handbook, 1911, 51

61 *"lameness is much more in evidence ..."* "153 Miles of Unimproved Roads Need
Oiling – Street Comm'r Harris," *Daily Star*, May 17, 1910, 21; Chief Constable
Annual Report, 1910.

61 *Motorists also benefited* ... "Modern Vehicular Traffic," Globe, Nov. 25, 1903, 6.

61 *a kind of swamp* ... A Taxpayer, "The Eclipse of the Bicycle," letter to the editor,
Globe, July 3, 1905, 4.

61 *chief accountant of the Imperial* ... "Toronto Streets Very Clean," *Daily Star*,
June 17, 1909, 1 "Bad Roadway Caused Accident," *Globe*, Oct. 26, 1908, 5; "Suit
against City," *Daily Star*, Oct. 24, 1908 15; and "Thrown from Wheel Under
Heavy Wagon," *Daily Star*, June 3, 1908, 1.

63 *supporting bike paths* ... "CWA Annual," *Globe*, Mar. 29, 1902, 34 – re BC initiative. CWA accepted bike paths – "in certain sections where conditions are such
that ridable roads cannot be constructed" – provided the paths were funded
with fees collected from wheelmen.

63 *circumnavigation of the globe* ... Kinsman, *Around the World Awheel*, 35–7, 121–3.
Creelman voluntarily augmented the challenge of his adventure by undertaking
the journey with no money, instead earning it along the way, but thereby facing
public criticism instead of admiration. Creelman learned to ride a bicycle mere
months before his trip. "Big Coup at Fort Erie," *Daily Star*, July 6, 1899, 5.

63 *streetcars posed the greatest hazard* ... Chief Constable Annual Report, 1910,
42 – 8 run over by "vehicle," 10 by train, 13 by trolley cars. Chief Constable
Annual Report, 1909, 15.

64 *defective equipment* ... "C.O. Rockwood Killed by Madly Rushing Street
Car," *Daily Star*, Oct. 10, 1905, 1. The motorman was initially charged with

manslaughter. "Street Railway," *Globe*, Oct. 10, 1905, 8; "C.O. Rockwood Fatal Race," *Globe*, Oct. 11, 1905, 12; and "Toronto Railway Settled," Feb. 6, 1906, 12; see also "Dr. A.K. Ferguson Fatally Injured by Street Car," *Daily Star*, Oct. 6, 1908, 1.

64 *few underground road passages ... Sims v. Grand Trunk R. W. Co.* 1905, CarswellOnt 274, 5 O.W.R. 664; see *Sims v. Grand Trunk Railway*, 1906 CarswellOnt 247, 7 O.W.R. 648, Ont CA. In July 1903, a Grand Trunk train hit carpenter Alexander Sims at a rail crossing on Bloor near Lansdowne. Sims was homeward bound along a "narrow pathway or bicycle track," presumably the bike path built in 1896 by James Lochrie. The court on appeal overturned the judgement for Sims, whose leg was amputated, concluding that he "was watching his wheel and the path and did not think to look for the train." By 1910, there was one underpass at the CPR crossing at Yonge near Yorkville and another at King in Parkdale.

64 *reaching the Ontario Court of Appeal ... Leslie v. McKeown,* 1909 CarswellOnt 590, 14 O.W.R. 846, 1 O.W.N. 106 (Ontario Court of Appeal).

64 *could cause pain and suffering ...* See, for example, "Death of Mrs. Paterson," *Globe*, Oct. 19, 1908, 1, 5, 12. She was the wife of prominent lawyer who, as she alighted from a streetcar, was killed by a young cyclist speeding downhill on Avenue Road (near Cottingham). There was no inquest. The criminal negligence charge appears to have been withdrawn.

64 *dusted off his clothes ...* "A Dangerous Pavement," *Daily Star*, June 28, 1902, 16.

65 *ran over a young "newsie"...* "Run Over by Auto – City Engineer's Car," *Daily Star*, May 22, 1907, 6.

65 *"biggest coups in Canadian finance ..."* "They Buy Up the Stock Readily," *Evening Star*, Sept. 6, 1899, 1.

65 *85 per cent of the Canadian market ...* Chen, "CCM, 1899–1982," 15.

65 *large-scale bicycle manufacturing ...* By 1890, with increasing Canadian manufacturing expertise, Comet Bicycle Co. (a successor to Thomas Fane & Co. of Brantford) was making Safeties on Adelaide Street, Toronto. By 1897, Comet bikes had wood frames and rims; see "Improvements in Bicycles," *Globe*, Apr. 15, 1897, 12. In 1891, Brooks & McLean – later the Planet Cycle Works – on Queen Street East was carrying on large-scale manufacturing. By 1900, Planet focused on a single model and style: Ad, *Cycling*, Mar. 8, 1900, vol. 10, no. 8, cover. Before the 1890s, bike-making in Ontario encompassed a range of operations from attaching name plates on imported bikes to actual manufacturing of at least some parts; see Norcliffe, *The Ride*, 95–115. For review of the development of the Canadian bicycle-making industry, see Babaian, *The Most Benevolent Machine*.

66 *Who's Who of Canadian finance* ... "They Buy Up the Stock Readily," *Evening Star*, Sept. 6, 1899, 1, 3. Other directors were Lyman Jones (Massey-Harris), Warren Soper (Ahearn & Soper), E.L. Goold (Goold Bicycle Co.), and E.R. Thomas (H.A. Lozier & Co.). The $2 million initial offering was quickly over-subscribed. Well-known principals provided investors with supposed guarantee of a "solid enterprise with an assured future," although subsequent lawsuits by investors suggested the guarantee was weak.

66 *appealing to patriotic fervour* ... See, for example, Ad, *Globe*, June 7, 1902, 7 – "Our Wheels Are Made by Canadian Workmen." The same ad promoted auto sales for Elmore, Baker, Toledo, Waverley, Rambler, and Peerless.

66 *cut out of the profits* ... See *Evans v. Jaffray*, 1903, CarswellOnt 468, 2 O.W.R. 678. Suit by Fred Evans, owner/manager Canadian Typographic Co., Windsor, maker of E&D Bicycles, against his former partner Robert M. Jaffray for breach of contract (relating to a partnership created to bring together sellers and investors to form a new bicycle-making company) and others for procuring a breach of contract, including Ryckman, Senator Cox, Soper, Jones, and the Walter E.H. Massey estate. See "Sues for Shares of $75,000 Cash," *Daily Star*, Nov. 3, 1902, 3.

66 *problematic fondness for gambling* ... M.G. O'Leary, "Cabinet Portraits," *Maclean's*, Oct. 15, 1930, 11, does not mention his cycling history. In 1923, the court ordered him to repay to a bookmaker $2,000 for a gambling debt.

67 *would open a factory in Hamilton* ... McKenty, *Canada Cycle & Motor*, 51–2. ABC was incorporated on May 12, 1899. National included Windsor, Ontario's Evans & Dodge (E&D) Bicycles, owned by Canadian Typographic Co. National's principals included Fred S. Evans along with Colonel Pope and A.G. Spalding. The steam-powered Locomobile was among National's products.

67 *too much bicycle production* ... Norcliffe, *The Ride*, 112. The bicycle craze started earlier in the United States where the number of bike-making factories jumped from seventeen in 1890 to 300 in 1895; production jumped from 1.2 million bicycles in 1896 (and only 50,000 in 1893) to 2 million in 1897; then it began to decline.

67 *a dubious acquisition* ... "Canada Cycle & Motor Company," *Globe*, Nov. 24, 1900, 16.

67 *CCM's early revenues* ... Chen, "CCM, 1899–1982." For riders more concerned about everyday utility, reliability became an important selling feature. CCM marketed its bikes, including Clevelands used by police, with the slogan, "Ask a policeman," see CCM, Ad, *Daily Star*, May 12, 1906, 8.

67 *"reached its perichelion ..."* "They Buy Up the Stock Readily," *Evening Star*, Sept. 6, 1899, 3.

67 *"the magnitude of this concern ..." "*The Canada Cycle Co.," *Evening Star*, Oct. 17, 1899, 2. CCM's head office moved to The Junction in 1902.

67 *Yes, it was big* ... Chen, "CCM, 1899–1982," 15. CCM bike sales fell in both 1900 and 1901 (to a low of 15,000) then climbed to 50,000 by 1904, not far off its 60,000 in 1899. CCM president Walter Massey died from typhoid in October 1901. When CCM was floundering, Joseph Flavelle started building a mansion near Queen's Park.

67 *head office and the operations* ... McKenty, *Canada Cycle & Motor*, 72. Massey-Harris's bicycle division quickly moved to the then recently expanded Lozier factory in The Junction. A plan to close the Welland-Vale factory in St. Catharines and to move its production to Brantford was sped up by a fire in the factory, and the suspiciously slow arrival of the fire brigade. See "Moving to Brantford the Manufacture of the Welland-Vale Chainless Bicycle – Another Important Industry," *Globe*, May 30, 1900, 8. In April 1896, a reporter cycled out to the Lozier factory (located at 201 Weston Road) to write about the operation. See "Making Bicycles," *Globe*, Apr. 18, 1896, 8. Lozier and Gendron were US-based companies.

67 *CCM expanded* ... Chen, "CCM, 1899–1982," 15. Sales levelled off in 1905, remained stable until 1911, then increased steadily. In 1910, CCM accounted for 80 per cent of bikes sold in Canada. See "Bicycle Board of Trade," *Globe*, Mar. 4, 1903, 14. The Bicycle (or Cycle) Board of Trade was established in 1890s. See, for example, "The Wheel: By the Way," *Globe*, Nov. 29, 1895, 6.

69 *the top three automobile retailers* ... Chen, "CCM, 1899–1982," 15.

69 *Ivanhoe electric runabout* ... "Electricity as Motive Power," *Daily Star*, July 27, 1901, 2. CCM also made the Flyer motorcar, under contract.

69 *spare capacity at The Junction* ... CCM's later success was helped by the English "sleeveless" Knight engine for which CCM had exclusive rights in Canada. The engine was first used on the Russell in 1909. By 1910, talk of free trade with the US had company officials worried about being displaced by US automakers who also held rights to the Knight engine.

69 *bought a 50-horsepower model* ... McKenty, *Canada Cycle & Motor*, 106–8.

69 *Willys-Overland* ... In December 1915, CCM's exclusive rights to the Knight engine expired. Willys Overland, then the world's second-largest automaker, took over the Russell Motor Car Company, building cars at CCM's former factory in The Junction. CCM prospered despite growing tensions with its workers, who after their sacrifices during the First World War, began demanding better working conditions and pay. See McKenty, *Canada Cycle & Motor*, 39.

69 *"Gentleman's Motor Cycle ..."* CCM, Ad, "Motosacoche," *Globe*, July 8, 1910, 4. CCM claimed the vehicle ran quietly and cleanly.

69 *side-by-side with bicycles ...* CCM, Ad for the Russell Car and the Cleveland Bicycle, *Daily Star,* June 9, 1908, 17.

70 *"one of the most expert drivers ..."* "Run Down by Motor Car," *Globe*, Nov. 2, 1908, 12; "Bicyclist Run into by Auto," *Daily Star*, Oct. 31, 1908, 1.

70 *A luxury Russell ...* Russell Motorcar, 1909 Model K, Ad, *Daily Star*, Oct. 31, 1908, 9.

70 *"free of any bicycle trust ..."* Lochrie's bikes were displayed at the Exhibition Transportation Building until at least 1906. Might's Directory, 1910, 1285, still lists Lochrie at 1403–1411 Bloor Street West under "bicycles." Comet Cycle Co., one of Canada's oldest bicycle-makers, went out of business in 1899. "Comet Company Fails," *Globe*, May 1, 1899, 7.

70 *death by the Spanish flu ...* "Wm Hyslop, Jr., died on Saturday," *Daily Star*, Apr. 28, 1919, 15.

71 *positions were filled by acclamation ...* "CWA Annual," *Globe*, Mar. 29, 1902, 34.

71 *"reached a low notch in Canada ..."* "CWA Annual," *Globe*, Mar. 29, 1902, 34; and "Bicycle Racing Again," *Globe*, Sept. 8, 1906, 13 – "As the bicycle became more of a necessity and a vehicle of every-day use bicycle racing died away."

71 *"the new means of travel ..."* "CWA Annual," *Globe*, Mar. 29, 1902, 34. CWA had already been accepted into the Canadian Amateur Athletic Union. The Canadian Road Club agreed to amalgamate with CWA.

71 *the "cycling insurgents" ...* See "CWA's Rival Association," *Globe*, Apr. 25, 1900, 12. In 1900, the rival body sanctioned forty-five races. See "Canadian Cyclists' Association Gives Up Control of Racing," *Daily Star*, Apr. 16, 1901, 8; "Insurgents Take a Name," *Daily Star*, Apr. 25, 1900, 8; "CCA Will Fight CWA's Claim," *Daily Star*, Apr. 8, 1901, 8; "CWA and Racing Control," *Cycling*, Mar. 8, 1900, vol. 10, no. 8, 3. *Cycling* encouraged CWA to give up racing control and to focus on touring and good roads.

72 *with forty members in attendance ...* "Lacrosse Men in Session," *Globe*, Apr. 2, 1904, 26. Howson admitted that some members remained purely out of loyalty. He blamed the decline in touring to bad roads, while the racing board chair attributed the cycling decline to bikes being geared too high (a common but weak rationale). See "Canadian Wheelmen's Annual," *Globe*, Apr. 2, 1904, 24; see also "CWA to Enter on a Campaign," *Daily Star*, Mar. 28, 1910, 12 – proposal to hire agent to go about country organizing new clubs for affiliation with CWA.

72 *country's oldest athletic association ...* "Cycling: The CWA To-day," *Globe*, Apr. 10, 1903, 10; see also Friss, *On Bicycles*, 79; "Organized Effort to Revive Cycle Racing in Ontario," *Daily Star*, Apr. 21, 1909, 10. In 1909, the chairman of the CWA Racing Board, ignoring wider trends, attributed the demise of racing to the lack of quality prizes, "dog-tag and tin-pan prizes."

72 *Percy McBride* ... "Toronto Bicycle Club Again Ready," *Daily Star*, Apr. 9, 1910, 24. McBride Cycle, which among others started supplementing bike sales with motorcycle sales, opened in 1909 and closed in 2006.

72 *feats of daring (or folly)* ... "Reengagement of Babcock," *Globe*, July 27, 1907, 24.

72 *an estimated 20,000 spectators* ... "Hamilton Boy Wins the Dunlop," *Daily Star*, Sept. 27, 1909, 9. see also "Sixty-Eight in the Road Race," *Daily Star*, Oct. 6, 1906, 8; and "The National Birthday – Dominion Day 5,000 at Bicycle Races," *Globe*, July 2, 1909, 1.

73 *Walton contributed significantly* ... "CWA Annual," *Globe*, Mar. 29, 1902, 34. The most popular clubs offered social events, dances, and concerts. See *Canadian Courier*, Mar. 14, 1908, vol. III, no. 15, 12. By 1905, the RCBC had lacrosse, baseball, football, and was considering hockey. See "Hockey RCBC for Senior Hockey," *Globe*, Nov. 9, 1905, 10. RCBC's last Dunlop victory was in 1908. The new facility had a large assembly hall, dining room, gymnastics area, and bowling alleys.

73 *178 motorcars in the city* ... "Automobile Club Organized," *Globe*, May 5, 1903, 16; "The Toronto Auto Club," *Globe*, July 30, 1903, 5; and "Automobile Owners," *Globe,* Aug. 28, 1903, 2 – CCM provided a charging station at the Ex for TAC members.

73 *the first motorcar owners* ... Norcliffe, *The Ride*, uses the term "trendsetters." John C. Moodie bought a gas-powered, 6-horsepower US-built Winton in 1898, a car later sold to Dr. Doolittle; see Ontario Motor League, *Six Glorious Years*, preface; see also Denison, *CCM: The First Fifty Years*, 12; and see Reynolds, "Technological Innovation," 17.

73 *no apparent animosity* ... Dr. Doolittle and Toronto Mayor McGuire remained honourary CWA presidents into the 1920s; see "Bicyclists to Compete for Title at Ottawa," *Globe*, Apr. 9, 1923, 8. See also Hodges, "Did the Emergence of the Automobile End the Bicycle Boom?

73 *mandatory vehicle registration* ... "Automobile Club's Run," *Globe*, June 20, 1901, 10.

73 *$2 registration fee* ... *Motor Vehicles Act – An Act to Regulate the Speed and Operation of Motor Vehicles on Highway,* s 3 Edw VII, (1903), c 27, 546.

74 *including The Half Way House* ... "The Toronto Automobile Club," *Globe*, Aug. 6, 1903, 12; "Automobile Club's Run," *Daily Star*, Nov. 6, 1903, 6. A.L. Massey (the son of Charles Massey and the subject of Charlotte Gray's *The Massey Murder*) was among those joining the club run.

74 *Canadian-made electric Victoria motorcar* ... "Auto Club's Run," *Globe*, June 28, 1901, 10.

74 *the advantage of easy starting ...* "Electricity as Motive Power," *Daily Star*, July 27, 1901, 2; and "The Automobile in Business," *Daily Star*, July 27, 1901, 4. See Ontario Ministry of Transportation, "The Ministry of Transportation 1916–2016: A History." Women were among early motorcar users, although typically relying on chauffeurs. By 1913, less than 2 per cent of Ontario's 17,300 motor vehicles were steam or electric-powered.

74 *small number of motorcars in the city ...* In 1903 there were 535 motorcars in Ontario; by 1910, there were 4,300 motorcars, of which approximately 2,000 were in Toronto. In 1903, there were an estimated 750,000 horses in Ontario. See Davies, "Reckless Walking," Appendix 1, citing Ontario Sessional Papers, 1942, Annual Report, Department of Highways, re MV registrations. *Motor Vehicles Act*, 1903, s 2, c 27, 3 Edw VII. $2 regis'n fee applied to local and non-residents (half of 1903 registrations were by visiting Americans).

74 *"automobilists so much detested ..."* "A Careless Driver?," *Daily Star*, Apr. 6, 1910, 8.

75 *the "devil-wagon" ...* See, for example, "The Gallery Clock," *Daily Star*, Apr. 5, 1906, 1.

76 *for lamps, bells, or reckless behaviour ...* "The Bicycle Bell Proposal Dropped," *Daily Star*, Dec. 9, 1908, 2; "No Restriction on Cyclists," *Globe*, Dec. 9, 1909, 7. The City Hall Committee concluded that bells and lamps would not diminish the number of collisions. See "Wants Bells on Bicycles," *Daily Star*, Mar. 16, 1910, 2; "Hold Pay Checks from Officials," *Daily Star*, Mar. 16, 1910, 2; and "Nay, Say Controllers," *Daily Star*, Apr. 7, 1910, 6. See also CoT Council Minutes, 1910, App A, Dec. 29, "Re Bicycle Riders," 1702.

76 *cyclists also lost their right ...* "No More Bicycles On The Street Cars," *Daily Star*, Nov. 20. 1908, 1.

76 *OML sought to entice aldermen ...* "Motor League Objects," *Daily Star*, Mar. 16, 1910, 2. A motion by Alderman Maguire claimed that in the last election, the OML sent twenty autos to defeat him. See CoT Minutes, 1910, Legislation and Reception Committee, "Regulating Automobile and Vehicular Traffic," Mar. 14, App A, 272.

76 *illegal for motorists to pass ... Motor Vehicles Act*, 1914, c 207, RSO 1914; "An Act to regulate the Speed and Operation of Motor Vehicles on Highways," s 15.

76 *"even the man on a bicycle ..."* "Reckless Driving May Be Curbed," *Daily Star*, Mar. 10, 1910, 1.

77 *"when he toots his horn ..."* "Reckless Drivers May Be Curbed," *Globe*, Mar. 10, 1910, 1. One MPP said that if any member of his family or his neighbours were injured by a motorist, "I would, if I could do nothing else to punish him, blow his brains out." See "To Blow His Brains Out," *Globe*, Apr. 28, 1906, 6.

77 *impose new obligations* ... Davies, "Reckless Walking," appendix 2. Motorists also had to avoid frightening horses and sounding a bell or horn to alert pedestrians and other road users of one's approach, and they had to equip their vehicles with lights.

77 *This "reverse onus"* ... *Highway Traffic Act*, s 193(1).

77 *"reckless driving" was added* ... The prohibition again immoderate cycling was later applied to car driving. As late as 1929, more than 17,000 charges were laid for driving at an "immoderate speed," contrary to the city by-law. Chief Constable Annual Report, 1929. The *Criminal Code* in 1912 added the offence of wanton or furious driving or racing that caused bodily harm.

77 *nine constables for the entire province* ... Davies, "Ontario and the Automobile," 224, 227. And when stopped, motorists were often simply given a warning.

77 *escape into the countryside* ... Davies, "Ontario and the Automobile," 315, 320, 343–4.

78 *an "urban amusement ..."* Davies, "Ontario and the Automobile," 182, 306, 309, 324

78 *"motor maniacs ..."* Davies, "Ontario and the Automobile," 172n139, 306, 324, 329. Drivers of rented cars also prompted anger: "The intoxicated reprobate in a hired motorcar [is] an earthquake on rubber." See "A New Terror," *Daily Star*, May 25, 1906, 8

78 *CCM's Tommy Russell* ... Davies, "Ontario and the Automobile," 310n25. MPP Ryckman complained he had "been held behind a farmer who refused to get out of the way."

78 *grumbled about the farmer* ... Davies, "Ontario and the Automobile," 313.

78 *to boycott the province* ... PEI's ban on automobiles was apparently in place from 1909 to 1913. Davies, "Ontario and the Automobile," 276. An Ontario MPP made a similar proposal for roads in rural Ontario, at least for weekends. See "Would Tie Up the Auto on Saturday and Sunday," *Daily Star*, Mar. 6, 1909, 1.

78 *"and sane use of them ..."* On occasion, the OML asked MPPs to advise it on cases of reckless driving. See Davies, "Ontario and the Automobile," 267n108, quoting "Debates," May 17, 1905. As a "quasi-elite social group," as Davies called them, OML had a limited appetite for calling out its members for misconduct. In 1908, the OML considered hiring a detective to prosecute reckless drivers, although in practice the OML's enforcement role usually meant little more than warning drivers about police speed traps. See "An Eye to the Vote," *Globe*, Mar. 28, 1908, 12; Davies, "Ontario and the Automobile," 270–3.

78 *Karl Benz's 1885 motorcar* ... Wilson, "Bicycle Technology," 88. The internal-combustion engine was successfully applied in 1885 by Gottlieb Daimler to a vélocipède of the Michaux type and by Carl Benz to a lightweight tricycle.

78 *"bad breath ..."* "Auto Day Is Advancing," *Daily Star*, June 4, 1904, 20, describing
the cost to buy and operate a motorcar as requiring "as many greenbacks as
we generally see while the earth is making several trips around the sun." The
reporter nonetheless predicted motorcars might one day become as common
as horses. John Eaton's Packard cost $7,000 Packard touring car but even the
cheapest one-cylinder car cost $750.

79 *dressed in flowing robes ...* "Pope Messiah Visits Toronto," *Daily Star*, May 18,
1908, 1. The man was a Wisconsin-born Methodist.

79 *bicycles offered the best option ...* "Street Car Men to Strike?," *Globe*, June 21,
1902, 1. The reporter noted that "while the craze for cycling which existed a
few years ago has disappeared, the wheel is still an important element in city
transportation."

79 *horse-drawn express wagons ...* Among railways serving Toronto were the CPR,
Great Western, Great Northern, and Canadian National (successor to the Grand
Trunk). See Schull, *Ontario since 1867*, 174 – "The great, redundant network."
Steam rail systems had been overbuilt, including three transnational lines. Since
1926, Toronto also had regional steamer service serving towns around Lake
Ontario.

79 *did what came naturally ...* "Toronto Trolleys Take a Day's Rest," *Daily Star*, June
21, 1902, 1 – city went about "almost entirely afoot ... only exceptions are a few
who hazarded taking their bicycles out in the drizzling rain this morning, those
who are wealthy enough to ride in carriages, and the few who can find accommodation on various express wagons, busses, and electric vans."

79 *over 98 million passengers ...* "Streetcar Statistics," Toronto Municipal
Handbook, 1910, 68.

80 *Toronto saloon keepers ...* "Saloon Keepers Grumbling, Claim Bicycles Hurt
Their Business," *Globe*, June 23, 1900, 23. The *Globe* mocked the proposal, suggesting that the "prudent and thrifty house-holder would rather water his grass
and trim his lawn than spend the evening treating at the bar."

80 *By 1910 the radials ...* Stamp, *Riding the Radials*, 10, 51, 59, 62, 92.

80 *bicycle liveries awaited ...* Stamp, *Riding the Radials*, 79. The Yonge line passed
through Glen Echo (now North York), Aurora, and Newmarket. In the summer,
there were seven round trips/day from Toronto. The GTR Lake Simcoe Junction
Railway (LSJR), since at least 1899, served the same route.

80 *demoralizing experience ...* The GO (Government of Ontario Transit) bus from
Toronto strands passengers at a car parking lot near the Town of Keswick, far
short of Jackson's Point. The local bus arrives at – and leaves – the lot before the
GO bus drops off passengers. An alternate transit option adds a few hours to
the trip.

80 *A bumpy stagecoach trip* ... Filey, *Not a One-Horse Town*, n.p., "Rapid Transit for All." Samuel Purdy began running Toronto-Kingston stagecoaches in 1817 along the recently opened Danforth and Kingston Roads. When Dr. Doolittle in 1896 chartered the Eurydice for wheelmen going to a CWA meet in Quebec City, it was for added comfort, not speed.

80 *seventeen hours, twenty-one minutes* ... H. English, "The Toronto Bicycle Club," *Outing*, Sept. 6, 1887, vol. 16, 491.

81 *lawyer Frederick Fetherstonhaugh* ... The *Globe* announced: "The dawn of the horseless era is approaching, weighing 700 lbs with 100 lb motor, storage batteries 270 lbs." See "Motorcarriage – First Appearance of the New Vehicle in Toronto," *Globe*, Dec. 7, 1896, 8. By 1901, some electric vehicles were being exported to Europe. See "Electricity as Motive Power," *Daily Star*, July 27, 1901, 2 – Electric Cab Co. of Toronto, Ltd., planned to offer electric vehicles, including Tally Ho coaches, for hire. Canadian Motors bought out John Still, and CCM later bought Canadian Motors.

82 *electric vehicles for hire* ... "Toronto's New Era," *Globe*, June 5, 1899, 7, describing them as a "movement for cheapening passenger and freight transportation in Toronto." See also "Automobile Supplement – Canadian History of Horseless Vehicles," *Daily Star*, July 27, 1901, 1; and "Electricity as Motive Power," *Daily Star*, July 27, 1901, 2. By 1899, motorcars were already being used as cabs in some US cities. For two summers in the early 1900s, a livery in Toronto offered electric cars for hire.

82 *The post office experimented* ... Chen, "CCM, 1899–1982," 15. From 1899 onwards, CCM built vehicles for the post office, including motor tricycles and quadricycles and parcel carriers and trailers. By 1901, the steam-powered Locomobile, acquired in the CCM takeover of National, and the Massey-Harris quadricycles were used to transport mail and parcels from Union Station to the post office.

82 *a radius of 35 to 40 miles* ... T.A. Russell, "The Automobile of 1904," *Canadian Magazine*, June 1904, vol. 23, no. 2, 142.

82 *for their recreational excursions* ... "Toronto's New Era," *Globe*, June 5, 1899, 5, made a similar point, listing drawbacks of gas or petroleum autos, for example, "vibration caused by the explosion of gas in the cylinders, the smell of gasoline and gas, the heat generated."

82 *railways offered a far easier* ... A commentator suggested motorcars (and previously, bicycles) liberated people from "bondage of the iron roadway," namely, the railways. A.G. Brown, "Automobiles in Canada," *Canadian Magazine*, Aug. 1903, vol. 21, no. 4, 327 – the bicycle would continue to serve "the man who desires quick locomotion with little investment."

83 *thirteen days just to cover* ... Rasenberger, *America 1908*, 80.

83 *about $50,000 today* ... See the CPI Inflation Calculator, https://www.in2013 dollars.com/us/inflation/1910?amount=1500#buying-power.

83 *downward price trajectory* ... "Reflections of the Editor," *Canadian Courier*, Oct. 1, 1910, 12; "The Car Question," *Daily Star*, Apr. 2, 1910, 1 – "The lure of automobiles is beginning to extend beyond the city's wealthy."

83 *ridiculed as "antiquated"* ... *Busy Man's Magazine*, 1908, quoted by Davies, "Ontario and the Automobile," 351.

83 *OML was still hiring men* ... Davies, "Ontario and the Automobile," 352–5. In 1901, through the *Highway Improvement Act*, Queen's Park committed to investing up to $1 million in highways. In 1910, Queen's Park offered to pay one-third of the cost of road construction undertaken by local bodies, but only half of the counties participated. In late 1914, work was underway to build Highway 5 between Toronto and Hamilton. Premier Hearst said it was "but the forerunner of a series of highways of like character."

83 *despite farmers' fear* ... "Reflections of the Editor," *Canadian Courier*, Mar. 12, 1910, 8 – "The cities have been so occupied with steam railway and suburban railway services that they have almost overlooked the value of good roads just beyond their boundaries." See also Davies, "Ontario and the Automobile," 345, noting a strong association between farmers, the good roads movement (which had a quasi-official status at Queen's Park), and the Ontario government before 1914.

83 *"farmers sing ..."* Peter McArthur, "All Things Considered," *Canadian Courier*, Mar. 12, 1910, 8.

84 *"The $20 a week man ..."* Nelson, *Toronto in 1928*, esp. 13, 14, 22, 23.

85 *Whitney's subsequent decline* ... See Charles W. Humprhies, "WHITNEY, SIR JAMES PLINY," *Dictionary of Canadian Biography*, vol. 14, University of Toronto/Université Laval, 2003. http://www.biographi.ca/en/bio/whitney_james_pliny_14E.html. Whitney died on Sept. 25, 1914, on the verge of his seventy-first birthday. In 1917, he was characterized among parliamentarians as the "most notable example of the retention of the cycling habit." See "Rode the Wheel to Parliament," *Globe*, Aug. 17, 1917, 9.

85 *"the people's power ..."* Schull, *Ontario since 1867*, 161.

85 *"Gruff and bluff ..."* "Life and Letters," *Globe*, July 13, 1929, 14, quoted in Henderson, *Great Men of Canada*: "strong and immovable as granite, yet at times tender as a woman."

1929 – Lethal Motorcars, Accidental Victims

87 *lauded for his zeal* ... "Doolittle Promoting Safety," *Globe,* Aug. 29, 1928, 4.

87 *best-known motor advocate* ... "Centenary – History Review," Ontario Safety League, https://ontariosafetyleague.com/public-advocacy/centenary/. He served as president of the OML in 1914 and as executive officer in 1929, and was vice president of the OSL in the mid-1920s. Dr. Doolittle was re-elected CAA president in September 1929. See "Auto Association Re-elects Doolittle," *Globe,* Sept. 25, 1929, 5. The CAA was formed in 1913 by nine motor clubs as the Canadian Automobile Federation. See "About Us, Our History," CAA, https://www.caasco.com/About-Us/History-of-CAA.aspx. In 1960, the OML merged into the CAA.

88 *no mention of the doctor's speed* ... Mrs. Marks was likely on her way towards the Avenue Road streetcar (taking her north to St. Clair, then a five-minute walk home), avoiding congested Yonge Street. According to Might's Directory, 1929, Mrs. Marks lived at 77 Oriole Road; Mrs. Mackay at 116 Belsize Drive; and Mrs. Lyman at 2 Farnham Avenue.

88 *released on $500 bail* ... "Dr. P.E. Doolittle in Motor Accident," *Mail & Empire,* Nov. 23, 1929, 4. According to one report, victims suffered bruises and abrasions. Dr. Doolittle was reported to have told police that he couldn't stop in time because the women had run suddenly into the roadway. The *Ottawa Citizen, Telegram,* and *Daily Star* also carried reports.

88 *"a token of its appreciation..."* "Dr. Doolittle Gets Cheque for $5000," *Daily Star,* Aug. 28, 1928, 3.

88 *the first time in several days* ... "Three Men Struck in Auto Accidents," *Mail & Empire,* Nov. 5, 1929, 8.

89 *as he alighted from a streetcar* ... "Reckless Auto Driver Kills Great Citizen," *Globe,* Apr. 12, 1920, 7.

89 *sentenced to three months in jail* ... "Careless Motorist Given Three Months," *Globe,* Nov 6, 1920, 17.

89 *"The modern juggernaut ..."* "The Slaughter of the Innocents," *Globe,* June 1, 1929, 4. The writer called for the creation of a Pedestrian League.

89 *cycling home for supper* ... "13-Year-Old Cyclist Killed," *Mail & Empire,* Nov. 6, 1929, 5; "Boy Is 81st Victim of Motor Accidents on Toronto Streets," *Globe,* Nov. 6, 1929, 13. The motorist was detained and released. The victim, Eddie Ecclestone, lived in the Bracondale Hill area.

89 *express-train speed* ... "The Neglected Cycle," *Globe* Apr. 9, 1929, 4, quoting the *Renfrew Mercury.*

89 *belonging to the same clubs … The Torontonian Society Blue Book* of 1921
(https://www.canadiana.ca/view/oocihm.8_03507_1/1) indicated that both
women belonged to the Imperial Order of the Daughters of the Empire (IODE)
and the Women's Canadian Club. Dr. Doolittle was among the leaders of the
Empire Club, to which Mr. Marks belonged.

89 *"I am a close friend …"* "Dr. Doolittle Freed of Reckless Driving," *Daily Star*,
Dec. 13, 1929, 40. There was no mention of the third woman. Other papers had
short reports, see, for example, "First Motorist Free After First Accident," *Mail
& Empire*, Dec. 14, 1929, 1.

90 *the scale, magnitude, and geography …* The *Globe* nonetheless gamely suggested
that the same anxiety had once been provoked by cyclists. "Terrors of the Nineties,"
Globe, Apr. 23, 1929, 4 – "We are being cured of 'jay-walking,' the 'stop' and 'go' signs
guard our intersections, and the dangers of our grandfathers are forgotten."

91 *driver's licence was introduced …* Chief Constable Annual Reports, 1927, 1928,
1929. "Forty Thousand Drivers' Permits Issued in Toronto in Two Weeks,"
Globe, July 16, 1927, 7. Until 1923, the OML opposed licences.

91 *laws governing motorcars …* Davies, "Ontario and the Automobile," appendix
2. Ontario's *Motor Vehicles Act* grew to fifty-five sections by 1912. In 1917, the
Provincial Highways Act was created, replaced by the *Highway Traffic Act* in
1923 to consolidate various acts.

91 *a toddler in a pram …* "Rabbi Has Narrow Escape," *Globe*, June 8, 1929, 17 – a
novice driver crashed into Allan Gardens, also narrow miss for "spooners"
on benches. See also "Policeman Injured," *Globe*, Apr. 22, 1929, 16; "Woman
Motorist Fined [$25]," *Daily Star*, Sept. 5, 1929, 3 – knocked down Patrol Sgt.;
"Magistrate's Verdict Reversed," *Globe*, Apr. 26, 1929, 16; "Three Dead; 19
Injured," *Globe*, Oct. 7, 1929, 16; "Little Girl Succumbs to Motorcar Injuries,"
Globe, Aug. 17, 1929, 15.

91 *boy's shocked father …* "Man Said to Have Run Over Own Son," *Globe*, Apr. 25,
1929, 2.

91 *pedestrian's status had descended …* Davies, "Ontario and the Automobile," 252.

92 *They did by 1929 …* Chief Constable Annual Report, 1928. Among the 2,000
collisions, crashes involving motorists dominated. See Chief Constable Annual
Report, 1910, App C, 73–4, and Chief Constable Annual Report, 1929, 17, 27–8.

92 *Toronto's motorcar population …* Might's Directory, 1929. In addition to cars,
there were 14,000 trucks. See also the Toronto Municipal Handbook, 1910 and
1931. In 1929, Ontario had 473,000 motorcars.

92 *a plague would provoke …* "Motor Accidents," letter to the editor, *Globe*, July 24,
1929, 4. It would be better "to curb our speed limit to a walking pace than that
one child per annum should go to its premature grave."

92 *suffered the death of a child* ... Chief Constable Annual Report, 1928, 16 – 1,600 collisions, 26 children killed, 650 injured. See also Chief Constable Annual Report, 1929, 17 – children were over-represented as road victims: 28 dead, 670 injured.

92 *sounded the alarm* ... Toronto Bureau of Municipal Research, "An Analysis of Motor Accidents in Toronto for the Year Ending April 30th, 1927," White Paper, no. 117, Nov. 16, 1927.

92 *"the menace to human lives ..."* "These Costly Week-Ends," *Globe*, Aug. 2, 1927, 4. The editorial followed the deaths of two women on the Dundas Highway, and a man injured when he went to their rescue.

92 *"An armistice is sadly needed ..."* "The Highway Terror," *Globe*, Nov. 17, 1929, 4.

92 *"Why does this tragedy go on ..."* "Notes and Comments," *Globe*, Nov. 12, 1929, 4.

93 *grief had curious limits* ... The *Evening Telegram, Mail & Empire*, and *Daily Star* all gave accounts of Dr. Doolittle's crash and charges on their first pages. Dr. Doolittle's son worked in a *Globe* office on Islington Avenue. On the day before the crash, Highways Minister Doucett said autos should be treated as potentially dangerous vehicles. "More Cancellation of Drivers' Permits," *Globe*, Nov. 20, 1929, 13.

93 *death by misadventure* ... "Hitching on Trucks Dangerous Practice," *Globe*, Oct. 4, 1929, 14; "Boy Cyclists Told of Crossing Perils," *Globe*, Nov. 23, 1929, 3; JFH Wyse (OSL) quoted in "Coasting on Bicycle Behind Motortruck Costs Another Life," *Globe*, Sept. 28, 1929, 17.

93 *"save many a young life ..."* "Regulate the Bicyclists," *Saturday Night*, Oct. 19, 1929, vol. 44, 1.

93 *"the turmoil of the city ..."* See, for example, "Mother, Mother, One Killed, Two Injured," *Globe*, Oct. 7, 1929, 15–16; "Young Cyclist Killed," *Daily Star*, Oct. 7, 1929, 3. Three boys on a ride from Christie Pits to New Toronto were crossing the Humber Bridge in Mimico (Highway 2) when they were struck head-on by a motorist who was charged with criminal negligence but exonerated at the trial and inquest; he was apparently blinded by the headlights of an oncoming vehicle.

94 *the rare weekend* ... "Safety-First Week-End on Streets," *Globe*, Aug. 12, 1929, 13. A mid-August weekend was one such exception, police reporting that although they had investigated crashes in which fourteen persons were injured, and arrested three motorists, not one of the fourteen had been critically injured.

94 *cyclists' influence had declined* ... CoT Council Minutes, 1929, App B, by-law 12051, "To licence residents owning and using bicycle on the highway."

94 *got scant media attention* ... Council rarely debated bikes in the 1920s, except for the 1925 motion (rejected) regarding rear lights. CoT Council Minutes,

1925, Minutes. See *VIM Magazine*, Jan. 1922, vol. 13, no. 1, 3 – re 1921
plebiscite for lights on all vehicles after dark. In London, Ontario, there were
"militant protests," mainly by boys and messengers, against bike licences.
"Crime Wave Ended by Arrest of Two," *Globe*, June 11, 1935, 3.

94 *set at 50 cents* ... By-law 14451 amended By-law 14319 to reduce the fine. CoT
Council Minutes, 1936, App B, 179, 199, adopted May 18, 1936. CoT, Ad,
"Bicycle Licenses 1935," *Globe*, June 1, 1935, 14.

94 *average reported value* ... Chief Constable Annual Report, 1929, "Reported
offences" – 1,408 bikes reported stolen. (Average cost of a bike was $17 in 1910.)

94 *offered a more plausible motivation* ... "30,000 Bicyclists to Pay City Licence,"
Globe, Mar. 7, 1929, 13. The $15,000 in revenues for bike licences was 9 per cent
of city licencing revenues of $170,000. See Chief Constable Annual Report,
19 – 4 bike liveries. Cigarette vendor's licences brought in over $65,000 revenue
from 2,400 vendors.

94 *moving picture shows* ... Chief Constable Annual Report, 1929, 19.

94 *bicycles to their rightful owners* ... "The Board of Works – No Bicycle
Regulations," *Globe*, Apr. 17, 1894, 3.

95 *Winnipeg's bicycle licence* ... "Bicycle Licences to Check Up Thefts," *Globe*, Mar. 29,
1928, 13 – suggesting licences "would eliminate much of the theft now prevalent."

95 *no research was offered* ... Recovery rates for stolen bikes were reported sporad-
ically in Toronto. In 1928, 25 per cent were recovered (Chief Constable Annual
Report, 1928); in 1902, 86 per cent were recovered (Chief Constable Annual
Report, 1902).

95 *an easier mark* ... After a rash of thefts in 1902, police chastized women who
left their bikes unlocked in front of Eaton's and Simpson's. See "Inspector Stark
Gives Warning," *Daily Star*, June 30, 1902, 1. See "Wholesale Thefts of Bicycles,"
Globe, June 30, 1902, 10. In 1895 a city magistrate said stealing a bike was more
serious than horse stealing, and it was much easier to walk off with a bike. See
"A Perjured Thief," *Daily Star*, Aug. 26, 1895, 4.

95 *an "epidemic"*... "By the Way," *Globe*, Apr. 3, 1895, 6. The Bicycle Accident
Repair Co., among others, offered insurance against theft, but 25-cent locks
were a cheaper option (Might's Directory, 1896, 1732). The bicycle trade considered a system under which members would communicate thefts (along with a
bike's number and description) to each other, then hold any bike (in absence of
explanation) brought in for repair or trade-in matching the information.

95 *ballooned to 1,100* ... Chief Constable Annual Report, 1910, 45–6 – total *reported* value of stolen bikes was $18,880. Chief Constable Annual Report, 1899, 28.
"Many Thefts of Wheels," *Daily Star*, Apr. 13, 1910, 1 – reported that bikes were
"getting to be a sure and safe source of revenue of the bicycle thief."

95 *had not risen so dramatically* ... Chief Constable Annual Report, 1921, 56, and Chief Constable Annual Report, 1928, 5.

95 *an increase of 220 per cent* ... "Chief Seeks Authority to Check Up on Bicycles," *Globe and Mail*, Mar. 14, 1935, 11; Chief Constable Annual Report, 1934, 45-6.

95 *easier to catch individuals* ... In November 1929, among three boys charged with non-compliance, one explained to the court that he was simply borrowing his elder brother's unused bike. See "Failed to Comply with Bicycle Law," *Daily Star*, Nov. 2, 1929, 11.

96 *walked off with a locked bicycle* ... "Men's Police Court," *Daily Star*, June 21, 1929, 2.

96 *in Toronto's Central Prison* ... Even an impoverished farmhand got a sixty-day sentence. See "Was in Hard Luck and His Baby Was Sick," *Daily Star*, Aug. 15, 1908, 1; "Bicycle Thief 17-Year Old Gets 6 Months," *Globe*, July 23, 1910, 9; "Bicycle Thief Sentenced," *Globe*, Feb. 23, 1909, 5 – eight-month sentence for poor boy.

96 *perhaps worth $17* ... Chief Constable Annual Report, 1929, 5 – average reported value of stolen car, $640. Automobile thefts had steadily increased since 1922, when such thefts hadn't merited a separate category. By 1929 motor thefts exceeded bicycle thefts. In fact, the dollar value of the 2,085 motorcar thefts in 1929 comprised the largest portion, by a wide margin, of the value of all thefts in Toronto.

96 *for the necessary amendment* ... "Bicycle Licences to Check Up on Thefts," *Globe*, Mar. 29, 1928, 13. Maximum allowable fee was $1. The Bicycle Dealers Association and the Canadian Manufacturers Association (CMA) were among the groups in support of bike licences, perhaps motivated by the impact on sales from thefts. Telegraph companies' support might also have been explained by the cost of thefts from their fleet of vehicles. Big Brothers, mentors to fatherless boys, also supported licensing, but their motivation was unclear.

96 *most of Toronto's neighbours* ... "Provincial Control of Wheels Urged," *Globe and Mail*, July 23, 1935, 10. Most if not all neighbouring municipalities in what became Metro Toronto followed the CoT example with their own bicycle licence, including Forest Hill (before 1935), Scarborough York (By-law 3588, Feb. 2, 1937), Mimico, East York, Long Branch, New Toronto, Leaside, Swansea, Weston, New Toronto, Etobicoke, North York (By-law 2174, Dec. 2, 1935), and York Township (issuing 4,150 licences in 1938 – see "Tobacco Licence Scheme Vetoed by York Township," *Daily Star*, Jan. 17, 1939, 6).

96 *absence of regular enforcement* ... Chief Constable Annual Report, 1929, 29.

97 *cyclists obliged to affix* ... CoT Council Minutes, 1929, By-law 12324, "To amend By-law No. 12051 respecting the licensing of bicycles," passed Sept. 23.

97 *not eager for the extra work* ... Chief Constable Annual Report, 1935, 40 – noting increased revenues "by reason of closer supervision of licenced persons, premises, etc."

97 *surged to 30,000 ...* Chief Constable Annual Reports, 1930, 1931, 1933, and
1934, noted issued bike licences: 1930, 11,925 (p. 25); 1931, 8,301 (p. 24); 1933,
11,059 (p. 22); 1934, 29,713 (p. 23).

97 *wanted larger licence plates ...* "Police Won't Enforce Law on Bicycles, Board
Told," *Daily Star*, Apr. 11, 1933, 1. One councillor chided Police Chief Draper
for wanting a plate "so big a boy couldn't carry it." "Like Licence with Cycle
Attachment," *Daily Star*, Apr. 5, 1933, 1.

97 *"twelve queues of boys ..."* "New Licence Plates Appeal to Cyclists," *Daily Star*,
June 2, 1934, 24.

97 *jump in dog licences ...* Chief Constable Annual Report, 1934, 23. From 1933 to
1934, dog licences almost *tripled* to 9,800 with revenues of $43,000.

97 *a fabricated serial number ...* "Bicycle Theft Pays Boys in Organization," *Daily
Star*, Nov. 6, 1934, 25. The *Daily Star* reported that boys in "hot bike" gangs
were paid from 25 cents to $2 per stolen bike, which might be quickly dissem-
bled and rebuilt, making them unrecognizable. The *Daily Star* suggested that as
many as three licences were associated with one bike. After stealing a bike, the
thief removed the licence plate, went to City Hall, "says he's Mahatma Gandhi or
somebody, his serial number 80,0006 and he wants a bicycle licence. He gets it
for 50 cents ... and delivers the bike [for resale] on York St. for ten bucks."

97 *bring stolen bicycles into Toronto ...* "Epidemic of Thefts in Mimico District Is
Believed Halted," *Globe*, Sept. 8, 1934, 4, referring to a gang of bike thieves in
Mimico.

97 *police would first verify ...* CoT Council Minutes, 1935, App B, May 20, 117–19.
By-law amendments gave the police responsibility to verify bike serial numbers,
while requiring metal plates to be affixed to the rear mudguard and obliging
cyclists to carry a paper licence (wishful thinking insofar as children were concerned). By-law 14139, "To licence residents owning and using bicycles on the
highways of the city" (replacing 1929 by-law no 12051.) See "'Old-Cold' Buyers
Must Be Licenced," *Globe and Mail*, Nov. 18, 1932, 9.

97 *complicate the process ...* "Chief Seeks Authority to Check Up on Bicycles,"
Globe, Mar. 14, 1935, 11. The chief also recommended that each bike have two
licence plates. The proposal was rejected.

98 *announcing a "vast" plan ...* "A Vision of Future Downtown Toronto," *Daily Star*,
Mar. 11, 1929, 6, described as "so vast a plan for downtown traffic arteries that
an offhand judgement upon its merits or demerits would be valueless."

98 *virtually every pastime ...* Might's Directory, 1929, vol. 1, "Miscellaneous,"
"clubs," and "misc societies."

98 *battles on the racecourse ...* The last race in Ottawa was won by Queen City
Bicycle Club. Denison, *CCM: The History of the First Fifty Years*, 16.

98 *added curling to its name* ... "New Curling Club ... RCBC Keeps Pace with the Times," *Globe*, Oct. 1, 1929, 13. Club members could also watch, from an indoor lounge, *fancy* skating and speed skating.

99 *"lacked nothing of the sporting spirit ..."* "The Neglected Cycle," *Globe*, Apr. 9, 1929, 4 – the bicycle, however, remained "an almost indispensable means of rapid locomotion in many branches of business"; "'Bike' Racing Not What It Used to Be," *Globe*, Apr. 1, 1929, 6; "Additional Sports; Increased Interest in Bicycle Racing," *Globe*, Apr. 1, 1929, 9.

99 *blessing of parishioners' vehicles* ... "Miles of Motors Receive Blessing," *Globe*, July 29, 1929, 13, 14. Mount Carmel Catholic Church.

99 *"bicycles are worse ..."* S. Ballachey, letter to the editor, *Globe*, July 30, 1929, 4. See also, "Boys and Bicycles," *Globe*, June 26, 1929, 4 – complaint that boys on bikes "seem to feel that the laws governing other wheeled traffic do not apply to them."

100 *"the better for all concerned ..."* G. Gordon, letter to the editor, *Globe*, July 19, 1929, 4 – "Bicyclists have become a positive nuisance in parts of Toronto ... The real trouble seems to be that the riders are 'Smart Alecks' and make an effort to show off and see how much they can frighten the motorist."

100 *dulled the appeal of car ads* ... Davies, "Ontario and the Automobile," 133n47, citing *Canadian Motorist*, Sept. 1923, 469. See also "Protect the Children," *Globe*, June 1, 1929, 3; "Make the Highways Safe," *Globe*, June 1, 1929, 3; and "Careless Delivery of Papers Discussed," *Globe*, July 26, 1929, 14.

100 *motorists were particularly careful* ... CCM, Ad, "100 Boys Tell Why They Feel Safe on a Bicycle," *Daily Star*, Apr. 10, 1928, 11.

100 *ten cycling commandments* ... Quoted in McKenty, *Canada Cycle & Motor*, 146, 149.

101 *streetcars as impediments* ... "Bloor St. Sidewalks," *Daily Star*, June 20, 1929, 3 – "If you are going to handle traffic to the satisfaction of the motorist you will have to have motor highways free from streetcar traffic."

101 *60 per cent of households* ... For the 60 per cent figure (albeit for Ontario), see Davies, "Ontario and the Automobile," 98. The 20 per cent figure is simply the population divided by total motorcar registrations, noted earlier. "Bloor St. Sidewalks Will Not Be Changed," *Daily Star*, June 20, 1929, 3. Works Commissioner Harris also estimated 20 per cent of people were motorists. Might's Directory, 1929, 1978 – second-hand cars could be bought for a few hundred dollars.

101 *against widening Bloor Street* ... "Adhere to Original Plan Bloor Gets 16-Foot Sidewalk," *Daily Star*, June 13, 1929, 1.

101 *"And bicycle paths! ..."* "A Little of Everything," *Daily Star*, June 20, 1929, 4; "Wide Bloor Sidewalk Is 'Colossal Mistake,'" *Daily Star*, June 12, 1929, 2.

102 *they would be worse off ...* Toronto Municipal Handbook, 1931, 91.

102 *30 per cent of its overall spending ...* Davies, "Ontario and the Automobile,"
appendix 5, quoting Pattison, *Historical Chronology of Highway Legislation in
Ontario, 1774–1961.* In 1910, Ontario spent only $680,000 on roads; by 1919, 17
per cent of Ontario's budget was spent on roads. At the time, a cross-town waterfront highway was in place, stretching 7 miles (11 kilometres) from Humber
River to Leslie St. See "City of Toronto Statistical Review," Might's Directory,
1953, 10.

102 *transitioning into a service organization ...* Davies, "Ontario and the
Automobile," 287–8: OML posted an estimated 60,000 road signs by 1924,
when the Ministry of Highways took over the task. In 1925, Doolittle, travelling
in a Ford Model T, with a Ford photographer, undertook a forty-day crossing
of Canada to make the case for a cross-Canada highway. "Pioneer Motorist,
Doctor Doolittle Dies at Age of 73," *Globe and Mail,* Jan. 1, 1934, 1 – calling
him the "Father of the Trans-Canada Highway" (completed in the 1960s). The
same trip could by 1899 be done by train in under five days. See R.L. Kennedy,
"Travel to and within Canada on Canadian Pacific," Old Time Trains.

102 *Mayor Sam McBride ...* CofT Council Minutes, 1929, Mayor's Inaugural
Address, App C, 5–7. Another goal was eliminating jogs between roads.

102 *need for wider highways ...* "Drive More Sanely, Retain Lower Rates," *Globe,* Feb.
5, 1929, 1.

102 *The wide median ...* "Public Clamouring for Safety Zones," *Daily Star,* Oct. 5,
1928, 2. The *Daily Star* found unanimous support for safety zones, including islands for patrons to access streetcars. By 2010, the wide median was reinstalled
on St. Clair Street West for the LRT.

103 *to facilitate private car use ...* One competitor the TTC no longer had to worry
about was the jitney, which had been popular in the mid-1910s. Jitneys were
large motorcars serving popular routes for a nickel, drawing patrons from
streetcars, presaging complaints against Uber and Lyft ride-hailing services a
century later. Jitneys had drawn the ire of the TRC as an unregulated, competing service. As to Uber and Lyft, see, RideFair, "Budgeting for the Uber Impact."

103 *chaired by the Minister ...* In theory, the OSL mission was to improve safety for
all road users, but the group's origin and leadership ensured it was the motor
lobby's priorities that prevailed. OML, Ad, "Hwy Safety Committee – Rules
20mph in Cities 35mph on Hwys," *Globe,* Aug. 30, 1929, 15.

103 *regulatory model from US ...* "Safety Ideas," *Globe,* Aug. 24, 1928, 42.

103 *"Greater Pleasure in Driving ..."* "Safety Ideas," *Globe,* Aug. 24, 1928, 42.

103 *conduct required reformation ...* Davies, "Ontario and the Automobile," 254. The
meeting included the trucking industry, freight traffic, W.G. Robertson (OML),

Dr. Doolittle (OSL), and the Board of Trade. See "Traffic Committee Also
Suggests Check on Pedestrians," *Globe*, June 29, 1929, 16.
103 *contributory negligence* ... "Chief Blames 'Jay Walkers,'" *Globe*, July 27, 1922,
17. (Dickson was chief constable from 1920 to 1928.) In his 2012 report, the
Ontario chief coroner offered a new perspective, pointing to an "inherent bias"
in cases involving a death where the motorist, but not the victim, could tell their
story. Coroner, Pedestrian Death Review, 2012.
104 *sophisticated and manipulative campaigns* ... Davies, "Ontario and the
Automobile," 53–96. Prior to 1910, ads focused on function "rather than as
object of beauty and admiration." After 1910, the focus was on lifestyle: "the automobile became as important symbolically as it did practically." Ads associated
the car with wealth even if targeting a market "significantly lower in income."
Automakers exploited middle-class desire for dream of upper-class leisure and
respectability. By the late 1920s, companies like GM adopted year-over-year
style changes. In the mid-1920s ads reflected possibilities for women as owners/
operators, highlighting independence but in pursuit of healthy, beneficial
recreation.
104 *automakers surpassed the food industry* ... Davies, "Ontario and the
Automobile," 100n6, quoting Lewis, *The Public Image of Henry Ford*, 36, 126–7.
104 *even if merely cosmetic* ... "Ontario and the Automobile," 38, 63, 64, 156–7. The
combined average price of closed and open models fell from $906 in 1921 to
$695 in 1926; and by 1919, GMAC had also started a Deferred Payment Plan.
Taxi services continued to expand.
105 *The capacity for speed* ... Davies, "Ontario and the Automobile," 131, 135–40.
Fascination with speed "blinded the public to its worst abuses." Speed (horsepower and acceleration) had become a prominent selling feature. When
distance is measured as time, miles become minutes. "Speed came to be seen as
some sort of inalienable right." But the general public saw speed as the cause for
the harm suffered by their loved ones. (Davies, "Ontario and the Automobile,"
125, quoting *Farmer's Sun*).
105 *a speeding horse* ... Davies, "Ontario and the Automobile," 132, citing *Hamilton
Herald*, Apr. 21, 1908.
105 *"mad scramble after the motors ..."* "The Motorcar in England," *Canadian
Wheelman*, Dec. 7, 1896, 19–20. Dr. Doolittle was among the spectators at the
celebrated 1896 London-Brighton motorcar race. The magazine wrote that the
British public was being "emancipated from the old time bondage of a red flag,"
and predicted that if "given highways free from absurd and hampering restrictions [they] may depend on British wealth and energy and Yankee ingenuity
succeeding and the result will at no distant day be as perfect as is the bicycle

locomotion of today." Harry Lawson, the inventor of the safety, organized the
event with the British Motor Syndicate.

105 *first pedestrian fatality* ... Green, *Original Highway Code,* 8.

105 *"an open air garage ..."* "Theft of Automobiles Increased in Toronto," *Daily Star,*
Feb. 24, 1927, 8.

105 *allocated to car parking* ... Shoup, *The High Cost of Free Parking.*

108 *a 10 mph (16 km/h) limit* ... Los, "A Danger and a Nuisance." See also the "Act
to Regulate the Speed and Operation of Motor Vehicles on Highways," a change
effected under the *Municipal Act,* 1903, c 27, 3 Edw VII, s 6. Motorists were
also required to slow down at intersections. However, cyclists were not beyond
criticism, one citizen writing that as to speed "a kind of intoxication" prevails,
endangering other road users, see A Citizen, letter to the editor, *Daily Star,* Nov.
4, 1903, 10.

108 *half of all road infractions* ... Chief Constable Annual Report, 1910, 35.

108 *social class drawn to motorcars* ... "Speeders' Stock Going Up," *Globe,* Dec. 9,
1909, 14.

108 *"war on the automobile ..."* "Timed the Autos," *Globe,* June 14, 1904, 12 – the
plate of each car was recorded, and the provincial secretary asked to provide
their names.

108 *"no scorching" rule* ... See, for example, "Young Cyclists Hurt in Crash with
Truck," *Daily Star,* June 18, 1929, 18.

108 *"forbidden to travel quickly ..."* Davies, "Ontario and the Automobile," 126,
citing *Maclean's,* May 1914, "The Law and the Motor: Why the future will be
completely changed in the legal viewpoint," 29–30 – the focus should be on safe
driving.

109 *motoring public was "held down"* ... Davies, "Ontario and the Automobile,"
126. The OML's lawyer recommended that speed limits be eliminated, replaced
by a system guided by rule, "that a motorist must drive reasonably and not
negligently." See "Abolish Speed Limit, Drop Half of Auto Laws," *Globe,* May 24,
1929, 13; "Dropping Speed Limit," *Globe,* May 29, 1929, 4.

109 *despite public concerns* ... Davies, "Ontario and the Automobile," 128, quoting a letter in the *Farmer's Sun,* Mar. 11, 1926: "The slaughter by the modern
Juggernaut of children, the old and infirm is appalling even now," fearing that
the 35 mph (56 km/h) highway speed limit, proposed for Ontario highways in
1929, would make matters worse. The higher speed was nonetheless implemented, along with 20 mph in cities. Henry, who in 1923 complained about
"speed fiends of motordom," raised the highway speed to 35 mph (56 km/h).
Henry had contemplated licence suspensions instead of fines as a more effective
penalty. See "Again Denounces Drunken Drivers," *Globe,* Nov. 30, 1929, 1. In

"An Auto Driver's Views," letter to the editor, *Globe*, Nov. 5, 1929, 4, urging that cars be constrained to 35 or 40 mph (56 or 64 km/h), a proposal that was technically feasible with speed governors. See also Davies, "Ontario and the Automobile," appendix 2. In 1914 a tax was imposed based on a motorcar's horsepower. C.W. Plaxton, letter to the editor, *Globe*, Nov. 13, 1928, 4 – high speed has more to do with these motor accidents than any other single factor."

109 *"Fastest Four in America ..."* Dodge Brothers, Ad, *Globe*, July 16, 1927, 7.

109 *producing 200,000 motorcars ...* Davies, "Ontario and the Automobile," 31, 40; in the same year, the industry was employing about 12,000 workers.

109 *exceeded bicycle production ...* Bike production data from Hodges, "Did the Emergence of the Automobile End the Bicycle Boom?"

109 *freedom, independence, and adventure ...* The gift of a bicycle became a reward for various life milestones. CCM, Ads, "Your Boy – Your Girl – Wants a BICYCLE ... Let 'Exam' Time Be Your Excuse for Gratifying that Desire" and "He or She Will Only Be Young Once," *Daily Star*, June 4, 1929, 7; CCM, Ad, "100 Boys Tell Why They Feel Safe on a Bicycle," *Daily Star*, Apr. 10, 1928, 11. Bicycles were also associated with wholesomeness: CCM, Ads, "Give Him a C.C.M and the Chance to Ride Away from Street Corner Influences."

109 *still holds much favour ...* "The Neglected Cycle," *Globe*, Apr. 9, 1929, 4.

110 *the socio-economic class ...* CCM, Ad, "Roll to Work," *Globe*, Apr. 11, 1929, 19, featuring a well-dressed man, presumably heading to work.

110 *"Rich Men Buy Them ..."* "Bicycle Once Again Coming to Its Own," *Daily Star*, July 29, 1918, 9 – the entire page was devoted to bicycling and ads, suggesting a substantial audience.

110 *prominent place to adults ....* See, for example, ads near the start of the decade, directed at adults: CCM, Ad, *Globe*, Apr 5, 1921, 13 and Hyslop Bros., Ad, *Globe*, Apr. 22, 1919, 11.

110 *"a professor of logic ..."* "A Bystander at the Office Window," *Globe*, May 10, 1928, 5. "What adult in this continent dares to ride a bicycle on the highway unless he is a mechanic going to work in overalls? Asks a writer in The Times (New York)."

111 *thousands of workers ...* In 1929, CCM announced another expansion to a 125,000-square-foot factory and head office at 2015 Lawrence Avenue West. Into the 1950s, CCM remained one of the most successful of Metro's 4,300 manufacturing entities, although management-labour relations continued to deteriorate. McKenty, *Canada Cycle & Motor*, 212–23. The union was established in January 1947, and a two-week strike followed in October 1947. In 1951, when CCM attributed an inability to meet workers' demands to a backlog

of unsold bikes, employees pointed to CCM's planned $350,000 factory expansion. A long strike ensued.

112 *Canadian Corps Cyclist Battalion ...* Norcliffe, *The Ride*, 216. The Corps had trained along the Humber River. Two bicycle divisions were sent overseas.

112 *war-tested sturdiness ...* "Yields a Return of 40 Per Cent on Your Investment of $65," *Daily Star*, Sept. 6, 1921, 9.

112 *"high-powered cars ..."* "Traffic Argument Leads to Police Patrol Try-Out," *Daily Star,* June 29, 1929, 1.

112 *special bicycle sheds ...* CCM, Ad, "Encourage Your Employees to Cycle to Work," *Daily Star*, June 19, 1924, 12.

112 *an invaluable tool for commerce ...* Tamblyn Drugs alone offered delivery from each of its thirty-six Toronto stores. Tamblyn, Ad, *Daily Star*, Aug. 22, 1929, 9, although it did not specifically mention bike deliveries. See, for example, the *Daily Star*, May 4, 1929, job ad: "Boy with wheel $9 Ferguson's Grocery."

112 *"skim over the country roads ..."* CCM, Ad, *Daily Star*, Apr. 2, 1929, 11, ending: "Roads are better now than they were in your day." See also CCM, Ad, "Why Not Give Him a CCM for His Birthday and Let Him Have the Health and Joy of the Open Road," *Globe*, Apr. 4, 1929, 16.

114 *a "Model T" bicycle ...* The Model T: CCM, Ad, *Globe*, Apr. 4, 1929, 16; Motorbike: CCM, Ad, *Globe and Mail*, May 10, 1930, 24, "Here's the New Motorbike '6' Superb." See Hyslop Catalogue, 1922, No. 34 for a range of its products directed at children, and adults (https://www.torontopubliclibrary.ca/detail.jsp?Entt=RDM297369&R=297369).

114 *"heaps of stores ..."* CCM, Ad, *Globe and Mail*, May 10, 1930, 24; "Beware of Cyclists," *Daily Star*, June 28, 1958, 6 – "The bicycle is a dangerous plaything, but it is a toy that most growing boys and girls demand."

114 *too old to play ...* GM, Ad, Dodge Ram pickup, Fall 2022.

115 *"The baron, astride the seat ..."* Today, vehicles modelled on this concept are again a popular children's toy.

115 *the "bone-shaker" ...* For a comprehensive review of the bicycle's development from *Laufmaschine* to safety, see Herlihy, *Bicycle*.

115 *"[s]udden wave of euphoria ..."* "City News," *Globe*, Feb. 25, 1869 1; and "Notes and Comments," *Globe*, Mar. 26, 1869, 4, characterizing *vélocipède* as a rich man's toy that would be "driven off the sidewalks if ... they should prove a nuisance."

115 *petition by vélocipède enthusiasts ...* CoT Council Minutes, 1869, Minutes 277, 281, May 10; and CoT Council Minutes, 1896, App, Board of Works, Report no. 5, May 27, pp 128–9.

116 *St. George's skating rink* ... Grants Riding Academy opened on Phoebe Street, see Norcliffe, *The Ride*, 30, illustration 1.8. As to utilitarian use, see "City News" *Globe*, Apr. 29, 1869, 1 – Dr. Robertson in Stratford made house calls. Eli F. Irwin, a Toronto medical student, regularly used the *vélocipède* to cycle 27 miles (43 kilometres) up Yonge Street to Newmarket to visit his mother.

116 *its popularity was fleeting* ... "Carriages – Velocipedes," *Globe*, Feb. 25, 1869, 3; Norcliffe, *The Ride*, 48. See also *Outing*, Apr. 1890–Sept. 1890, vol. 16, 491 – Doolittle as a seven-year-old apparently built a *vélocipède*, and as a fifteen-year-old built a high-wheel from a *Scientific American* drawing; he built another in 1879, using a musket barrel for the backbone.

116 *"such a fashionable fury ..."* Humber, *Freewheeling*, 27, quoting *Canadian Illustrated News*, Dec. 9, 1876. *Vélocipèdes* survived as a toy, especially for boys, into and after the high-wheel era, but were unwelcome on the sidewalks. See, for example, "City News," *Globe*, May 4, 1881, 6. A Canadian adaptation (patented in 1869) outlasted the fury when the rear wheel was replaced with a ski, an early version of the snowmobile – Norcliffe, *The Ride*, 84. Years later, a Chicago company offered an updated version with the ski replacing the front wheel (giving it rear-wheel drive). See Ad, *Canadian Wheelman*, Apr. 5, 1897, vol. 14, no. 10.

116 *a logical next step* ... With a 54-inch-diameter (1.4 metres) wheel, one full turn advanced the bike by 13.5 feet (4.2 metres).

116 *bravado of high-wheeling* ... See Friss, *The Cycling City*, 25. Pope designed some bikes for commercial deliveries like mail, messages, and food, and even designed a cold-weather "Yukon" for prospectors headed to the Alaskan gold rush. Riders could reach speeds of 20 mph (32 km/h).

116 *high-wheel riders looked down* ... "The Wheel," *Globe*, Mar. 30, 1898, 2.

117 *chain drive* ... The chain drive made it possible for a single revolution of the pedal crank to advance the rider as much as a single turn of the high-wheel's pedal. This could be achieved with the chain drive when the chain wheel (affixed to the pedal crank) was larger than the sprocket on the rear wheel.

118 *William Mackenzie's monopoly* ... The 1927 amendment to the Ontario *Railway Act* gave streetcars priority over other vehicles, but the provision was rarely enforced. Radials beyond the city had the advantage of clear passage when lines were located along private rights of way. By 1927, the TTC portfolio included city motorbuses, ferries, radial cars, and interurban buses, including the Gray Coach.

118 *TRC had refused to act* ... Stamp, *Riding the Radials*, 89 – Bloor Street (west of Dundas Street), 1915; Gerrard Street (1912); Lansdowne Avenue (1917); and portions of St. Clair and Danforth Avenues (1912). The Toronto Civic Railways

(TCR) was established in Sept. 1911 and was later integrated with the TTC. See "Street Railway Is Next Big Problem for City Council," *Daily Star*, Oct. 31, 1908, 1. The TTC in 1923 took over the Toronto Suburban Railway Co. (TSR; owned by Mackenzie), with lines operated on segments of St. Clair Avenue and Davenport and Weston Roads. The TSR also built the Toronto-Guelph radial operated by CN in the 1920s; see Stamp, *Riding the Radials*, 89. The Scarborough, Long Branch, and Yonge lines were operated by Mackenzie's T&YRR.

118 *increasing competition from motorcars ...* The TTC had 270 miles (434 kilometres) of track, but ridership trajectory was unclear, even though in 1928, it carried almost 200 million passengers in the city and the suburbs. CoT Council Minutes, 1929, App A, Sept. 30, Board of Control Report 24; and CoT Council Minutes, 1929, App A, Special Meeting of TTC, No 24, 1792. In April 1929, acting TTC chair E.J. Lennox, who touted the low fares and high frequency of the transit service, alleged that some TTC commissioners were lazy, inexperienced, and incompetent after a majority voted against the purchase of new streetcars. See "Lennox Promises Improved Service for Patrons," *Globe*, Apr. 9, 1929, 1; and "TTC Commissioners Vote Down Proposal," *Globe*, July 26, 1929, 14.

118 *"rubber-tired competition ..."* See "Traffic Congestion Points to City's Needs," *Daily Star*, July 3, 1929, 22.

118 *survived until 1949 ...* Davies, "Ontario and the Automobile," 112. See also "Controllers in Favour of Abandoning Radials if Legally Feasible," *Daily Star*, May 28, 1929, 1, 3; "TTC Asked to Continue Radial Line to Lake Simcoe for 2 Months," *Daily Star*, Sept. 25, 1929, 1. The TTC took over the Yonge line in 1927; Ontario Hydro had run it at a deficit, 1922–7. See "TTC Will Buy Gray Coach Lines; Weston-TO Service by CNR Stopped," *Globe*, Apr. 9, 1929, 13. The TTC got provincial authority to operate regional bus lines. The TTC argued that acquiring bus lines and abandoning radials would allow for substantial savings.

119 *the biggest drop in ridership ...* From 1923 to 1926, combined ridership on the Mimico, Scarborough, and Yonge radials had fallen from 7 million to 5.3 million passengers. Ridership decline (1.2 million) was largely attributable to the Mimico line, with competition from cheaper, faster rails and buses. Transfer at Dundas and Keele Streets was a long-standing problem for the Mimico line, a result of prohibitions against interurbans entering the city, a problem that Beck sought to remedy with a high-speed waterfront entry.

119 *Toronto-Guelph radial ...* The Guelph line had various other problems, and it also had to compete with a rail line. The last electric passenger interurban in Canada was the Port Colborne-Thorold line until 1959. See Stamp, *Riding the Radials*, 7.

120 *the proposed Hydro Radials ...* Might's Directory, 1920, "Transportation," 32.

120 *talking about electric trains* ... Schull, *Ontario since 1867*, 157, 159. Beck's radial network was originally premised on using surplus electric power from Niagara Falls, but when surplus became a shortage, radials became the reason to generate more power from the Falls.

120 *strong public support* ... Schull, *Ontario since 1867*, 244–7. In early 1915, Beck spoke of 1,000 miles of radials in Ontario. Before the end of the war, Beck was planning three lines: Toronto-Markham-Brooklin-Whitby; Toronto-Port Credit-Guelph-London; and Toronto-Niagara Peninsula. Beck's plan was supported by the city's working class (for access to the suburbs) and business for the potential of lower rates relative to rail, but farmers generally opposed them since around 1922 there were plentiful rail lines and new roads.

121 *"in about a hundred years ..."* "Called to Oppose Hydro-Radial, Stay to Cheer Beck," *Globe*, Dec. 21, 1922, 17.

121 *antagonistic to his interurban* ... See generally Stamp, *Riding the Radials*, chap. 8.

121 *"roads on all sides of him ..."* "Scores Biggs for Reckless Extravagance," *Globe*, June 2, 1921, 3. The subsequent royal commission further undermined government support and public confidence in Beck's plan, pointing to increased competition from autos, heavy provincial and municipal debt, and the floundering radial system in the United States. (Beck's radials would also have competed with existing railways and radials.)

121 *fighting for a single radial* ... Beck's stubborn insistence that the six-track waterfront line should exclude TTC vehicles was another factor that doomed his cause. The curiously named "Toronto Radial Association," among other Toronto groups, opposed Beck's plan. See "Says New Association Not Anti-Hydro at All," *Daily Star*, Aug. 26, 1920, 2.

122 *motorcar had harnessed society* ... Davies, "Ontario and the Automobile," 293, suggests that Sapir's critique in 1924 was aptly applied to cars: "The great cultural fallacy of industrialism ... is that in harnessing machines to our uses it has not known how to avoid the harnessing of the majority of mankind to its machines." See Edward Sapir, "Culture, Genuine and Spurious," *American Journal of Sociology* 29, no. 4 (Jan. 1924): 411, https://www.journals.uchicago.edu/doi/abs/10.1086/213616.

1953 – The Bicycle Endures

125 *a boy thought dead* ... "Downsview Boy, 14, Killed Weeping Sisters Identify Lad in Error," *Daily Star*, Apr. 10, 1953, 1; "Dead Boy," *Toronto Telegram*, Apr. 10, 1953, 1 – collision reported as having occurred "last night," i.e., Thurs, April 9. Obit shows death as April 10 (Friday), presumably on operating table.

125 *"controlled access" highways* ... Under the *Highway Improvement Act*, RSO 1937,
c 56, s 74, the minister could designate highways as "controlled access," which
was applied to the QEW and the 401. By 1942, bikes were banned on the QEW,
though this was a rare designation. See "Cycling's a Cinch to Good Old Days,"
Daily Star, Apr. 23, 1942, 3.

125 *direct route home* ... Even by 1968, when a boy was killed pushing his bike
across the DVP to reach a park, there was still no Metro by-law against walking
on the Don Valley Parkway (DVP) or the Gardiner, over which Metro had authority. See "Ban Pedestrians on Parkway, Metro Is Urged," *Globe*, Oct. 10, 1968,
5. Cycling on highways did occur from time to time, even in later years. George
Fotopoulos recounted to the author that as young immigrant he commuted by
bike on the DVP from 1972 to 1975.

126 *signs to warn them* ... "Thorns to Line Bypass as Pedestrian Guard," *Globe*, Dec.
4, 1952, 5.

126 *easily gain access* ... The absence of signage for cyclists is suggested by the
fact that such signage wasn't developed by the transportation ministry
until 1956.

126 *many adults and children* ... See, for example, "Boy Cyclist Dies, Highway
Mishaps Kill Four Others," *Globe and Mail*, Sept.17, 1951, 10; "Hit on Bicycle
Hurled 45 Feet," *Globe and Mail*, July 10, 1952, 8; and "Boy, 14, Killed Riding
Bicycle," *Globe and Mail*, Jan. 29, 1951, 8.

126 *misidentified by police* ... Gilchrist's death occurred on a provincial highway.
Newspapers reported that the North York police, not the OPP, investigated the crash.

126 *western terminus of the highway* ... Toronto's by-pass was completed in July
1952, between Yonge Street and Humber River. The highway was built in sections from Windsor to Cornwall and completed in the 1960s. In 1952, Highway
400, running north out of Toronto, was the first of the 400 series highways.

126 *The supposed victim* ... Ironically, Grant's elder brother, Harry Wyldes, was
well-known to police for a bizarre case of "joy-riding" in a police car in July
1952. Harry Wyldes fled the scene, only to be apprehended after overturning his
car. He was placed in the back of the police car but jumped into the driver's seat
and drove away, eluding police by listening to the police radio. "Joy Riding in
Cruiser Fine Man $300, Costs," *Daily Star*, July 23, 1952, 15 – plus a $10 fine for
having alcohol in the car.

126 *dead boy's background* ... "Mr. and Mrs. Frank Munro, Sheppard Ave.,
Downsview," were reported as Robert's parents, but no directory listing can be
found for them. No mention of his mother, Margaret Gilchrist. She had likely
given up custody as an unwed mother. Obituary, *Toronto Telegram*, Apr. 11,

1953. Robert was buried beside his grandmother, Jessie Bain Gilchrist (d. 1952), and his uncle Thomas (d. 1945, Battle of Normandy).

127 *only requires a reflector* ... *Highway Traffic Act, RSO 1950*, c 167, ss 10(10), required the front of the bike to have a "white or amber lighted lamp, or reflector approved by Dept," and on the back "a red lighted lamp, or reflector approved by Dept, as well as white surface not less than 10" long and 2" wide." In 1955, the act was amended to require a white light on the front of bikes. See "Revisions in Highway Traffic Act," *Globe and Mail*, May 13, 1955, 17.

127 *he will be acquitted* ... David Cousins of Willowdale was charged with dangerous driving (*Criminal Code*) and careless driving (*Highway Traffic Act*) but charges were dismissed. See "Charges Dismissed in Death Collision," *Globe and Mail*, Apr. 30, 1953, 5.

127 *50 per cent more cars* ... R.S. McLaughlin, "Future Highways Built for Speed Foreseen as Need," *Globe and Mail*, Nov. 6, 1937, 21.

127 *father's giant carriage works* ... Robertson, *Driving Force*, 78–9.

128 *1943 Master Plan* ... White, *Planning Toronto*, 27–42. The plan was the product of the city's new planning board. (The Richview, along Eglinton West, and the Scarborough superhighways had no assigned letters.)

128 *Toronto and its twelve neighbours* ... Bill 80 of *The Municipality of Metropolitan Toronto Act*, c 73, SO, 1953, included the Townships of North York, York, Etobicoke, and Scarborough; Towns of East York, Leaside, New Toronto, Mimico, Long Branch, and Weston; and the Villages of Swansea and Forest Hill. Metro, a 240-square-mile area, was also responsible for regional planning, mass transit, water, and sewage. Metro was preceded by the Toronto and Suburban Planning Board, established by the province in 1947. Metro Council's twenty-five positions were dominated by Toronto (its mayor, two controllers, nine aldermen); the twelve other municipalities had a total of four mayors and eight reeves.

128 *govern cross-boundary matters* ... "This was the transportation problem, not enough capacity, and engineers devoted all their efforts to move more traffic, whatever the cost." Kulash, "The Third Motor Age," 42.

128 *except Premier Leslie Frost* ... "Super-Mayor," *Toronto Telegram*, Apr. 9, 1953, 1–2. Gardiner was the former reeve of the wealthy Town of Forest Hill, where sanitation workers still collected garbage bins from backyards.

128 *the new strongman* ... "Is Super-Mayor a Superman Too?," *Toronto Telegram*, Apr. 8, 1953, 1.

128 *With Metro in charge* ... Hayes, *Historical Atlas of Toronto*, 151–2. See also "Arteries of Progress," *Globe and Mail*, Mar. 29, 1946, 6.

129 *began a long fight* … The Avenue Road Safety Coalition, the author among the founders, was formed by local residents' groups in November 2017. The city proposed safety improvements, including bike lanes and wider sidewalks, in the fall, 2023.

130 *straighten out the kinks* … "Super-Mayor," *Toronto Telegram*, Apr. 9, 1953, 2. Gardiner's appointment ran to December 31, 1954. He was elected for a new term in a vote by Metro Council.

130 *best served by cars* … Mass transit wasn't forgotten. White, *Planning Toronto*, 89. Metro's 1959 plan was to spend 35 per cent on public transit and 65 per cent on arterials and expressways, though the suburban reality makes this hard to believe, at least in practice, given the dominance of cars.

130 *the motorcar population* … Chief Constable Annual Report, 1953, 51. The figure includes passenger cars, trucks, motorcycles, and service cars. In 1953, the total automobile registrations fell to 214,000, perhaps due to population flight to the suburbs. See Chief Constable Annual Report, 1951, 48–9; and Chief Constable Annual Report, 1955, 71.

130 *faster in the suburbs* … Metro Toronto Police Annual Report, 1955, 10, "Traffic."

130 *an untapped resource* … "Super-Mayor," *Toronto Telegram*, Apr. 9, 1953, 2. Despite massive roads spending, traffic engineer Sam Cass still lamented in 1957 that his biggest headache was "lack of money" in making Metro a motorist's dream. See "My Biggest Headache," *Daily Star*, Dec. 13, 1957, 8.

130 *Sunnyside was demolished* … An early plan was to spare the park with a by-pass. "Move Sunnyside First," *Globe and Mail*, Sept. 23, 1950, 6. Gardiner got an expressway, the DVP, in the Don Valley, although Metro's ravines were generally protected from development by assertive parks departments in Metro and the city. White, *Planning Toronto*, 183.

131 *shove the poles back* … "Cut 5 or 6 Feet Off Sidewalks for Lanes of Traffic," *Daily Star*, Apr. 14, 1953, 3. Gardiner was reported as telling the Young Men's Canadian Club: "Many municipalities don't have sidewalks because people don't want them."

131 *park their idle vehicles* … On residential streets, local motorists likewise needed permission to park their cars overnight. Laneways built in the 1940s behind homes in the central city solved part of the problem. It had once been a "principle" that carriages had to park on private property. See White, *Planning Toronto*, 158–9.

132 *road building was tempered* … CoT Council Minutes, 1953, App C, Inaugural Address, 3, 5. See also CoT Council Minutes, 1953, Saunders, Mar. 10, re 1953 Civic Estimates, 41–3, including the anticipated widening or expansion of the Lake Front Highway, Spadina Avenue, Eglinton Avenue, Avenue Road, St. George Street, Don Valley Road, Keating Street, and Dundas Street extension;

the Clifton Road extension (now the southern part of Mount Pleasant Road) was already in place by 1950.

132 *"salute the authorities ..."* "What about the Poor Pedestrian?," letter to the editor, *Daily Star*, Mar. 13, 1953, 6.

132 *partially underground ...* CoT Council Minutes, 1953, App C, Inaugural Address, 3, 5. The Yonge subway was approved by city residents in January 1946, who were spurred by traffic congestion studies in 1942 and 1945, highlighting anticipated increase in auto traffic after the war. See "Something Toronto Cannot Afford," *Toronto Star*, May 13, 1952, 6.

132 *freeing up more road space ...* Officially, Metro sought to balance mass transit with road expansion. Among the streetcar lines removed in Toronto were ones on Dupont Street and Avenue Road. The lines on Yonge and Bloor-Danforth were moved underground. Streetcar lines elsewhere in Ontario were already facing an uncertain future; indeed, some lines were already removed. Niagara Falls, Sudbury, Welland, Windsor, St. Catharines, Hamilton, Ottawa, Peterborough, and Chatham had either lost or were soon to lose their streetcars.

132 *where cycling was popular ...* My father arrived in 1952 at age twenty-two from Germany where he regularly cycled to work, but once in Canada, he never again owned a bike – very much like others in his community of newcomers. This anecdote is supported by the recent Nanos *City of Toronto Cycling Study*, 11, which shows that immigrants of less than five years in Canada are the least likely of any group to own a bike.

132 *low-density neighbourhoods ...* The TTC initially divided the city into four zones, requiring an additional fare when crossing one of the zones, but these were later eliminated, further reducing TTC fare box revenues.

133 *with a small margin ...* "Controllers on Seesaw over Spadina Widening," *Daily Star*, Jan. 5, 1948, 2.

133 *days as a bicycle messenger ...* Colton, *Big Daddy*, 6.

133 *big developers ...* Harris, *Creeping Conformity*, 129–41.

134 *lack of materials ...* "No Increase in Bicycle Licences," *Globe and Mail*, July 19, 1941, 5. See also "Bicycle Sales Rocket as 'Gas' Ration Result," *Globe and Mail*, Apr. 7, 1942, 4.

134 *the lowly two-wheeler ...* CCM, Ad, "Wartime Voluntary Rationing," *Globe and Mail*, Apr. 20, 1944, 15. Bike demand spurred by rationing of oil and gas (as of summer 1941), and material shortages such as rubber for car tires suspended car manufacturing. In his letter to the editor, *Daily Star*, May 21, 1940, 3, Basil Rayhnam noted the low status of the bicycle (calling the attitude "ignorance sublime"), and adding, "Many people here won't ride a bicycle because their neighbours have a car."

134 *put aside their prejudices ...* "Cycling's a Cinch to Good Old Days," *Daily Star*, Apr. 23, 1942, 3.

134 *buried in cellars* ... "Wartime Voluntary Rationing," *Globe and Mail,* Apr. 20, 1944, 15. Second-hand bikes were likewise hard to find.

134 *give priority to buyers* ... "Sales of Bicycles Restricted," *Globe and Mail,* Apr. 1, 1943, 4; and CCM, Ad, "Wartime Voluntary Rationing," *Globe and Mail,* Apr. 20, 1944, 15. A buyer couldn't simply walk into a shop and buy a bike, but first had to complete an application, then wait, perhaps months, given that manufacturing was geared towards the war effort; "In War as in Peace," *Daily Star,* May 14, 1945, 11.

134 *converted to bike parking* ... "Car Parks Converted to Handle Bicycle Boom," *Globe and Mail,* Nov. 10, 1943, 4.

135 *a mom with her infant* ... "Cycling's a Cinch to Good Old Days," *Daily Star,* Apr. 23, 1942, 3.

135 *modest comeback* ... "Cycling's a Cinch to Good Old Days," *Daily Star,* Apr. 23, 1942, 3. "The bicycle ... is here to stay." Combined bicycle-train trips were common, apparently with no extra charge for bikes. A.E. Walton, seventy-two and still a member of the RCCC said that scarcity of gas allowed people to rediscover simple joy of cycling.

135 *for weekend outings* ... "Here Are Two Tours," *Daily Star,* Apr. 23, 1942, 3.

135 *alongside the QEW* ... "Modern Long-Distance Bicycling," *Daily Star,* July 10, 1942, 6. The *Daily Star* suggested that motorists slow their speed and politely honk their horn when passing a touring cyclist on a highway.

135 *indication of bicycle usage* ... Chief Constable Annual Report, 1952, 34.

135 *Between 1934 and 1947* ... In 1945, only 30,000 licences were issued but the numbers jumped to 36,500 in 1946 and to 36,100 in 1947. Chief Constable Annual Report, 1948, 57. In 1948, 4,000 fewer licences were issued relative to 1947.

135 *20 per cent of all registered vehicles* ... In 1939 a tiny contingent of horse-drawn wagons remained on the roads for the delivery of goods. Eaton's replaced its horses with motorcars in 1935; "Horses Vanishing from City Streets," *Globe and Mail,* Dec. 24, 1936, 6. In Might's Directory, 1929, there were 10 listings for "horse dealers," "horse nail mfrs.," and "horseshoers"; 5 listings for "Livery, Sale, and Boarding Stables"; and 57 blacksmiths, but the Directory was already overwhelmed by auto listings.

135 *50,000 bicyclists on city streets* ... Toronto Police Department, *Bicycle Regulations with Safety Suggestions for Pedestrians and Cyclists,* 1946 (Toronto Museums Living History Collection). See "Bicycle Licences Sold Ahead of All Time High of 50,000 Seen," *Daily Star,* June 1, 1942, 9.

135 *"Mayor Robert Saunders ..."* "Popular Mayor Often Takes Bicycle Rides Around City," *Daily Star,* Oct. 11, 1947, 3.

136 *"human bric-a-brac ..."* Six-day races were originally held at Mutual Street
      Arena before moving to venues such as Cycledrome on Dundas Street and, after
      1931, to Maple Leaf Gardens. See "'Torchy' Peden and Bobby Walthour to Meet
      in Match Race," *Globe*, July 5, 1929, 10; "Bike Race to Nowhere Returning after
      Skipping Full Generation," *Globe*, May 1, 1965, 27.

136 *"men sober and drunk ..."* "Star Sport Rays," *Daily Star*, May 13, 1935, 10 –
      describing "thronging riders on saucer-like, wooden track" and "throbbing
      grind." In the 1930s, the Dundas Street Velodrome was also used. See "The Babe
      Ruth of Bicycle Racing Streets Return of Six-Day Races," *Globe and Mail*, Aug.
      26, 1961, 33. The original six-day race in Toronto (c. 1912) was in the Mutual
      Street Arena; McKenty, *Canada Cycle & Motor*, 161.

136 *including Torchy Peden ...* Tabitha de Bruin, "William 'Torchy' Peden,"
      Canadian Encyclopedia, https://www.thecanadianencyclopedia.ca/en/article/
      william-j-peden. See also "Sports Digest," *Globe and Mail*, May 16, 1952, 18.
      Peden counted dozens of victories among 148 six-day races between 1929
      and 1948. CCM, Ad, "Boys 'Torchy Peden' Rides a CCM on the Streets and
      Highways and on the Race Tracks," *Daily Star*, May 3, 1935, 18. Road rac-
      ing, occasionally including women, retained an audience. CWA organized a
      popular High Park race each year, covering a 25-mile (40-kilometre) circuit. In
      1953, CWA had sixteen affiliated clubs, including the Toronto Cycle Club, see
      "Toronto CC Officers," *Globe and Mail*, Sept. 20, 1950, 19. Women, including
      Nora Young, had begun to appear among the city's bicycle racers.

136 *quirky or eccentric individuals ...* "Trucker Catches Holdup Suspect Escaping on
      Bike," *Globe and Mail*, Apr. 28, 1952, 5 – man fled on delivery boy's unattended
      bicycle after aborted drug store robbery; "UK Immigrants to Cross Canada on
      Bike for 3," *Daily Star*, Apr. 3, 1953, 1; "Bicycle Rider Ends 8th Trip Around the
      World," *Globe and Mail*, June 8, 1952, 5; and "Wife's Eyes See Twice for Tourists
      on Tandem," *Globe and Mail*, May 8, 1952, 7 – local couple Europe-bound for
      tandem adventure, wife in front seat of tandem and spouse, a war veteran blind-
      ed during invasion of Normandy, in back.

136 *who fell off bridges ...* "Boy, 11, Saves Mother from Chilly Lake Water," *Globe
      and Mail*, May 2, 1952, 5; and "Cyclist Rescued from Eastern Gap," *Globe and
      Mail*, Aug. 16, 1952, 5.

137 *cities too dangerous ...* "Weston Man Has Cycled 300,000 Miles since 1914,"
      Globe and Mail, Oct. 11, 1950, 7.

137 *adults continued to cycle ...* Chief Constable Annual Report, 1952, 77–95. In
      1952, among the 210 *reported* cycling injuries, almost half of victims were age
      fifteen and over, although most fell into the fifteen to twenty-four age category.
      The fifteen to twenty-four year age group accounted for 33 per cent of injuries,

almost all among men. Children ten to fourteen accounted for 52 per cent of
injuries. By the late 1940s, there was a steep decline in traffic offences committed
by adult cyclists, dropping from several thousand to hundreds, consistent with a
drop in adult cycling. In fact, by the late 1940s, police no longer segregated adult
cycling violations (totalling 3,500 in 1938). B.H.B., letter to the editor, *Daily Star*,
Mar. 15, 1940, 7 – "thousands of young and old rely on bicycles as their mode of
transportation."

137 *"dependable for transportation ..."* Canadian Tire, Ad, *Daily Star*, June 25, 1953,
19; A. Humphries, letter to the editor, *Globe and Mail*, Apr. 20, 1957, 1B; "Voice
of the People: A Mean Theft," *Daily Star*, Aug. 17, 1953, 6 – a mother, writing
about the theft of her son's bike lamented: "By the time my son saves enough
money to buy another bike he will be too old to enjoy it."

137 *"I think it stinks ..."* "Boosted License Fee 'Last Straw,'" *Globe*, Mar. 12, 1948, 4.

137 *Diminished police interest ...* In 1949 police refused to enforce some licence
types, although the impact on bike licences is unclear. In 1948, 7,000 fewer dog
licences were issued – see "Finds Dogs, Bikes Unlicensed if It's Left to Owners'
Honor," *Globe*, Nov. 23, 1949, 4. Bike licences dropped by 2,000 from 1948
to 1949. By 1950, bike licences dropped to 29,000; and by 1952, to 24,500, by
which year bikes comprised only 8 per cent of *all* Toronto vehicle registrations
(CoT Council Minutes, 1948, Special Committee, App A, 517).

137 *a far greater drop ...* Chief Constable Annual Report, 1944, 59.

137 *22,000 bike licences ...* In 1954, there were – 19,500 issued licences (Chief
Constable Annual Report, 1954, 73; and Annual Report 1955, 79). There are no
numbers available for 1956. In 1956, the Metro Licensing Commission made it
clear that bike licencing would not be maintained, citing administrative burdens
and asking all municipalities to abandon their regimes. Toronto first announced
the end of bike licences in 1954, then extended it. See "City Abolishes Bicycle
Licences," *Globe and Mail*, Sept. 30, 1954, 17 – end of bike licence prematurely
reported. Police chief reported that cost outstripped value; and "Halt Licensing
of Bicycles, Metro Advises," *Globe and Mail*, Oct. 25, 1956, 5. The chief admitted
that having a licence gave little protection from theft.

139 *revenues – dropped precipitously ...* "$1 Bicycle Licence Not Worth Trouble,"
Globe and Mail, June 25, 1953, 5 – Mayor Lamport agreed that eliminating the
licence was "a good idea," provided the owner recorded the bike's serial number.

139 *$18,000 into city coffers ...* Chief Constable Annual Report, 1947, 60–1.
Accounting for 6 per cent of all licensing revenues (total $300,000) in 1950. See
Chief Constable Annual Report, 1948, 50.

139 *adult-like formality of a bike licence ...* Annual police reports showed children's violations of by-laws and HTA offences (most for cycling violations)

as "Application for Summonses forwarded by the Summons Division to the Juvenile Court during the year." It is unclear how courts decided which children were summoned, or whether these summonses included all cycling violations.

140 *a pretext for police* ... See, for example, "Accused Says Officer Struck Him in Cells," *Daily Star*, June 6, 1935, 16; and "Asking Boy's License Leads to Arrest of Four," *Daily Star*, June 30, 1930, 13.

140 *Magistrate Arthur Tinker* ... "Parking Violators Pay in $250 Daily," *Daily Star*, July 14, 1936, 27. Tinker took sidewalk riding more seriously.

140 *200 people in his court*... Among other common cycling offences under by-laws and the HTA were the carrying of a passenger, riding on the sidewalk, failure to have lights, and making illegal turns. The 1952 cycling violations by children included 810 for boys under the age of sixteen, and twelve violations for girls. The number of violations fluctuated wildly from 170 in 1952 to 1,320 in 1948 (Chief Constable Annual Report, 1948, 36; and Annual Report 1952, 38). Until 1951, bike offences were subdivided into age groups, for example, the sixteen to nineteen age group.

141 *eyeing Powley's bike* ... Roger Powley, interview with author, Feb. 13, 2020. The incident likely occurred in 1954 or 1955 when Powley (b. 1943) was twelve years old.

141 *rebuke from child welfare experts* ... The *Young Offenders Act*, 1984, replaced the JDA and restricted its application to criminal acts. Youth justice experts lambasted the JDA approach. See, for example, "Minutes of Federal-Provincial Conference on Juvenile Delinquency," Ottawa, Jan. 10–11, 1968 (Public Safety Canada, Archived Content, https://www.publicsafety.gc.ca/lbrr/archives/hv%20 9058%20f4%201968-eng.pdf). BC's Deputy AG: "We were troubled by the fact that juveniles were receiving records as juvenile delinquents for such things as not having bicycle licences, riding bicycles on sidewalks and other minor offences. See Sherri Davis-Barron, *Canadian Youth and the Criminal Law*, 40 – the juvenile court's role was *not* to ask "what has the child done?" but "How can this child be saved?" (citing Bolton et al., "The Young Offenders Act," 40). The JDA codified a paternalistic, welfare-oriented approach focused on curing the delinquent. Other officials also critical: "Cigarettes a Money-Maker, Licences Hint Bicycle on Way Out," *Globe and Mail*, Mar. 26, 1954, 17 – Police chief, Chisholm, said juvenile court authorities and school principals considered summoning of kids to court for licence violations poor public policy. Chief Constable Annual Report, 1929, 5 – letter to Board.

141 *authority to impose any penalty* ... Chief Constable Annual Report, 1948 (summary 1945–8), 36. At 6–7 – among dispositions for juveniles: sentence to industrial school, strapped, put on probation, or sent to a farm. A simple by-law

violation became an opportunity, out of all proportion to actual violation, for the state to intervene in child's life, perhaps to address issues such as truancy, an unstable family situation, or homelessness.

141 *the heading "Crime"* ... Chief Constable Annual Report, 1952, 38. Subheading "Juvenile Crime."

142 *"ashamed to be seen chasing boys ..."* J.V. McAree, "Circle Bar, Fourth Column," *Globe and Mail*, June 7, 1951, 5.

142 *police weren't as ashamed* ... Bike licence infractions by children (1947–52 charges for licence non-compliance ranged betw 1,950 and 2,300 – Chief Constable Annual Report, 1952, 70) almost equalled all other licence violations combined, including cigarette vendors, dog owners, and restaurants. Bike licence violations by adults are not listed as separate category. By comparison, there were 200 charges against children for major crimes. See Chief Constable Annual Report, 1952, chap. 4, "Crime," 37, 38.

142 *provoked public anger* ... J. Goodwin, letter to the editor, *Globe*, Aug. 10, 1937, 6, complained about the inequity of requiring delivery boys to obtain a bike licence when horse-drawn wagons working for corporations (which Eaton's then still used for deliveries) had no similar obligation but caused more damage to roads while leaving behind manure. "Licence Increase Opposed," *Globe and Mail*, Mar. 15, 1948, 6. Refusal to obtain a licence could be considered another form of protest.

142 *killed by a heavy truck* ... "Turns to See if Pal Okay, Cyclist Killed by Trailer," *Daily Star*, May 1, 1952, 2; "Just Got New Bicycle, Boy, 14, Killed by Truck," *Globe and Mail*, May 1, 1952, 1; "Death of Cyclist Held Accidental," *Globe and Mail*, May 20, 1952, 5. After obtaining his annual bicycle licence (imprinted with a tidy #10300) from City Hall, John Sweeney was cycling home with a friend, both Grade 9 students at De La Salle High School, riding east along Queen. A truck's rear wheels caught Sweeney's bike. The driver said: "The first I saw of the boys was in my rear-view mirror just as the first one slipped under the wheel."

142 *nothing changed* ... "Urge 'Child-Catchers' on Trucks," *Daily Star*, May 3, 1953, 1. The *Daily Star* offered an artist's rendition of a proposed *child-catcher* or guard for the rear wheels, especially valuable for someone caught in a driver's blind spots. The Automotive Transport Association supported the guards or some type of skirting in front of or behind the rear wheels. See "Urge Child-Catchers on Trucks," *Daily Star*, May 3, 1952, 1–2. Safety cradles on front of streetcars served a similar function. See, for example, "Carried 50 ft. by Tram 'that Was Close' – Boy," *Daily Star*, May 4, 1953, 4; W.J. Lucas, Regional Coroner, "A Report on Cycling Fatalities in Toronto, 1986–1996," July 1998. Coroner

recommended study of side-guards. See the 2010 report by the Office of the Chief Corner of Ontario, *Pedestrian Death Review*, 38, in which the Ontario Chief Coroner recommended side-guards for trucks.

142 *at schoolyard racks ...* "Police Check Unsafe Bicycles," *Globe and Mail*, Apr. 10, 1959, 5. Traffic Safety Division 8 officers planned to return to each school to re-check bikes. See "Bicycle Check Brings Results," *Globe and Mail*, Apr. 28, 1959, 5 – checks of 5,600 bikes in Metro schools over a three-week period revealed 3,900 defects.

142 *"prowled racks ..."* D. Waller, letter to the editor, *Globe and Mail*, July 31, 1957, 13 – "Children who learn and practice the rules of safe cycling will be well prepared to meet traffic problems as a motorist."

142 *The Kiwanis Club ...* "Fit Reflective Tape on 3,000 N. York Bikes," *Daily Star*, May 30, 1952, 22. Occasional crackdowns on offences such as failing to have lights was another strategy – "Orders Crackdown on Cycle Lighting," *Globe and Mail*, Oct. 21, 1952, 5.

142 *Thefts remained high ...* In 1938, a high number of bike and car thefts prompt-ed Chief Constable Draper to chastise owners for leaving "unchained bicycles leaning against the wall." (Car and homeowners were similarly criticized for unlocked doors and windows.) Thefts based on Chief Constable Annual Report, 1938, 36–7 – 2,200 bike thefts; 1,770 car thefts. Thefts based on Chief Constable, Annual Reports 1929 to 1952: 1929 – 1,408; 1934 – 3,075; 1935 – 3,400; 1948 – 1,300; 1952 – 1,700.

143 *He didn't elaborate ...* "To Check Bike Thefts," *Daily Star*, Sept. 19, 1942, 34. York Township had its own innovative solution to thefts. Licence plates came in two parts – when the upper portion of the plate was removed from the bike, the words "Stop Thief" remained on the part of the plate left behind. See "'Stop Thief' Shout New License Plates," *Daily Star*, Dec. 31, 1938, 6.

143 *fluctuated dramatically ...* Recovery numbers might spike if a theft ring was broken up in a particular year, thus recovering bikes stolen in a previous year. Police didn't always report recovery rates. Chief Constable Annual Reports reported recovery rates between 1933 to 1952 ranging from a low of 23 per cent (1933) to 62 per cent (1937).

143 *to recover stolen bikes ...* In the 1990s, a voluntary registration initiative called the "Bike Tracks" (to be sold through bike stores for a fee) was proposed, to be supported by a national registry. The initiative failed. The Bicycle Guild Corp. offered voluntary bike registration for a fee with the advantage of national reach, calling on Toronto to review its licence system – CoT Council Minutes, 1950, Minutes, 105, Mar. 20. The Tyden Seal Method was used by some municipalities.

143 *forfeiting the opportunity* ... Some bikes did not have serial numbers. In theory, cyclists could buy theft insurance, but at $5 annually, the fee could, over several years, exceed the value of the bike.

143 *plate was itself costly* ... CoT Council Minutes, 1953, App A, Board of Control, June, 767, "Purchase of Bicycle Licence Plates." In 1953, the city paid $2,000 for the 30,000 licences on order. Smaller municipalities might pay more, given economies of scale.

143 *tags into a snack* ... Frank Tumpane, "At City Hall: Metal Dog Tags Again," *Globe*, Jan. 29, 1946, 3.

144 *risk travel on arterials* ... See, for example, "Teen-Age Transport Workers Ride in Autos, Bicycle Maker Reports," *Globe and Mail*, Feb. 14, 1951, 5 – presentation to Canadian Bicycle & Sports Goods Dealers' Association. "Bicycles used to be ridden to the factory or shop ... But today workers in industry ride to work in automobiles. The bicycle has become teen-age transportation."

145 *"One child's life saved ..."* "Advocates Bicycle Paths," *Globe and Mail*, June 26, 1947, 13. As to bicycle paths, the same point had been made in the 1920s: "The Neglected Cycle," *Globe*, Apr. 9, 1929, 4 – "cycling would be just as prevalent today were more provision made for the safety of cyclists on our roadways."

145 *playing in the streets* ... "Police Chief Draper Favors New By-Law Outlined by Coroner," *Globe*, July 26, 1929, 14.

145 *push for playgrounds* ... Quoted in Davies, "Ontario and the Automobile," 158, citing *Hamilton Times*, July 6, 1918. "Playgrounds are becoming more a necessity than ever. The automobile and the motor truck have driven the children off the streets."

145 *his own grandchildren* ... Phillips had considered a ban for children under ten, under eleven, or under twelve – "Why Mayor Phillips Proposed Bicycle Ban," *Globe and Mail*, May 29, 1958, 7. Children could legally cycle on sidewalks – "Uniform Traffic By-Law Bikes Up to 24 Inches Allowed on Sidewalks for Metro," *Globe and Mail*, June 25, 1958, 5. Sidewalk riding had its own risks, including cars backing out of driveways or at intersections when children emerged unexpectedly from sidewalks.

146 *"raising a bunch of sissies"* ... "Mayor Urges Bicycle Ban," *Globe and Mail*, May 13, 1958, 11.

146 *"not going to be lucky ..."* "Street Hazard Claimed Bid to Ban Children on Bicycles Defeated," *Globe and Mail*, June 25, 1958, 5.

146 *developed some positive ideas* ... "No, Mr. Phillips Ban Is Not Way to End Bike Hazard," *Globe and Mail*, May 21, 1958, 15 – characterizing Phillips's ban as akin to prohibiting swimming to address drowning accidents. Young pointed to London, England, as a model, for bike and foot paths. He also proposed that

motorists refrain from cutting off cyclists when making right or lefts turns or passing other cars on two-lane roads. Similarly, Ron Haggard, "Metro Toronto By-Law Problem Seen for Boy with Bicycle," *Globe and Mail*, June 5, 1958, 7, argued that issue was particularly difficult because decision-makers were "weighing the joys of childhood against the possibilities of personal tragedy."

146 *rarely enforced* ... *Highway Traffic Act*, R.S.O. 1990, c. H.8, s. 148 (6.1). Patrick White, "Windsor Police Issue 0 Tickets in 4 Years for One-Metre Cycling Safety Rule Violations," *CBC News*, Dec. 23, 2019.

146 *Blaming children* ... "Struck by Truck, Boy, 5, Killed in North York," *Globe and Mail*, Feb. 18, 1953, 7 – child was playing in front of home warned several times by truck driver, who nonetheless ran over the child. See also "'Stay Off Road' Mum Told [3-yr-old] Tot Truck Killed," *Toronto Telegram*, Apr. 6, 1953, 37. The police inspector claimed that above all else parental instruction and supervisions would save children – "Child Death Toll Rises in '66-67 School Year," *Globe*, Aug. 15, 1967, 6. As for injurious crashes, the police inspector urged parents to "preach" safety – "Ten Children Hurt Parents Urged to 'Preach' Safety," *Daily Star*, Apr. 4, 1953, 1. Also, "Chief Calls for Safety," *Globe and Mail*, Sept. 24, 1934, 6 – pedestrians to be discouraged from deliberately provocative behaviour, and urged to cross street as quickly as convenient to "allow the cars to proceed without needless loss of time."

146 *Constant vigilance* ... "Cub, 11, on Way to Apple Meeting, Killed by Car," *Globe and Mail*, Oct. 18, 1952, 1. Another fatality on Highway 27 happened when the cyclist "suddenly swerved out of control" and crashed into the automobile – "Bicycle Hit, Boy, 14, Dies in Hospital," *Globe*, May 25, 1969, 5. Also "Hit Side of Car, Cyclist, 7, dies," *Globe and Mail*, June 17, 1968, 5.

147 *as if he were sick* ... "Farmer Plowing Hears Scream," *Globe and Mail*, Sept. 30, 1950, 1.

147 *"Give them room ..."* L. Coates, "You Can Help Cut Bicycle Accidents," *Daily Star*, Sept. 15, 1979, F10.

147 *what police knew best* ... Oft-cited cyclist, Raynham, who dismissed police-taught cycling skills programs, asked rhetorically, "What does the average police officer today know about a modern bicycle?" See "Safety for Bicyclists," *Globe and Mail*, May 24, 1958, 6.

148 *Elmer the Safety Elephant* ... OSL helped create in 1947 (and still runs today) the program, supported by the *Toronto Telegram*, motor groups, and the Toronto Traffic Safety Council (staffed by police).

148 *Elmer was lowered* ... Chief Constable Annual Report, 1953, "School Traffic Safety," 72 – schools needed thirty accident-free days before Elmer returned in a similar ceremony. See Chief Constable Annual Report, 1948, 51.

148 *bespectacled terrier* ... See, for example, "Star's Knee-High Tells of Safety on
Bicycles at Blythwood School," *Daily Star*, Sept. 21, 1949, 25. Smiling children
crowded around the dog, often accompanied by police inspector Sam Wheeler
(his real name).

148 *a wide range of goods* ... New uses of telegrams became popular, including to
order flowers. See, for example, ads in the *Daily Star*, Apr. 10–11, 1953, 42.

148 *"speedy messenger service ..."* "Yes, Mrs. Smith, At Once," *Daily Star*, May 13,
1936, 16. The model shown has racing handlebars, rat-trap pedals, a light-
weight frame, and hand-operated rim brakes, resembling a ten-speed of the
1970s bike revival, but without derailleur and ten gears. Ad, "A Light-Weight
Marvel," *Globe and Mail*, May 16, 1935, 9.

148 *the ages of fourteen and eighteen* ... "Messenger Girls Flit Quickly to Other Jobs,"
Globe and Mail, Sept. 10, 1942, 4, estimating sixty girl telegram messengers in
Toronto alone.

148 *their Flyte bicycles* ... Reynolds, "Technological Innovation," 37. CCM "produced no ground-breaking technological innovation" in its eighty-three-year
history. Morris and McKenty, "The 1936 CCM *Flyte*."

149 *amputation of both his legs* ... See "Dying Telegraph Boy Begs Man to Deliver
Messages for Him," *Daily Star*, May 12, 1938, 25. See also "Pinned by Trolley,
Boy Thinks of Job," *Globe and Mail*, May 12, 1938, 1.

149 *minimum wage of $8* ... Margaret Gould, "Child Workers Plead for 60 Hour
Week," *Daily Star*, Oct. 13, 1937, 1.

150 *Toronto Welfare Council* ... Cited in "Appeal for Delivery Boys," *Daily Star*,
Feb. 23, 1940, 6; and "Helping to Protect Boys," letter to the editor, *Daily Star*,
Nov. 22, 1940, 6. In the end, council merely supported voluntary measures
by Retail Druggists Assoc to educate its members about the problem – CoT
Council Minutes, 1941, App A, "Regulation and Control of Employment of
Delivery Boys and Store Messengers," p 1432.

150 *"[c]old, dark winter nights ..."* Big Brothers Bulletin, cited in "An example
to Ontario," *Daily Star*, Dec. 26, 1940, 6. The *Daily Star* called for provincial
legislation to protect the boys. It supported better work conditions and minimum wage. On the same day, the paper reported the hit-and-run Christmas
Eve death of a young bike messenger on Lakeshore Highway – "Smashed Glass
Gives Clue in Highway Hit-Run Death," *Daily Star,* Dec. 26, 1940, 8.

150 *"fire and daring of youth ..."* Judith Robinson, "How to Curb Traffic Toll and
Tempers," *Globe and Mail*, May 18, 1940, 13, recommending cycling instruction
for boys by Sir Ellsworth Flavelle's Cyclists' Safety Council. (No other references
to this group have been found.)

151 *appealed to drug store owners* ... "No Bike Parking," *Daily Star*, May 14, 1940, 11.

151 *limits proposed in 1941 ...* In 1941, the City of Toronto proposed a *Municipal Act* amendment to Queen's Park to limit the size and weight of goods carried by messengers. It was unclear if the proposal was motivated by concern for messengers' welfare or whether the death of a drug store messenger weeks earlier (on icy roads on Avenue Road) was a pretext for dealing with unrelated complaints about messengers, or even to support car-based delivery. See "Messenger, 14, Is Killed; Medical Student Held," *Globe and Mail*, Jan. 25, 1941, 5. See also "Group Passes Bill to Limit Loads Carried by Bicycles," *Globe and Mail*, Mar. 27, 1941, 4.

151 *an obvious dilemma ...* F. Anglin-Johnson, letter to editor, *Globe*, May 10, 1940, 6.

151 *gangster-like threat ...* "Bandits 12 and 8, Rob East End Delivery Boy," *Globe*, Oct. 28, 1952, 5.

151 *sitting on his handlebars ...* "12-Year-Old Drug Store Given Fake Order," *Globe and Mail*, Apr. 12, 1950, 3. There were a variety of other cases: "Boy Alleges Masked Man Kidnapped and Robbed Him," *Daily Star*, Jan. 4, 1940, 8; "Messenger Scared 'Ghost' Steals $24," *Daily Star*, Apr. 8, 1953, 19 – the thief jumped out from behind bushes wearing a white sheet over his head. See also "Masked, Armed Robs Store Boy," *Toronto Telegram*, Apr. 8, 1953, 44.

152 *"rode into a car door ..."* "11 Hurt or Shaken Up," *Daily Star*, Feb. 28, 1953, 2; "Delivery Boy, 14, Critically Hurt by Hit-Run Car," *Daily Star*, Dec. 5, 1953, 18 – Weston boy was delivering fish and chips.

152 *"a swell bike ..."* "25 Subscriptions Wins Free Bicycle for Boy and Girl," *Globe and Mail*, Mar. 21, 1950, 1; "Proud of Their Whizzers," *Globe and Mail*, July 30, 1949, 16; "Delivery Stars, Two Boys Even Buy Sisters Bikes," *Daily Star*, Mar. 3, 1953, 8 – membership, and award for children twelve and older, attained with twenty-five newspaper subscriptions.

152 *a happy connection ...* See, for example, "Riding Bicycle, Carrier Killed, Driver Charged," *Globe and Mail*, Apr. 16, 1953, 31.

153 *road users' conduct ...* Police also routinely conducted vehicle inspections, exposing defects such as poor brakes. See, for example, "Find 60 P.C. of Cars Defective 1st Day Testing," *Daily Star*, Apr. 8, 1953, 19. Inspections in 1929 detected 8,900 defective brakes in 50,000 car inspections. Chief Constable Annual Report, 1929, 15. By comparison, by 2018 in Ontario, only 1 per cent of vehicles involved in injury or fatal collisions had defects. Ministry of Transportation, Ontario Road Safety Annual Report, 2018, 63.

153 *face the scrutiny ...* Doolittle, as OML president, distinguished between "safe use of the highway and hysterical legislation that would penalize careful sane motorists." See "Dr. Doolittle's Speech," *Globe*, Sept. 13, 1927, 4.

153 *"the root of the evil ..."* Lauriston, "Motor Murder," *Maclean's*, Aug. 1, 1933. See also Warren Hastings, "Speed Limit," *Maclean's*, Oct. 15, 1933 – the acting OML

secretary responded that "arbitrary" speed limits should be replaced by an enforcement focus on unsafe driving practices.

154 *"more thoughtfulness and care ..."* "55 Lives Sacrificed to Traffic in Year on Toronto Streets," *Globe,* June 16, 1922, 13. J.F.H. Wyse, said "automobile in motion is proving itself to be a very deadly weapon when in careless or inexperienced hands."

154 *aimed at reducing crashes ...* Minister of Highways, Ontario, Ad, "Try Courtesy on Highways," *Globe,* July 10, 1937, 9.

154 *but lauded him ...* Chief Constable Annual Report, 1938, 44 – "if he's a gentleman he's a careful, competent and considerate driver."

154 *"lack of good manners ..."* "Bad Manners, Not the Auto, Cause Most Traffic Accidents," *Toronto Telegram,* Apr. 10, 1953, 2. According to the *Toronto Telegram:* "The same habits [of care, consideration and courtesy] exhibited behind the wheel would reduce the appalling loss of life on the roads of this province." Doucett said: "[W]e must go back to three places, the home, the church and the school ... The starting place for good driving habits – and I may add, good walking habits – is in the home."

154 *pent up consumer demand ...* "84th Day of the Year Traffic Deaths 16," *Daily Star,* Mar. 25, 1938, 3.

155 *death as "accidental" ...* "Killed by Automobile," *Globe,* June 15, 1905, 14. The chauffeur-driven car owned by Frederick Robins, owner of a real estate company, driving at a "fairly fast rate of speed." The chauffeur (not named) testified that he slowed down behind the trolley but didn't see the victim (Lenton Williams) in time. Working-class victim, upper-class car owner. In September 1906, Jane Porter was killed when she was run over and dragged by an automobile. The deaths of Williams, Porter, and Delia Hazelton, who was killed in October 1907 at Yonge and Bloor, were all determined at subsequent inquests as "accidental." See "Police Should Control Cars," *Globe,* Oct. 11, 1907, 12.

155 *predictable, constantly repeated reality ...* Lauriston, "Motor Murder," called the term "accidental" a curious one when applied to road deaths that continued day after day.

155 *claimed more lives ...* "Motors Not Dangerous," *Globe,* Jan. 15, 1909, 12. In 1899–1908, the OML listed 111 individuals killed by trolley cars (an average of 11 annually); 76 by trains, mainly at level crossings; and 19 by wagons. In the same period, three people were killed by motorists. See also Chief Constable Annual Report, 1909, 33: three road fatalities resulted from individuals being run over by "vehicles," which may or may not have been motorcars. The OML ignored various factors, but numbers supported the OML's inference that motorists' poor reputations were not entirely deserved. See also Chief Constable Annual Report, 1897,

37–8: 3 fatalities from bicycle collisions, 3 by trolley, 1 fell from trolley, 1 jumped from train, 4 "on railways" (presumably the tracks), 1 by fire engine, and "one run over by vehicle," presumably a horse-drawn cart or carriage.

155 *generic category "vehicle"* … Chief Constable Annual Report, 1910, 42: "Return showing the number of accidental deaths and fatal casualties." Among 27 total road deaths, 13 people were killed by streetcars, 8 were run over by a "vehicle" (likely including motorcars), and 6 fell from a "vehicle" or trolley; 10 others were killed at level rail crossings.

155 *dulled the public outrage* … Chief Constable Annual Reports, 1945 and 1952. Injuries in 1945, 2,800 per year rising to 3,800 per year by 1952; collisions in 1945, 4,400 per year and rising to 9,400 per year by 1952. See Chief Constable Annual Report, 1952, 47, 75, 78 (Table B). See Chief Constable Annual Reports, 1939–45. On average, there were 78 road deaths from 1935 to 1945. Road deaths peaked at 102 in 1941.

155 *"Death on Wheels …"* Royd Beamish, "Death on Wheels," *Maclean's*, Feb. 15, 1946.

155 *"for tragedy and violence …"* "The Black Year," *Globe and Mail*, Jan. 1, 1953, 4. The Minister of Highways tried to dull the pain of the 1953 numbers by offering (accurately) that a jump in the road casualty toll in Ontario "had been expected" from the increase in vehicle registrations and motor traffic – a comment for which he was quickly rebuked. "Slaughter on the Highways," *Globe and Mail*, Jan. 2, 1954, 6. In 1953, Toronto had 69 road fatalities (compared to 11 murders). In 1935, there were 50 road deaths, and, by 1941, there were 102 fatalities. Road deaths remained consistently high in the post-war years. See also Chief Constable Annual Report, 1955, 71.

156 *poisoned by carbon monoxide* … Robert G. Gilchrist (1939–1953) shares a gravestone with his grandmother, Jessie Bain Gilchrist (1881–1952). In the same Sanctuary Park Cemetery plot, hidden by a yew tree, lies Margaret Gilchrist (1914–1983), wife of Robert G. Loftus (1911–1995). "Gas Poisoning Kills Wife of Safety Expert," *Toronto Star*, Dec. 29, 1983, A6.

156 *"general verdict …"* A pedestrian's letter to the editor, responding to "The Slaughter of the Innocents," *Globe*, June 1, 1929, 4.

156 *the case failed at trial* … In 1952, three of seven manslaughter cases in Toronto were related to fatal road crashes, none resulted in a conviction (one was dismissed; two sentenced for dangerous driving). CC, 1952 Annual Report, 47, 76–9.

156 *"vote of condolence to the man-slayer"* … "Motor Accidents," letter to the editor, *Globe*, July 24, 1929, 4 – "If, as sometimes happens, an inquest is held, we are told that 'death was due to accident,' or, as in most cases, 'the driver was exonerated from all blame.'"

157 *"came out of nowhere ..."* "Jury in Open Court Acquits," *Daily Star*, Oct. 23, 1929, 35. See also "Dawes Road Fatality Blames on Poor Light and Slippery Roadway," *Globe*, July 13, 1929, 15.

157 *The rogue motorist* ... The OSL characterized drunk drivers as "probably the greatest menace." See "Safety Ideas Promulgated," *Globe*, Aug. 24, 1928, 42.

157 *a check on reckless driving* ... Davies, "Ontario and the Autombile," 249.

157 *a lucrative enterprise* ... "Empty Bottles along Ontario Highways Tell Impressive Tale," *Daily Star*, Sept. 25, 1929, 1 – Boys collected 500 liquor bottles along deadly three-mile stretch of Highway 2. Editorials mocked "portly political potentates" more concerned that boys might drink alcohol dregs – "Behind Boys and Bottles," *Globe*, Oct. 1, 1929, 4.

157 *the "blackguard"* ... *The Canadian Courier*, Mar. 28, 1908, vol. 3, no. 17, 7 – to protect "healthful pleasure" of motorcars the magazine asked readers to secure the safety of the public and "punish the blackguard" among motorists.

158 *"banish the witless driver ..."* R.S. McLaughlin, "Future Highways Built for Speed," *Globe*, Nov. 6, 1937, 21.

158 *the motor vehicle an outlaw* ... *Campbell v. Pugsley* (1912), 7 D.L.R. 177, 180, concluded that danger was not inherent to "construction and use of the vehicle, so as to prevent its use." A 1913 Ontario Court of Appeal cited the New Brunswick decision with approval. *Bernstein v. Lynch* 1913 CarswellOnt 796, 13 D.L.R. 134, 28 O.L.R. 435

158 *except in the US* ... Kevin Quealy and Margot Sanger-Katz, "Comparing Gun Deaths by Country: The U.S. Is in a Different World," *New York Times*, June 13, 2016.

158 *had ballooned in size* ... "Auto Drivers Warned to Heed All Stop Signs," *Daily Star*, May 29, 1929, 1 – Chief Constable Draper, after observing routine disobedience of stop signs, concluded there were too many infractions to allow for meaningful action.

159 *"an open air garage ..."* "Theft of Automobiles Increased in Toronto," *Daily Star*, Feb. 24, 1927, 8.

159 *municipal, provincial, and federal laws* ... Chief Constable Annual Report, 1929, 21; and Annual Report, 1951, Table 4, "Breach of Hwy Traffic Act and City Traffic Regulations," 60–1. The total included 135 charges against cyclists.

159 *"can't avoid getting a ticket ..."* "10,000 in Fines for Day Proof Road Problem Acute – Gardiner," *Daily Star*, Apr. 17, 1953, 25.

159 *record-keeping process* ... Chief Constable Annual Report, 1938 – adopting National Safety Council of America's standardized system for recording and summarizing collision information.

159 *chapter for (motor) "traffic"* ... Chief Constable Annual Report, 1934, 30.
160 *"clean up this menace ..."* "Crusader for Safety on Ontario Highways," *Globe*, May 27, 1948, 7.
160 *didn't spare Doucett* ... "Condition Serious Travelling to Meeting Doucett Hurt in Crash," *Globe and Mail*, Nov. 9, 1951, 1.

1979 – The Bicycle Revival

163 *its first winter* ... Irvin Lutsky, "Bay Window," *Toronto Star*, Nov. 19, 1980, D12, quoting Barbara Weiner – ten-speed tricycle for winter, wider tires, better brakes, enclosed gears, and weather-proof bags.
163 *an adding machine* ... Carol Vyhnak, "Bike Courier Idea Pedalled into Business," *Toronto Star*, Oct. 14, 1980, A6; "Pedal Power Saves Energy, Money," *Globe*, June 18, 1981, T2. In the 1950s and 1960s, commercial delivery work was dominated by cars and small trucks, but many neighbourhood shops continued to rely on boys (and some girls) with bikes. Each group competed with consumers who were by then accustomed to using their own cars to pick up goods at a shop or mall, often encouraged by abundant free parking.
164 *commercial documents* ... Michael Valpy, "Bicyclist Almost Wins Uphill Rush-Hour Race," *Globe and Mail*, May 3, 1972, 5. To show the slow pace of cars, a race was organized between a motorist, a cyclist, and a pedestrian. The car, averaging, 12 mph (19 km/h) beat the cyclist, on a strongly uphill course. The transit user came last. See "Victory Not So Sweet," *Globe and Mail*, May 3, 1972, 5.
164 *Sunwheel's raison d'être* ... Tiessen, in an interview for CBC, said that she wanted a business that brought together the bicycle, concern for the environment, equity, and a cooperative work atmosphere. "The bicycle being present on the streets of Toronto is a transformational kind of vehicle ... it is small, ...it is quiet, ...it flows with the energy that you put into it." See Zielinski and Sutherland, "Bicycle," 4–5:
164 *Federal ParticipAction* ... "Yes, the Average 60-Year-Old Swede Really Is More Fit," *Globe and Mail*, June 8, 1974, A2.
164 *"Bicycling is back ..."* Edna Hampton, "Cycle Goes Full Circle," *Globe and Mail*, Aug. 28, 1969, W1. "Nowadays natty Rosedale housewives cycle over to Yonge Street for groceries. Office girls wheel down University Avenue on their way to work and some of the prettiest girls cycle along Bloor Street." See also "Metro Adults Saddling Up in New Bike-Riding Boom," *Daily Star*, June 18, 1969, B47 – 'a real boom,' not only kids on high-rise bikes.

165 *"a nostalgic yearning ..."* "Recycled," *Globe and Mail,* July 10, 1979, 6.

165 *adult cyclists back on city streets ...* "Toward a Metro Toronto Bicycle Route System" (Mar. 1973) noted that while the sale of children and youth bicycles comprised 98 per cent of retail sales in 1968 in Metro, that figure had dropped to 78 per cent by 1971 and was trending towards 50 per cent within three to four years.

166 *"automobile already rules ..."* E.A.H. Banks, letter to the editor, *Globe and Mail,* June 11, 1971, 6; John Cameron, letter to the editor, *Globe and Mail,* July 23, 1976, 7.

166 *"four-fold solution ..."* *Globe and Mail,* Aug. 11, 1973, A12.

166 *"stirrings that may not be denied ..."* "The Bicycle Fights Back," *Globe and Mail,* July 10, 1978, 6.

166 *"the most benevolent of machines ..."* Wilson, "Bicycle Technology" – "By riding a bicycle instead of walking, a person uses one fifth less energy and becomes more efficient than any other animal or machine." See also Illich, *Toward a History of Needs.* Illich calculated that a typical American motorist travels at 5 mph (8 km/h) when one includes the amount of time a motorist invests in paying for the vehicle, driving, looking for parking, and so on.

166 *a major retailer ...* See Bloor Cycle, Ad, *Globe and Mail,* June 21, 1979, 43.

167 *entailed a substantial outlay ...* Annual bicycle sales figures for Canada, which stood at approx 500,000 in 1968, increased gradually in 1971, then surged, reaching a peak of 1.4 million (most of them imported) in 1973. The subsequent decline in sales nonetheless left sales figure above 1971 levels. Kosny, Anthony, and Chow, "The Bicycle as a Mode," table 1.1, "Bicycle Sales in Canada."

167 *500,000 bicycles in Metro ...* "Toward a Metro Toronto Bicycle Route System," Report to Metro Commissioners of Planning, Parks, Roads & Traffic from H. Abrams et al, Metro Roads & Traffic, Mar. 23, 1973, (page) A.3.

167 *survey of Metro households ...* Strok & Associates, "Bikeway System," 2. See the "Summary" in Kosny, Faulds, Anthony, and Chow, "The Bicycle." The report included a phone survey for Metro and a Bike Week Survey at City Hall.

167 *decade-by-decade increase ...* Barton-Aschman, "Planning for Urban Cycling," 1.

168 *"the bike as a status symbol ..."* Scott Young, "A Briefing on Bikes," *Globe and Mail,* May 24, 1972, 7; "Sex and the Bicycle," *Toronto Star,* May 14, 1976, 14.

168 *Bicyclists' Day ...* "2,000 Expected in Bike-a-Thon," *Globe and Mail,* Sept. 14, 1972, 5.

168 *"a sport of social etiquette ..."* "A Sprocket and a Subculture Analysis," *Maclean's,* Mar. 1, 1971.

168 *selling meat and produce ...* Edna Hampton, "Cycle Goes Full Circle," *Globe and Mail,* Aug. 28, 1969, W1 – photo, delivery boy for Jack's Meat Market.

168 *telegram itself slowly becoming redundant* ... Herbert Bryce, "Messengers Are Sympathetic," *Globe and Mail*, Sept. 15, 1962, 19 – estimating approximately a dozen high school students working as part-time telegraph messengers (at 85 cents per hour and with their own bikes) in Metro. Fax machines then replaced the telex, allowing documents to be sent using the phone system. See T. Gobspill, "Decline in Telegram Traffic Expected to Ease," *Globe*, Feb. 22, 1972, B1.

169 *"look out for the cops ..."* Robert Stall, "You Don't Send a Boy to Do a Phone's Job," *Globe and Mail*, Oct. 13, 1973, A8.

169 *"even proprietary pride ..."* Denison, *CCM: The Story of the First Fifty Years.* Quebec's Procycle bought CCM's bike assets and name, then manufactured "CCM" bikes. CCM's skate division continued under independent management.

169 *with extracting profits* ... Its closure brought to an end to large-scale bike manufacturing in Ontario, with the exception of Jim Miele's short-lived, state-of-the-art factory in Mississauga in the 1980s. Miele was a contemporary of Mike Barry's early bike-making days. Miele (d. 2012) went bankrupt in 1996. The Miele name was bought by Procycle. Several other bike-makers served niche elements of the market, but all were gone by 2019.

170 *a device that counted cars* ... CoT Council Minutes, 1965, By-law 01-392 and By-law 03-22458; and Minute 01-650, re making "licences and bells mandatory." And "Bicycle fall," App A, 2349. "Traffic matters," however, filled many pages of minutes.

170 *ban cyclists from riding* ... By-law 2518, Nov. 1965, "To regulate traffic on Metropolitan Roads." By-law Sch XIX "Bicycle riding prohibited" on Don Valley and on Gardiner. See "Regulations for Bicycles," ss 17–20. Bike livery on island approved.

170 *400-page textbook* ... White, *Planning Toronto.*

170 *ran as candidates* ... "Bicycle Built for Two Carries Candidate," *Globe and Mail*, Oct. 9, 1965, 11. A *Daily Star* columnist, noted for her adventuresome spirit, merited several photos simply for being on her new bicycle, which she planned to use for grocery shopping. See "Writer Abandons 'Jet Set' Pace for Cycling," *Daily Star*, Jan. 31, 1966, B37.

170 *too young, too poor* ... B. Rahme, "Rediscovering Bikes," *Daily Star*, July 1, 1967, 98. Cycling remained common on Toronto Island.

170 *distinguished from bicycles* ... "Power Ousts Pedal," *Globe and Mail*, Dec. 25, 1965, 5; "5-hp Scooters Hamilton Rage," *Globe and Mail*, May 25, 1965, B1. "Moped" came from "motor" and "pedal." Mopeds became so popular among teenaged students that the Toronto Board of Education banned them from school properties. See "Scooter Parking Ban Favoured," *Globe and Mail*, Nov.

25, 1965, 47. "The bike boom," which included motorbikes with smaller motors, provoked debate about helmets prior to the same debate for cyclists.

172 *road with no sidewalk* ... "Walking Man Hit by Wagon Towed by Bike," *Globe and Mail*, Aug. 8, 1969, 5. See also "Bicycle Hit, Boy 14 Dies," *Globe and Mail*, May 15, 1969, 5; "Girl Cyclist, Boy, 3, Die in Traffic," *Globe and Mail*, Oct. 13, 1969, 5; and "Hit-and-Run," *Globe and Mail*, July 28, 1969, 5 – North York boy, age 9, on bike. "No wonder there were 47 cyclists killed in Ontario in 1968," see DW Marchant letter to the editor ("Killer Bicycles"), *Daily Star*, Oct. 25, 1969, 13.

172 *popular "high-rise" model* ... See, for example, "Police Check Unsafe Bicycles," *Globe and Mail*, Apr. 10, 1959, 5.

172 *Britannia, Italia, and Berolina* ... Gene Glisky, "Cycling Regaining Popularity," *Globe and Mail*, May 26, 1961, 15.

174 *to intimidate them* ... Mike Barry, interview with author, July 16, 2018. Bicycle club members could still be counted on for impressive feats of endurance. In one case, two racers cycled to Ottawa to prove that delivery of a letter by bicycle was faster than the postal service. They easily won, although their toes fared poorly in the freezing temperatures. See "Beating the Postman," *Cycling*, May 18, 1974, 11 – Britannia racers in March 1974, temperature of 25 degrees Fahrenheit (-4 degrees Celsius), raced 265 miles (426 kilometres) to Ottawa to prove a letter could travel faster by bike.

174 *a slate of expressways* ... The Gardiner Expressway was completed in 1957; the Don Valley Parkway in two phases, 1961 and 1967; and Highway 427 in 1971.

174 *a ring around the city* ... See also "Speed Expressways – Metro Traffic Chief," *Daily Star*, Dec. 28, 1963, 41. Queen's Park also planned to extend Highway 400 south to at least St. Clair Avenue West but faced strong opposition.

174 *"a Batmobile out of hell ..."* Bruce West, "Men and Machines," *Globe and Mail*, Aug. 22, 1972, 31. A "flivver" is a cheap or decrepit vehicle.

175 *one of ten expressways* ... "Okay, So You Ban the Car ...," *Maclean's*, Mar. 1, 1971.

175 *"building a city for people ..."* Milligan, "The Board Has a Duty," para. 51.

176 *"as obsolete as the horse and buggy ..."* "Why Toronto Is Still a Streetcar City," *Globe and Mail*, Aug. 29, 2014.

176 *envy of many US transit agencies* ... Levine, "Streetcars for Toronto Committee."

176 *55 kilometres of subways* ... Extension to North York's Wilson station completed in 1978; Yonge line on March 30, 1954; University Line on February 28, 1963; Bloor Danforth line completed on February 26, 1966, and later extended into Etobicoke and Scarborough.

176 *Passenger rail travel ...* Jean Dupuis, "VIA Rail Canada Inc. and the Future of Passenger Rail in Canada," Library of Parliament, Aug. 31, 2015.

176 *"bring a ton of steel ..."* CoT Council Minutes, 1973, Mayor's Inaugural Address, App C, pp 4–8.

177 *transfer to the TTC ...* Toronto Official Plan, 1969, Toronto Planning Board, Official Plan, Part 1, 2: "the linkage of the rapid transit system with the regional system of expressways and long distance mass transit by means of facilities, including parking areas or structures, designed to permit easy transfer."

177 *uttered in polite conversation ...* K. Bagnell "Post-Car Era?," *Globe and Mail,* June 26, 1972, 27.

177 *to reduce the size and weight ...* "Thinking Small," *Globe and Mail,* July 23, 1976 35. But see "Big Car Makes a Comeback," *Toronto Star,* July 3, 1976, A2.

177 *undignified to his office ...* "A Difference in Tastes," *Globe and Mail,* Apr. 14, 1972, 4. John Sewell (b. December 8, 1940; mayor at age thirty-seven) had been cycling since 1972. "Name Is All That's Left of Leave the Car at Home," *Globe,* June 11, 1970, 5.

178 *award-winning structure ...* Councillors retained access to a small fleet of cars for city business, but not chauffeured limousines, as had been the case for the city's Board of Control, which was dissolved 1969, and as Metro continued to do. See John Barber, "Hail to the Stunt King," *Globe,* May 31, 1994, A9.

178 *blue jeans and a casual jacket ...* Kilbourne, *Toronto Remembered,* 7, articulated the changed city – "Then, quite suddenly, things changed. In the 1970s Toronto was something unique and glorious ... a place to praise, extravagantly."

178 *efficient form of transportation ...* CoT Council Proceeding, 1976, Executive Committee Report, no. 50, App A, p 8497. The policy continues: "and as a means of recreation, can make a significant contribution to the quality of city life."

178 *1930s bicycle racing star ...* Pollution Probe also called for lower speed limits. See "25 m.p.h. Limit Urged for City's Residential Streets," *Toronto Star,* May 23, 1973, 1. Public Works Commissioner Bremner suggested that the focus should be on changing motorists' attitudes. By 1973, 73 miles (110 kilometres) of city roads had 25 mph (40 km/h) limits.

180 *remained an open question ...* The August 2022 rally was organized by personal injury lawyer Dave Shellnut, who bills himself as "The Biking Lawyer LLP." Shellnut, who has a strong social media presence, prominently advertises his services to both sport and utilitarian cyclists.

180 *"International Cyclists' Day ..."* "June 4th Rally," *City Cyclist,* May 1978, vol. 1, no. 1, 1.

180 *cyclists heeded the call ...* "Setting Wheels in Motion," *Globe and Mail*, June 5, 1978.

181 *qualified as a double "century" ...* The "Niagara Hair Shirt" ride is still run today as an event of the Toronto Bicycle Network.

181 *"Nothing could cloud our view ..."* Norm Hawirko, Pollution Probe, interview with author, Aug. 15, 2019. CCC member Robin Mautner (later a teacher/labour activist) showed equal energy, planning a cross-country high-wheel ride to bring attention to cycling potential. He settled on founding a new cycling advocacy group.

181 *"hard-headed transportation planners ..."* "No Simple Matter," *Globe and Mail*, Oct. 9, 1972, 29. An advocate ascribed the problem to civic officials who were reluctant "to tamper with the established order to do anything that will restrict motor traffic."

181 *cyclists were a "nightmare..."* Bruce West, "No Simple Matter," *Globe and Mail*, Oct. 9, 1972, 29.

182 *"those nuisance committees ..."* Janice Dineen "The Cyclist Still Isn't the Big Wheel," *Toronto Star*, Apr. 24, 1976, B4; David White, interview with author, Dec. 28, 2017, Toronto.

182 *tripling to over 1.1 million ...* In 1979 Metro's human population was 2.131 million compared to 1.148 million registered motor vehicles (an increase from 290,000 vehicles in 1953). Metro Police, Annual Statistical Report, 1979, pp 4, 16. Strok & Associates, "Bikeway System." Ironically, 1971, the year of the so-called Bicycle Boom in Metro, was the only year when motor vehicle registrations in Metro actually declined.

182 *"wheel traps ..."* Hood, *Practical Pedalling*, 15.

182 *Population Control, Too?..."* Marsha Williams, letter to the editor, *Globe and Mail*, May 11, 1974, 7; P. Whelan, letter to the editor, *Globe and Mail*, July 27, 1972, 5 – "Drains are the sort of thing you learn to watch out for when you're 5."

182 *replace tens of thousands of grates ...* CoT Council Minutes, 1971, App A, 3072, Bicycle Committee report. Public Works Commisioner reported on possible realignment of storm drains to align slots perpendicular to travel direction.

182 *a pace that, if maintained ...* CoT Council Minutes, 1981, Report no. 16, App A, 8545, City Services Committee, "Bicycle Proof Catch Basin Covers," with chart showing total number of remaining unsafe grates (Toronto – 31,000 and Metro – 8,000) with 1,850 replaced in period 1977–9. Roads under suburban authority appeared to get far less attention.

183 *the average cast iron grate ...* "The Cyclist Still Isn't the Big Wheel," *Toronto Star*, Apr. 24, 1976; *Toronto, 1976*, CCC, PW Committee report no. 21, App A, 3916.

184 *"no longer know their place ..."* Christie Blatchford, "A Curse on Sweaty, Unwanted Cyclists," *Toronto Star*, May 28, 1979, A3 – "All week, Torontonians

will be bombarded with falsehoods about car drivers, while cyclists are painted as fine and decent human beings." Her article provoked angry and sarcastic letters to the editor, for example, "Grossly Insulted by Bicycling Article," letters to the editor, *Toronto Star*, June 1, 1979, A9, and *Toronto Star*, June 4, 1979, A9.

184 *were zealous guardians* ... See, for example, Donald Shoup, *The High Cost of Free Parking*. Approximately four parking spaces, ranging in size from 130 square feet for a curbside spot to 330 square feet for a spot in a parking lot, are required for each car.

184 *"angry tyre squeals ..."* R. Coneybeare, "How about the Pedal-Pusher Party," letter to the editor, *Globe and Mail*, Oct. 12, 1972, 7; T. Dodgson, letter to the editor, *Toronto Star*, Aug. 21, 1971, 7.

185 *"risk asphyxiation ..."* "The Curbed Cyclist Scared Stiff," *Globe and Mail*, Aug. 1, 1975, 23. See also "Osgoode Hall by Bicycle," *Globe and Mail*, Oct. 8, 1966, 5 – the Law Society Secretary said motorists were pretty tolerant but added, with a grin, "some of the buses show homicidal tendencies."

185 *"heralded the bicycle craze ..."* J. Simpson, "Metro Still No Cyclists' Dream," *Globe and Mail*, Aug. 4, 1973, 33.

185 *"we want the bicycle ..."* "Cycling Without Safety," *Globe and Mail*, Oct. 26, 1974, 6 – "European cities have for years had reserved bicycle lanes on the streets."

185 *"fit for pleasant Sunday afternoons ..."* "Safety for the Bicycle," editorial, *Globe and Mail*, July 19, 1976, 6.

186 *"a take-it-or-leave-it basis ..."* "The Bicycle Fights Back," *Globe and Mail*, July 10, 1978, 6.

186 *"car worshipper ..."* Bicycle "has no place on Toronto's busy main roads." "Safety Standards Needed for Bikes," *Toronto Star*, July 7, 1972, 6.

186 *remained disturbingly high* ... Z.S. Ciesielski, "The Problem of Bicyclists," letter to the editor, *Globe and Mail*, Sept. 6, 1957, 6 – "A bicycle seems to be an instrument giving full impunity to the user."

186 *135 road deaths in Metro* ... Metro Police Annual Report, 1979 16–18. For 1979, the 90 road deaths far exceeded 51 murders – "Criminal Code Offences," 5. Metro numbers excluded deaths on provincial highways (numbering twenty in 1964 alone). Children (14 and under) accounted for 9 per cent of fatalities and 11 per cent of injuries. Also 15,400 injury collisions; 1,211 cyclists injured, approximately 8 per cent of injuries and deaths. There were 209,000 *Criminal Code* charges, among which 40,000 were for driving-related offences, a figure that rose to 46,000 (22 per cent of the total) when including auto theft. *Criminal Code* driving-related charges (20 per cent of the total) included criminal negligence, failure to remain, impaired, failure to stop, dangerous driving, refused breathalyzer test, limit over 80 milligrams, and driver disqualified.

187 *stern lecture of the victims* ... Ministry of Justice and Correctional Services, "Verdict of Coroner's Jury" re Glenn McNickle," July 13, 1976.

187 *the edge of the crosswalk* ... The media reported that the boys made a right turn off Lawrence onto northbound Brimley, but the jury made no such finding. The location of the arcade was on the south-east corner of Lawrence and Brimley. Marilyn McNickle, interview with author, Oct. 2, 2019.

187 *0.9 metres (36 inches) of space* ... "Cyclist Told Don't Double-Up Inquest Hears," *Toronto Star*, July 13, 1976, B1 – the bus driver said he only saw boys after passing them and didn't have time to move to the other lane. He suggested the bike's handlebars got caught by the bus rear doors.

187 *media rendered its judgment* ... "Scarborough Boy Killed Riding Double on Bike," *Toronto Star*, Apr. 20, 1976, 1, quoting TTC spokesman: the boys "hit the rear of the bus, near the back door. They fell off their bike and underneath the rear wheel." The article "Cyclist, 11, Killed by Rush-Hour Bus," *Toronto Sun*, Apr. 21, 1976, 1, even bizarrely (and wrongly) claimed, that Glenn's sixteen-year-old sister Marilyn was on the bus that killed her brother.

188 *strapping a $2 pool noodle* ... Peter Goffin, "Cyclist Says His Pool Noodle Makes Toronto Streets Safer for Him," *Toronto Star*, June 27, 2016, https://www.thestar. com/news/gta/cyclist-says-his-pool-noodle-makes-toronto-streets-safer-for-him/article_488dc2d4-9f5a-5113-af2c-901b340caf20.html.

188 *on a bike similar to Glenn's* ... "Cop Warns Cyclists on Shunning Safety," *Toronto Sun*, Apr. 22, 1976, 59; and "Second Bike Boy Dies," *Toronto Sun*, Apr. 22, 1976, 59. See also "Safety Check", *Globe and Mail*, Aug. 6, 1976, 4, which took a similar approach, with a photo showing the Safety Bureau officer inspecting an eight-year-old girl's bike with the implicit message, "cyclists are safe if complying with the law *and* keeping bikes in working order."

188 *narrower handlebars* ... "Cyclist Told Don't Double-Up Inquest Hears," *Daily Star*, July 13, 1976, B1. "Banana Seats, Handlebars Suspect in High Cyclist Toll," *Daily Star*, July 31, 1969, 35; and "Researchers Want to Learn Whether Some Bikes Are Killers," *Daily Star*, Oct. 21, 1969, 35. See also CoT Council Minutes, 1971, App A, PW Report no. 24, p 3072–4 (referencing OTC, Bicycle Committee report), recommending that Metro Council be requested "to engage CSA to establish standards for bikes and equipment, including size, shape and location of handlebars." Brezina and Kramer, "Rider, Bicycle."

189 *young cyclists to be punished* ... Speed, whether the posted limit or the actual speed, rarely got attention. See, for example, "3 Boys on 2 Bicycles Killed by Car," *Globe and Mail*, Aug. 5, 1958, 1 – three boys were killed at dusk on a country road, hit so hard that the hood of the car popped open. Bodies were spread around a 25-yard area. Headline noted that the boys were riding side-by-side, with two on one bike, but it did not mention the motorist's speed.

189   *chalk marks directly over a sewer grate* ... David Cooper, Photo, *Toronto Sun,* April 21, 1976, 1.

189   *"but for the grace of God ..."* Lauriston, "Motor Murder." Lauriston noted a case where the motorist was fined $10 for negligence where one person was killed and another seriously injured. Years earlier a letter writer suggested that "No motorist should be permitted on a jury dealing with the slaying of a pedestrian by the death car." "Pedestrian," letter to the editor, *Globe,* June 1, 1929, 4.

189   *"has to give a bike-rider a lane ..."* "Coroner's Jury, Restrictions Urged for Young Cyclists," *Globe and Mail,* July 14, 1976, 4. At the time bicycles were apparently not allowed on the sidewalks of Scarborough roads. Brimley was a Metro road, but legal status of sidewalk riding on Metro roads was not addressed. See "Alderman's Rush Hour Plan: Allow Bicycles on Sidewalks," *Toronto Star,* Sept. 7, 1976, 2; "Scarborough Battles Wheelchair Menace," *Toronto Star,* Feb. 5, 1977, B2.

189   *"in this urban world ..."* "Metro Traffic Accidents Kill a Soaring Number of 'Carefree' Children," *Toronto Star,* June 21, 1972, 1 – John Marjury of the Metro Traffic Safety Bureau said: "In most cases, the children are to blame. When they're out playing, they're carefree, not careless. They just forget ... I really don't know what the answer is when they're in the charge of their parents." In terms of the "particularly dramatic increase" in child casualties, see, Strok & Associates, "Bicycle System," 16–17, 67, 74, referring to 1972–4.

191   *the Scarborough tragedy ...* Brezina and Kramer, "Rider, Bicycle," 24, 25, reported that among the 1,400 boys surveyed, 20 per cent rode to school, and among those riding after school the most common destinations were to visit friends, go to parks or recreational areas, and run errands. Both the city and Metro considered the study, but little action came of it.

191   *a safe place to ride ...* "Boys Killed on Bikeway Route," *Toronto Star,* Apr. 24, 1976, B4. See also R. Silverman, letter to the editor, *Globe and Mail,* July 16, 1976, A6 – "The real fault for the number of deaths and accidents is that there just isn't any space on the roads for cyclists." The narrative that children were safe if they obeyed road rules and maintained their bikes was repeated with the photo in "Safety Check," *Globe and Mail,* August 13, 1976, 4

191   *cycling was at a crossroads ...* CoT Council Minutes, 1976, App A, PW Committee, Report no. 25, p 6760, relying on CCC report.

192   *nothing came of the initiative ...* CoT Council Minutes, 1971, App A, PW report no. 24, p 3074 – to "investigate, and report on, the provision of a special lane in a highway for bicycle riders, on an experimental basis." The initiative was also referenced in a report adopted by Metro. Metro Council Minutes, 1972, Transportation Committee, Mar 21, "Safety, Licensing, Parking and the Sale of Bicycles," Report 5, Clause 12,

192 *Statement of Policy* ... General Policy Statement, 1975. "To further the integration of cycling within the urban transportation system. 1. To develop exclusive bicycle lanes on those roads containing major attractors or carrying high vehicle traffic volumes ..." Use of the word "integration" does not suggest Forester's concept of vehicular cycling but instead contemplated various types of cycling facilities. In 1978, the CCC, working with a consultant, again noted the "integration of cycling in the traffic system" but continued to embrace facilities such as bike lanes. "Proposed Statement of Policy – City Cycling Committee," PW Committee, Report no. 1, Jan. 30, 1978. CTA, Fonds 200, Series, 2178, File 1.

192 *alongside the boardwalk* ... Winona Gallop, interview with author, Sept. 18, 2018.

193 *network of bike "freeways"* ... "He Wants to Build 100 Miles of 'Bicycle free-ways,'" *Daily Star*, Nov. 28, 1964, 8. The city planner Murray Pound envisioned recreational paths (separating cyclists and pedestrians) along ravines, river valleys, and hydro right-of-ways.

193 *ribbon-cutting ceremony* ... The city's oversight in not inviting Gallop was note-worthy given that her work had then recently been featured in a newspaper article. Albert Koehl, "The Small Step that Paved the Way for Toronto's Waterfront Trail," *Globe and Mail*, Nov. 26, 2018.

193 *"choice of a core route ..."* Letter from Gallop to David White, Nov. 15, 1978 (CTA, Fonds 200, Series 2178, File 6).

194 *from the Warden subway station* ... The students, including Hawirko (b. 1948), Leonard Steele, Richard Seypka, Rodney Daw, and Brian Guzzy, quickly learned that though governments wouldn't take the lead, they could be counted on for funding, including a very significant sum (at the time) of $70,000 to the group for three environment initiatives, including the pathway. Pollution Probe, "The Scarborough Bicycle Pathway System," 1973 (n.p.). The proposed path crossed Lawrence and Brimley where the boys were killed in 1976. Energy Probe, a break-away group from Pollution Probe, also organized cycling initiatives, including Spokes (led by Robin Mautner), to increase bike commuting into downtown. See CoT Council Minutes, 1981, City Services Committee, App A, Report no. 17, pp 9192, 9198; and arrive-by-bike, see E. Agger, "Energy Probe: A Great Idea," *City Cyclist*, 1984, 6.

194 *"you've got to start small ..."* Michael Valpy, "Scarborough Balks at Tax Loss," *Globe and Mail*, Apr. 20, 1972, 61. See "Scarborough Rejects Free Bikeway Bid," *Toronto Star*, Apr. 20, 1972, 23; and "Putting the Brakes on Bikes," *Globe and Mail*, July 12, 1972, 3.

194 *"the thanks you get ..."* "Scarborough Council Won't Issue Receipts for Bike Path Gifts," *Globe and Mail*, Aug. 29, 1972. 5. Hawirko oversaw the project while demonstrating (on a bet) the bicycle's versatility, cycling the entire length of a proposed path in the creek itself, only to be thwarted by a large rock near the end of the route.

195 *the value of the path ...* Pollution Probe, "The Scarborough Bicycle Pathway System." Metro likewise took up path building, though slowly, including some paths proposed as part of the students' plan.

195 *could only be a mystery ...* Kirkham's Road between Sheppard and Finch Avenues. By-law 63-73, Apr 17, 1973. Pursuant to Ontario Municipal Board No H 4255.

196 *"convert to the Bicycle Revolution ..."* "The Cyclists Get Another Friend," *Toronto Star*, May 27, 1972, 18. The original bike path was installed between Islington Avenue and Martin Grove Road. Cass died in 2022 at the age of ninety-nine, never giving up his belief in expressways. Oliver Moore, "Toronto Roads Czar Championed Spadina Expressway Plan," *Globe and Mail*, Feb. 22, 2022.

196 *85-kilometre Pan Am Path ...* Jesse Winter, "Construction and Confusion on the Pan Am Path," *Toronto Star*, May 12, 2017. Strok & Associates' 1974 report included a similar arterial trail – resembling Tommy Thompson's arc – beginning in the city's west end at Eglinton and Highway 427 then dipping down to Queen's Park (instead of the waterfront) before climbing up to the zoo in the city's northeast corner. Strok & Associates, "Bicycle System," 16, table 1 and figure 13.

196 *Dutch-style bicycle tracks ...* "The Cyclists Get Another Friend," *Toronto Star*, May 27, 1972, 18 – "Though Cass's planners recognized the traffic-clogged arterials of downtown – Yonge and Bloor, for example – as a cyclists' killing ground, they were seeing the cycling potential of the more recent highway system in suburbia – on Keele Street, perhaps, or Finch and Sheppard." By 2022, only Sheppard Avenue East had (disconnected) segments of a bike lane.

196 *"not sit on it ..."* "Cycling without Safety," *Globe and Mail*, Oct. 26, 1974, 6; "Strok Study on Bikeway a Bestseller," *Toronto Star*, June 11, 1974, 33. Strok & Associates proposed a three-year first phase; Metro adopted a five-year timeline and a $1.8-million budget. Strok wasn't the first at the time to suggest trails; see, for example, "Pedalling Has Its Problems," *Globe and Mail*, Aug. 19, 1971, B4, referencing a 1971 call by the Social Planning Council, Etobicoke branch, for 200 miles (320 kilometres) of recreational bike trails in Metro ravines and river valleys.

197 *trails suitable for cycling ...* "Towards a Metro Bike Route System," Mar. 23, 1973, D2, summarizes paths in place under Metro jurisdiction,

though it appears to include both Metro and local paths. The report listed these paths as "special facilities used by cyclists" with only the Eglinton Avenue path and Winona Gallop's eastern beaches path described a "principally cycle."

197 *nine kilometres at the time* ... "Earmark Ravine Land for Parks, Board Asks," *Globe and Mail*, May 11, 1960, 5. *Toronto's 1969 Official Plan* encouraged creation of parks, ravines, Toronto island, waterfront, etc., with continuous paths suitable for use by pedestrians, equestrians, skiers and cyclists, connecting the individual parks making up the system.

197 *a pleasant outing by bike* ... Esther and Robert Kaplan, "Bicycle Routes in Toronto," *Toronto Life*, 1972.

197 *a ban on cycling* ... "Putting the Brakes on Bikes," *Globe and Mail*, July 12, 1972, 3. Parks By-law 1551 was amended to allow a ban on bikes.

198 *sympathetic to the idea* ... Cass's letter, dated Oct. 25, 1972, and addressed to the Metro Transportation Committee, is found in *Toward a Metro Toronto Bicycle Path System*.

198 *Initial Trial Bikeway System* ... "A Metropolitan Toronto Bicycle Route System," Mar. 23, 1973, G1, including "Initial Trial Bicycle Route System" to "assess the strength of apparently increasing demand for cycling facilities." The report was the result of two study requests: (1) May 29, 1972, from the Transportation Committee for a conceptual plan of bicycle paths; and (2) September 5, 1972, from Transportation and the Parks and Recreation Committee for future bike paths on Metro roads and in Metro parks.

198 *maintain the degree of stability* ... Strok & Associates, "Bikeway System," 41.

198 *borrowing his daughter's bike* ... "Long Overdue Bicycle System Finds Beginning," *Globe and Mail*, June 11, 1974, 33.

199 *motorcycle-riding cops* ... Strok & Associates, "Bikeway System," 2, 38, 65, 83, 102, panel 29 – "Security."

199 *complex regulatory regime* ... Strok & Associates, "Bikeway System," 88; "Cyclists Need Test," *Toronto Star*, July 28, 1978, 7.

199 *"each residential sidewalk ..."* Strok & Associates, "Bikeway System," 16, 102, rationalized that sharing sidewalks was a fair trade-off given lower cyclist fatalities vis-à-vis roads, despite a likely increase in pedestrian injuries.

199 *"an expressway without ramps ..."* "Metro's Cyclists Are Seeking 246 Miles of Paths," *Toronto Star*, May 15, 1975, E7.

199 *predominantly for school* ... Strok & Associates, "Bikeway System," 2, 6–8, 12, 14, 15, 19, 29, 38, 65, 83, panel 29, and 102 – "Bicycles, even if they are allowed to be motorized, are not expected to become a significant transportation mode" (3).

200 *"the bicycle problem ..."* "Safety, Licensing, Parking and the Sale of Bicycles," Report 5, Clause 12, Transportation Committee, Metro Council, Mar. 21, 1972.

200 *too child-oriented ...* See "Canada Is Lagging with Bikeway," *Globe and Mail*, Aug. 19, 1971, B4.

200 *regard bikes as playthings ...* L.K. Humphreys, letter to the editor, *Globe and Mail*, June 26, 1974, 7. Humphreys was the chair of CCA.

200 *"overwhelming bias ..."* N. Roth, Memo, City of Toronto Planning Board re Strok report, Apr. 10, 1975, CCC files, 1975–77, TA. Highlighting lack of access to downtown. Sewell, interview. He recalled the report as being "crazy" for pushing cyclists off of roads.

201 *officially abandoned on April 16, 1982 ...* Metro Council Minutes, 1982, App A, Transport Committee, Report 6, p 710. See also Metro Roads & Traffic Commissioner, Sept. 19, 1984, Letter, Cass to Transportation Committee, "Use of Bicycles on Arterial Roads." When Metro abandoned the trail system in 1982, it had 83 kilometres in place or slated for completion by end of the year. Cass called the termination a "modified version of the recommended system."

201 *"loves a bike ..."* M. Daly, "In Toronto Almost Everybody Loves a Bike," *Toronto Star*, July 1, 1975, A1.

201 *a boon to commuters ...* Bob Pennington, "1975 Is the Year of the Bike in Metro," *Toronto Star*, July 12, 1976, H1.

201 *Metro approved 26 kilometres ...* "Building 16 Miles of Bike Paths Gets Approval of Metro Council," *Globe and Mail*, June 19, 1975, 5; "Bike Pathway Plan Wheeling Right Along," *Toronto Star*, Mar. 26, 1975, B1. See also Metro Council Minutes, 1976, Transp Committee, App A, 405, v 1, Report No. 3 noting total Metro Roads and Traffic capital budget for 1976 of $8 million, of which $300 thousand was scheduled for extensions to Metro Bicycle Path System. Metro likely built about 19 kilometres of new bike paths in 1975.

201 *"within one mile of a bikeway ..."* Bob Pennington, "1975 Is the Year of the Bike in Metro," *Toronto Star*, July 12, 1975, H1. Strok & Associates, "Bikeway System," 9, had recommended the one-mile proximity.

201 *"splendid for the weekend ..."* Janice Dineen, "The Cyclist Still Isn't a Big Wheel," *Toronto Star*, Apr. 24, 1976, B4. Despite a slim portfolio of bike trails, there were detractors, including Ontario's finance minister who questioned further investments, mocking Metro for spending $500,000: "I wish we could be Lady Bountiful forever, but we can't." See "Raise Taxes or Cut Costs Metro Told," *Toronto Star*, Feb. 4, 1976, A3. One letter writer went further: D. Miller, "Bicycle Paths Are Pure Frills," letter to the editor, *Toronto Star*, Feb. 4, 1976, A3.

201 *"philosophical split ..."* Janice Dineen, "The Cyclist Still Isn't the Big Wheel," *Toronto Star*, Apr. 24, 1976, B4.

202 *"discretionary" bikeways* ... See, for example, Leonard Steeles, Urban Bikeways, Inc. (a group that existed from 1974–7) to Works Committee, "Bike for a Better City," Apr. 7, 1975. In the mid-1970s, the City of Toronto also planned (then installed in the 1980s) a 2-kilometre separated walking/cycling path along Rosedale Valley Road. (Slated for reconstruction in the 2020s.)

202 *liability for cyclists' injuries* ... CoT Council Minutes, 1976, PW Report 25, p 6761. See also Beddoes, "Let Those Wheels Roll!," *Globe and Mail*, July 4, 1976, 8; "Report Suggests Route for Bikes on Yonge Street," *Globe and Mail*, Apr. 22, 1978, 2.

202 *approving a series of bike lanes* ... Michael Moore, "City Approves Bike Lanes on Streets," *Globe and Mail*, Dec. 1, 1976, S8. The north-south bike lane was interrupted, however, by a gap through the University of Toronto. (At the time, St. George and Beverley Streets were Metro roads.) Queen's Quay and Wellesley Street were also approved. CoT Council Minutes, 1976, App A, Nov 29, Exec Committee, citing CCC brief, pp 8496–7. See CoT Council Minutes, 1976, App A, Nov 30, Exec Committee, p 8499, re Bremner's Nov 8, 1976 report.

202 *"serious consequences ..."* Michael Moore, "City Approves Bike Lanes on Streets," *Globe and Mail*, Dec. 1976, S8, with map.

202 *exclusive bike lanes* ... City Solicitor to CCC, May 31, 1977, re "Bicycle lane designation" as cited in City Solicitor to CCC, July 17, 1978, CTA, Fonds 200, Series 2178, File 1. See also CoT Council Minutes, 1976, App A, PW Report, pp 3916–17, re Letter dated June 9, 1976.

202 *bike lanes were stalled* ... The amendment was made in Bill 80 (s. 28), 1978, An Act to Amend the *Municipal Act*. See also Letter from McMurtry, Attorney General, re amendment to *Municipal Act*, writing, "I look forward to the creation of additional bicycle lanes in Toronto." (In fact, there were none in place.) CTA, Fonds 200, Series 2178, File 3. See also HTA, RSO 1950, c 243, s 479, paras 1–4 re bike paths, a provision that dated from at least RSO 1937, c 266, subs 507(4). Province allowed municipalities to set aside so much of any highway "as the council may deem necessary for the purposes of a cycle path."

202 *had largely been forgotten* ... Barton-Aschman started a study in August 1977, for completion within twenty weeks. It delivered three working papers on November 23, 1977, and three others on January 26, 1978, followed by a summary: Barton-Aschman, "Planning for Urban Cycling." See also CoT Council Minutes, 1976, Exec Committee Report no. 50, Nov. 30, pp 8498–9, recommending $50,000 budget; CoT Council Minutes, 1976, PW Report 21, "Measures to promote safety for bicyclists," p 3915; and CoT Council Minutes, 1978, PW Report no. 1, Jan 30, Clause 23. See also "Cyclists Trying to Peddle Idea of Commuter Bike Lanes," *Toronto Star*, May 17, 1977.

203 *profile of the Toronto cyclist ...* By contrast to Metro, in the City of Toronto less than half of cycling trips were by children (under the age of sixteen). Barton-Aschman, "Planning for Urban Cycling," 1 – 44,000 trips/day for utilitarian purposes. See also Barton-Aschman, WP1, 5–8, 9–10. Barton-Aschman's cycling data was for October 1976, but much of it was extrapolated from Minneapolis and St. Paul. See Mars and Kyriakides, "Riders, Reasons and Recommendations," 3.

203 *"relatively 'hazardous' experience ..."* Barton-Ashman, WP1, 5–8. In Toronto, 35 per cent of cyclists were aged five to fifteen; 40 per cent were in the sixteen to twenty-nine age group. The 7.5 per cent of *destinational* trips for work understated the amount of such trips given the inclusion in the group of riders under age sixteen, who were less likely to be employed.

203 *cyclists and motorists used the same ...* Barton-Aschman, "Planning for Urban Cycling," 1979 CTA, Fonds 2, Series 1143, Item 289.

203 *the preferred east-west route ...* Barton-Aschman, WP2, 11–12 and table 2-8. CoT Council Minutes, 1979, App A, PW Report 25, p 6760. Ranking based on such factors as cycling numbers, potential growth, and danger of collisions.

204 *"ensure the continuing viability ..."* Barton-Aschman, WP3, 7, 8, 14–15.

204 *precisely the opposite conclusion ...* The Centre for Active Transportation, "Bloor Street Bike Lane Economic Impact Studies, 2009–2017." A 2017 study for Bloor Street found that 50 per cent of merchants drove to their shops (compared to 10 per cent of their customers). Merchants then occupied some customer parking spots.

204 *created by restriping ...* Wider curb lanes were proposed for Harbord-Wellesley, Gould, Sherbourne, and portions of St. George Street. Barton-Aschman, "Planning for Urban Cycling," 1979, 11, called for more study into access across the University of Toronto campus to connect Harbord and Wellesley. Harbord's narrow width meant reconfiguration would mean loss of one car lane. Left turn lanes for intersections were recommended to pre-empt turning cars blocking traffic. Barton-Aschman, WP3, 6.

204 *one of three options ...* Barton-Aschman, "Planning for Urban Cycling," 1979, 9–10.

204 *"major re-allocation of space ..."* Barton-Aschman, WP4, 5.

204 *Bremner remained cranky ...* "Toronto Gets Bikes-Only Traffic Lane," *Globe and Mail*, May 16, 1979, 42. CoT Council Minutes, 1979, App A, "Harbord-Wellesley Bicycle Route," PW Report 12, p 5606; and CoT Council Minutes, 1979, App A PW report no. 12, "Harbord-Wellesley Bicycle Route," June 11, pp 5606–9.

204 *"significant disagreement ..."* Barton-Aschman, WP-3, Table 3-9, p 28.

204 *"for practical purposes, impossible ..."* Barton-Aschman, "Planning for Urban Cycling," 1979, 4.

205 *"the road system should be designed ..."* Barton-Aschman, "Planning for Urban Cycling," 1979, 5–6, suggesting road design elements were potentially *as effective as* bike lanes: wider curb lanes, pavement markings, prohibitions on cars stopping, lower speeds, signing of routes, motorist turn restrictions, bus bays, high quality road surface, and street lighting.

205 *cycling education courses ...* Forester, *Effective Cycling*; and Beames, "City Cycling Skills."

205 *"you drive a bike ..."* Ontario Ministry of Transportation and Communications: "Sam the Safety Duck Learns to Drive a Bicycle," YouTube, https://www.youtube.com/watch?v=bo2jSFq70aQ.

205 *"Cyclists fare best ..."* Forester, *Effective Cycling*.

206 *about 600 metres in length ...* CoT Council Minutes, 1979, App A. Mar 8, PW Approval, adopted by council Apr 2; and CoT Council Minutes, 1979, App A, Feb 28, "Bicycle Lane – Poplar Plains Rd," pp 3097–100. Original approval for Macpherson to Clarendon (700 m), but this was likely shortened to Cottingham at the southern end. Bike lane varied from 1.2 to 4.8 m. See Michael Moore, May 16, 1979, "Toronto Gets Bikes-Only Traffic Lane," *Globe and Mail*, May 16, 1979, 42; and "Ottawa Beats Hogtown," *Toronto Star*, May 30, 1979, 39.

206 *"already intolerable traffic ..."* "There's a Limit to Bike Lanes," *Toronto Star*, Oct. 14, 1979, A8. See Michael Moore, "Toronto Gets Bikes-Only Traffic Lane," *Globe and Mail*, May 16, 1979, 42 – Senior Traffic Engineer said, "The inconvenience of providing such special facilities for cyclists is not really justified by the number who would benefit ... If we start to see a trend, planning will change but we don't see anything yet."

207 *"[W]e have fat reports ..."* "Long Overdue Bicycle System Finds Beginning," *Globe and Mail*, June 11, 1974, 33.

207 *"10 years is a short time ..."* W. Gunter Plaut, "Think the Unthinkable! Safety for Cyclists," letter to the editor, *Globe and Mail*, Oct. 5, 1978, 7.

2019 – A Changing City

209 *coordinated global protest ...* Extinction Rebellion organized the protest. At mid-day police arrested nineteen protesters for mischief under the *Criminal Code*. Protesters appeared in court on November 18, 2019. The Crown withdrew all charges, against all individuals (including John Liss, represented by the author), likely fearing a show trial.

209 *eco-systems will begin collapsing ...* United Nations, "Only 11 Years Left to Prevent Irreversible Damage from Climate Change," Media Release, Mar. 28, 2019, https://www.un.org/press/en/2019/ga12131.doc.htm.

210 *Toronto's 1.3 million cars and trucks* ... Ontario Ministry of Transportation, emails to author, Aug. 26 and 28, 2018. The precise figure (for 2016) was 1,257,409, among which 1.1 million are passenger vehicles, including light trucks. For GHG figures, see CoT, *Transform TO: 2019 Implementation Update*, June 2020, https://www.toronto.ca/wp-content/uploads/2020/11/96aa-TTO-2019-Update-June2020-FINAL-AODA.pdf.

210 *bicycle basket being crushed* ... Lyn Adamson, "Bike Lane Scare," *Cyclometer*, Nov. 1994/Jan. 1995.

211 *early calls to climate action* ... "Toronto Conference on the Changing Atmosphere: Implications for Global Security," Canadian Meteorological and Oceanographic Society, 1988, https://cmosarchives.ca/History/ChangingAtmosphere1988e.pdf.

211 *rally easily counted 25,000* ... See, for example, Gabby Rodrigues, "Toronto's Climate March Takes Over Downtown," *Global News*, Sept. 27, 2019, https://globalnews.ca/news/5960005/toronto-climate-strike-march-friday/.

212 *inventory of bike lanes* ... "On-road cycling facilities" include bike lanes, cycle tracks, contra-flow lanes, and boulevard (or sidewalk-level) paths – and, technically, wider curb lanes, sharrows, and signed routes, which are marginal applications. In some cases, I use bike lanes (usually interpreted as paint-only) more generically to include cycle tracks, contra-flows, and boulevard paths, although each has its own features. The broader term "bikeways" also includes off-road bike trails. The 5,600-kilometre figure for roads excludes provincial highways 400, 427, and 401 within the city. In 2019, the DVP and Gardiner were still under the city's jurisdiction.

212 *as many cyclists had died* ... In the period 1971–2019, about 160 cyclists died in road collisions, based on author's compilation of data from Toronto Police Service and City of Toronto, Transportation Services.

212 *University of Toronto report* ... Imani, Miller, and Saxe, "Cycle Accessibility and Level of Traffic Stress."

212 *prioritized human life* ... CoT, "Vision Zero 2.0 – Road Safety Plan Update."

213 *confirmed the growing number of cyclists* ... Nanos, *City of Toronto Cycling Study*, 2.

213 *the number of utilitarian cyclists* ... The population was 2.3 million in 1999 and 2.8 million in 2019. The survey was of people age fifteen and over (suggesting an adult population of 1.9 million in 1999, and 2.3 million in 2019).

213 *100,000 utilitarian cyclists* ... Mars and Kyriakides, "Riders, Reasons and Recommendations," 40. The earlier report qualified its numbers as *conservative*.

213 *40 per cent in North York* ... Nanos, *City of Toronto Cycling Study*, 3, 25. By the same measure, the percentage of Etobicoke residents who reported to be "non-cyclists" fell from 53% (1999) to 29% (2019).

214 *dropped to 20 per cent* ... Nanos, *City of Toronto Cycling Study*, 3. Distance had become a less important factor for cyclists, perhaps the result of e-bikes. Mars and Kyriakides, "Riders, Reasons and Recommendations," 40, for 1986 figures.

214 *showed majority support* ... EKOS, "Public Attitudes to Bicycle Lanes in Toronto," July 2018, https://drive.google.com/file/d/1izk3DITNsaDLY_UC6Yd2YA3MabiJBqN7/view?usp=sharing.

214 *Council incumbents* ... Tai Huynh, "How Toronto's Councillors Became Nearly Unbeatable," *The Local*, Sept. 15, 2022. The average length of a Toronto councillor's duration was 13.8 years, the longest among major Canadian and American cities.

214 *40 per cent of trips* ... Ostler, *Trends, Issues, Intensification*, 41. See also CoT, "Downtown Mobility Strategy."

214 *condo building booms* ... "Trips Made by Residents of City of Toronto," TTS, 2016 – the percentage of trips on foot and bikes almost doubled from 7 per cent in 1986 to 13 per cent in 2016.

214 *third-highest population growth* ... See Matt Elliot (@GraphicMatt), "Figure 7: Population Growth, 2016–2021, City of Toronto Federal Electoral Districts (FEDs), Ranked by Highest Percent Change," Twitter, May 10, 2023, https://twitter.com/GraphicMatt/status/1656368423130001414. City wards with little or negative growth, including four wards in Scarborough, generally retained their councillors.

214 *cycling across the mega-city* ... For the 1.2 per cent, see Metro, "Review of Bicycle Facilities," 22, 27, based on the 1991 TTS. The TTS figures for 2016 and 2011 are summarized in CoT, "Cycling Network Plan Update," 14. (The 2016 Census, also cited, puts the figure at 2.2 per cent for 2011.) The TTS numbers exclude trips that were for school purposes or were not work-related. The numbers continued to show low levels (and high potential) for cycling to school, which was only 2.2 per cent in 2016.

214 *In Cabbagetown* ... CoT, "Cycling Network Plan Update," 10–11, citing StatsCanada, "2016 Census Topic: Journey to Work," Nov. 2017, https://www12.statcan.gc.ca/census-recensement/2016/rt-td/jtw-ddt-eng.cfm.

215 *1,000 per cent on Richmond-Adelaide* ... CoT, "Cycling Network Plan Update," 14.

215 *55 per cent of trips to work* ... Ontario Ministry of Transportation analysis, based on TTS 2016, https://drive.google.com/file/d/1H21g6SHtpkQA1MLqjxlFUaMPPfCQVXV8/view?pli=1.

215 *ongoing trend away from cars* ... EKOS, "Public Attitudes to Bicycle Lanes in Toronto," July 2018, https://drive.google.com/file/d/1izk3DITNsaDLY_UC6Yd2YA3MabiJBqN7/view?usp=sharing. The 2016 census showed the

Toronto metro area with highest levels (42.5 per cent) of sustainable transport use for commuting among largest Canadian metro areas. See Statistics Canada, "Commuters Using Sustainable Transportation in Census Metropolitan Areas" (2017), https://www12.statcan.gc.ca/census-recensement/2016/as-sa/98-200-x/2016029/98-200-x2016029-eng.cfm.

215 *households didn't own a car* ... TTS, 2016.

215 *faster than the car population* ... In 1960 there were 2.8 people for each motor vehicle; by 1970 this figure had dropped to 2.3 people and to 1.9 people per motor vehicle by 1979, then rising to 2.2 by 2016. Source: Toronto Police Service, Annual Statistical Reports, 1960 to 1980, and MTO, email to author, July 30, 2018.

215 *quickly ridiculed* ... Edward Keenan, "More Lanes Won't Help Highway 401," *Toronto Star*, June 29, 2018.

215 *disfigured the city* ... Shoup, *The High Cost of Free Parking*.

216 *eliminated minimum parking requirements* ... Madison Polidoro and Craig White, "Explainer: Changing Parking Requirements in Toronto, *Urban Toronto*, Mar. 31, 2022.

216 *most comprehensively studied* ... CoT Council Proceedings, 2017, Committee Debate, PWIC24.9, "Bloor Street West Pilot Bike Lane," Oct. 18, 2017, Questions by Joe Cressy to Transportation Services, General Manager, Barbara Gray, Video Archive at 4:48:20. Cressy's mother Joanne Campbell (wife of Councillor Gordon Cressy, 1978–82) was a sitting councillor when Joe was born.

216 *made them easy to ignore* ... Mass transit, especially when underground, had similar attributes. A 2023 study reported that of the 156,000 people that moved daily through the Bloor Street West corridor (Runnymede to Kipling Avenue), only 26,000 were motor vehicles; the remainder travelled on foot, bikes, and transit. (Assuming 1.5 people per car, the figure would rise to 39,000.) "Mode Share and Traffic Volumes," Bloor West Complete Street Extension, Online Materials," Apr. 2023, Slide 13, https://www.toronto.ca/wp-content/uploads/2023/03/956c-TZS-BWB-PIC1-FINAL-ONLINEAODAcompressed.pdf.

216 *the importance of bike counts* ... Barton-Aschman, "Planning for Urban Cycling," 11. *Toronto Bike Plan, 2001*, 2–9, recommended "a bicycle specific data collection program."

217 *"what you count ..."* Jan Gehl, "Green and Grey / What You Want to Do & What You Must Do," A Walk in the Park Series, Jan. 11, 2022 (at 17:14), https://www.youtube.com/watch?v=uGgY0ke97JQ.

217 *video-recorded count* ... The five-day bike count recorded between 5,900 and 6,700 cyclists per day. Bells on Bloor, "Bike Count – Final," Sept. 18, 2017, "How many cyclists are using the Bloor bike lanes?," Biking in a Big City, Sept. 28,

2017, https://jnyyz.wordpress.com/2017/09/28/how-many-cyclists-are
-using-the-bloor-bike-lanes/. See also John Reiti, "Bloor Street Bike Lane
Debate Heating Up as Final Report Nears," *CBC News*, Sept. 17, 2017, https://
www.cbc.ca/news/canada/toronto/bloor-bike-lane-alert-1.4308633.

217 *obliged to use Tower Road* ... See, for example, James Ham (University of
Toronto) to David White, "Bicycle Path on University Property," July 13, 1979,
Fonds 1142, Series 2674, File 55.

217 *some motorists on Harbord* ... R.M. Bremner, PW to City Services, Oct. 11,
1983, CTA, Fonds 1361, Series 683, File 266 (marked as Box 6, File 25).

218 *"a veritable death trap ..."* Joe Robert, "A Not So Trivial Pursuit," *City Cyclist*,
Spring 1984, and Linda Pim to Jack Layton, May 29, 1987, CTA, Fonds 1361,
Series 683, File 266 (marked as Box 6, File 25).

218 *preferred parallel Bloor* ... R.M. Bremner, PW to City Services, Oct. 11,
1983, CTA, Fonds 1361, Series 683, File 266 (marked as Box 6, File 25).
Comparing the busiest eight hours on Bloor Street to Harbord-Wellesley
showed the difference: August 1978 – 768 cyclists on Bloor compared to 495 on
Harbord-Wellesley; August 1981 (with the wider lane in place) – 1,161 to 483;
and September 1983 – 1,437 to 986.

218 *traffic-calming measure* ... Installed circa 1983, the bike lane was actually
extended at the behest of local residents worried about motor traffic near the
local school. In 1999, a portion of the bike lane in front of the school was
removed under By-law 723-1999, presumably for student drop off and pick up.

218 *city's second bike planner* ... David McCluskey, "True Grid," *City Cyclist*, Winter
1985, 4, argued that "the designation of separate bike lanes or signed-routes is
not cost effective on a large scale."

218 *"prevailing view ..."* David Nobbs and Kate Sutherland, "Still Talking Strok;
Metro's Hardening Arteries," *City Cyclist*, Summer 1985, 3.

219 *"cyclist-inferiority phobia ..."* See, for example, John Forester, "The Effect of
Effective Cycling," *Bicycle Forum*, Fall 1978, CTA, Fonds 1142, Series 2674,
File 54.

219 *"macho militants ..."* Charles Harnik, "The Spokes of a Wheel," Spokespeople,
Energy Probe Conference on Bicycle Advocacy, 9, Apr. 1985, CTA, Fonds 1361,
Series 683, File 270 (marked as SC 361, Series 1, Box 6, File 29). See also Hood,
Practical Pedaling, 20, 32, who summarized Forester's position, according to his
critics, as "best suited to the more naturally aggressive, physically strong rider."

219 *"Bicycles Belong ..."* The fear that cyclists might be banned from roads had a
basis in a (short-lived) ban imposed on some New York City streets in the late
1980s. Friss, *On Bicycles*, 142.

219 *tourism pages of local papers* ... See, for example, Lucy Izon, "Netherlands a Wonderful Place to Ride a Bicycle," *Toronto Star*, Dec. 12, 1987, H27.

219 *1980 survey by Ryerson* ... Kosny, "The Bicycle as a Mode of Urban Transporation," including Appendix A, Bicycle Week Survey, June/July 1980, 8 – noting that Metro residents most favoured or demanded exclusive bike lanes. Common answers included "More bicycle pathways are desperately needed" and "More bike routes along thoroughfares as in Holland are essential."

220 *among the top concerns* ... Mars and Kyriakides, "Riders, Reasons and Recommendations," 49. Respondents could choose several concerns. Traffic conditions were chosen by 33 per cent while bike lanes were listed by 8.6 per cent.

220 *64 per cent of respondents* ... Marshall, Macklin, Monaghan, "Route Selection Study," 9 – citing Healthy City Office report, May 1989, building on CCC findings that 89 per cent of cyclists didn't cycle more often because of safety concerns.

220 *"adopt as a high priority ..."* Healthy City Office, "Evaluating the Role of the Automobile: A Municipal Strategy," 1991, vol 2, 59; and Toronto Public Health, "Roads for Cyclists too," 1989, 56.

220 *"it's about families ..."* Lyn Adamson, interview with author, Aug. 10, 2018. See also Nancy Smith Lea, "Cycling Safety," 3, who characterizes the division as a reflection of society's power structure, one side dominated by middle- and upper-class males and the other by society's more vulnerable groups, including the elderly, women, immigrants, and the lower-income.

221 *"Road Warrior ..."* Canada Market Research, "Road Warrior: The Toronto City Cycling Committee Bicycle Safety Campaign," Aug. 1989, CTA, Fonds 1361, Series 683, File 265; see also Beames, "City Cycling Skills."

221 *cyclists stopped by police* ... The HTA already defined "vehicle" as "any vehicle drawn, propelled or driven by any kind of power, including muscular power." The conference also opposed persistent calls for bike licensing, although this was perhaps a curious position for vehicular cyclists, given the desire to be treated like motorists. D. Graves, "Cycling Licences Rejected," *City Cyclist*, Winter 1985, vol. 7, no. 2, 1. Section 218 of the HTA – failure to identify oneself could lead to arrest.

222 *cycling skills education* ... See Brezina and Kramer, "An Investigation of Rider," 34, identifying children's lack of road skills and judgment in cycling as a problem to be addressed by special training.

222 *replaced by 2041* ... By 1981, 2,350 grates had been replaced on Toronto roads, leaving 17,000 (at a cost of $11 million) plus thousands on Metro roads within

city borders. CoT Council Proceeding, 1981, App A, City Services Committee, Report 16, p 8543.

222 *paltry $13,000 cost* ... Doug Graves, "Grating News," *City Cyclist*, Spring 1984, 7.

222 *his tire stuck in a grate* ... Layton quickly issued a press release calling on the city and Metro to address the problem. Jack Layton, Media Release, Aug. 2, 1984, CTA, Fonds 1361, Series 683, File 265 – "Action on sewer grates desperately needed." See also "Paralysis Fails to Slow Down Student's Active Life," *Globe and Mail*, Oct. 10, 1983, 13.

222 *accelerated replacement schedule* ... "Rejection of Grate Warnings Assailed," *Globe and Mail*, July 23, 1984, M6; D. McCluskey, "Public Works Commissioner Okays Increase in Grate Replacement," *City Cyclist*, Winter 1985, vol. 7, no. 23, 1.

222 *attempt to mount the curb* ... Ferguson, "Boy's Bike Didn't Strike Sewer Grate," *Globe and Mail*, Aug. 31, 1984, E6; "Cyclist Didn't Mention Grate Inquest Told," *Globe and Mail*, Aug. 30, 1984, A6.

223 *credited for its invention* ... Jack Layton and David Dennis of the city's Urban Design Unit claimed credit. See Tammy Thorne, "Who Was First Past the Post?," *Spacing*, Feb. 12, 2010; and *Toronto Bike Plan, 2001*, 9–1. Many car parking metres had been removed (replaced by centralized devices) thus depriving cyclists of lock-up spots.

223 *cycling guidebooks* ... See, for example, Daniel B. Benson, *The Toronto Cycling Guide*, and Elliott Katz, *The Great Toronto Bicycling Guide*, which also advised on how to get to trails, often most easily reached by car. By 1994, Katz had another guidebook, this time for the Canadian Cycling Association (CCA), which had published a similar guide, *Wheel Outings*, a century earlier. See Elliott Katz, *Canadian Cycling Association's Complete Guide to Bicycle Touring in Canada*.

223 *Gardiners who loved bikes* ... Frederick Gardiner, *Ten Bike Tours in and around Toronto*.

223 *"murderer ..."* Sarah Hood, interview with author, Feb. 7, 2019.

223 *"alone in the world ..."* John Forester, *Effective Cycling*, 780.

223 *28,000 signatures* ... For the petition by Deborah Reid, see Garry Wice, "Is Metro Ready for Bicycle Lanes on Roads," *Toronto Star*, July 5, 1992, B5.

224 *installed over twenty kilometres* ... "Bike Lanes Proposed for Toronto," *Toronto Star*, Apr. 8, 1993, A6.

224 *"a mouse in the room ..."* Dan Egan, interview with author, Nov. 20, 2018: "My goal wasn't to be loud ... but getting people to buy in and take things over as their project." City staff working on cyclng issues, pre-amalgmation, included Egan, Zielinski, and Barb Wentworth (the bicycle safety planner).

224 *"why not one for cyclists ..."* Kevin Scanlon, "Biking in a City a Way of Life," *Toronto Star*, Aug. 13, 1980, A3.

224 *"three bike lane routes ..."* "Building the Bike Lane Network," *Cyclometer*, Mar. 1994.

224 *1,000 kilometres of new bikeways ...* "Toronto Cyclists Call for Inquest," *Globe and Mail*, Aug. 2, 1996, A6. In 1996, the CCC proposed "Bicycle City 2001: Creating a Bicycle Transportation Plan for the City of Toronto," which was adopted by city council in 1997.

224 *despite Metro's "policy" ...* Metro Roads Commissioner described arterial policy by quoting from the 1974 Strok & Associates report, which, after noting bikes already banned from expressways, recommended extension of a ban "to other roads *as bikeway systems develop* and alternative access to properties be ensured or bicycle operation along the road be clearly defined" (emphasis added).

225 *no loss of motor vehicle capacity ...* Dan Egan, interview with author, Nov. 20, 2018.

225 *reaching 3,100 daily ...* Nick Gamble, "Bikes Mean Business!," 1995, 18. See also "Cyclists Gearing Up for Bike to Work Week," *Toronto Star*, June 9, 1991, E2.

225 *despite its predictablility ...* See Claire Pfeiffer, "Does New Cycling Infrastructure Really Lead to More Cycling?," City Building Toronto Metropolitan University, May 31, 2021.

225 *"an ideal east-west route ..."* Marshall, Macklin, Monaghan, "Route Selection Study," vi. Also proposed for 1992 was a 2.3-km westward extension of the Bloor Viaduct bike lane to Spadina, given "negligible" impacts on other road users.

225 *rethink old ways ...* Consultant Dave Richardson, email to author, Dec. 3, 2019: "The vision for Bloor-Danforth was genuine given roadway width and opportunity for some type of dedicated bike facility, provided on-street parking issue could be solved." A bike lane on Yonge Street (from Front Street to the northern city limit) was also considered but rejected by consultant as a "non-starter" given the impact on car parking.

225 *local councillor's proposal ...* Howard Levine, interview with author, Nov. 5, 2019

226 *novel clearway ...* The Bay Street clearway was a curb lane designated by a diamond symbol to be shared by taxis, buses, bikes. See Katie Lazier, "Bike Lanes – Riding into Conflict," *NOW Magazine*, July 12–18, 1990, 8.

226 *"no bike lanes, period ..."* J. Barber, "Bike Lanes Rally Cry Might Face Uphill Battle," *Globe and Mail*, Apr. 24, 1994, A9.

226 *"reallocated to bicycles ..."* Andrew Macbeth, "Bicycle Lanes in Toronto," 39. See also *Toronto Bike Plan, 2001*, Table 1, "Before and After Traffic Volumes for Selected Streets with Bicycle the Lanes," 2–10, re: installations (1993–7), bike traffic increased on average by 23 per cent. Highest bike traffic levels were on

College and St. George at 1,900 bikes per day. Egan believed that new left turn lanes ensured that the same motor traffic volumes could be moved through intersections despite the installation of bike lanes.

227 *to publish and distribute* ... Zielinski organized the 1993 Bikes Mean Business Conference, and as part of Transportation Options collaborated with other levels of government for events such as the 1998 Moving the Economy Conference. She also leveraged CCC to help grassroots groups, including the Community Bicycle Network, to access government funds. See also Sue Zielinski and Gordon Laird, *Beyond the Car.*

226 *dynamic and diverse cycling community* ... Dan Egan, "Bicycling Magazine Names Toronto the Best Cycling City in North America," *Cyclometer,* Nov./Dec. 1995.

227 *"Business sucked ..."* Crank's Corner – "Watch Out! It's Crank," *Ontario Bicyclist Magazine,* July/Aug. 1995, vol. 2, no. 1, 10.

227 *motivated by a cash prize* ... "Councillor Ever Ready to Step into Spotlight," *Globe and Mail,* Feb. 15, 1994, A16. And see John Barber, "Bike Lanes Rally Cry Might Face Uphill Battle," *Globe and Mail,* Apr. 24, 1994, A9.

227 *Mayor Doug Holyday* ... By-laws 1996-170 and 1997-0200, City of Etobicoke, amending Municipal Code, Chapter 240, Article IV, Bicycle Lanes, Schedule A.

228 *"the public attitude ..."* Metro, "Review of Bicycle Facilities," 200.

228 *bikes in (West) Germany* ... Metro, "Review of Bicycle Facilities," 22 – 642 bikes per 1,000 inhabitants in Metro.

228 *69 per cent of arterial roads* ... Metro, "Review of Bicycle Facilities," 194, 200.

228 *"other users of the road ..."* Metro, "Review of Bicycle Facilities," 192.

228 *nicknamed Pink Floyd* ... Nancy Smith Lea, interview with author, Jan. 24, 2018.

228 *curb lane approach* ... Professor Kay Teschke, email to author, Feb. 22, 2018, noting the absence of consistent evidence about safety benefit of wide curb lanes; one report found greater severity of cycling injuries (consistent with higher motor speeds).

228 *"curb lane in every pot ..."* John Barber, "Bicycle Gang Puts Spoke in Proposal," *Globe and Mail,* Nov. 5, 1993, A18, quoting Shannon Thompson. At a Metro Council debate on Oct. 14, 1993, long-haired advocate Phil Piltch was dubbed "the Scarborough Cyclist" as a reference point. Councillor Marie Labatte complained, "I thought we were doing something good," venting her anger by calling for bike licensing. Councillor Mike Colle denounced cyclists' opposition as "the total negative trashing of the report."

229 *segment of Danforth Avenue* ... Dan Egan, "New Danforth Design," *Cyclometer,* Sept./Oct. 1995.

229 *truncated bike lanes ...* The total of 5.5 kilometres included the Bloor Viaduct, Steeles Avenue (two sections), Lakeshore West, Millwood Bridge, and Bayview (near Lawrence). Metro By-law 62-91, Schedule A.

229 *"taking the bicycle more seriously ..."* "Pedal Power," *Maclean's*, July 26, 1993. It is noteworthy that countries with the lowest cycling injury rates are usually those with the best cycling infrastructures and not the ones with the most helmeted cyclists. The helmet issue was raised as early as the 1970s. See "Bike Helmets Urged," *Toronto Star*, May 13, 1977, 1.

229 *later became mandatory ...* HTA subs 104(2.1)

229 *coal-fired power plants ...* *Toronto Bike Plan, 2001*, E-7. In a 1999 survey, 42 per cent of utilitarian cyclists reported not riding on smog days.

230 *reached 68 per cent ...* *Toronto Bike Plan, 2001*, 2–15.

230 *excavation was filled in ...* The project was restarted as an LRT in 2011, albeit with underground sections. Only an ill-advised subway on Sheppard Avenue East proceeded, championed by the then mayor of North York, Mel Lastman.

231 *"bicycle friendly environment ..."* *Toronto Bike Plan, 2001*, ES1.

231 *mega-city had 166 kilometres ...* *Toronto Bike Plan, 2001*, ES2.

231 *"pragmatic approach ..."* Bike lanes on Wellesley, Richmond, and Adelaide were among the few significant proposals for downtown. *Toronto Bike Plan, 2001*, 5–5, 5–6, 10–2.

231 *grid of bikeways ...* Dan Egan, interview with author, Nov. 20, 2018. "It was a well-planned grid but not doable." He said that in retrospect, the bike plan should have focused on the downtown, even if that that would have been politically difficult, then expanded out from there, as was proposed in the later "Changing Gears" report.

231 *to bridge barriers ...* *Toronto Bike Plan, 2001*, 10–4.

232 *prior to intersections ...* *Toronto Bike Plan, 2001*, 5–5. Metro had authority over the city roads on the approach to intersections with Metro roads.

232 *Pedestrian and Cycling Infrastructure ...* In 2009, pedestrian matters were separated out from the City Hall unit, then added back a decade later. Post-amalgamation, Egan had to apply to become manager (a new position). His staff had two engineers (working primarily, but not exclusively, on cycling) and one assistant planner dedicated to pedestrian issues.

232 *zero bike lanes ...* Robert Zaichkowski, Two Wheeled Politics, Bike Lane Tracker, http://www.twowheeledpolitics.ca/p/bike-lane-tracker.html.

232 *"expressway crazy ..."* Jack Layton, "Speak Up," *City Cyclist*, Spring 1984. In *The Bad Trip*, David and Nadine Nowlan recount that the 1960s fight against Spadina Expressway involved "the relentlessly pro-expressway material being fed Council by Metro civil servants" (70).

233 *the project would proceed* ... Heaps's announcement pre-dated (by several days) the release of the "Toronto Bike Plan – New Strategic Directions," Transportation Services to PWIC, May 25, 2009, including a report on the feasibility of a bikeway on Bloor-Danforth from Royal York Road to Victoria Park Avenue. The initiative was related to the city's 2007 climate action plan.

234 *incited by local merchants* ... Jeff Gray, "Danforth Businesses Divided over Bike Lanes," *Globe and Mail*, May 21, 2009, A8. Dan Egan, interview with author, Nov. 20, 2018, said there was "huge pushback" from Danforth councillors. Councillors were "put out" that Heaps was imposing this in their wards.

234 *dubious legal foundation* ... In 2015, Queen's Park purported to "clarify" the Municipal Class EA so that EAs were not required for bike lane construction. Tess Kalinowski, "Bike Lanes and Paths Easier to Build Under New Rules," *Toronto Star*, Oct. 22, 2015. This did not, however, stop the city from suggesting that an EA was required for some bike lanes.

234 *reclassify the project* ... Provincial planning policies had been marginally improved to encourage, but not legally require, cities to install a cycling infrastructure. See, for example, Government of Ontario, *A Place to Grow: Growth Plan for Greater Golden Horseshoe* esp. 3.2.3, "Municipalities will ensure that active transportation networks are comprehensive and integrated into transportation planning to provide: (a) safe, comfortable travel for pedestrians, bicyclists ..."

234 *flash point for motorists* ... Egan attributed the problems to Heaps's dispensing with public consultation; and Heaps to the fact that he was a novice councillor strongly influenced by the staff's recommendation.

234 *shifted the planning focus* ... "Changing Gears," Transportation Services, 2009.

235 *a wedge issue* ... Michelle Berardinetti, campaign literature, 2010 (courtesy of Jonathan Schmidt). Another consequence of the experience was the formation of a local cycling advocacy group that became Toronto East Cyclists (TEC), reviving the work in Scarborough of the 1970s Pollution Probe student group. TEC remains active today.

236 *served politicians well* ... *Toronto Bike Plan, 2001*, 10–5, did, however, allow flexibility to build bike lanes not articulated in the plan, while providing for annual progress reports.

236 *"champion of bike thieves ..."* Ian Austen, "In a Cyclist-Friendly City, a Black Hole for Bikes," *New York Times*, Aug. 21, 2008. It took police years to charge Kenk, even though his Queen Street bike shop was a well-known "chop shop" for bikes. He was arrested after a sting operation and sentenced to thirty months in jail for bike thefts and possession of cocaine. He was released in 2010. See "Bike Thief Igor Kenk Released from Jail," *Toronto Star*, Mar. 6, 2010.

236 *"Don't Steal My Bike ..."* Betsy Powell, "Registering Bicycle May Help if It's Stolen," *Toronto Star*, Aug. 13, 2007, A9.

237 *"my heart bleeds ..."* "Rob Ford on Cyclists," CoT Council Proceedings, 2007, Capital Plan Debate, Mar. 7, YouTube, https://www.youtube.com/watch?v=nySs1cEq5rs. See also Sue Zielinski and Kate Sutherland, "Bicycle: The Wheels of Change," 5–6: When the crash occurred, it's like: "You asked for it ... You were riding in a place that wasn't safe enough for you."

237 *meme wasn't new ...* The meme was once popular in England. See Longhurst, *Bike Battles*. See also Joanna Walters, "War on the Car Sparks Driver Rage," *The Observer*, Aug. 26, 2011.

237 *cyclists as "pinkos" ...* "Don Cherry Rips 'Left-Wing Pinkos' at Council Inaugural," *Toronto Star*, Dec. 7, 2010. Buttons emblazoned with "Bike-Riding Pinko" enjoyed a brief popularity.

238 *capable of speed ...* The removal of the bike lane and restoration of Jarvis Street, along with the removal of two Scarborough bike lanes, cost $400,000 – a 5.3 kilometre setback.

238 *"don't send us any more cyclists ..."* "Quoted: Deputy Mayor Doug Holyday Has Had Enough of Activists, Unionists and Cyclists," *National Post*, Apr. 11, 2012.

238 *Bikeway Trails ...* CoT Council Proceedings, 2012, Public Works and Infrastructure Committee, "The Bikeway Trails Implementation Plan," adopted June 6, 2012.

238 *meandering trails ...* Metro, "Review of Bicycle Facilities," 46, cautioned that "joint use of sidewalks or paths by pedestrians and bicycles is generally *not* recommended" (emphasis in original).

240 *length of bike trails ...* By 2019, 300 kilometres of bike trails were in place, double the length of bike lanes.

240 *"long-term" projects ...* Strok & Associates, "Bikeway System," 15, 19, and map. See also *Toronto Bike Plan, 2001*, 5–6.

240 *the waterfront path ...* Only the Beaches to the Humber River portion is actually known as the Martin Goodman Trail, although the trail by 2019 reached 5 kilometres to the west of the Humber.

240 *"Jewel in the Crown ..."* Kingston Road, the best eastward route, remained inhospitable to cyclists. By the early 1990s, the waterfront bike trail, despite gaps, had over 4,000 riders (9 a.m. to 4 p.m.) on a typical summer day, the highest of any city bikeway. *Toronto Bike Plan, 2001*, 2–9.

240 *five-year-old boy ...* Chris Fox, "Barrier along Martin Goodman Trail Would Have Saved 5-Year-Old Cyclist: Grandfather," *CTV News*, June 3, 2017. Despite its initial reluctance, the city installed a temporary, later permanent, barrier along the trail.

240 *"stick to his knitting ..."* David Rider, "McKeown Immune to Criticism," *Toronto Star*, May 3, 2012, G2.

240 *hit by a car at 30 km/h ...* See Andersen et al., "All-Cause Mortality Associated with Physical Activity."

241 *advice to be more active ...* Medical Officers of Health in GTHA, "Improving Health by Design in the Greater Toronto-Hamilton Area," May 2014. In Toronto alone, there were 280 deaths per year and over 1,000 hospital admissions (20). See also CoT, "TransformTO Net Zero Strategy," Nov. 2021, 40.

241 *downtown cycling circuit ...* the circuit was proposed to the previous council by Alan Heisey, former chair of the Toronto Police Service.

244 *"subways, subways, subways ..."* For example, A. Paperny, "Rob Ford Transit Plan Focuses on Subways, Roads," *Globe and Mail*, Sept. 10, 2010.

244 *ballooning cost projections ...* The 19-kilometre Eglinton Crosstown (started in 2011, but incomplete by the end of 2023) survived Rob Ford's mayoralty, while the Finch West LRT was revived in 2012 as a more modest project, running between Keele Street and Humber College.

244 *became Conservative Party leader ...* Ford replaced Conservative Party leader Patrick Brown who had resigned over allegations, never proven, of sexual impropriety. Brown later became mayor of Brampton.

245 *fines under the HTA ...* In a 1980 case in Burlington, Ontario, a motorist who struck five cyclists, killing three, was fined $200 and his licence suspended for one year under an HTA careless driving charge. The Crown decided that a dangerous driving charge could not be proven. The sentence was appealed but then side-tracked by an unrelated issue. "Crown Will Appeal Sentence of Motorist Who Killed 3 Cyclists," *Globe and Mail*, Apr. 28, 1981, 1.

245 *additional cost of $20 million ...* David Rider, "Mayor John Tory Pressured to Drop Opposition to Yonge Street Bike Lanes," *Toronto Star*, Feb. 2, 2018.

246 *enthusiasm for a new bike plan ...* CoT Council Proceedings, 2016, Memo from General Manager of Transportation to PWIC, May 16, 2016, regarding the Ten-Year Cycling Network Plan – described as "a comprehensive roadmap and workplan, outlining planned investments in cycling infrastructure for 2016 to 2025 period," and including 335 kilometres of new bike lanes, cycle tracks, and sidewalk-level paths. The plan lacked implementation benchmarks or strategy, and priorities. CoT Council Proceedings, 2016, PW 13.11, June 7, adopted the plan "in principle" (http://app.toronto.ca/tmmis/viewAgendaItemHistory.do?item=2016.PW13.11).

246 *a pleasant euphemism ...* CoT Council Proceedings, 2016, "The Ten-Year Cycling Networking Plan," May 3, 2016, 4–5.

246 *"will be achieved ..."* CoT Council Proceedings, 2016, PW 13.11, Ten Year Cycling Network Plan, Comments by Mayor Tory, June 9, Video Archive at 3:32:30. "The old way was to set targets that were very ambitious, and sometimes too ambitious, to be frank; not to fund them and then not to achieve them." By the end of 2019, the most noteworthy new bike lanes were on Richmond-Adelaide (an initiative launched under Rob Ford), and a 2.4-kilometre bike lane stub on Bloor Street.

246 *list of justifications ... Cycling Network Plan Update, 2019,* 25. In fact, the Budget Committee in preparing the 2020 budget asked staff to explain the significant *underspending* in 2019. CoT Council Proceedings, 2020, Transportation Services, Jan. 28, Response, "2020 Capital Budget Briefing Note," https://drive. google.com/file/d/1Gq2OiyqE_FI1scCRbTf1SW9etdooh1-L/view.

247 *"to get nothing done ..."* Hamish Wilson, CoT Council Proceedings, 2019, IEC 6.11, Cycling Network Plan Update, Video Archive, June 27, Part 1 at 2:35:04.

247 *double that of Toronto ...* By end of 2018, Montreal had 314 kilometres of bike lanes. Marianne Giguère, Conseillère associée, transports actifs et développement durable, email to author, Mar. 25, 2019.

248 *confirmed advocates' suspicions ...* Over $100 million was available for cycling infrastructure between 2016 and 2019, including an annual cycling capital budget of $16 million plus $47 million from the province's Ontario Municipal Commuter Cycling (OMCC) program and from the federal government. The chair of PWIC had called for funding from other levels of government. See Toronto Community Bikeways Coalition, letter to Mayor John Tory, Dec. 10, 2020, https://drive.google.com/file/d/1bWvUbhiAVaALOsKeBNxAtUZAetYR0jr1/view.

248 *"everything except bike lanes ..."* Albert Koehl, "The Bike Budget That Pays for Everything except Bike Lanes," *dandyhorse,* Apr. 2, 2019. In 2018, a total of $11 million was spent from the cycling capital budget but only $1.26 million (under 12 per cent) for bike lanes or cycle tracks. Other spending went to bike lane upgrades, trails, showers, and parking.

248 *glass-enclosed tubes ...* Rosie DiManno, "Visionary Plan for Cycling City No Pie in the Sky," *Toronto Star,* June 7, 1991, A7. See also Canadian Urban Institute, "Laneways as Bikeways Opportunities Report," Jan. 29, 2018, https://canurb.org /publications/laneways-as-bikeways-opportunities-report/.

248 *"prioritization metrics ..." Cycling Network Plan Update, 2019.*

249 *"It's my wheelchair ..."* Jutta Mason, age seventy-two, comment to author, Oct. 1, 2019, adding "I feel like I'm twenty-five again;" and John Beckwith, age ninety-two, interview with author, Mar. 7, 2018.

249 *a homeless man* ... Verdict of the Coroner's Jury for Grant Faulkner, June 2018, Ontario Chief Coroner, EC7.11, no. 24, https://www.toronto.ca/legdocs /mmis/2019/ec/bgrd/backgroundfile-136738.pdf.

249 *latté-sipping elites* ... There was some basis for the belief in higher overall incomes among cyclists, though this might be explained by the prevalence of cycling in the older parts of the city. *Toronto Bike Plan, 2001*, 2–5. "As household income rises, so does the probability that one is a utilitarian cyclist."

251 *corners of parking garages* ... In the 1990s, the city amended its zoning by-law to require that new buildings have secure bike parking. *Toronto Bike Plan, 2001*, 2-2.

252 *popularity of ten-speed bikes* ... By comparison, in 1986 Mars and Kyriakides, "Riders, Reasons," 27, noted that 75 per cent of all cyclists used ten- to twelve-speed bikes, while only 4 per cent of utilitarian cyclists used the newer mountain or city bikes.

252 *mittens, and a tuque* ... According to a 2018 study, 27 per cent of student cyclists continued to ride during winter, facilitated by city's increasingly diligent snow clearing in bike lanes. See Mitra and Nahal, "Facilitators and Barriers to Winter Cycling."

252 *sold cycling outfits* ... Upside Cycle Style operated in Kensington Market in 2018 but had left by 2023.

252 *Courier chic* ... T. Livingstone, "Courier Tribe," *Globe and Mail*, Aug. 17, 1995, E6.

252 *celebrated on social media* ... See, for example, Sara Elton, "A Bicycle Built for Three (Plus Groceries)," *Maclean's*, Aug. 23, 2010; and Andrea Yu, "Toronto Families Turning to Cargo Bikes for the School Drop Off," *Toronto Star*, Sept. 4, 2019.

252 *preaching to the converted* ... Tammy Thorne, interview with author, Nov. 30, 2018.

253 *potential audience for cycling* ... Wice's cycling column appeared in the "Life" section from 1990 to 1992. Among other cycling publications were the Bicycle User Group's *BUGle*, until about 1998; the *CBNquirer*; and *Ontario Bicyclist*, beginning July/Aug. 1994.

253 *conversion from shrill opponent* ... See, for example, "Bike Lanes on Bloor Should Be Kept and Extended," Editorial, *Toronto Star*, Oct. 11, 2017.

253 *two full pages of the paper* ... Norris McDonald, "Traffic Jams on Bloor, Yorkville in the Sixties and a Cop Car in a Bike Lane," *Toronto Star*, Sept. 11, 2020.

253 *contingent of twenty officers* ... "Bike couriers and Police Bike Squad Officers Use Bikes on the Job," *Cyclometer*, June 1993, and Toronto Police Service, Annual Statistical Report, Update, 2012. Police on bikes project launched as a pilot in July 1990.

253 *shaming the perpetrators* ... Kyle Ashley, interview with author, Nov. 16, 2018. Ashley convinced superiors to set up a bike unit of three officers to patrol bike lanes and sidewalks.

254 *attending Sunday worship* ... Dan Egan, "Divine Intervention on Bloor," *Cyclometer*, Nov./Dec. 1995.

254 *"just be a minute ..."* Kyle Ashley, interview with author, Nov. 16, 2018, recounted that one motorist returning to her illegally parked car in front of Starbucks
attempted to defend her conduct with, "I have diarrhea." Ashley issued a ticket
anyway, unconvinced about the medicinal value of a Double Frappuccino.

255 *the cyclist that suffered ...* Ashley resigned, believing his termination imminent,
soon after a home visit by his superiors asking for the return of his social media
accounts.

255 *a more modest initiative ...* BikeShare had about 150 bikes; by comparison, Bike
Share by 2019 had 5,000 bikes located at 450 stations. A much earlier, modest
initiative, with little success, in the 1970s involved donated, white-painted
"liberated" bikes made available for free public use, with drop off by users in
conspicuous places. Alexander Ross, "Why City Hall Won't Help You Cycle to
Work," *Daily Star*, Oct. 13, 1971, 29.

255 *bikes on the subway ...* Mars and Kyriakides, "Riders, Reasons and
Recommendations," 35. See Doug Graves, "Breakthrough in TTC Policy," *City
Cyclist*, Winter 1985, 2. GO trains, beginning in 1993, allowed bikes, except
during rush hour – Alan Belaiche, "Bike and GO," *Cyclometer*, July/Aug 1993.
GO buses were also retrofit with bike racks.

255 *cycling and transit trips ....* See also Nanos, *City of Toronto Cycling Study*, 5. Mitra
and Nahal, "Facilitators and Barriers," 35, noted untapped potential of bike-transit
trips, especially in the suburbs given that most of the city's population lived within
a fifteen-minute bike ride to a transit station; and *Toronto Bike Plan, 2001*, 8-1.

257 *number of document couriers ...* Jason McBride "The Secret Life of Food
Couriers," *Toronto Life*, Sept. 25, 2019. As to the figure of 500 document couri-
ers, see "Messenger Appreciation Day," *Cyclometer*, Oct. 2002; and for the 500
Foodora couriers, Alex Paterson, interview with author, Mar. 7, 2018.

257 *15,000 food couriers ...* The estimate of 15,000 is extrapolated, conservatively,
from New York City numbers and adjusted for Toronto's smaller population.
Aude White, "The Revolt of New York City's Delivery Workers," *New Yorker
Magazine*, Sept. 13, 2021.

257 *victim of competition ...* C. Vyhnak, "Bike Courier Idea Pedalled into Business,"
Toronto Star, Oct. 14, 1980. See also Joe Hendry, "Toronto Messenger History –
'Modern' Era," Mess Media, http://messarchives.com/toronto-modern.html,
who estimated that Sunwheel had $1.9 million annual revenue by 1988. See also
"Cyclists and Motorists Fight for Fair Share of Road," *Toronto Star*, July 25, 1982,
A8. Other factors for demise of Sunwheel were an economic recession, and a
dispute with Sunwheel's new corporate partner. By 1990 Tiessen was forced to
put the company into receivership. "I didn't have the resources or the emotional
will to continue." See John Stackhouse, "Uneasy Riders of the Courier Business,"
Globe and Mail, July 19, 1991, 8. Reimer's Express Lines bought Sunwheel for

$1, building the bike courier business back to 75 per cent of its earlier volume. Tiessen died in December 1996, age fifty-four.

257 *temporary storage depots* ... James "Jimjamr" Rooney, interview with author, Feb. 1, 2018. Other bike delivery services had emerged at the time, including one for soiled diapers. Document and parcel couriers on bikes might yet see a revival. In 2017, City Hall collaborated with Purolator to pilot a delivery service using an electric-assist cargo bike. (The service became permanent several years later.) The use of cargo bikes would continue to expand, including for city park maintenance staff. Pembina Institute, "Modernizing Urban Freight Deliveries with Cargo Cycles," 2019, https://www.pembina.org/reports/cargo-bikes-v4 -online.pdf; and Pembina, "Cyclelogistics: Opportunities for Moving Goods by Bicycle," 2017, https://www.pembina.org/reports/cyclogistics-final.pdf.

257 *announced its departure* ... *Canadian Union of Postal Workers v Foodora Inc*, 2020 CanLII 16750 (ON LRB).

258 *range of cycling groups* ... Newer groups that emerged included Cycle55+, Bike Brigade, BikePOC, and Gyaldem and ManDem bicycle clubs.

259 *Le Monde à Bicyclette* ... Albert Koehl, "The Life and Times of Bicycle Bob," *dandyhorse*, Oct. 19, 2016. On one occasion, Bicycle Bob dressed as Moses, stood on the banks of the St. Lawrence River, then raised his arms to part its waters to give safe passage for his two-wheeled followers. The cyclists eventually succeeded in getting a proper crossing on a nearby bridge.

259 *Bicycle Works!* ... Joe Robert, "A Not So Trivial Pursuit," *City Cyclist*, Apr. 1984, 7. Doiron complained that "[t]he CCC is always underserviced ... the city is supportive but in practice little is done." J.H. Cuff, "Make Way for the Pedal Pushers," *Globe and Mail*, Aug. 4, 1984, L1.

260 *promotion of utilitarian cycling* ... The original masthead for the Toronto Bicycle Network (TBN) Newsletter, March 1983, included a range of utilitarian cyclists such as commuters and shoppers.

260 *The BLT* ... Nick Gamble, interview with author, Dec. 11, 2018.

261 *cycling advocacy group* ... The word "union" in the original name was seen as limiting the group's appeal for new members. The new name was adopted in May 2012.

261 *funded by members* ... Dave Meslin, interview with author, May 17, 2018.

261 *executive director* ... Yvonne Bambrick became the Cyclists' Union's executive director (and only employee). The Metcalf Foundation provided seed money. By 2019, Cycle Toronto had grown modestly to as many as six staff, with 3,000 members, 25,000 social media followers, a ward-based volunteer network, and a $500,000 annual budget, including large City Hall contributions to run *Bike Month*.

262 *onto the roof of a car* ... Nick Kovats, email to author, Oct. 27, 2023. Critical Mass rides were an example of the fact that couriers, despite the solitude and

challenges of their work – or perhaps because of them – shared a strong bond. Alleycat races, starting in the late 1980s, were among the competitions that also brought together bike couriers. In the 1990s, Toronto was an attractive destination for couriers from abroad, given the loose work arrangements.

263 *"a determined dreamer ..."* Steve Brearton, "The Long Road to a Bike Path," *dandyhorse*, Summer 2008, no. 1.

263 *activism and advocacy ...* I use "activism" and "advocacy" interchangeably, albeit appreciating the differences in meaning: advocacy works within the law and activism beyond it. In practice, advocates and activists usually engage in both activities, for example, a die-in that blocks motor traffic on a road, followed by a deputation at City Hall.

264 *previous warnings ...* Letter from Lorne Falkenstein to David McCluskey, Planning and Devt Dept, Aug. 23, 1984, CTA, Fonds 1361, Series 683, Files 265–8.

264 *install a bike lane on Spadina ...* Garry Wice, "Spadina Is a Crucial Test of Bike versus Car," *Toronto Star*, Nov. 15, 1992, G5. A bike lane petition was signed by 14,000 people.

264 *review of cycling deaths ...* ARC also initiated a variety of creative advocacy stunts, including parking meter parties where car parking spaces were occupied to highlight superior uses of the public road. "Advocacy Group Puts Bikes First," *Toronto Star*, July 14, 2002, A9.

264 *obscured by fuzzy dice ...* Tony Boston, "The Lessons We Learn from the Death of a Cyclist," *City Cyclist,* Winter 1987, vol. 9, no. 1, 3. Neither prosecutor nor judge appeared to understand that Adrienne. who taught cycling safety in her native Scotland, should have been safe from (attentive) motorists.

264 *road safety research group ...* TCAT started as a grassroots coalition before becoming a project of the Clean Air Partnership, an arm's-length city agency. Today, the acronym's underlying words have been changed to *The Centre* for Active Transportation.

265 *"Don't take chances ..."* "Cycling Safety: Tom Samson's Widow Wants Probe into Teacher's Death Reopened," *Toronto Star*, July 22, 2013. The driver later turned himself in, charged only with "failing to remain," instead of careless or dangerous driving. He was sentenced to a six-month weekend jail term. See also Toronto Public Health, "Road to Health – Improving Walking and Cycling in Toronto," which found that in 69 per cent of pedestrian injuries in crashes, the motorist had violated a traffic law leading to a crash. See also Office of the Chief Coroner, "Cycling Death Review," 2012.

265 *(mis)informed public perceptions ...* Subsequent civil trials, where errors in police investigations are often exposed, typically take years but the outcomes are generally subject to confidentiality clauses. As to police investigatons, on

Metro Morning, Sept. 6, 2019, personal injury lawyer Pat Brown stated, "In my experience, although not in all cases, the investigation is cursory, witnesses are not spoken to, videos are not obtained, personal devices and cell phones are not looked at and the narrative taken from the offending party is given far too great a weight." Oliver Moore, "Family Seeking Justice, 'Closure' in Case of Toronto Cyclist's Hit-and-Run," *Globe and Mail*, Dec. 21, 2015. Tom's father lamented, "I blame myself for his death because I taught him to ride."

268 *who toiled on streets …* "Food as Fuel," *ABC World News Tonight*, Jan. 18, 1999, YouTube, https://www.youtube.com/watch?v=R-WYFZs2_XQ. For the court case, Scott recorded each delivery (on foot or transit) and food consumed in the course of a 150-kilometre day, calculating the need for an extra 1,300 calories per day. The tax agency rejected the modest claim, the cost of an extra meal per day, but offered Scott a settlement if he would agree that it only applied to him and not to all couriers. He rejected the offer. In a later case, Scott (represented by the author) challenged the city for violating the *Labour Relations Act*, alleging that it failed to provide a safe workplace, namely city streets, for its Road and Trail Safety Ambassadors, a program established in 1995. See *Alan Wayne Scott v. Toronto (City)* 2010 CanLII 34213 (ON LRB). Scott lost on a technical ground.

268 *concepts which are outdated …* *Alan Wayne Scott v. Her Majesty the Queen*, FCA, 1998

269 *soliciting a bribe …* Betsy Powell, "Former Immigration Judge Sentenced to 18 Months," *Toronto Star*, July 29, 2010.

269 *the Mink Mile …* Bryant was charged with "operating motor vehicle in manner dangerous to public and thereby caused death of Darcy SHEPPARD contrary to subs 249(4), *Criminal Code*" and criminal negligence, subs 220(b).

269 *prosecutor withdrew all charges …* *R. v. Michael James Bryant*, Court Proceedings, May 25, 2010, available on Canadian True Crime: The Death of Darcy Allan Sheppard, at https://darcyallansheppard.files.wordpress.com/2013/05/das-court-proceedings.pdf. In withdrawing the charges, the Crown meticulously detailed the troubled childhood of the "deceased," his addictions, his recent threatening encounters with other motorists, and several criminal convictions. Bryant's own turbulent personal life escaped mention.

269 *"You are my witnesses …"* Jennifer Wells, "Lost Boy: The Death of Darcy Allan Sheppard," *Toronto Star*, Dec. 26, 2013. A witness told police: "I was shouting 'I'm calling the police' because I wanted him (the driver of the car) to know this was not appropriate behaviour." Victoria Switzman, Police Interview, Canadian True Crime podcasts, "The Death of Darcy Allan Sheppard," May 25, 2022, https://vimeo.com/user24450920.

270 *"out to kill this guy …"* "Darcy Allan Sheppard – Witness 9–12," *NOW Magazine*, Apr. 6, 2015 – police recording.

270 zines, photo essays … See, for example, Derek Chadbourne's zine in the 1990s for couriers, *Hideouswhitenoise*, archived at Mess Media, http://www .messarchives.com/messville/HWN.HTM.

2020–2023 Pandemic – and a Familiar Friend

276 *"In times of crisis …"* Gideon Foreman, "The Bike as COVID-19 Solution," *Toronto Star*, Apr. 27, 2020.

276 *by 130 per cent* … Aaron Enchin, email to author, Nov. 24, 2023.

276 *responding to public pressure* … See, for example, letter from 120 community groups to Mayor Tory, May 14, 2020. The author was among the organizers. https://docs.google.com/document/d/1d5Ine3-Zehb4qe2zm5y6luOk6bZlXxr4 /edit?usp=sharing&ouid=108842432101551679190&rtpof=true&sd=true.

276 *embracing the bicycle* … In 2020, Montreal installed 60 kilometres of bike lanes. Marianne Giguere, Montreal Conseillère associée au comité exécutif, email to author, Oct. 16, 2020.

276 *"the largest expansion …"* CoT, Media Release, "Toronto City Council Approves 40 km of Expanded and Accelerated Bike Routes for ActiveTO," May 28, 2020, https://www.toronto.ca/news/toronto-city-council-approves-40-km-of-expanded -and-accelerated-bike-routes-for-activeto/. In Scarborough, past mistakes were repeated by building unconnected cycle tracks. A 4-kilometre bike lane on Brimley Rd. was removed in October 2020, months after installation. Bike lanes on Eglinton and Finch avenues (20 and 11 kilometres long, respectively), though not part of the pandemic initiatives, were also taking shape, running along or above multi-billion-dollar LRT lines. The provincial transit agency Metrolinx built the Eglinton bike lane east of Leslie Street, quickly proving that it had little idea about how to install a safe bikeway. "Cyclist Critically Injured after Being Hit by Vehicle in Toronto," *CBC News*, Aug. 12, 2022, https://www.cbc.ca/news/canada /toronto/cyclist-struck-life-threatening-injuries-vehicle-toronto-1.6550075.

277 *"make that European trip …"* Gordon Coutts, letter to the editor, *Toronto Star*, Sept. 2, 2020.

279 *"catastrophic" impacts* … Mark Garner, "Future of Yonge Should Be Flexible," *Toronto Star*, Jan. 10, 2021.

279 *decline in road casualties* … CoT, "Fatalities – Vision Zero," https://www.toronto .ca/services-payments/streets-parking-transportation/road-safety/vision-zero /vision-zero-dashboard/fatalities-vision-zero/. The pandemic confirmed a

particular anomaly: when motor traffic drops, some motorists will take advantage of freed up space to speed and act carelessly. Chris McCahill, "Traffic Congestion Vanished and More People Died on the Roads," State Smart Transportation Initiative, Mar. 16, 2021.

279 *thousands of infractions* ... The Hospital for Sick Children, "The City of Toronto Automated Speed Enforcement Program Evaluation," Final Report, Mar. 28, 2023, 18.

281 *greater danger to pedestrians* ... Sarah C. Plonka, Sara Volo, Patrick A. Byrne, Ian Sinclair, and Thadshagini Prabha, "Ontario Pedestrian Crash Causation Study: A Focus on the Impact of Large-Scale Trends on Road Safety," Ontario Ministry of Transportation, June 2020, 16.

283 *Ford's petty meddling* ... During the 2018 municipal election, for example, Ford cut the number of Toronto council seats in half. In the run up to the June 2023 mayoral election, Ford oafishly warned that Olivia Chow would be an "unmitigated disaster," given her "lefty" politics. "Ford Says Toronto Would Be 'Toast' if 'Lefty' Mayor Elected," *Canadian Press*, Feb. 13, 2023; Rob Ferguson, "Doug Ford Says Olivia Chow Would Be an 'Unmitigated Disaster' as Toronto's Mayor," *Toronto Star*, June 21, 2023.

283 *increasingly irrational* ... Edward Keenan, "As We Near the Finish, Here's How the Toronto Mayoral Rivals Stack Up," *Toronto Star*, June 24, 2023. Local residents challenged a proposal to install a bike lane on Bloor Street in Mississauga, claiming a violation of their right to enter and exit their driveways under the *Canadian Charter of Rights and Freedoms*. Andrea Meno, "Weird World: 12 Times Utterly Bonkers Stuff Happened on This Planet," *Cracked*, Feb. 26, 2022, https://www.cracked.com/image-pictofact-8186-weird-world-12-times-utterly-bonkers-stuff-happened-on-this-planet.

287 *"out-of-touch position ..."* Comments by Amber Morley to City Council, June 14, 2023, IE4.3 Cycling Network Plan, Video Archive at 7:52:58, https://secure.toronto.ca/council/#/committees/2462/23195.

287 *would be abolished* ... CoT, "City Council Approves Changes to Regulations for Car and Bike Parking Spaces in New Developments," News Release, Dec. 15, 2021, https://www.toronto.ca/news/city-council-approves-changes-to-regulations-for-car-and-bike-parking-spaces-in-new-developments/. See also, Shoup, *The High Cost of Free Parking*, 21–65.

287 *a bicycle "little changed"* ... "A Hundred Years Hence," *Cycling!*, 19–21. (The article's author is not named.)

287 *"No Bravado ..."* Tweet by @tomflood1, https://twitter.com/search?q=No%20Bravado.%20No%20Celebrities.%20No%20Big%20Budget.%20No%20Stunts.%20&src=typed_query.

Bibliography

By-Laws

City of Toronto, By-law 2464, For the Regulation of the Streets, and for the Preservation of Order.

City of Etobicoke, Municipal Code, Chapter 240, Article IV, Bicycle Lanes, Schedule A.

City of Toronto, Chapter 866, Footpaths, Pedestrian Ways, Bicycle Lanes and Cycle Tracks, Schedules C to E.

Municipality of Metropolitan Toronto, By-law No. 62-91, Respecting Reserved Lanes for Bicycles on Certain Metropolitan Roads, Schedule A.

Caselaw

Alan Wayne Scott v. Toronto (City), 2010 CanLII 34213 (ON LRB)

Bernstein v. Lynch, 1913 CarswellOnt 796, 13 D.L.R. 134, 28 O.L.R. 435 (Ontario Court of Appeal)

Canadian Union of Postal Workers v Foodora Inc., 2020 CanLII 16750 (ON LRB)

Evans v. Jaffray, 1904 CarswellOnt 483, 3 O.W.R. 877 (Ontario Court of Appeal)

Hannah Evans v. City of Toronto, July 5, 2004, Court file no. TO-64013/02 Ont Court of Justice (Small Claims Court)

Johnson v. Town of Milton, [2008] 239 O.A.C. 122 (Ontario Court of Appeal)
Leslie v. McKeown, 1909 CarswellOnt 590, 14 O.W.R. 846, 1 O.W.N. 106 (Ontario Court of Appeal)
Preston v. Toronto Railway Co., 1905 CarswellOnt 630, 11 O.L.R. 56, 5 C.R.C. 30, 6 O.W.R. 786
R. v. Justin, (1894), 24 OR 327, (Ontario Court of Appeal)
Rowan v. Toronto Railway Co., 1899 CarswellOnt 18, 29 S.C.R. 717
Sims v. Grand Trunk Railway, 1906 CarswellOnt 247, 7 O.W.R. 648 (Ontario Court of Appeal)
Wayne Scott v. Canada, 98 DTC 6530 (FCA) 1998
William Ashley China Ltd. v. Toronto (2008), 243 O.A.C. 89 (Divisonal Court)

Directories, Handbooks, Guidebooks, Maps

Bryers, Fred. "Cyclists' Road Guide of Canada with Map." Toronto: W.H. Miln, 1896.
City of Toronto Planning and Development Department and Toronto City Cycling Committee. "Recreational Bicycle Route Guide." Oct. 1984.
Doolittle, Perry E., ed. *Wheel Outings in Canada and C.W.A. Hotel Guide*. Toronto: Canadian Wheelmen's Association, 1895.
Foster, J.G. "Cyclists' Road Map for the County of York with portions of Ontario, Peel, and Simcoe." Toronto: 1896
Gardiner, Fred. *Ten Bike Tours in and around Toronto*. Toronto: 1985.
Hayes, Derek. *Historical Atlas of Toronto*. Toronto: Douglas & McIntyre, 2009.
Kaplan, Esther, and Robert Kaplan. "Bicycling in Toronto." *Toronto Life*, 1972.
Katz, Elliott. *The Canadian Cycling Association's Complete Guide to Bicycle Touring in Canada*. Toronto: Doubleday Canada, 1994.
 – *The Great Toronto Bicycling Guide*. 3rd ed. Toronto: Great North Books, 1990.
Kron, Karl [pseud.] [Lyman Hotchkiss Bagg]. *Ten Thousand Miles on a Bicycle*. New York: Karl Kron, 1887.
Might's (Telephone) Directory, Toronto (Might's Directory)
Toronto Municipal Handbook (various years)

Municipal Reports, Plans, and Studies

City Cycling Committee
- Beames, Denys. "City Cycling Skills." Toronto: 1985
- Cycling and the Law Conference, Jan. 4–5, 1985 (CTA, Fonds 1361, Series 683, Files 267, 271, 274, 289; and Fonds 2, Series 1143, Item 2888)

- "Bicycle City 2001: Creating a Bicycle Transportation Plan for the City of Toronto," 1996
- Canada Market Research. "Road Warrior: The Toronto City Cycling Committee Bicycle Safety Campaign." 1989
- Koch, Tom. "Creating a Cycle Efficient Toronto: A Program to Increase Utilitarian Bicycle Use in the Metropolitan Region." 1992
- Kyriakides, Michael I. "Phase II of the Toronto Cycling Survey: Views and Perceptions of Utilitarian Cyclists in Metropolitan Toronto." Report for City Cycling Committee and Planning and Development Dept, May 1988
- Mars, James H., and Michael I. Kyriakides. "Riders, Reasons and Recommendations: A Profile of Adult Cyclists in Toronto." Report prepared for City Cycling Committee and Toronto Planning and Development Department. Toronto: Ryerson Polytechnical Institute, School of Urban and Regional Planning, 1986
- Ranger, Pierre. "The First Nine Years: The Early History of the City Cycling Committee." Toronto: 1984
- Wallace, Will. "Slow and Steady Progress: The Evolution of the Toronto City Cycling Committee." Strategies and Politics Series. 1998

City of Toronto (1869–Present)

- Barton-Aschman Canada Limited. Working Paper (WP) 1 to 6, Nov. 1977 to Mar. 1978
- Barton-Aschman Canada Limited and Peat Marwick and Partners. "Planning for Urban Cycling." 1979 (CTA Series 1143, Item 2892)
- "Bicycle/Motor Vehicle Collision Study." Works and Emergency Services Dept, Transportation Services, Transportation Infrastructure Management, 2003
- "Bike Plan: Shifting Gears." June 2001. https://www.toronto.ca/wp-content/uploads/2018/12/93b7-bike_plan_full.pdf
- Bikeway Trails Implementation Plan. PW15.2, June 12, 2012
- "Bloor Street West Bike Lane Pilot Evaluation." Transportation Services, Oct. 2017
- City Engineer's Annual Report (various years)
- City of Toronto Council Minutes (various years), including Minutes, Chief Constable's Annual Report (until 1925), and Committee Reports, 1869–2023
- "Cycling Network Plan Update." Transportation Services, June 2019
- "Downtown Mobility Strategy." April 2018. https://www.toronto.ca/wp-content/uploads/2018/04/9700-downtown-mobility-strategy-city-panning.pdf
- Marshall, Macklin, and Monaghan. "Route Selection Study for On-Street Bike Lanes." Final Report, February 1992

- Minutes, "Subcommittee re Bicycle Paths." Board of Works. Mar. 6, 1896. (CTA, Fonds 200, Series 582, File 1, p 35)
- Nanos Research. "City of Toronto Cycling Study." 2019. https://www.toronto .ca/wp-content/uploads/2021/04/8f76-2019-Cycling-Public-Option-Survey -City-of-Toronto-Cycling.pdf
- "Rosedale Trail Report." Consulting Group No 9, City of Toronto, Commissioner of Roads, Rosedale Ravine Bicycle Pathway, 1972
- "Ten Year Cycling Network Plan." May 3, 2016. https://www.toronto.ca /legdocs/mmis/2016/pw/bgrd/backgroundfile-92811.pdf
- Toronto Healthy City Office. "Evaluating the Adverse Health Impacts of the Automobile: A Municipal Strategy." Sept. 1991
- TransformTO Net Zero Strategy. https://www.toronto.ca/services-payments /water-environment/environmentally-friendly-city-initiatives/transformto/
- Transportation Options and the City of Toronto. "Proceedings from Moving the Economy: Economic Opportunities in Sustainable Transportation." International Conference. July 9–12, 1998
- Victor Ford & Associates. "Inventory of Cycling Trail Opportunities in Rail and Hydro Corridors." Dec. 1998
- "Vision Zero 2.0 – Road Safety Plan Update." June 13, 2019. https://www .toronto.ca/legdocs/mmis/2019/ie/bgrd/backgroundfile-134964.pdf

Municipality of Metropolitan Toronto (1954–1997)

- "Bikeway System within Metropolitan Toronto." W. Strok & Associates, Apr. 1974
- "A Metropolitan Toronto Bicycle Route System," H. Abrams, Metro Roads and Traffic, R. Bristow, Metro Parks, and F. Crann and C. Halen, Metro Toronto Planning Board to Metro Commissioners for Planning and Parks, and for Roads and Traffic, Mar. 23, 1973
- Municipality of Metropolitan Toronto Annual Council Minutes (various years), 1954–97
- "Review of Bicycle Facilities on Metropolitan Roads, Research Report." Metro Transportation, Oct. 1993
- "Termination of Metro Arterial Bikeway System." Transportation Committee, Manager's Report 6, 1982, 710

Police Reports

- "Bicycle Regulations with Safety Suggestions for Pedestrians and Cyclists," 1946
- Chief Constable Annual Reports, City of Toronto, 1869–1956

- Metropolitan Toronto Police, Annual Reports, 1957–1997
- Metropolitan Toronto Police, Statistical Reports, 1957–1997
- Toronto Police Service, Annual Statistical Reports, 1998–Present

Toronto Public Health

- "Air Pollution Burden of Illness from Traffic in Toronto – Problems and Solutions," 2007
- "Healthy Toronto by Design," Oct. 2011
- "Road to Health: Improving Walking and Cycling in Toronto," Apr. 2012
- "The Walkable City: Neighbourhood Design and Preferences, Travel Choices and Health," April 2012

Newspapers, Journals, and Magazines

- *Canadian Courier* (esp. 1906–1918)
- *Canadian Home Journal*
- *Canadian Wheelman: The Official Gazette of the Canadian Wheelmen's Association* (CWA, 1883–1900)
- *City Cyclist* (City Cycling Committee, 1978–1989)
- *Cycling: A Mirror of Wheeling Events – Devoted to the Interest of Cyclists in General* (1896–1901)
- *Cyclometer* (City Cycling Committee/Cycling Advisory Committee, 1989–2009)
- *dandyhorse* (2008–2019)
- *Daily Star* (1900–1971)
- *Evening Star* (1892–1900)
- *Globe* (1844–1936)
- *Globe and Mail* (1936–Present)
- *Maclean's* (formerly *Busy Man's Magazine*) (1905–Present)
- *Mail & Empire* (1895–1936)
- *Massey's Magazine* (esp. 1894–1900)
- *Outing: An Illustrated Monthly Magazine of Sport, Travel, and Recreation* (USA)
- *Pastime and The Canadian Wheelman* (1900–1901?)
- *Saturday Night* (only 1887–1937)
- *The Bicycle: The Official Organ of the Canadian Wheelmen's Association* (1882–1883)
- *Toronto Star* (1971–Present)
- *VIM Magazine* (CCM, 1917–?)

Province of Ontario Reports, Plans, Policies, Studies

Ministry of Transportation

- *A Place to Grow: Growth Plan for Greater Golden Horseshoe.* 2020. https:// files.ontario.ca/mmah-place-to-grow-office-consolidation-en-2020-08-28 .pdf
- Brezina, E., and M. Kramer. "An Investigation of Rider, Bicycle and Environmental Variables in Bicycle Collisions." Technical Bulletin SE-70-01. Toronto: Ontario Department of Transportation, 1970
- #CycleON: Action Plan 1.0 and Action Plan 2.0
- "Cycling Skills – Ontario's Guide to Safe Cycling"
- Municipal Class Environmental Assessment, Municipal Engineers Association
- Ontario Cycling Policy, 1982, 1993
- Ontario Road Safety Annual Reports (ORSAR)
- Plonka, Sarah C., S. Volo, P.A. Byrne, I. Sinclair, and T. Prabha, "Ontario Pedestrian Crash Causation Study: A Focus on the Impact of Large-Scale Trends on Road Safety." June 2020
- Provincial Policy Statement, 2020. https://www.ontario.ca/page/provincial -policy-statement-2020
- "The Ministry of Transportation 1916–2016: A History." Toronto, 2016. https://collections.ola.org/mon/30005/334765.pdf

Office of the Chief Coroner for Ontario

- Cass, Dan. "Cyclist Death Review: A Review of All Accidental Cyclist Deaths in Ontario from January 1st, 2010 to December 31st, 2010." 2012. https://www.publicsafety.gc.ca/lbrr/archives/cnmcs-plcng/cn29871 -eng.pdf
- Lucas, W.J. (Regional Coroner). "A Report on Cycling Fatalities in Toronto, 1986–1996." July 1998
- McCallum, Andrew. "Pedestrian Death Review: A Review of All Accidental Pedestrian Deaths in Ontario from January 1st, 2010 to December 31st, 2010." Sept. 2012. https://www.mcleishorlando.com/wp-content/uploads/2012 /09/ec161058.pdf
- Verdict of Coroner's Jury (Glenn McNickle, July 1976; Dean Pace, Sept. 1984; Louis Faulkner, 2015)

Select Articles, Books, Brochures, Reports

Aass, Carl. *The Canadian Urban Bikeway Compendium*. Ministry of State, Urban Affairs Canada, 1976.

Armstrong, Christopher, and H.V. Nelles. *The Revenge of the Methodist Bicycle Company: Sunday Streetcars and Municipal Reform in Toronto, 1888–1897*. Toronto: Oxford University Press, 1977.

Babaian, Sharon. *The Most Benevolent Machine: A Historical Assessment of Cycles in Canada*. Ottawa: National Museum of Science and Technology, 1998.

Bambrick, Yvonne. *The Urban Cycling Survival Guide*. Toronto: ECW Press, 2015.

Beausaert, Rebecca. "'Young Rovers' and 'Dazzling Lady Meteors': Gender and Bicycle Club Culture in Turn-of-the-Century Small-Town Ontario." *Canadian Journal of the History of Science, Technology and Medicine* 36, no. 1 (2013): 33–61.

Boles, Derek. *Toronto's Railway Heritage*. Charleston, SC: Arcadia Publishing, 2009.

Bolton, Janet, Jane Caskey, Suzanne Costom, Richard Fowler, Sivan Fox, Kirsten Hillman, Matthew Taylor, and Rhonda Yarin. "The Young Offenders Act: Principles and Policy – The First Decade in Review." *McGill Law Journal* 38, no. 4 (1993): 939–1052.

Bureau of Municipal Research, Annual Reports, 1914–1983. http://bomr.ca.

Canadian Institute of Planners. *Community Cycling Manual: A Planning and Design Guide*. March 1990.

Chen, Patrick Y. "CCM, 1899–1982." In Rob van der Plas, ed., *Cycle History 15: Proceedings of the 15th International Cycle History Conference*, 98–101. San Francisco: Cycle Publishing, 2005.

Colton, Timothy. *Big Daddy: Frederick G. Gardiner and the Building of Metropolitan Toronto*. Toronto: University of Toronto Press, 1980.

Courtney, Kristin E. "Sustainable Urban Transportation and Ontario's New Planning Regime: The *Provincial Policy Statement, 2005* and the *Growth Plan for the Greater Golden Horseshoe*." *Journal of Environmental Law and Practice* 19, no. 2 (April 2009): 71–104.

Davies, Stephen D. "Ontario and the Automobile, 1900–1930 – Aspects of Technological Integration." PhD diss., McMaster University, 1987.

– "Reckless Walking Must Be Discouraged: The Automobile Revolution and the Shaping of Modern Urban Canada to 1930." *Urban History Review* 18, no. 2 (1989): 123–38.

Davis-Barron, Sherri. *Canadian Youth and the Criminal Law: One Hundred Years of Youth Justice Legislation in Canada.* Markham, ON: LexisNexis, 2009.

Denison, Merrill. *CCM: The Story of the First Fifty Years.* Toronto: Canada Cycle & Motor Co., 1946.

Doolittle, Perry E. "Cycling for Women." *Canadian Practitioner* 21, no. 5 (May 1896).

– "Cycling of To-day." *Massey's* 1, no. 6 (June 1896): 407.

Energy Probe. "Spokespeople, Conference on Bicycle Advocacy." Apr. 27–28, 1985. CTA, Fonds 1361, Series 683, File 279 (marked as SC 361, Series 1, Box 6, File 29).

Ferguson, Ted. *Kit Coleman: Queen of Hearts.* Toronto: Doubleday Canada, 1978.

Filey, Mike. *Not a One-Horse Town: 125 Years of Toronto and Its Streetcars.* Toronto: Filey, 1986.

Filey, Mike, and Victor Russell. *From Horse Power to Horsepower, 1890 to 1930.* Toronto: Dundurn Press, 1996.

Forester, John. *Effective Cycling.* 7th ed. Cambridge, MA: MIT Press, 2012.

Freed, Josh. *Les bons, les méchants et la bicyclette* [The good, the bad and the bicycle]. Documentary. Montreal: Mediatique, 2015.

Friss, Evan. *The Cycling City: Bicycles and Urban America in the 1890s.* Chicago: University of Chicago Press, 2015.

– *On Bicycles: A 200-Year History of Cycling in New York City.* New York: Columbia University Press, 2019.

– "The Path Not Taken: The Rise of America's Cycle Paths and the Fall of Urban Cycling." In Gary W. Sanderson, ed., *Cycle History 20,* 68–72. Cheltenham, England: John Pinkerton Memorial Publishing Fund, 2010.

Goheen, Peter. *Victorian Toronto, 1850 to 1900: Pattern and Process of Growth.* Chicago: University of Chicago Press, Department of Geography, 1970.

Hall, Ann M. *Muscle on Wheels: Louise Armaindo and the High-Wheel Racers of Nineteenth-Century America.* Montreal: McGill-Queen's University Press, 2018.

Harris, Richard. *Creeping Conformity: How Canada Became Suburban, 1900–1960.* Toronto: University of Toronto Press, 2004.

Hawirko, Norman R. "A Brief Compendium of Information Pertaining to the Planning, Designing and Implementation of Bicycle Facilities for the Canadian Urban Bikeway Design Competition." 1975. Toronto Reference Library.

Henderson, John. *Great Men of Canada: Life Stories of a Few of Canada's Great Men Told in Narrative Form.* Toronto: Government of Ontario, 1929.

Herlihy, David V. *Bicycle: The History*. New Haven, CT: Yale University Press, 2004.

Hodges, Karl. "Did the Emergence of the Automobile End the Bicycle Boom?" In Rob van der Plas, ed., *Cycle History 4: Proceedings of the 4th International Cycle History Conference*, 39–42. San Francisco: Cycle Publishing Van der Plas Publications, 1994.

Hood, Sarah. *Practical Pedaling: A Companion for Everyday Cycling in Toronto*. Toronto: Detour, 1998.

Humber, William. *Freewheeling: The Story of the Bicycle in Canada*. Erin, ON: Boston Mills Press, 1986.

Humphries, Charles W. *"Honest Enough to Be Bold": The Life and Times of Sir James Pliny Whitney*. Toronto: University of Toronto Press, 1985.

Illich, Ivan. *Energy and Equity*. New York: Harper & Row, 1974.

Imani, Ahmadreza Faghih, Eric J. Miller, and Shoshanna Saxe. "Cycle Accessibility and Level of Traffic Stress: A Case Study of Toronto." *Journal of Transport Geography* 80 (2019): 102496.

Kilbourn, William. *Toronto Remembered: A Celebration of the City*. Toronto: Stoddart, 1984.

Kinsman, Brian. *Around the World Awheel: The Adventures of Karl M. Creelman*. Hantsport, NS: Lancelot Press, 1993.

Kosny, Mitchell, J. Faulds, W. Anthony, and H. Chow. "The Bicycle as a Mode of Urban Transportation in Metropolitan Toronto." Prepared for Ontario Ministry of Energy. Toronto: Ryerson Polytechnical University, 1980.

Kulash, Walter. "The Third Motor Age." *Places* 10, no. 2 (1996): 44–9.

Lauriston, Victor. "Motor Murder." *Maclean's*, August 1, 1933.

Lehr, John C., and H. John Selwood. "The Two-Wheeled Workhorse: The Bicycle as Personal and Commercial Transport in Winnipeg." *Urban History Review* 28, no. 1 (1999): 3–13.

Levine, Howard. "Streetcars for Toronto Committee: A Case Study of Community Activism in Transit Planning and Operations." *Policy and Planning Considerations* (1973): 190–8.

Levy, Edward J. *Rapid Transit in Toronto: A Century of Plans, Projects, Politics, and Paralysis*. Toronto: BA Consulting Group, 2015.

London, Daniel. "Keeping a Respectable Distance: Bicycling and Class Consumption in fin-de-siècle New York." *International Journal of Bicycling History* (2010).

Longhurst, James. *Bike Battles: A History of Sharing the American Road*. Seattle: University of Washington Press, 2015.

Los, Christopher. "A Danger and a Nuisance: Regulating the Automobile in Ontario, 1903–1912." *Ontario History* 106, no. 2 (2014): 143–64.

Loucks Don, and Leslie Valpy. *Modest Hopes: Homes and Stories of Toronto's Workers from the 1820s to the 1920s.* Toronto: Dundurn Press, 2021.

Macbeth, Andrew. "Bicycle Lanes in Toronto." *ITE Journal* 69, no. 4 (1999): 6.

Mackintosh, Phillip G. "A Bourgeois Geography of Domestic Cycling: The Responsible Use of Public Space in Toronto and Niagara-on-the-Lake, 1890–1900." *Journal of Historical Sociology* 20, no. 1–2 (2007): 126–57.

– *Newspaper City: Toronto's Street Surfaces and the Liberal Press, 1860–1935.* Toronto: University of Toronto Press, 2017.

Mapes, Jeff. *Pedaling Revolution: How Cyclists Are Changing American Cities.* Corvallis: Oregon State University Press, 2000.

McKenty, John A. *Canada Cycle & Motor: The CCM Story, 1899–1983.* Belleville, ON: Essence Publishing, 2011.

Metro by Cycle. "Two Wheeling into the Future: A Snapshot of Cycling in Metro Toronto." Toronto: Metro by Cycle, 1993.

Milligan, Ian. "This Board Has a Duty to Intervene." *Urban History Review* 39, no. 2 (2011): 25–39. https://www.erudit.org/en/journals/uhr/2011-v39-n2-uhr1521619/1003460ar/.

Mitchinson, Wendy. *The Nature of Their Bodies: Women and Their Doctors in Victorian Canada.* Toronto: University of Toronto Press, 1991.

Mitra, Raktim, Nancy Smith Lea, Ian Cantello, and Greggory Hanson. *Cycling Behaviour and Potential in the Greater Toronto and Hamilton Area.* Toronto: TRANSFORM, 2016.

Mitra, Raktim, and Tamara Nahal. "Facilitators and Barriers to Winter Cycling: Case Study of a Downtown University in Toronto, Canada." Toronto: School of Urban and Regional Planning, Ryerson University, 2018.

Morris, Christopher, and John McKenty. "The 1936 CCM *Flyte*, Canada's Contribution to the Streamlined Decade." Paper presented at the 25th International Cycling History Conference, Baltimore, Maryland, USA, August 2014.

Nelson, Frederick. *Toronto in 1928: A Novella.* Toronto: National Business Methods & Publishing Company, 1908.

Norcliffe, Glen. *The Ride to Modernity: The Bicycle in Canada, 1869–1900.* Toronto: University of Toronto Press, 2001.

Norton, Peter D. *Fighting Traffic: The Dawn of the Motor Age in the American City.* Cambridge, MA: MIT Press, 2008.

Nowlan, David, and Nadine Knowlan. *The Bad Trip: The Untold Story of the Spadina Expressway.* Toronto: New Press, 1970.

Oddy, Nicholas. "Cycling's Dark Age? The Period 1900–1920." In Rob van der Plas, ed., *Cycle History 15: Proceedings of the 15th International Cycle History Conference*. San Francisco: Cycle Publishing, 2005.

Ontario Medical Association. "Enhancing Cycling Safety in Ontario." August 2011.

Ontario Motor League. *Sixty Golden Years, 1915–1975: The Story of Motoring in Ontario*. Toronto: Ontario Motor League, 1975.

Ostler, Thomas. *Trends, Issues, Intensification: Downtown Toronto*. Toronto: City of Toronto, 2014. https://www.toronto.ca/legdocs/mmis/2014/te/bgrd/backgroundfile-69192.pdf.

Pattison, Irma E. *Historical Chronology of Highway Legislation in Ontario, 1774–1961*. Toronto: n.p., 1964.

Pollution Probe. "The Scarborough Bicycle Pathway System – Design and Construction Concepts." Toronto: Pollution Probe, 1973.

Pratt, Charles E. *The American Bicycler: A Manual for the Observer, the Learner, and the Expert*. Boston: Houghton, Osgood, 1879.

Pucher, John, and Ralph Buehler, eds. *City Cycling*. Cambridge, MA: MIT Press, 2012.

Rasenberger, Jim. *America 1908: The Dawn of Flight, the Race to the Pole, the Invention of the Model T*. New York: Scribner, 2007.

Reid, Carlton. *Roads Were Not Built for Cars: How Cyclists Were the First to Push for Good Roads and Became the Pioneers of Motoring*. Washington, DC: Island Press, 2015.

Reynolds, Brian. "Technological Innovation in Canadian Cycling Industry." In Rob van der Plas, ed., *Cycle History 17: Proceedings of the 17th International Cycling History Conference*, 31–40. San Francisco: Cycling Publishing, 2008.

Ride Fair. "Budgeting for the Uber Impact: How Uber/Lyft Cost the TTC $74 Million in 2019." February 2021.

Robertson, Heather. *Driving Force: The McLaughlin Family and the Age of the Car*. Toronto: McClelland & Stewart, 1995.

Robertson, William Norrie. *Cycling!* Stratford: F. Pratt, 1894.

Rubenson, Paul. "Missing Link: The Case for Bicycle Transportation in the United States." In Rob van der Plas, ed., *Cycle History 16: Proceedings of the 16th International Cycle History Conference*, 73–84. San Francisco: Cycle Publishing, 2006.

Rush, Anita. "The Bicycle Boom of the Gay Nineties: A Reassessment." *Material History Bulletin* 18 (1983): 1–12.

Sanderson, Gary. W. *Cumulative Index to the Proceedings of the International Cycle History Conferences, 1990–2014*. February 2015. https://www.ichc.biz/documents/ICHC-CUMULTIVE-INDEX-1-25.pdf.

Schull, Joseph. *Ontario since 1867*. Toronto: McClelland & Stewart, 1978.

Sewell, John. *How We Changed Toronto: The Inside Story of Twelve Creative, Tumultuous Years in Civic Life, 1969–1980*. Toronto: James Lorimer, 2015.

Shoup, Donald. *The High Cost of Free Parking*. New York: Routledge, 2011.

Smith, Ken, ed. *The Canadian Bicycle Book*. Toronto: D.C. Heath Canada Limited, 1972.

Smith Lea, Nancy. "Cycling Safety: Shifting from an Individual to a Social Responsibility Model." MA thesis, University of Toronto, 2001.

Stamp, Robert. *Riding the Radials*. Erin, ON: Boston Mills Press, 1989.

Teschke, Kay, et al. "Route Infrastructure and the Risk of Injuries to Bicyclists: A Case Crossover Study." *American Journal of Public Health* 102 (2012): 2336–43.

The Centre for Active Transportation (TCAT). "Bloor Street Bike Lane Economic Impact Studies, 2009–2017." https://www.tcat.ca/resources/bloor-street-economic-impact-studies/.

Toronto Bicycle Club. "Announcement of the 11th annual meet of the Toronto Bicycle Club on the Grounds of the Toronto Lacrosse and Athletic Assoc., 13 and 15 August, '92." https://www.canadiana.ca/view/oocihm.60808/1.

Toronto Cycling Think & Do Tank. "Mapping Cycling Behaviour in Toronto." 2016. https://www.torontocycling.org/uploads/1/3/1/3/13138411/mapping_cycling_behaviour_in_toronto_final_23_may_printer_tl.pdf.

Toronto Transit Commission. "Bike and Ride Study: Final Report." 1994.

Toronto Railway Company. "Toronto As Seen from the Streetcars: A Passenger Souvenir for Visitors and Residents of Toronto." 1894. TRL Digital Archive.

University of Toronto, Engineering, Data Management Group. "Transportation Tomorrow Surveys (TTS)." 2006, 2011, 2016. http://dmg.utoronto.ca/transportation-tomorrow-survey/tts-reports/.

Waters, Christopher. *Every Cyclist's Guide to Canadian Law*. 2nd ed. Toronto: Irwin Law, 2022.

– "The Rebirth of Bicycling Law?" *Canadian Bar Review* 91, no. 2 (2013): 395–416.

White, Richard. *Planning Toronto: The Planners, the Plans, Their Legacies, 1940–80*. Vancouver: UBC Press, 2016.

Willard, Francis E. *A Wheel within a Wheel: How I Learned to Ride the Bicycle*. New York: Fleming H. Revell, 1895. https://www.gutenberg.org/files/60356/60356-h/60356-h.htm.

Wilson, S.S. "Bicycle Technology." *Scientific American* 228, no. 3 (1973): 81–91.

Zaichkowski, Robert. "Bike Lane Tracker." *Two-Wheeled Politics* (blog).
October 27, 2023. http://www.twowheeledpolitics.ca/p/bike-lane-tracker
.html.

Zielinski, Sue, and Gordon Laird, eds. *Beyond the Car: Essays on the Auto
Culture.* Toronto: Steel Rail Publishing and Transportation Options, 1995.

Zielinski, Sue, and Kate Sutherland. "Bicycle: Wheels of Change." *CBC Ideas*,
Transcript, 1988.

Index

Note: Page numbers in bold refer to images

182, 215, 228–30, 264; old, **xiv**,
213, 215; support for cycling, 25,
151, 160–1, **179**, 272; support for
motorists, 16, 130, 176, 200, 237.
See also City Hall
classes, social: love of cycling across,
8, 110; markers of, 29, 100–1, 249,
269; upper, x, 18, 30, 32–3, 52, 72,
108, 197; working, 19, 67, 187
climate change, 244; activism,
209–11, 258; bicycle's importance
in response to, ix, xiii, 249, 258,
288; city experiences of, 209–11,
247; city planning for, 231–2, 272,
283–5; greenhouse gas emissions,
209–10, 268, 285; impacts on
bike commuting, 199; vehicle
marketing amid, 114
Coleman, Kit (a.k.a. Kit Blake), 31,
305n31
College Street, 1, 32, 41, 61, 64, 155,
211
Comet Cycle Co., 30, 319n65
Community Bicycle Network (CBN),
255, 260, 384n227
Complete Streets Guidelines, 247
coroner's inquests, 142, 187, 249, 264,
337n103
couriers, bicycle. *See* messengers
Creelman, Karl, 63, 318n63
Cressy, Joe, 216, 379n216
Critical Mass rides, 261, **262**, 263,
393n262
Crombie, David, 176, 226
Curbside Cycle, 251, 276
Cycle Toronto, xviii, 260–1
Cycling, 30, 39, 42, 52, 180
cycling academies, 8–9, 31
Cyclometer, 224

dandyhorse magazine, 248, 252, **254**
Danforth Avenue, 72, 182, 229, 233,
241, 277. *See also* Bloor-Danforth
bike lane

Davis, Bill, Premier, 175, 207
Dennison, William, Mayor, 168, 177,
195, 248
Depression, Great, 130, 154, 276
devil strip, the, 2, 11; accidents
involving, 12, 57, 64
Dickson, S.J., Chief Constable, 103,
105, 159, 337n104
discretionary ("experimental")
bicycle routes, 196, 202, 369n192
dogs, 144, 350n138; licensing, 11, 94,
97, 112, 139, 334n97; stray, 10–11,
32, 298n14; walking, 261; war on,
10–11
Doiron, Joan, 184, 224, 259–60
Don Valley Parkway (DVP), 79, 130–
1, 170, **171**, 174, 201, 344n125
Doolittle, Perry: automobile
organization roles, 73, 88–9, 105,
118, 261; braking adaptation by, 3,
17; cycling organization roles, 1–3,
36, 39, 261; fight for better roads,
1, 16, 24, 102
publications of, 36–7; reckless
driving charge, 87–9, 93, 121–2;
views on cycling, 1, 3, 14, 18, 33,
43, 52–3
Drais, Baron Karl von, xvi, 115, 198,
272
Draper, Dennis, Chief Constable,
143, 145, 154, 334n97,
360n159
Dundas Street, 68, 83, 88, 227
Dunlop Cup, 38, 72, 98, 323n73

East York, 93, 149, 182, 199, 213
Eaton family, 42, 69, 73
Eaton's, 81, 83; bicycle prices, 7, 49
Egan, Dan, 218, 221, 223–4, 232
Eglinton Avenue, 79, 211; bike path,
195–8, 227; transit lines to, 132,
176, 230
electric bicycles, xix, 82, 84, 229,
279, 287

Tory, John, Mayor, **241**, 244–6, 275, 278
touring, bicycle, 174; decline of, 53, 71–2; popularity of, 15, 38–9, 135, 172, **282**; publications on, 36, 52, 223
trains, 105; electric, 85, 120; GO (diesel), 176, 251, 391n257; steam, xvii, **49**, 80, 90–1, 120; into suburbs, xi, **49**, 58–9, 79, 244; as transportation option, 83–4, 117–18
transit, mass: in low-density neighbourhoods, 133; TTC takeover of, **90**, 103, 118, 133; use of, 80, 117, 285
Transportation Options, 226, 384n227
Transportation Tomorrow Survey (TTS), 378n214
tricycles, 3, 304n29; for children, **111**, 115–16; electric, 82, 327n82; popularity of, 34, 306n34

Urban Bikeways Inc., 178, 191

vehicular cycling, 28, 200, 223; approach, xviii, 205, 217–21
vélocipède, xvii, 95, 115–16, 325n78
Vision Zero road safety plans, 147–8, 212, 247

war, bicycle use in, 60, 66
Warden Avenue, 171, 194–5

Weston, Ontario, 126, 137, 149, 281, **282**; CCM relocation to, xvi **68**, 93, **111**, 169; cycling tours to/in, 32, 35, 93, 135
Weston Road, 35, 65, 281
Wheeling Gazette, 39, 52, 180
White, David, **179**, 182
Whitney, James, Premier, 45–6, **47**, 64, 76, 85, 91, 120
wider curb lanes, 132, 152, 204–5, 217, 226–8, 264, 276–7
Williams, Lenton, 155, 358n155
women, 143–4, 309n39; bicycle clubs and groups for, 32, 42, 258; bicycle etiquette, 30–2, 34–5; bicycles for, xvii, 2, 7, 29–30, 34, 43, 116; cycling clothing for, 29–32, **33**, 34–5, 252; cycling injuries, 32; cycling races, 34–5; older, 31, 249; upper-class, 29–30, 32–3
World War. *See* First World War; Second World War

Yonge Street, 81; bicycle-related retailers on, 7–9, 30; calls for bike lanes on, 182, 202–4, **241**, 278–9; cycling on, 3, 14, 35, **49**; pedestrian crossing, 5, 22; proposed pedestrian spaces for, 177, 245, 279; radial lines on, 38, **49**, 80, 118
Young, Scott, 146, 148, 168

Zielinski, Sue, 226–7

About the Author

Albert Koehl has been an environmental lawyer for thirty years, and is a former adjunct professor of law, dedicated to issues of transportation, energy (mis)use, and climate change. His writings and interviews are regularly published in a variety of media. He has represented (*pro bono*) cycling groups before courts, tribunals, public forums, and at City Hall. Albert's name has been called "synonymous with cycling in Toronto," his work inspired and sustained by a commitment to social justice and the belief that how we get around should be based on fairness and respect for each other and our community, instead of on power and wealth. Among his proudest achievements at home or abroad, he counts his leadership in the successful, decades-long fight for a Bloor Street (-Danforth Avenue) bike lane that transformed this dangerous arterial into a model for safer, happier, and more climate-friendly public spaces.